D0667529

CE

# THE THEORY OF SOCIAL CHOICE

BY PETER C. FISHBURN

# The Theory of
# Social Choice

PRINCETON UNIVERSITY PRESS

DEDICATED TO THE MEMORY OF

Leonard J. Savage

THIS BOOK IS motivated by the democratic premise that social policy, group choice or collective action should be based on the preferences of the individuals in the society, group, or collective. It is based on the notion of a social choice function, which assigns a nonempty subset of feasible alternatives to each potential combination of a feasible set of social alternatives and a profile of individuals' preferences on the alternatives. Individual preferences are assumed to be irreflexive and transitive, but individual indifference relations are not necessarily assumed to be transitive. Transitive indifference is noted explicitly when it is used.

The first chapter outlines the plan of the study and acknowledges some of its limitations. The text is divided into three parts: social choice between two alternatives, which examines a variety of majority-like functions; simple majority social choice, which focuses on social choice among many alternatives when two-element feasible subset choices are based on simple majority; and a general study of aspects and types of social choice functions for many alternatives. I have tried to provide in-depth coverage of the topics included in the book without attempting a broad survey of the subject.

A modest knowledge of elementary set theory and linear algebra is a useful prerequisite.

The work was supported by a grant from the Alfred P. Sloan Foundation to The Institute for Advanced Study. I am indebted to the Institute for providing the environment in which the book was written. Special thanks are offered to Catharine Rhubart and Anna Holt, who typed the manuscript, to Professor Bengt Hansson, who kindly shared some of his recent research findings with me and allowed substantial improvements in the text, and to Professor Julian H. Blau whose careful analysis of the entire work was extremely valuable.

Peter C. Fishburn

*University Park, Pennsylvania*
*January 1972*

# CONTENTS

CONTENTS

# THE THEORY OF SOCIAL CHOICE

# CHAPTER 1

# Introduction

DEMOCRATIC THEORY is based on the premise that the resolution of a matter of social policy, group choice or collective action should be based on the desires or preferences of the individuals in the society, group or collective. Following a tradition established by Arrow (1963), Black (1958), Murakami (1966), Sen (1970), and others, this book is primarily motivated by this premise of democracy. In brief, our study will be concerned with relationships between individuals' preferences and social choices.

The medium through which the investigation will proceed is provided by the notion of a social choice function. The purpose of the present chapter is to define this notion in a precise manner and to provide a suitable orientation for the chapters that follow. In doing this we shall also mention some topics that are not dealt with in detail in the present volume.

## 1.1 SOCIAL CHOICE FUNCTIONS

In general, we shall let $n$ denote the number of individuals in the group or society under consideration, with $n$ a positive integer. The types of groups that might be considered seem almost endless. The group might be a husband and wife ($n = 2$), the United States Supreme Court ($n - 9$), a faculty senate, the eligible voters in a political district, a corporation's common stockholders, a labor council or labor union, a religious congregation, a farmers' cooperative, a board of directors, a jury, the General Assembly or Security Council of the United Nations, and so forth. In some cases the group may have well-recognized subgroups or be built up in a hierarchy of levels.

The generic situation for our study is characterized by a group of $n$ individuals who must select one alternative from a set $X$ of social alternatives. It is presumed that the alternatives are so structured that the choice of any one of them implies the rejection of every other alternative. Moreover, by inclusion of alternatives such as "delay the decision to a later time" or "maintain the status quo," we can assure that some alternative in $X$ must be selected.

To provide a general framework for the analysis, two aspects of the generic situation will be open to variation. First, in any specific realization of the situation, it will be presumed that each individual or "voter" prefers some social alternatives to others. However, we shall

3

not presume to fix these preferences in advance. That is, we want to be able to deal with any set of individual preference orders that might arise.

Second, in any specific realization of the situation it need not be true that every alternative in $X$ is feasible or available for implementation. For example, in an election of some kind, the only feasible candidates may be those who have qualified to have their names placed on the ballot. As in the case of individuals' preferences, we shall not presume to fix the feasible alternatives in advance. That is, we want to be able to deal with any set of feasible alternatives that might arise.

Suppose in fact that $Y$ turns out to be the feasible subset of $X$ and that $D$ specifies the individual preference data in a specific realization of the generic situation. Based on the pair $(Y,D)$, a nonempty subset $F(Y,D)$ of $Y$ is specified as the "choice set" for this specific case. In a manner of speaking, $F(Y,D)$ might be viewed as the "socially best" alternatives in the feasible set $Y$ when the preference data specified by $D$ obtain. If $F(Y,D)$ is a unit subset of $Y$, containing only one social alternative, the social choice is unambiguous in the case at hand. However, when $F(Y,D)$ contains more than one alternative in $Y$, the issue before the group may not be fully resolved and some form of tie-breaking procedure might be required. Although we have specified that $X$ is structured so that exactly one social alternative will be implemented, we shall permit $F(Y,D)$ to contain more than one alternative in order to allow a degree of generality in the analysis. Our basic approach might thus be characterized as an examination of group decision, excepting tie-breaking procedures. We shall say more about this at later points in the study, especially in Chapters 6 and 18.

SOCIAL CHOICE FUNCTIONS

For different possibilities of feasible sets and individual preference data we will have different choice sets. The choice set for the possibility $(Y,D)$ will be $F(Y,D)$, as before. The collection of all possibilities in conjunction with their respective choice sets constitutes a social choice function.

In abstract terms a *social choice function* is a function $F: \mathfrak{X} \times \mathfrak{D} \to \mathcal{P}(X)$ where $\mathfrak{X}$ is a nonempty set of nonempty subsets of a nonempty set $X$, $\mathfrak{D}$ is a nonempty set, $\mathcal{P}(X)$ is the set of all subsets of $X$ and, for each $(Y,D) \in \mathfrak{X} \times \mathfrak{D}$, $F(Y,D) \in \mathcal{P}(X)$ is a nonempty subset of $Y$. In terms of the preceding interpretations, $\mathfrak{X}$ is the set of all subsets of $X$ that might turn out to be feasible subsets of $X$, $\mathfrak{D}$ is the set of all configurations or profiles of individual preference data that might arise, and $F(Y,D) \in \mathcal{P}(X)$ with $\emptyset \subset F(Y,D) \subseteq Y$ is the choice set when $(Y,D)$ obtains.

An example might help to make the idea of a social choice function somewhat clearer. Suppose that $X$ contains two social alternatives and that only $X$ itself is considered as a feasible possibility so that $\mathfrak{X} = \{X\}$. Suppose further that there are three individuals or voters, each of whom either prefers one alternative to the other or is indifferent between them. Let $D$ specify the preferences (or indifferences) of the three voters. Since each individual has three options, the set $\mathfrak{D}$ of all possible $D$ has $3 \times 3 \times 3 = 27$ elements. For each of the $27D$, $F(X,D)$ can take one of three values: it can specify exactly one of the two alternatives, or it can specify both (a tie). Thus there are $3^{27}$ different social choice functions that can be defined on $\mathfrak{X} \times \mathfrak{D}$. Hence, even in this simple case there are more than 7 trillion ($7 \times 10^{12}$) possible social choice functions. Naturally, a great many of these will violate one or more conditions that are felt to reflect the basic premise of democracy.

## 1.2   INDIVIDUAL PREFERENCES

Until fairly recently, most studies of individual or group decision theory that are based on individual preference have assumed that an individual's preference order on a set of alternatives is a weak order. This means that if $>$ denotes preference on $X$, with $x > y$ meaning that $x$ is preferred to $y$, then $>$ is assumed to be asymmetric (if $x > y$ then not $y > x$) and transitive ($x > y \, \& \, y > z \Rightarrow x > z$); moreover, with indifference $\sim$ defined as the absence of preference, so that

$$x \sim y \Leftrightarrow \text{not } x > y \, \& \, \text{not } y > x,$$

it is assumed that indifference is transitive.

In this book we shall retain the assumption that each individual preference relation $>$ is asymmetric and transitive (i.e. a strict partial order), but individual indifference will not generally be assumed to be transitive. Those cases where $\sim$ is taken to be transitive will be clearly identified in context. Although the question of transitive indifference does not arise when $X$ has only two alternatives, and hence will have no affect on Part I of the book, it will be very much in evidence in Parts II and III, which consider social choices from larger sets of alternatives. Additional background on order relations is presented in the initial chapter of Part II.

As pointed out by Armstrong (1939, 1948, 1951), Luce (1956), and many others, it is rather unrealistic to suppose in general that individual indifference is transitive. Luce's coffee example, where an individual will be indifferent between $x$ and $x + 1$ grains of sugar in his coffee for a reasonable range of $x$ but will not be indifferent between $x$ and $x + m$ for sufficiently large $m$, is a case of intransitive or nontransitive indifference.

For another example, suppose that Mr. Jones is a member of a group that must decide how much money to allocate to a certain project. Mr. Jones favors an amount in the vicinity of $1000. He likes each of $900, $1060 and $1070 less than $1000, and he prefers $1060 to $1070. However, he is indifferent between $900 and $1060 and also indifferent between $900 and $1070, so that his indifference relation is not transitive.

For a third example, suppose that the Browns are going to buy a new car and have agreed to buy either a certain model of Ford or a certain model of Chevrolet. Mrs. Brown prefers (Ford, at $2800) to (Ford, at $2830), but is indifferent between (Ford, at $2800) and (Chevrolet, at $2900), and also indifferent between (Chevrolet, at $2900) and (Ford, at $2830).

Additional material on intransitive individual indifference is presented in the surveys by Roberts (1970) and Fishburn (1970d), and in Fishburn (1970).

## SOCIAL CHOICE AND INDEPENDENCE FROM
### INFEASIBLE ALTERNATIVES

The general characterizati n of $\mathfrak{D}$ in the foregoing section leaves open the question of just what types of individual preference data are to be included in the domain of the social choice function. In this book it will generally be assumed that each $D \in \mathfrak{D}$ is an $n$-tuple of strict partial orders on $X$, one order for each individual in the group or society. Thus, if $>_i$ is the preference relation on $X$ for the $i$th individual in a possible realization of the situation then $D = (>_1, >_2, \ldots, >_n)$ for this possible realization. Section 1.4 notes some other things that might be included in the elements of $\mathfrak{D}$ but which will not be considered in detail in later chapters.

It should be observed that, by taking each $>_i$ on all of $X$ and not just on the particular subset $Y$ of $X$ that happens to be feasible, we are leaving open the possibility that individual preferences that involve infeasible alternatives may influence the social choice. My present feeling, which is shared by some but certainly not all social choice theorists, is that such preferences ought not to affect the social choice from the feasible set. In terms of the social choice function, this feeling can be expressed by the condition that $F(Y,D) = F(Y,D')$ whenever $D = (>_1, \ldots, >_n)$ and $D' = (>'_1, \ldots, >'_n)$ are identical on $Y$, although they may differ on $X$. This says that, when $Y$ is the feasible set in each of two possible realizations and when each individual has the same preference order on $Y$ in each of the two possible realizations (the restriction of $>_i$ on $Y$ equals the restriction of $>'_i$ on $Y$, for each $i$), then the choice sets should be identical in the two possible realizations. We shall call this condition the *condition of independence from infeasible alternatives*. It is proposed in the same spirit as Arrow's condition of the independence of irrelevant alternatives (1963, p. 27).

This condition will be used, either implicitly or explicitly, in much of the book. The most notable exception arises in Chapter 17, which presents some general theory for social choice functions that are based on sums of individual utilities.

Because independence from infeasible alternatives plays a significant role throughout this study, a word on its possible merits is in order. First of all, when $Y$ is recognized as the relevant feasible set, there may be serious question about the significance or meaning of individual preferences that involve infeasible elements in $X - Y$. When independence applies, the question of preferences that involve infeasible alternatives becomes academic, and individuals need only specify preferences within the feasible subset.

If in fact the social choice can depend on infeasibles, which infeasibles should be used? For with one set of infeasibles, feasible $x$ might be the social choice, whereas feasible $y \neq x$ might be the social choice if some other infeasible set were adjoined to $Y$. Hence, the idea of allowing infeasible alternatives to influence the social choice introduces a potential ambiguity into the choice process that can at least be alleviated if not removed by insisting on the independence condition.

This obviously ties into the choice of the universal set $X$ of alternatives in a particular situation. If independence is adopted, then the contents of $X$ are not especially important as long as they include, at least conceptually, anything that might qualify as a feasible candidate or alternative. If independence is not adopted, the ambiguity noted in the preceding paragraph may cause significant problems in attempting to specify just what should and should not be included in $X$.

The question of just what is or is not a feasible alternative may also present problems in a group decision process, but the independence condition says nothing about this as such. Related to this, we may consider a maneuver in which an alternative is legally placed in nomination not because its sponsors think it has any chance of being elected but because they feel that its introduction will increase the chance of the election of their favored alternative. This is more a question of the

7

process of identifying feasible alternatives than it is of the independence condition, which deals only with the feasible set that arises. It is also a question of the design of the choice procedure, and other conditions might play a part in its analysis. It is also clearly connected with individual and coalition strategies in social choice processes. This book will not go into the fascinating subject of voter strategy in any detail, although a few comments on the topic are presented in the final section of Chapter 8.

It should also be pointed out that our use of the independence condition is not, in itself, an argument against the inclusion of individual intensities of preference. For example, if individual intensities of preference were taken to be relevant along with the basic preference orders, then we would have to change our viewpoint about the contents of $\mathfrak{D}$. If each $D$ included data on intensities as well as basic preferences, then the intention of the independence condition would be preserved if the form of the condition were not changed. In this case the condition would say that $F(Y,D) = F(Y,D')$ whenever the data in $D$ and $D'$ are the same (including any data on intensities) within $Y$. We shall say more about the matter of intensity and the related subject of interpersonal comparisons in the final section of this chapter.

## 1.3 PREVIEW

With the foregoing introductory material at hand, a brief sketch of the contents of later chapters will indicate the scope of the present study. The text is presented in three parts, as follows:

Part   I. Social Choice with Two Alternatives.
Part  II. Simple Majority Social Choice.
Part III. Social Choice Functions.

Parts II and III are generally concerned with the case where $X$ contains more than two social alternatives.

The initial emphasis in Part I is on the structure of individual preference profiles $D \in \mathfrak{D}$ and social choice functions when $X$ contains only two alternatives. In the spirit of the independence condition, only preferences that involve the two alternatives will be considered as relevant. Potential conditions for social choice functions, such as monotonicity, unanimity, duality, and anonymity, are introduced, and their effects on social choice functions are analyzed. Various types of majority functions, including simple, weak, weighted, and representative majorities, are characterized in terms of such conditions. Each of these types of majorities satisfies the duality condition, which requires equal treatment for the two alternatives.

The final chapter of Part I discusses several forms of special majority which do not generally treat the two alternatives equally—the "status quo" usually has a built-in advantage.

Part II focuses on social choice functions for larger $X$ whose binary parts agree with simple majority. This says that, for any feasible subset $Y = \{x,y\}$ that contains just two elements from $X$, $F(\{x,y\},D) = \{x\}$ if more individuals prefer $x$ to $y$ than prefer $y$ to $x$, and $F(\{x,y\},D) = \{y\}$ if more $i$ prefer $y$ to $x$ than prefer $x$ to $y$. It is generally assumed in Part II that $\mathfrak{X}$ is the set of all nonempty subsets of $X$.

Following some comments on the well-known fact that simple majorities may be intransitive when $X$ contains more than two alternatives, the central segment of Part II examines structural features of situations that give rise to transitive majorities or, short of that, to one alternative having a simple majority over every other alternative. This analysis begins with the case of single-peaked preferences, which dates at least to Galton (1907) and was studied extensively some years later by Black (1948, 1958).

The penultimate chapter of Part II examines the contention of Condorcet (1785) that an alternative that has a simple majority over every other alternative should be the social choice, assuming that the simple-majority rule is sanctioned in any case where the feasible set contains just two alternatives. The final chapter of Part II looks at several explicit social choice functions that agree with simple majority.

Part III begins with a general classification of conditions for social choice functions. The categories of this classification are then related to several topics, including the transitivity of binary (but not necessarily simple-majority) choices, an analysis of structural conditions in conjunction with order-related conditions, and Arrow's impossibility theorem (1963) and some of its close relatives.

As noted earlier, Chapter 17 presents a general theory of summation social choice functions. The final chapter discusses the use of lotteries to make social choices. If a group decides to use a lottery, an alternative is then chosen randomly according to the probabilities specified by the lottery. As in preceding chapters, individual preference orders will be assumed to be strict partial orders, on lotteries in this case. Other assumptions for individual preferences in the lottery context will generally be weaker than the typical von Neumann-Morgenstern (1947) axioms for expected utility.

## 1.4 PREFERENCE INTENSITY

Because the present study concentrates on social choice functions in which the elements of $\mathfrak{D}$ are $n$-tuples of preference orders on social alternatives, data on intensities of preferences will not be included in $\mathfrak{D}$. This is not to say that such data ought not to be used in determining social choices, and it by no means implies that the author regards the intensity topic as sterile or unimportant. Rather it points out one of the self-imposed limitations on the present volume.

As we have mentioned intensities, a few words about what is being excluded in later chapters seem appropriate. There are at least two distinct senses in which the phrase "preference intensity" is used. The first is an intrapersonal sense and the second is an interpersonal sense.

Intrapersonal preference intensity (degree of preference, strength of preference) applies solely to a particular individual. If, for example, you prefer $x$ to $y$ and $y$ to $z$, it asks whether your "degree of preference" for $x$ over $y$ exceeds, equals, or is less than your "degree of preference" for $y$ over $z$. If you preferred Nixon to Humphrey to Wallace in the 1968 United States Presidential election, was the intensity of your preference for Nixon over Humphrey greater than, equal to, or less than the intensity of your preference for Humphrey over Wallace?

Theories of intrapersonal preference intensity go back at least to Pareto (1927) and Frisch (1926). Later contributors include Lange (1934), Alt (1936), Armstrong (1939), Weldon (1950), and Suppes and Winet (1955). The inclusion of vagueness in preference-difference comparisons, which is related to the phenomenon of intransitive indifference, is discussed by Fishburn (1970e; 1970, Chapter 6).

A simple example will illustrate one way in which intrapersonal intensity might be taken into account in social choice theory. Suppose that $Y = \{x,y,z\}$, $n = 2$, the first person prefers $x$ to $y$ to $z$, and the second prefers $z$ to $y$ to $x$. If the first person feels that $y$ is closer to $x$ than to $z$ in terms of his relative preference differences, and the second feels that $y$ is closer to $z$ than to $x$ in his own view, then it might seem appropriate to "elect" $y$ as the social choice. On the other hand, if the reverse holds and $y$ is nearer to the worst rather than the best alternative for each person, then $y$ might be excluded from the choice set.

### INTERPERSONAL PREFERENCE COMPARISONS

As the name suggests, interpersonal preference comparisons purport to compare preference differences of different individuals. For example: Mr. Smith's intensity of preference for Nixon over Humphrey exceeds Mr. Jones' intensity of preference for Humphrey over Nixon. Another example: the husband would rather stay home than go to a movie, but he really doesn't feel strongly about this; on the other hand, his wife is "dying to get out of the house" and has a very "strong" preference for "movie" over "stay home." A third example concerns the intense and passionate minority versus the apathetic majority.

Needless to say, the idea of accounting for interpersonal preference comparisons has received a great deal of attention in the literature of social choice theory. Rather than attempting to survey this, we shall simply indicate several resources that present various points of view on the topic. The following list is by no means complete, but will lead the interested student to additional references: Dahl (1956), Buchanan and Tullock (1962), Kendall and Carey (1968); Harsanyi (1955), Rothenberg (1961), Arrow (1963, pp. 108–118), Sen (1970), Luce and Raiffa (1957, Chapter 14); Churchman (1966).

At several places in the present study it might appear that questions of interpersonal comparisons are very much at issue. Some cases in point are the theory of weighted majority in Chapter 5 and the theory of summation social choice functions in Chapter 17. Indeed, it has been suggested by several authors that any specific social choice function or social choice procedure incorporates some notion of interpersonal comparisons, whether or not this is explicitly recognized by its sponsor. Regardless of how one feels about this, it should be remembered that this study is based on $n$-tuples of individual preference orders, and does not, at any point, explicitly include intensity data (either intrapersonal or interpersonal) in the elements of $\mathfrak{D}$.

# SOCIAL CHOICE WITH
# TWO ALTERNATIVES

MANY INTERESTING facets of social choice theory appear only when a choice is required among three or more alternatives. However, a significant body of theory has been developed for two-alternative situations. Since we can examine this theory in its own right without becoming involved in the added complexities of more general situations, we shall do so in Part I of the book. As will be seen, the two-alternative theory itself provides enough complexities to occupy our attention for several chapters.

In a practical sense, the case of two alternatives is of paramount importance since groups often concentrate their attention on two competing alternatives, and since many different types of choice procedures are in fact used to resolve such competitions.

Although we shall look at some specific choice procedures and identify conditions for social choice functions that characterize such procedures, our focus will be somewhat broader than this. In particular, the primary purposes of Part I will be to examine the structure of social choice functions for two alternatives and to investigate the effects that certain conditions, such as monotonicity and duality, have on social choice functions.

# CHAPTER 2

# Social Choice Functions for
# Two Alternatives

THIS CHAPTER has three purposes. The first is to set forth some nota-
tions and conventions that will be used throughout Part I. The second
purpose is to examine structures of preferences and social choice functions for two alternatives. Thirdly, we shall investigate the conditions
of monotonicity and unanimity for social choice functions. These conditions are used throughout the succeeding chapters of Part I.

## 2.1 NOTATIONS AND STRUCTURES

For any set $S$ let $\#S$ be the number of elements in $S$, and let $S^n$ be the
$n$-fold Cartesian product of $S$ with itself so that $S^n = \{(s_1, \ldots, s_n):
s_i \in S$ for each $i\}$. We write $f: S \to T$ to denote a function $f$ with
domain $S$ and codomain $T$. $S^n$ can be viewed as the set of all functions
$f: \{1, \ldots, n\} \to S$.

In mathematical terms, Part I will deal with the set of all functions
$F: S^n \to S$ when $\#S = 3$ and $n$ is a positive integer. The symbols used
for the three elements in $S$ can be anything we want them to be. However, for mathematical and interpretive purposes it is very efficient to
take $S = \{1, 0, -1\}$.

Our interpretation of this structure in terms of choice between the
two alternatives in the set $X = \{x, y\}$ is the following. First, $n$ is the
number of individuals in the group or society, and $i = 1, \ldots, n$
indexes these individuals. Let $D_i$ be a variable whose values represent
the possible preferences of individual $i$ on $X$. It is assumed that individual preference is asymmetric, so that $D_i$ has three possible values,
identified as follows:

$$D_i = \phantom{-}1 \Leftrightarrow i \text{ prefers } x \text{ to } y$$
$$D_i = \phantom{-}0 \Leftrightarrow i \text{ is indifferent between } x \text{ and } y$$
$$D_i = -1 \Leftrightarrow i \text{ prefers } y \text{ to } x.$$

The set $\mathfrak{D} = \{1, 0, -1\}^n$ is the set of all *individual preference profiles*,
of the form $D = (D_1, \ldots, D_n)$, that might obtain in a particular
situation. In terms of voting we can think of $D_i = 1$ as a vote for $x$,
$D_i = -1$ as a vote for $y$, and $D_i = 0$ as an abstention.

The function $F:\mathfrak{D} \to \{1,0,-1\}$ assigns a social choice $F(D) \in \{1,0,-1\}$ to each preference profile $D \in \mathfrak{D}$. To maintain consistency with the foregoing 1, 0, $-1$ interpretation for individual preference, we interpret

$F(D) = \quad 1 \Leftrightarrow x$ is the social choice under $D$
$F(D) = \quad 0 \Leftrightarrow x$ and $y$ are tied under $D$
$F(D) = -1 \Leftrightarrow y$ is the social choice under $D$.

Because the situation that arises when only one of $x$ and $y$ is available is of no real interest, $F$ as here defined is to be viewed as the choice function when both $x$ and $y$ are feasible alternatives. In terms of the notation of Chapter 1, $F(D) = F(\{x,y\},D)$. Since our definition of social choice function requires $F(\{x\},D) = \{x\}$ and $F(\{y\},D) = \{y\}$ for all $D \in \mathfrak{D}$, we dispense with these trivial cases and simply refer to $F:\mathfrak{D} \to \{1,0,-1\}$ as a social choice function.

### GEOMETRIC INTERPRETATION

Since $\mathfrak{D} = \{1,0,-1\}^n$, $\#\mathfrak{D} = 3^n$. Figure 2.1 illustrates the 27 points in $\mathfrak{D}$ when $n = 3$. The central point is the origin $\mathbf{0} = (0,0,0)$ of a

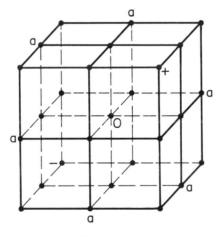

FIGURE 2.1

three-dimensional Euclidean space. The point labeled $+$ is $(1,1,1)$ and the point labeled $-$ is $(-1,-1,-1)$. Each point labeled "$a$" has $D_1 + D_2 + D_3 = 0$.

A particular social choice function $F$ for $n = 3$ can be identified on the figure by labeling each point $D$ with its corresponding $F(D)$ value from $\{1,0,-1\}$. This will partition the set of 27 points into three subsets (one or two of which may be empty) according to the three values.

More generally, for any $F: \{1, 0, -1\}^n \to \{1, 0, -1\}$ let

$$F^*(k) = \{D : D \in \{1, 0, -1\}^n \text{ and } F(D) = k\} \qquad (2.1)$$

for $k = 1, 0, -1$. $F^*(k)$ is thus the *inverse image* of $k$. Any social choice function $F$ is completely described by the triple $(F^*(1), F^*(0), F^*(-1))$. Correspondingly, any triple $(\mathfrak{D}^1, \mathfrak{D}^0, \mathfrak{D}^{-1})$ of disjoint subsets of $\mathfrak{D}$ whose union equals $\mathfrak{D}$ determines a social choice function $F$ in the obvious way.

Our intuitions about "acceptable" social choice functions suggest that the elements in a given $F^*(k)$ should be bunched together, or that the sets in the triple $(F^*(1), F^*(0), F^*(-1))$ should form clusters that are simply described in a figure such as Figure 2.1. For example, we may feel that it is reasonable to prescribe $F(+) = F(1,1,1) = 1$, so that $x$ is the social choice when everyone prefers $x$ to $y$, and that other $D \in F^*(1)$ should be in the vicinity of $+$. Similarly, $F(-) = -1$, with other $D \in F^*(-1)$ in the vicinity of $-$, may seem reasonable. As we shall see, the conditions for social choice functions that we investigate tend to separate the $F^*(k)$ into more or less cohesive groupings.

## VECTOR OPERATIONS AND HYPERPLANES

The usual operations on vectors in $n$-dimensional Euclidean space $Re^n$ will be used extensively in Part I.

For any $\lambda \in Re$ and $a = (a_1, \ldots, a_n)$ and $b = (b_1, \ldots, b_n)$ in $Re^n$, $\lambda a = (\lambda a_1, \ldots, \lambda a_n)$ and $a + b = (a_1 + b_1, \ldots, a_n + b_n)$. Also, $-a = (-1)a$. The *inner product* $a \cdot b$ of $a$ and $b$ is

$$a \cdot b = a_1 b_1 + \cdots + a_n b_n = \Sigma_i a_i b_i. \qquad (2.2)$$

Equality and inequality between vectors $a, b \in Re^n$ will be denoted in the following way:

$a = b \Leftrightarrow a_i = b_i$     for each $i$
$a > b \Leftrightarrow a_i \geq b_i$     for each $i$, and $a_i > b_i$ for some $i$
$a \geq b \Leftrightarrow a = b$     or $a > b$.

Naturally, $a < b \Leftrightarrow b > a$, and $a \leq b \Leftrightarrow b \geq a$.

Consider the set

$$\{a : a \in Re^n \text{ and } \rho \cdot a = \lambda\} \qquad (2.3)$$

where $\rho$ is a fixed vector in $Re^n$ and $\lambda \in Re$. This set is a *hyperplane* in $Re^n$. It is a *hyperplane through the origin* if $\lambda = 0$. If $\rho = 0$ then $\{a : \rho \cdot a = \lambda\}$ equals $\emptyset$ or $Re^n$ according to whether $\lambda \neq 0$ or $\lambda = 0$. If $\rho \neq 0$, then the hyperplane is neither $\emptyset$ nor $Re^n$.

Every hyperplane of the form (2.3) partitions $Re^n$ into three disjoint subsets (some of which can be empty) according to whether $a \cdot \rho > \lambda$, $a \cdot \rho = \lambda$, or $a \cdot \rho < \lambda$. Thus, we see that a host of social choice functions can be characterized by using hyperplanes. In particular, $\rho$ and $\lambda$ determine a social choice function $F$ as follows:

$$
\begin{aligned}
F(D) &= \phantom{-}1 \Leftrightarrow \rho \cdot D > \lambda & F^*(1) &= \{D : \rho \cdot D > \lambda\} \\
F(D) &= \phantom{-}0 \Leftrightarrow \rho \cdot D = \lambda & F^*(0) &= \{D : \rho \cdot D = \lambda\} \quad (2.4) \\
F(D) &= -1 \Leftrightarrow \rho \cdot D < \lambda & F^*(-1) &= \{D : \rho \cdot D < \lambda\}.
\end{aligned}
$$

The following are some examples.

(i) $F \equiv 0$, the completely indecisive social choice function ($x$ ties $y$ regardless of $D$), is described by $\rho = 0$ and $\lambda = 0$.

(ii) $F \equiv 1$, the imposed function which prescribes $x$ as the social choice regardless of $D$, is described by $\rho = 0$ and $\lambda = -1$.

(iii) $F \equiv -1$, the imposed function which prescribes $y$ as the social choice regardless of $D$, is described by $\rho = 0$ and $\lambda = 1$.

(iv) The *simple majority* social choice function has $\rho = (1, \ldots, 1)$ and $\lambda = 0$ so that $x$ beats $y$ whenever more individuals prefer $x$ to $y$ than prefer $y$ to $x$ (i.e. $\Sigma D_i > 0$), and $y$ beats $x$ whenever the converse holds. The hyperplane that defines simple majority for Figure 2.1 is the plane that contains the origin and the "$a$" points. Each "$a$" point has $F(a) = 0$, each $D$ on the $+$ side of the plane has $F(D) = 1$, and each $D$ on the $-$ side has $F(D) = -1$.

(v) Simple majority with a tie-breaking chairman, individual 1, can be described by $\rho = (3, 2, 2, \ldots, 2)$ and $\lambda = 0$. A tie can arise in this case only if the chairman does not vote. The greater weight for the chairman makes a difference as compared to simple majority only when there is a simple majority tie.

(vi) The case where $x$ wins if the number of votes for $x$ exceeds the number for $y$ by at least a positive integer $r$, and $y$ wins otherwise, is described by $\rho = (1, \ldots, 1)$ and $\lambda = r - \frac{1}{2}$. Since $\rho \cdot D$ must be an integer in this case, ties cannot arise.

(vii) We shall call $F$ a *weighted majority* social choice function if and only if it can be described as in (2.4) with $\rho > 0$ and $\lambda = 0$. Of the foregoing examples, only (iv) and (v) are weighted majorities. In terms of Figure 2.1, the weighted majorities are described by planes through the origin with $\rho$ a nonzero vector or point in the nonnegative octant ($+$ octant) of the space.

## 2.2 Sign Functions

Many interesting social choice functions cannot be expressed in the linear way as in (2.4). To deal with some of the nonlinearities that will arise, we shall use the sign function $s: Re \to \{1, 0, -1\}$ defined by

$$\begin{aligned} s(r) &= \phantom{-}1 \Leftrightarrow r > 0 \\ s(r) &= \phantom{-}0 \Leftrightarrow r = 0 \\ s(r) &= -1 \Leftrightarrow r < 0. \end{aligned} \tag{2.5}$$

A hint of the usefulness of $s$ comes from observing that the social choice function $F$ defined by (2.4) is specified by

$$F(D) = s(\rho \cdot D - \lambda) \qquad \text{for all} \qquad D \in \mathcal{D}.$$

We shall let $s$ operate on vectors $a = (a_1, \ldots, a_n)$ in $Re^n$ in the following way:

$$s(a) = s(a_1, \ldots, a_n) = s(\Sigma a_i). \tag{2.6}$$

It should be noted here that $s(a_1, \ldots, a_n)$ is a number in $\{1, 0, -1\}$ and not an $n$-tuple in $Re^n$. An alternative way of writing (2.6) is $s(a) = s(1 \cdot a)$, where $1 \in Re^n$ has 1 for every component.

Thus $s(\rho_1 D_1, \ldots, \rho_n D_n, -\lambda) = s(\rho \cdot D - \lambda)$, simple majority is described by $F(D) = s(D)$, and any weighted majority social choice function is given by $F(D) = s(\rho_1 D_1, \ldots, \rho_n D_n)$ with $\rho_i \geq 0$ for all $i$ and $\rho_i > 0$ for some $i$.

OPERATIONS ON FUNCTIONS

The real usefulness of $s$ requires its extension to operations on social choice functions.

Let $\mathcal{F}$ be the set of social choice functions $F: \mathcal{D} \to \{1, 0, -1\}$. Then with $F_1, \ldots, F_K \in \mathcal{F}$, $s(F_1, \ldots, F_K)$ is defined to be the function on $\mathcal{D}$ specified by

$$s(F_1, \ldots, F_K)(D) = s(F_1(D), \ldots, F_K(D)) \qquad \text{for all} \qquad D \in \mathcal{D}. \tag{2.7}$$

It is clear from this definition that $s(F_1, \ldots, F_K)(D) \in \{1, 0, -1\}$, so that we may designate $\{1, 0, -1\}$ as the codomain of the function. Hence we see that

$$F_1, \ldots, F_K \in \mathcal{F} \Rightarrow s(F_1, \ldots, F_K) \in \mathcal{F}. \tag{2.8}$$

A standard interpretation of $F = s(F_1, \ldots, F_K)$ goes as follows. The society uses $F$ to specify its decision. The society has $K$ councils or legislatures. These councils may have overlapping memberships or they may be disjoint. $F_k$ is the social choice function for the $k$th council. To determine the social choice, a "vote" is taken in each council with outcomes specified by the $F_k$. The overall outcome is then determined by $F$, which operates by simple majority on the outcomes of the votes of the councils.

Readers familiar with group theory will note that, with $F \oplus G = s(F,G)$ for all $F,G \in \mathfrak{F}$, the algebraic system $(\mathfrak{F},\oplus,F^0)$ with $F^0 \equiv 0$ has all the properties of an idempotent abelian group, except for associativity. For example, for all $F,G \in \mathfrak{F}$,

$$
\begin{aligned}
F \oplus G \quad &= G \oplus F & \text{(commutative, or abelian)} \\
F \oplus F^0 \quad &= F^0 \oplus F = F & \text{(identity)} \\
F \oplus -F &= -F \oplus F = F^0 & \text{(inverse)} \\
F \oplus F \quad &= F & \text{(idempotent).}
\end{aligned}
$$

However, associativity fails since $(F \oplus G) \oplus H = s(s(F,G),H)$ is not necessarily the same function as $F \oplus (G \oplus H) = s(F,s(G,H))$. For nonassociativity it suffices to observe that $s(s(-1,1),1) = 1$, whereas $s(-1,s(1,1)) = 0$.

In the preceding paragraph we have suggested that it makes sense to put one s function inside of another. Indeed, we can structure any finite hierarchy in this way, such as

$$s(F_1,F_2,F_2,s(F_3,F_4),s(F_1,F_4,s(F_5,F_6))), \tag{2.9}$$

and the resultant expression still defines a social choice function in $\mathfrak{F}$. For (2.9), $s(F_5,F_6)$ is a social choice function. Call it $F_7$. Then $s(F_3,F_4)$ and $s(F_1,F_4,F_7)$ are social choice functions. Call them $G$ and $H$. Then (2.9) has the form $s(F_1,F_2,F_2,G,H)$, which, as we observed above, is a social choice function in $\mathfrak{F}$.

Hierarchies of the form of (2.9) will be referred to as *representative systems* when it is possible to write the $F_k$ as simple majority social choice functions that apply to subsets of individuals. If for (2.9), each $F_i$ except $F_1$ is such a simple majority, and $F_1(D) = s(D_1,D_1,D_2,D_4)$, then we can write this as $F_1(D) = s(F_{11}(D),F_{11}(D),F_{12}(D),F_{14}(D))$ where each $F_{1i}(D) = s(D_i)$ is a simple majority for the subset $\{i\}$ that contains only the individual $i$. Replacing $F_1$ in (2.9) by $s(F_{11},F_{11},F_{12},F_{14})$, we see that (2.9) can in fact be written in the manner required to make it a representative system.

Representative systems, which were first studied extensively by Murakami (1966, 1968), will form the basis of our analysis in the next three chapters.

## 2.3 MONOTONIC SOCIAL CHOICE FUNCTIONS

Henceforth, Part I will concentrate on specific conditions for social choice functions. We shall examine structural characteristics and functional forms of social choice functions that satisfy these conditions.

All social choice functions of further interest in Part I will be monotonic.

DEFINITION 2.1. $F:\mathfrak{D} \to \{1,0,-1\}$ *is* monotonic *if and only if* $D \geq D' \Rightarrow F(D) \geq F(D')$, *for all* $D,D' \in \mathfrak{D}$.

Imagine two possible realizations of individual preferences in a given situation, say $D$ and $D'$. With regard to preferences between the two alternatives $x$ and $y$, $D \geq D'$ means that any change in preference from $D'$ to $D$ favors $x$. $F(D) \geq F(D')$ then requires that

1. if $x$ is chosen under $D'$, then $x$ is chosen under $D$,
2. if $x$ and $y$ tie under $D'$, then either $x$ is chosen under $D$ or $x$ and $y$ tie under $D$.

Conversely, if $y$ is chosen under $D$ then $y$ must be the group choice under $D'$, and if $x$ and $y$ tie under $D$ then $x$ cannot be the unique choice under $D'$.

Another way to look at this is with a "lost votes" example. Suppose a society uses a monotonic $F$, and a secret ballot is taken. Each person votes for $x$ or for $y$ or abstains. Before the ballots can be processed, a fire breaks out and consumes the ballot box. A second ballot is taken. Suppose that every voter who voted for $x$ the first time votes for $x$ again and that each voter who abstained the first time either abstains or votes for $x$ the second time. Monotonicity says that if $x$ would have won with the first ballot then $x$ must win with the second ballot, and that if $x$ and $y$ would have tied on the first ballot then they either tie or $x$ wins on the second ballot.

On Figure 2.1 consider any path from $-$ to $+$ that proceeds only in positive directions. Monotonicity says that $F$ must not decrease as we proceed along the path from $-$ to $+$.

Monotonicity can also be defined in terms of a change by a single voter thus: $F(D) \geq F(D')$ whenever $D_i = D'_i$ for all but one $i$, say $j$, for which $D_j > D'_j$. This is easily seen to be equivalent to Definition 2.1 since $D > D'$ implies that we can go from $D'$ to $D$ by a succession of single changes.

We can easily verify that monotonicity holds for each of the seven examples following (2.4), and that every representative system is monotonic.

BASIC THEOREMS AND UNANIMITY

The "inverse" or *dual* of $F$ is $-F$, where $(-F)(D) = -F(D)$ for every $D$. $F$ is *constant* $\Leftrightarrow F(D) = F(D')$ for every $D,D' \in \mathfrak{D}$. The three constant functions in $\mathfrak{F}$ were specified in examples following (2.4).

THEOREM 2.1. *Let* $\mathcal{G}$ *be the set of all monotonic social choice functions* $F:\mathfrak{D} \to \{1,0,-1\}$. *Then*

$$F_1, \ldots, F_K \in \mathcal{G} \Rightarrow s(F_1, \ldots, F_K) \in \mathcal{G},$$

*and there are exactly three functions in* $\mathcal{G}$ *whose duals are in* $\mathcal{G}$, *namely the three constant functions.*

*Proof.* If $F_1, \ldots, F_K \in \mathcal{G}$ and $D \geq D'$, then $F_k(D) \geq F_k(D')$ for each $k$. Therefore, $s(F_1(D), \ldots, F_K(D)) \geq s(F_1(D'), \ldots, F_K(D'))$. For the latter part of the theorem, suppose that $F, -F \in \mathcal{G}$. Then $D \geq D' \Rightarrow F(D) \geq F(D')$ and $-F(D) \geq -F(D')$, and therefore, $F(D) = F(D')$. Since $1 \geq D \geq -1$ for every $D \in \mathfrak{D}$, only constant functions in $\mathcal{G}$ can have duals in $\mathcal{G}$. Each constant function is clearly monotonic. ◆

We shall now consider the inverse sets $F^*(k)$ defined by (2.1). To avoid the uninteresting possibility that $F^*(1) = \emptyset$ or $F^*(-1) = \emptyset$ we shall introduce the unanimity condition at this point.

DEFINITION 2.2. $F:\mathfrak{D} \to \{1,0,-1\}$ *is* unanimous *if and only if* $F(1) = 1$ *and* $F(-1) = -1$.

This simply prescribes that $x$ wins when everyone prefers $x$ to $y$, and that $y$ wins when everyone prefers $y$ to $x$. Although hindsight may suggest cases where the unanimous choice was judged to be a bad choice, temporal considerations prevent inclusion of this in the social decision. (This is not to say that experience and foresight should not affect the decision.)

Instead of using unanimity directly, it would suffice to use a weaker condition of nonimposition which says simply that $F^*(1) \neq \emptyset$ and $F^*(-1) \neq \emptyset$. Then this and monotonicity imply unanimity.

The effect of unanimity on Theorem 2.1 is obvious.

THEOREM 2.2. *Let* $\mathfrak{K}$ *be the set of all monotonic and unanimous social choice functions* $F:\mathfrak{D} \to \{1,0,-1\}$. *Then*

$$F_1, \ldots, F_K \in \mathfrak{K} \Rightarrow s(F_1, \ldots, F_K) \in \mathfrak{K},$$

*and no* $F \in \mathfrak{K}$ *is constant.*

For $F \in \mathfrak{K}$ the *boundary* of $F^*(1)$ is

$$BF^*(1) = \{D : D \in F^*(1) \text{ and } D > D' \text{ for no } D' \in F^*(1)\},$$

and the *boundary* of $F^*(-1)$ is

$$BF^*(-1) = \{D : D \in F^*(-1) \text{ and } D < D' \text{ for no } D' \in F^*(-1)\}.$$

According to these definitions, $BF^*(k)$ supports $F^*(k)$ in the sense that

$$F^*(1) = \{D : D \geq D' \text{ for some } D' \in BF^*(1)\}$$
$$F^*(-1) = \{D : D \leq D' \text{ for some } D' \in BF^*(-1)\}.$$

Figure 2.2 shows two $F \in \mathcal{X}$ for $n = 2$. In each case the points in $BF^*(1)$ and $BF^*(-1)$ are circled and squared respectively. Given $D \in BF^*(-1)$, Figure (a) shows that there may be no $D' \in BF^*(1)$ with $D' > D$. Figure (b) shows that $D \in F^*(0)$ may have no $D' \in BF^*(1)$ for which $D' > D$.

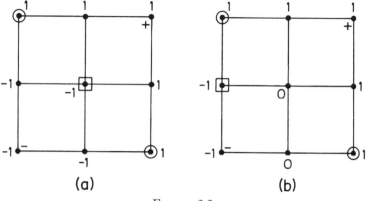

(a)                     (b)

FIGURE 2.2

Given $F \in \mathcal{X}$, the boundaries are unique and determine $F$ by the preceding "support" equalities, with $F^*(0)$ the complement of $F^*(1) \cup F^*(-1)$ in $\mathcal{D}$. In general, any two "boundaries" determine a unique $F \in \mathcal{X}$ in the sense of the following theorem.

THEOREM 2.3. *Let $A$ and $B$ be nonempty subsets of $\mathcal{D}$ such that, for all $D, D' \in \mathcal{D}$:*

(i) $D, D' \in A$ *or* $D, D' \in B \Rightarrow$ *not* $(D > D')$.
(ii) $D' \in A$ *and* $D \in B \Rightarrow$ *not* $(D \geq D')$.

*Then there is a unique $F \in \mathcal{X}$ such that $BF^*(1) = A$ and $BF^*(-1) = B$.*

*Proof.* Given the hypotheses, define $F$ by

$$F(D) = \ \ 1 \Leftrightarrow D \geq D' \text{ for some } D' \in A$$
$$F(D) = -1 \Leftrightarrow D \leq D' \text{ for some } D' \in B$$
$$F(D) = \ \ 0 \ \ \text{ otherwise.}$$

Suppose there are $D' \in A$ and $D'' \in B$ such that $D \geq D'$ and $D \leq D''$. Then $D'' \geq D'$, which contradicts hypothesis (ii). Hence

**23**

$F \in \mathfrak{F}$, and by (i), $A = BF^*(1)$ and $B = BF^*(-1)$. Since $A$ and $B$ are not empty, $F$ must be unanimous. To verify monotonicity suppose that $D \geq D'$. If $F(D') = 1$ then, since $D' \geq D^*$ for some $D^* \in A$, $D \geq D^*$ and therefore $F(D) = 1$. If $F(D') = 0$, then $D^* \geq D'$ for no $D^* \in B$; consequently, $D^* \geq D$ for no $D^* \in B$, and therefore $F(D) \neq -1$. Therefore $F(D) \geq F(D')$. Uniqueness follows from the paragraph that precedes the theorem. ◆

The following theorem states that common support points carry through s.

THEOREM 2.4. *Suppose that* $F_1, \ldots, F_K \in \mathfrak{IC}$ *and* $F = \mathrm{s}(F_1, \ldots, F_K)$. *Then*

$$\bigcap_{k=1}^{K} BF_k^*(j) \subseteq BF^*(j) \qquad \text{for each } j \in \{-1, 1\}.$$

*Proof.* For $j = 1$, suppose that $D \in BF_k^*(1)$ for each $k$. Since $F(D) = 1$, $D \notin BF^*(1) \Rightarrow D > D'$ for some $D' \in BF^*(1)$, which requires $F_k(D') = 1$ for some $k$. But then $D \notin BF_k^*(1)$ for any such $k$, a contradiction. Hence $D \in BF^*(1)$. The $j = -1$ proof is similar. ◆

STRONG MONOTONICITY

Monotonicity allows $F(D) = 0$ when $F(D') = 0$ and $D > D'$. This says that if $x$ ties $y$ under $D'$, and if one or more individual preferences change in favor of $x$ but none changes in favor of $y$ in going from $D'$ to $D$, then $x$ and $y$ may still tie under $D$. Strong monotonicity prevents this.

DEFINITION 2.3. $F: \mathfrak{D} \rightarrow \{1, 0, -1\}$ *is strongly monotonic if and only if it is monotonic and, for all* $D, D' \in \mathfrak{D}$,

$$\begin{aligned} F(D) = 0 \qquad &and \qquad D' > D \Rightarrow F(D') = 1 \\ F(D) = 0 \qquad &and \qquad D > D' \Rightarrow F(D') = -1. \end{aligned}$$

This condition has a very practical appeal. Compared to monotonicity, it tends to limit the region $F^*(0)$ of ambiguity or ties. It says that any abstainer under a tie vote can break the tie so long as others do not change their votes or abstentions. If in fact ties are prohibited by $F$, so that $F^*(0) = \emptyset$, then monotonicity and strong monotonicity are equivalent.

One argument against strong monotonicity that is not also an argument against monotonicity concerns the ability of a "change" by any person to resolve a tie. For example, there may be situations where an individual may be "ineligible," or may not be able (or allowed) to influence the social choice by his vote. Short of this, there may be cases where the power to break a tie is allowed only to certain individuals in certain cases.

A simple example where monotonicity holds but strong monotonicity fails is the bicameral representative system $F$ defined by

$$F(D) = \mathbf{s}(\mathbf{s}(D_1, D_2, D_3), \mathbf{s}(D_4, D_5, D_6)).$$

This function decides the social choice by simple majority on the outcomes of two three-member simple majority councils. Observe that $F(1,1,0,-1,-1,0) = \mathbf{s}(\mathbf{s}(1,1,0), \mathbf{s}(-1,-1,0)) = \mathbf{s}(1,-1) = 0$, but neither individual 3 nor individual 6 (nor both together) can change the $F = 0$ outcome by changing $D_3$ or $D_6$.

Structurally speaking, the important aspect of *strong* monotonicity is given by the following obvious implication:

$$D, D' \in F^*(0) \qquad \text{and} \qquad D \neq D' \Rightarrow D_i > D'_i \qquad \text{for some}$$
$$i \in \{1, \ldots, n\}.$$

This can fail under monotonicity, when $D' > D$ and $D, D' \in F^*(0)$.

STRONG UNANIMITY

DEFINITION 2.4. $F : \mathfrak{D} \to \{1, 0, -1\}$ *is* strongly unanimous *if* $D > 0 \Rightarrow F(D) = 1$, *and* $D < 0 \Rightarrow F(D) = -1$, *for all* $D \in \mathfrak{D}$.

This says that only Pareto optimal alternatives can be chosen.
I leave it to the reader to check the following simple implications:

$F(0) = 0$ and strong monotonicity $\Rightarrow$ strong unanimity,
$F$ not constant and strong monotonicity $\Rightarrow$ unanimity.

# CHAPTER 3

## Duality and Representative Systems

IN THIS CHAPTER we shall first examine the condition of duality for social choice functions in conjunction with monotonicity and unanimity. Representative systems are then defined recursively and discussed in some detail. The chapter centers on the Fundamental Theorem for Representative Systems, which is stated and proved in section 3.4. The Theorem of The Alternative, which concerns the existence of a solution for a set of linear inequalities, is used in the proof. Two versions of the Theorem of The Alternative are presented in section 3.3. These will be used also in later chapters of Part I.

Several corollaries of the fundamental theorem are proved in sections 3.4 and 3.5. The main corollary is Corollary 3.2. Other corollaries state the following: $F$ is a representative system if it is strongly monotonic and dual; $F$ is a representative system if it is monotonic, dual, and $F^*(0) = \{0\}$; if $F$ is monotonic, strongly unanimous and dual then it can be written as the product of an odd number of representative systems $F_1, \ldots, F_K$ for which $F^*(1) \subseteq F_k^*(1)$ for each $k$. The chapter concludes with the weak majority social choice function, which is monotonic, unanimous, and dual, but which is not strongly unanimous and cannot be written as a product of representative systems as just noted.

Necessary and sufficient conditions for representative systems are given in the next chapter.

### 3.1 DUALITY

For $D = (D_1, \ldots, D_n) \in \mathfrak{D}$, the *dual* of $D$ is

$$-D = (-D_1, \ldots, -D_n).$$

In terms of $x$ and $y$, the dual of a preference profile is obtained by reversing each individual preference. The condition of duality for a social function $F$ says that if $x$ and $y$ tie under $D$ then they tie under $-D$, that $x$ wins under $D$ if and only if $y$ wins under $-D$, and that $y$ wins under $D$ if and only if $x$ wins under $-D$.

DEFINITION 3.1. $F:\mathfrak{D} \to \{1,0,-1\}$ *is dual if and only if* $F(-D) = -F(D)$, *for all* $D \in \mathfrak{D}$.

Such a function $F$ is also called "self-dual" and "odd." Duality is also referred to as "neutrality" and "neutrality of alternatives."

The essential feature of duality is that it treats the two alternatives equally, apart from the actual preferences of the individuals in the society. In other words, duality prohibits the social choice function from having a built-in bias or favoritism for one of the two alternatives. The prime examples of social choice functions that are *not* dual are the special-majority functions in which one alternative (the "challenger") requires a two-thirds or three-quarters majority to defeat the other alternative (the "status quo"). Nondual social choice functions are discussed in Chapter 6.

If $\mathcal{E}$ is a subset of $\mathcal{D}$, $-\mathcal{E} = \{-D : D \in \mathcal{E}\}$. We shall refer to $-\mathcal{E}$ as the *dual* of $\mathcal{E}$. Clearly, $\mathcal{D}$ is the dual of $\mathcal{D}$, and if $F$ is dual then $-F^*(0) = F^*(0)$ and $-F^*(1) = F^*(-1)$. Obviously, duality requires $F(0) = 0$, and it and strong monotonicity imply strong unanimity. Some other basic facts are summarized in the following theorem.

THEOREM 3.1. *Let* $\mathfrak{M}$ *be the set of all monotonic, unanimous, and dual social choice functions* $F : \mathcal{D} \to \{1, 0, -1\}$. *Then*

$$F_1, \ldots, F_K \in \mathfrak{M} \Rightarrow s(F_1, \ldots, F_K) \in \mathfrak{M},$$

*and* $-BF^*(1) = BF^*(-1)$ *for every* $F \in \mathfrak{M}$.

The last part of the theorem states that the dual of the boundary of $F^*(1)$ is the boundary of $F^*(-1)$, which is easily seen to follow from $-F^*(1) = F^*(-1)$ and the definitions of section 2.3. Closure in $\mathfrak{M}$ under s follows from Theorem 2.2 and

$$s(F_1, \ldots, F_K)(-D) = s(F_1(-D), \ldots, F_K(-D))$$
$$= s(-F_1(D), \ldots, -F_K(D)) = -s(F_1, \ldots, F_K)(D).$$

## 3.2 REPRESENTATIVE SYSTEMS

We now define an important subfamily of $\mathfrak{M}$, namely the set $\mathfrak{R}$ of all representative systems.

For each $i \in \{1, \ldots, n\}$ let $S_i : \mathcal{D} \to \{1, 0, -1\}$ be defined by $S_i(D) = D_i$ for all $D \in \mathcal{D}$. If $F - S_i$ then individual $i$ completely dictates the social choice.

Let $\mathfrak{R}_0 = \{S_1, S_2, \ldots, S_n\}$ and, proceeding recursively, for each $m > 0$ let $\mathfrak{R}_m$ be the set of all functions $s(F_1, \ldots, F_K) : \mathcal{D} \to \{1, 0, -1\}$ with $K$ any positive integer and $F_k \in \mathfrak{R}_{m-1}$ for each $k$. Finally, let $\mathfrak{R}$ be the union of the $\mathfrak{R}_m$ so that $F \in \mathfrak{R} \Leftrightarrow F \in \mathfrak{R}_m$ for some $m \geq 0$.

DEFINITION 3.2. $F : \mathcal{D} \to \{1, 0, -1\}$ *is a* representative system *if and only if* $F \in \mathfrak{R}$.

Several remarks about this definition are in order. First, it differs from Murakami's definition, which requires that $F$ be nondictatorial in the sense that there is no $i$ such that $F(D) = D_i$ whenever $D_i \neq 0$. Because this nondictatorship condition is not essential to the rest of our analysis, it will be deferred until later.

Second, the definition does not require $F$ to be *given* in the terms of an s hierarchy in order for it to be a representative system. However, $F$ is a representative system only if it is possible, in principle, to write it in terms of an s hierarchy. To illustrate this point, let $n = 4$ and let $F$ be defined by simple majority except that $F(D) = D_1$ when two $D_i$ equal 1 and the other two $D_i$ equal $-1$. This $F$ is not given in terms of an s hierarchy, but it is a representative system, as will be noted below.

Thirdly, since $s(F) = F$ for any social choice function $F$, $\mathfrak{R}_0 \subseteq \mathfrak{R}_1 \subseteq \mathfrak{R}_2 \subseteq \cdots$. Since $\#\mathfrak{F}$ is finite ($= 3^{3^n}$), $\#\mathfrak{R}$ is finite and therefore there is an $m$ such that $\mathfrak{R} = \mathfrak{R}_m$.

From the definition of $\mathfrak{R}$ and our preceding observations it is obvious that

$$F_1, \ldots, F_K \in \mathfrak{R} \Rightarrow s(F_1, \ldots, F_K) \in \mathfrak{R}$$

and that $\mathfrak{R} \subseteq \mathfrak{M}$. Thus, every representative system is monotonic, unanimous, and dual. In fact, $\mathfrak{R} = \mathfrak{M}$ only when $n = 1$. For $n = 2$, one can show that $F$ defined by $F(1,1) = 1$, $F(-1,-1) = -1$ and $F(D) = 0$ otherwise is in $\mathfrak{M}$ but not in $\mathfrak{R}$.

Since $\mathfrak{R} = \mathfrak{R}_m$ for some $m$, it is clear that a given $F \in \mathfrak{R}$ can be written in many different ways as an s hierarchy. Indeed, note that $F = s(F) = s(s(F)) = s(s(s(F))) = \cdots$ and that $F = s(F,F) = s(F,F,F) = \cdots$. A nontrivial example of equal representations will be stated shortly.

ADDITIONAL NOTATION

An evaluational form for $F \in \mathfrak{R}$ is obtained by replacing each $S_i$ by $D_i$. For example, if $F = s(S_2, s(S_1, S_1, S_2, S_3))$, then $F(D) = s(D_2, s(D_1, D_1, D_2, D_3))$ for every $D \in \mathfrak{D}$. For any given $D \in \mathfrak{D}$, this is obviously evaluated from the inside outward. Thus $F(1,-1,1) = s(-1, s(1,1,-1,1)) = s(-1,1) = 0$, and $F(1,-1,-1) = s(-1, s(1,1, -1,-1)) = s(-1,0) = -1$.

Identical and contiguous expressions in a string of this form will often be pre-added to shorten the string, as in $s(D_1, D_1, D_2, D_3) = s(2D_1, D_2, D_3)$. Another example is

$$s(s(D_1,D_2), s(D_1,D_2), s(D_3,D_3,D_3,s(D_2,D_3)), s(D_1,D_3), s(D_1,D_2)))$$
$$= s(2s(D_1,D_2), s(3D_3, s(D_2,D_3)), s(D_1,D_3), s(D_1,D_2))).$$

An even simpler notation results when the s are omitted, with the understanding that s is applied *immediately before* each left parenthesis. Under this convention, the preceding string is $(2(D_1,D_2), (3D_3,(D_2,D_3), (D_1,D_3),(D_1,D_2)))$.

Consider again the case where $n = 4$ and $F$ is defined by simple majority except that $F(D) = D_1$ when two $D_i = 1$ and the other two $D_i = -1$. One evaluative form for this $F$ is

$$F(D) = ((2D_1,D_2,D_3,D_4),(D_1,2D_2,2D_3),(D_1,2D_2,2D_4),(D_1,2D_3,2D_4)).$$

It is a useful exercise to show that this agrees with the given definition of $F$. Although the above string presents $F(D)$ in a two-level hierarchical form, it can be written in other ways. One of these is the following three-level form:

$$
\begin{aligned}
F(D) = (&((3D_1,2D_2,2D_3,2D_4),(D_2,D_3)),\\
&((3D_1,2D_2,2D_3,2D_4),(D_2,D_4)),\\
&((3D_1,2D_2,2D_3,2D_4),(D_3,D_4)),\\
&(D_2,D_3,D_4)).
\end{aligned}
$$

Using duality and the natural symmetry in $D_2$, $D_3$ and $D_4$, it is not too hard to show that this also agrees with the given $F$.

INTERPRETATION

As in the interpretation following (2.8), we can think of a representative system as a hierarchy of voting councils, although, as we have just seen, there may be a number of different hierarchical structures that have identical social choice functions. The outcomes of the votes of lower councils act as votes in higher councils. This continues up through the hierarchy until a final aggregation is made at the highest level. The interest in representative systems obviously stems from the large number of social choice procedures that operate (more or less) in this fashion.

As Murakami notes, the definition of a representative system prohibits fixed ballots, or votes from outside the system, from influencing the social choice. For example, $F$ defined by $F(D) = (D_1,D_2,1)$ is not a representative system. The definition also prohibits the choice process from reversing an individual's vote. For example, $F$ defined by $F(D) = (D_1, -D_2)$ is not a representative system. In this regard, it would appear from the definition that if a person votes in a certain way in one of the councils of which he is a member, then he must vote the same way in every other council to which he belongs. Although this is true in a sense, it may be relaxed by treating one person as different individuals in different councils. This can be effected by assigning more than one subscript $i$ to the same person for his voting in different councils.

**29**

To illustrate a case where an individual might vote differently in different councils, suppose a society is partitioned into two disjoint groups of approximately equal size. The chairman of the society is in one of these groups. A simple-majority vote is taken in each group. If the simple-majority aggregation of the outcomes of the two groups, as given by $s(s(\text{group } 1), s(\text{group } 2))$, yields a tie between $x$ and $y$, then the chairman can break the tie by another vote. With $D_1$ for the chairman in his tie-breaking capacity, the process can be represented as $s(D_1,2s(s(D_2, \ldots ,D_m),s(D_{m+1}, \ldots ,D_n)))$, or simply as $(D_1,2((D_2, \ldots ,D_m),(D_{m+1}, \ldots ,D_n)))$. Suppose that the chairman, in his role as a member of a group, votes for $x$, which he personally prefers to $y$. Suppose further that $x$ beats $y$ by a slim margin in group 1, and that $y$ overwhelms $x$ in group 2. Then the chairman, in his role as tie-breaker, might very well vote for $y$. The temporal aspects of this example suggest a complex formulation that incorporates certain informational variables, but we shall not pursue this here.

The effects of monotonicity, unanimity, and duality relate to the foregoing aspects of representative systems. Monotonicity and unanimity tend to require a social choice function to be faithful to the preferences of the individuals, and duality tends to prevent the intervention of fixed votes or outside interests from affecting the decision. (Needless to say, pressures from outside the voting group can influence the votes of individuals in the group.)

## 3.3 THE THEOREM OF THE ALTERNATIVE

Before presenting the fundamental theorem for representative systems, we shall state a theorem that will be used in its proof and in later chapters.

Let $A = \{a^1, \ldots ,a^K\}$ and $B = \{a^{K+1}, \ldots ,a^M\}$ be finite sets of vectors in $Re^n$, with $1 \leq K \leq M$ so that $A \neq \emptyset$. Our first form of the Theorem of The Alternative concerns the possibility of passing a hyperplane $\{a:\rho \cdot a = 0\}$ through the origin $\mathbf{0}$ of $Re^n$ so that all points in $A$ lie completely on one side of the hyperplane, and all points (if any) in $B$ lie in, or on the other side of, the hyperplane. The theorem states explicitly what must happen when it is not possible to separate $A$ and $B$ by such a hyperplane.

Figure 3.1 pictures three situations in $Re^2$, where hyperplanes through the origin are straight lines. In figure (a), $A$ has four points and $B$ has three points, and there are many lines that separate $A$ and $B$. This separation depends on precisely the fact that the convex closure $\bar{A}$ of $A$ does not intersect the convex cone with origin, $B'$, that is generated by $B$. (If $B = \emptyset$, then $B' = \{\mathbf{0}\}$.) In figure (b), $B$ is empty but $\bar{A}$ contains the origin, and no line through the origin can

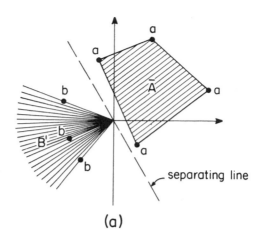

(a)

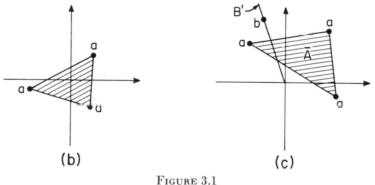

(b)                              (c)

FIGURE 3.1

have the three points in $A$ on only one side. In figure (c), $0 \notin \bar{A}$ but $B'$ and $\bar{A}$ have a nonempty intersection.

A vector $a \in Re^n$ is *rational* if each component $a_i$ is a rational number, and *integral* if each $a_i$ is an integer. The following theorem remains valid when "rational" and "integral" are deleted and "integers" is replaced by "numbers."

THEOREM 3.2. (THEOREM OF THE ALTERNATIVE). *Suppose that* $a^1, \ldots, a^K, \ldots, a^M$ *are rational vectors in* $Re^n$ *with* $1 \le K \le M$. *Then* EITHER *there is an integral* $\rho \in Re^n$ *such that*

$$\rho \cdot a^k > 0 \quad for \quad k = 1, \ldots, K \qquad (3.1)$$
$$\rho \cdot a^k \le 0 \quad for \quad k = K+1, \ldots, M \qquad (3.2)$$

OR *there are nonnegative integers* $r_1, \ldots, r_K$ *at least one of which is positive, and nonpositive integers* $r_{K+1}, \ldots, r_M$ *such that*

$$\Sigma_{k=1}^{M} r_k a_i^k = 0 \quad for \quad i = 1, \ldots, n. \tag{3.3}$$

Although theorems on the existence of solutions for systems of linear inequalities such as (3.1) and (3.2) date at least from early in this century, alternative forms such as Theorem 3.2 appeared more recently. For example, apart from the rational-integral aspects of Theorem 3.2, that theorem is equivalent to Theorem 2 in Goldman (1956).

The following theorem can be seen as a corollary of Theorem 3.2 by replacing each $\rho \cdot a^k = 0$ equality in (3.4) with the pair ($\rho \cdot a^k \leq 0$, $\rho \cdot (-a^k) \leq 0$), to be used as in (3.2).

THEOREM 3.3. *Suppose that* $a^1, \ldots, a^K, \ldots, a^M$ *are rational vectors in* $Re^n$ *with* $1 \leq K \leq M$. *Then* EITHER *there is an integral vector* $\rho \in Re^n$ *such that*

$$\rho \cdot a^k > 0 \quad for \quad k = 1, \ldots, K$$
$$\rho \cdot a^k = 0 \quad for \quad k = K+1, \ldots, M \tag{3.4}$$

OR *there are nonnegative integers* $r_1, \ldots, r_K$ *at least one of which is positive, and integers* $r_{K+1}, \ldots, r_M$ *such that*

$$\Sigma_{k=1}^{M} r_k a_i^k = 0 \quad for \quad i = 1, \ldots, n.$$

This version of the Theorem of The Alternative is similar to the form used by Aumann (1964).

## 3.4 THE FUNDAMENTAL THEOREM

One more definition is needed before we can state the Fundamental Theorem for Representative Systems.

DEFINITION 3.3. *With respect to a social choice function F, individual i is* essential *if and only if* $F(D_1, \ldots, D_{i-1}, 1, D_{i+1}, \ldots, D_n) = F(D_1, \ldots, D_{i-1}, 0, D_{i+1}, \ldots, D_n) = F(D_1, \ldots, D_{i-1}, -1, D_{i+1}, \ldots, D_n)$ *is false for some* $(D_1, \ldots, D_{i-1}, D_{i+1}, \ldots, D_n) \in \{1, 0, -1\}^{n-1}$.

If $i$ is not essential, then $F$ is completely insensitive to his preference. Unanimity and duality require some $i$ to be essential, for if no $i$ were essential then $F(1) = F(0, 1, \ldots, 1) = F(0, 0, 1, \ldots, 1) = \cdots = F(0)$. If $F$ is a representative system and $i$ is not essential, then no s hierarchy for $F$ can contain $S_i$ (or $D_i$).

Many succeeding results in this and the next chapter will be based on the following theorem.

THEOREM 3.4. (FUNDAMENTAL THEOREM FOR REPRESENTATIVE SYS-TEMS). *Suppose that $F: \mathfrak{D} \to \{1, 0, -1\}$ is monotonic, unanimous and dual, so that $F \in \mathfrak{M}$. Suppose further that $\mathcal{E}$ (possibly empty) is a subset of $F^*(0)$ such that*

$$D, D' \in \mathcal{E} \Rightarrow D_i > -D'_i \text{ for an essential } i \in \{1, \ldots, n\}. \quad (3.5)$$

*Then there is a representative system $G \in \mathfrak{R}$ such that $i$ is essential for $G$ only if $i$ is essential for $F$, and*

$$G(D) = 1 \quad \text{for all} \quad D \in F^*(1) \cup \mathcal{E}. \quad (3.6)$$

One immediate corollary of this is

COROLLARY 3.1. *If $F$ is monotonic and dual and $F^*(0) = \{0\}$ then $F$ is a representative system.*

Expression (3.5) has no effect on the corollary: any $\mathcal{E}$ that satisfies (3.5) cannot contain $0$. More generally, if $\mathcal{E}$ satisfies (3.5) then $\mathcal{E} \cap (-\mathcal{E}) = \emptyset$ since $D_i > -(-D_i)$ is false for all $i$. A second corollary of Theorem 3.4 involves (3.5) and will serve as the basis of further results to be deduced using the fundamental theorem.

COROLLARY 3.2. *Suppose that the hypotheses of Theorem 3.4 hold, and suppose further that (3.5) holds when $\mathcal{E}$ therein is replaced by $-\mathcal{E}$. Then there is an $H \in \mathfrak{R}$ such that $i$ is essential for $H$ only if $i$ is essential for $F$, and*

$$\begin{aligned} H(D) &= 1 &\quad \text{for all} \quad & D \in F^*(1) \\ H(D) &= 0 &\quad \text{for all} \quad & D \subset \mathcal{E} \cup (-\mathcal{E}) \\ H(D) &= -1 &\quad \text{for all} \quad & D \in F^*(-1). \end{aligned}$$

*Proof.* Under the hypotheses of the corollary, let $G$ satisfy (3.6). Since (3.5) is assumed to hold for $-\mathcal{E}$, Theorem 3.4 implies also that there is a $G' \in \mathfrak{R}$ such that $i$ is essential for $G'$ only if $i$ is essential for $F$, and

$$G'(D) = 1 \quad \text{for all} \quad D \in F^*(1) \cup (-\mathcal{E}).$$

Let $H = s(G, G')$. Then $D \in F^*(1) \Rightarrow H(D) = s(G(D), G'(D)) = s(1, 1) = 1$. Since $H$ is dual, $H(D) = -1$ when $D \subset F^*(-1)$. Finally, if $D \in \mathcal{E}$ then $H(D) = s(G(D), G'(D)) = s(1, -1) = 0$, and if $D \in -\mathcal{E}$ then $H(D) = s(-1, 1) = 0.$ ◆

Other corollaries are given in the next section. The rest of this section proves Theorem 3.4.

PROOF OF THE FUNDAMENTAL THEOREM

Throughout this proof, $F$ and $\mathcal{E}$ are as specified in the hypotheses of the theorem. Before applying the Theorem of The Alternative, we shall prove two lemmas. The conclusion of the second lemma will be pivotal in the later use of Theorem 3.2.

LEMMA 3.1. $D,D' \in F^*(1) \cup \mathcal{E} \Rightarrow D_i > -D_i'$ for an essential $i$.

*Proof.* If $D,D' \in \mathcal{E}$, (3.5) gives the conclusion. Henceforth assume that $D \in F^*(1)$. Then, by duality, $F(-D) = -1$. If $D_i' \leq -D_i$ for every essential $i$ then, by monotonicity and Definition 3.3, $F(D') = -1$. This contradicts $D' \in F^*(1) \cup \mathcal{E}$. Therefore $D_i' > -D_i$ for an essential $i$. This is the same as $D_i > -D_i'$ for an essential $i$. ◆

Since nonessential $i$ have no effect on $F$, *all $i$ to be used henceforth will be assumed to be essential.* Without any loss in generality, $\{1, \ldots, n\}$ will be the set of essential $i$.

LEMMA 3.2. *Suppose that $m$ is a positive integer and that $D^1, \ldots, D^m$ are all in $F^*(1) \cup \mathcal{E}$. Then*

$$\Sigma_{k=1}^m H(D^k) > 0 \qquad \text{for some} \qquad H \in \mathcal{R}. \qquad (3.7)$$

*Remark.* The various $D^k$ in $D^1, \ldots, D^m$ need not all be distinct. For example, with $m = 5$, we could have $D^1 = D^2$ and $D^3 = D^4 = D^5$.

*Proof.* We shall prove the lemma by constructing an $H$ that satisfies (3.7). The proof is accomplished by induction on even $m$ in $\{2,4,6, \ldots\}$. This proof serves also for odd $m$, for if $m$ is odd then the number of terms in the sequence $D^1, \ldots, D^m, D^1, \ldots, D^m$ is even, and (3.7) holds $\Leftrightarrow 2\Sigma_{k=1}^m H(D^k) > 0$.

Given $D^1, \ldots, D^m$ with each $D^k \in F^*(1) \cup \mathcal{E}$ and $m$ even, $\{1, \ldots, m\}$ has $m(m-1)/2$ two-element subsets. For each subset $\{j,k\}$ with $j \neq k$, Lemma 3.1 implies that there is an $i \in \{1, \ldots, n\}$ for which $D_i^k > -D_i^j$ (and hence $D_i^j > -D_i^k$ also). Let $i\{j,k\}$ be such an $i$ for $\{j,k\}$. $i\{j,k\} = i\{k,j\}$.

Clearly, $(D_{i\{j,k\}}^j, D_{i\{j,k\}}^k) \in \{(1,0),(0,1),(1,1)\}$ for each $\{j,k\}$ pair. With $j$ fixed, suppose that $\#\{k : k \neq j$ and $(D_{i\{j,k\}}^j, D_{i\{j,k\}}^k) = (1,0)\} \geq m/2$. If this were true for each $j \in \{1, \ldots, m\}$, then there would be at least $m(m/2)$ distinct $\{j,k\}$ pairs with $k \neq j$. Since there are in fact only $(m-1)(m/2)$ such pairs, it follows that there is a $j$, which for definiteness we shall suppose is $j = 1$, such that

$$(D_{i\{1,k\}}^1, D_{i\{1,k\}}^k) \in \{(0,1),(1,1)\} \qquad \text{for at least} \qquad m/2 \ k > 1.$$

Re-indexing these $k$ as required, we obtain the array of components shown in Figure 3.2. Only the components that we shall use (except for $m = 4$) are shown. Some of the columns may represent the same $i \in \{1, \ldots, n\}$ since it is possible to have $i\{1,k\} = i\{1,k'\}$ when $k \neq k'$. Apart from this, the blank spaces could be filled in any way from $\{1, 0, -1\}$ and the end result would not vary. The last column $(i')$ in the figure must be used when all entries in the first row preceding the last column are zeros: Lemma 3.1 ensures that $D_i^1 = 1$ for some $i$.

The number of $D^k$ in Figure 3.2 exceeds $m/2$. To satisfy (3.7) we shall construct an $H \in \mathfrak{R}$ such that $H(D^k) = 1$ for $k = 1, \ldots, 1 + m/2$.

For $m = 2$, $H(D) = s(2D_{i\{1,2\}}, D_{i'})$ gives $H(D^1) = H(D^2) = 1$. For $m = 4$, we have the situation shown in Figure 3.3, where an additional

| | i{1,2} | i{1,3} | i{1,4} | . . . | i{1,$\frac{m}{2}$} | i{1,$\frac{m}{2}$ + 1} | i' |
|---|---|---|---|---|---|---|---|
| $D^1$ | 0 or 1 | 0 or 1 | 0 or 1 | . . . | 0 or 1 | 0 or 1 | 1 |
| $D^2$ | 1 | | | | | | |
| $D^3$ | | 1 | | | | | |
| $D^4$ | | | 1 | | | | |
| . . . | | | | | | | |
| $D^{m/2}$ | | | | | 1 | | |
| $D^{1+m/2}$ | | | | | | 1 | |

FIGURE 3.2. Matrix of $D_i^j$

| | i{1,2} | i{1,3} | i' | i{2,3} |
|---|---|---|---|---|
| $D^1$ | 0/1 | 0/1 | 1 | |
| $D^2$ | 1 | | | 0 |
| $D^3$ | | 1 | | $\perp$ |

FIGURE 3.3

column has been added for $i\{2,3\}$. [The $(0,1)$ in this column can be replaced by $(1,0)$ or $(1,1)$ and the same end result can be obtained.] With

$$H(D) = ((2D_{i\{1,2\}}, D_{i'}), (2D_{i\{1,3\}}, D_{i'}), (D_{i\{1,2\}}, 2D_{i\{2,3\}}))$$

we obtain $H(D^k) = 1$ for $k = 1, 2, 3$.

Continuing by induction on even $m'$, suppose that the result just established for $m' = 2$ and $m' = 4$ holds for each even $m'$ less than $m \geq 6$. Let Figure 3.2 apply to $m$. By ignoring the last row and next-to-last column of Figure 3.2, we have precisely the Figure 3.2 situation for $m' = m - 2$. The induction hypothesis then gives a representative system $H_1$ with

$$H_1(D^k) = 1 \quad \text{for all} \quad k \leq 1 + m/2 \quad \text{except} \quad k = 1 + m/2.$$

**35**

Similarly, by ignoring the next-to-last row and second-from-last column of Figure 3.2, the induction hypothesis gives $H_2 \in \mathfrak{R}$ with

$$H_2(D^k) = 1 \qquad \text{for all} \qquad k \le 1 + m/2 \qquad \text{except} \qquad k = m/2.$$

Finally, deletion of the second-from-last row and third-from-last column gives an $H_3 \in \mathfrak{R}$ for which

$$H_3(D^k) = 1 \qquad \text{for all} \qquad k \le 1 + m/2 \qquad \text{except} \qquad k = m/2 - 1.$$

It follows that $H = \mathbf{s}(H_1, H_2, H_3)$ has $H(D^k) = 1$ for all $k \le 1 + m/2$. ◆

We shall now use the Theorem of The Alternative. Let $\mathfrak{R} = \{F_1, F_2, \ldots, F_T\}$ with $\#\mathfrak{R} = T$. We note first that (3.6) holds if and only if there are positive integers $\rho_1, \ldots, \rho_T$ such that

$$\mathbf{s}(\rho_1 F_1, \ldots, \rho_T F_T)(D) = 1 \qquad \text{for all} \qquad D \in F^*(1) \cup \mathcal{E}. \quad (3.8)$$

If this is true, then $G = \mathbf{s}(\rho_1 F_1, \ldots, \rho_T F_T)$ satisfies (3.6), where $\rho_t F_t$ denotes $F_t$ repeated $\rho_t$ times. Conversely, suppose that $G \in \mathfrak{R}$ satisfies (3.6). Then $G$ is one of the $F_t$. For definiteness let $G = F_1$. Then $G' = \mathbf{s}(TF_1, F_2, \ldots, F_T)$ also satisfies (3.6).

We shall use only the (3.1) part of Theorem 3.2. The theorem is applied to $Re^T$, with $K = \#(F^*(1) \cup \mathcal{E}) + T$. The $K$ vectors $a^k$ for (3.1) are the vectors $(F_1(D), \ldots, F_T(D))$ for each $D \in F^*(1) \cup \mathcal{E}$ and the vectors $(0, \ldots, 0, 1, 0, \ldots, 0)$ for each $t \in \{1, \ldots, T\}$. Theorem 3.2 states that *either* there is an integral vector $\rho \in Re^T$ such that

$$\rho \cdot (F_1(D), \ldots, F_T(D)) > 0 \qquad \text{for each} \qquad D \in F^*(1) \cup \mathcal{E},$$
$$\rho_t = \rho \cdot (0, \ldots, 0, 1, 0, \ldots, 0) > 0 \qquad \text{for each} \qquad t \in \{1, \ldots, T\},$$

in which case (3.8) holds, since $\mathbf{s}(\rho_1 F_1, \ldots, \rho_T F_T)(D) = \mathbf{s}(\rho \cdot (F_1(D), \ldots, F_T(D))) = 1$ for each $D \in F^*(1) \cup \mathcal{E}$; *or* the stated alternative holds.

Suppose that the alternative holds. Then, with $A = \#F^*(1) \cup \mathcal{E}$ and $\{D^1, \ldots, D^A\} = F^*(1) \cup \mathcal{E}$, there are nonnegative integers $r_1, \ldots, r_A, s_1, \ldots, s_T$, at least one of which is positive such that

$$\Sigma_{k=1}^A r_k F_t(D^k) + s_t = 0 \qquad \text{for} \qquad t = 1, \ldots, T. \quad (3.9)$$

If some $s_t > 0$ then at least one $r_k > 0$. Consequently, at least one $r_k$ is positive. Let $m = \Sigma r_k$ and let $E^1, \ldots, E^m$ be a sequence of $D \in F^*(1) \cup \mathcal{E}$ that contains $D^k$ $r_k$ times for $k = 1, \ldots, A$. Then, according to (3.9), since $s_t \ge 0$ for each $t$,

$$\Sigma_{k=1}^m F_t(E^k) \le 0 \qquad \text{for} \qquad t = 1, \ldots, T.$$

Hence, since $\mathcal{R} = \{F_1, \ldots, F_T\}$, there is no $H \in \mathcal{R}$ such that $\Sigma_{k=1}^m H(E^k) > 0$. But this contradicts Lemma 3.2. Hence the alternative is false and (3.8) holds for positive integers $\rho_1, \ldots, \rho_T$. ◆

## 3.5 TWO THEOREMS

We shall now use Corollary 3.2 of the fundamental theorem to establish theorems that use strong monotonicity (Definition 2.3) and strong unanimity (Definition 2.4). These theorems add new results to Corollary 3.1, whose conditions imply that $F$ is both strongly monotonic and strongly unanimous. The conditions of the following theorem also imply strong unanimity, but they permit $F^*(0)$ to contain elements in $\mathcal{D}$ other than $0$.

THEOREM 3.5. *If $F$ is strongly monotonic and dual then it is a representative system.*

*Proof.* Let $\mathcal{D}^0$ equal $F^*(0)$ minus $0$. If $\mathcal{D}^0 = \emptyset$ then Corollary 3.1 implies that $F \in \mathcal{R}$. Henceforth suppose that $\mathcal{D}^0 \neq \emptyset$. Since the dual of $\mathcal{D}^0$ is $\mathcal{D}^0$, we can partition $\mathcal{D}^0$ into $\mathcal{E}$ and its dual $-\mathcal{E}$. Each of $\mathcal{E}$ and $-\mathcal{E}$ satisfies (3.5). To show this for $\mathcal{E}$, suppose that (3.5) fails with $D, D' \in \mathcal{E}$ and $D_i > -D_i'$ for no essential $i$. Then $D_i \leq -D_i'$ for every essential $i$. Since the hypotheses of the theorem imply that every $i$ is essential, $D \leq -D'$. Now $-D' \in -\mathcal{E}$, and since $\mathcal{E} \cap (-\mathcal{E}) = \emptyset$ we must have $D < -D'$. But this contradicts strong monotonicity since both $D$ and $-D'$ are in $F^*(0)$. Therefore $D_i > -D_i'$ must hold for some $i$. The proof of (3.5) for $-\mathcal{E}$ is similar. Corollary 3.2 then completes the proof. ◆

THEOREM 3.6. *Suppose that $F$ is monotonic, dual and strongly unanimous. Then there are representative systems $F_1, \ldots, F_K$ with $K$ odd such that*

$$F^*(1) \subset F_k^*(1) \quad for \quad k = 1, \ldots, K, \qquad (3.10)$$
$$F(D) = F_1(D)F_2(D) \cdots F_K(D) \quad for\ every \quad D \in \mathcal{D}. \qquad (3.11)$$

*Proof.* As in the preceding proof let $\mathcal{D}^0$, if it is not empty, be partitioned into $\mathcal{E}$ and $-\mathcal{E}$. Let $D$ be any preference profile in $\mathcal{E}$. Then $D_i > -D_i$ for some $i$, for otherwise we get $D_i \leq 0$ for every $i$, and hence $D \leq 0$, and hence $D < 0$ (since $D \neq 0$), which contradicts strong unanimity since $F(D) = 0$. Hence (3.5) holds for the singleton subset $\{D\}$, and by a similar proof (3.5) holds also for $\{-D\}$. Corollary 3.2 then gives the representative systems $F_k$, one for each $D \in \mathcal{E}$, that satisfy the conclusions of the theorem. If $\#\mathcal{E}$ is even (and positive) then one of these $F_k$ can be repeated in the product to ensure that $F_1(D) \cdots F_K(D) = -1$ when $D \in F^*(-1)$. ◆

37

A somewhat naive interpretation of the representation in Theorem 3.6 suggests itself if we view the $F_k$ as $K$ parallel councils. Each council actively involves all voters and is a representative system. For every $D \in F^*(0)$ there will be at least one council that gives $F_k(D) = 0$. Because of the product form this will negate the votes of other councils and require an overall tie between $x$ and $y$. Alternative $x$ is the group choice when it is the choice of every council, and similarly for $y$.

WEAK MAJORITY

We conclude this chapter with a social choice function which shows that the conclusions of Theorem 3.6 can be false when "strongly unanimous" is replaced by "unanimous" in the hypotheses.

The social choice function that we shall use for this purpose is the so-called *nonminority* or *weak majority* social choice function, defined by

$$
\begin{aligned}
F(D) &= 1 \Leftrightarrow \#\{i : D_i = 1\} > n/2 \\
F(D) &= -1 \Leftrightarrow \#\{i : D_i = -1\} > n/2.
\end{aligned}
\tag{3.12}
$$

Thus, $x$ is the unique winner only if more than half of the voters vote for $x$, and similarly for $y$. A tie results when neither candidate receives a clear majority. If at least half the voters abstain then, regardless of how the others vote, a tie will result.

The weak majority social choice function is neither strongly unanimous nor strongly monotonic. However, it is monotonic, unanimous, and dual, so that $F \in \mathfrak{M}$.

To show the effect of this $F$ on the conclusions of Theorem 3.6, let $n = 3$, and let $G$ be any representative system that satisfies (3.10). That is, $F^*(1) \subseteq G^*(1)$ and $G \in \mathfrak{R}$. Any evaluative form for $G$ must contain all of $D_1$, $D_2$ and $D_3$. For example, if $G$ were a function of $D_1$ only, say $G(D) = D_1$, then we have $G(-1,1,1) = -1$, contrary to $F^*(1) \subseteq G^*(1)$. Or suppose that only $D_1$ and $D_2$ appear in $G(D)$. Then, since we require $G(1,-1,1) = 1$ and $G(-1,1,1) = 1$ and since duality would require $G(-1,1,*) = -G(1,-1,*)$ if only $D_1$ and $D_2$ were essential with respect to $G$, we see that this supposition is false. Thus all of $D_1$, $D_2$, and $D_3$ must be essential with respect to $G \in \mathfrak{R}$. But then every such $G$ has $G(1,0,0) = G(0,1,0) = G(0,0,1) = 1$ and the product of any number of $G$'s that satisfy (3.10) will yield 1 for each $D \in \{(1,0,0),(0,1,0),(0,0,1)\}$. However, $F(D) = 0$ for each of these three $D$'s by (3.12), and therefore (3.11) must be false.

In the latter part of Chapter 5 we shall note conditions on $F$ which are necessary and sufficient for weak majority and compare these with the necessary and sufficient conditions for simple majority which are given in Chapter 5 also.

# CHAPTER 4

# Decisive Coalitions and Representative
# Systems

THIS CHAPTER concludes our study of general representative systems by establishing a set of necessary and sufficient conditions for them. The next chapter examines some specialized representative systems.

We have already seen that every representative system is monotonic, unanimous, and dual. A fourth condition, which we shall call condition *RS*, completes the set of necessary and sufficient conditions. Condition *RS*, which shares some of the aspects of strong unanimity, will be introduced in section 4.2. The theorems that make use of it are in section 4.3.

Condition *RS* is somewhat difficult to interpret as a reasonable prescription for a social choice function. Because of this we shall begin the chapter with another condition which is also necessary for representative systems and which has a rather easy interpretation. This other condition asserts the possibility of simple majority winning coalitions and contains much of the essence of condition *RS*. However, it is not sufficient for the existence of a representative system in the presence of the three basic conditions of monotonicity, unanimity, and duality. It must of course be implied by the four necessary and sufficient conditions: we shall note in section 4.2 that it is implied by monotonicity and *RS*.

## 4.1 DECISIVE COALITIONS

Let $F$ be a social choice function in an $n$-voter context and let $J$ be a subset of $\{1, \ldots, n\}$. With respect to $F$, $J$ is *decisive for $x$ over $y$* if $x$ wins under $F$ when all $i \in J$ vote for $x$ and all $i \notin J$ vote for $y$. That is, $J$ is decisive for $x$ over $y$ if $F(D) = 1$ when $D_i = 1$ for all $i \in J$ and $D_i = -1$ for all $i \notin J$. The decisiveness of $J$ for $y$ over $x$ is defined similarly. If $F$ is dual, then $J$ is decisive for $x$ over $y$ if and only if $J$ is decisive for $y$ over $x$. Hence, when $F$ is dual, we simply say that $J$ is *decisive* when $J$ is decisive for $x$ over $y$.

If $F$ is imposed with $F \equiv 1$ then every $J$, including $\emptyset$, is decisive for $x$ over $y$, and no $J$ is decisive for $y$ over $x$. If $F$ is unanimous then $\{1, \ldots, n\}$ is decisive (both ways). If $F$ is monotonic and if $J$ is decisive for $x$ over $y$, then $F(D) = 1$ when $D_i = 1$ for all $i \in J$, regardless of the values of the $D_i$ for $i \notin J$. If the group contains a dictator $j$ in the sense that $F(D) = D_j$ whenever $D_j \neq 0$, then $J$ is decisive if and only if $j \in J$. Under both simple majority and weak majority (3.12), $J$ is decisive if and only if $\#J > n/2$.

Suppose that $F$ is monotonic and dual, and let $N$ be an integer that exceeds $n/2$ but not $n$. Thus, if $\#J = N$, then $J$ contains more than half of the individuals. Now some coalitions of size $N$ might not be decisive. However, in view of the facts that a tie vote does not resolve an issue and that "majority will" in some form or other plays a part in most social choice procedures, it would seem somewhat strange if no $J$ with $\#J = N$ were decisive. The condition that we shall develop in this section asserts the existence of at least one decisive coalition $J$ of size $N$ for each $N$ for which $n/2 < N \leq n$. For example, if there are nine voters in the group then there is some subset of five voters who can ensure the election of $x$ by voting for $x$. Depending on $F$, other subsets of five voters may or may not be able to ensure the election of $x$.

There might also be decisive coalitions that contain less than half of the voters, but we shall not focus on these here.

## DECISIVE COALITIONS WITHIN SUBSETS

We shall now extend the notion of decisive coalitions to account for cases where some voters abstain or are indifferent.

DEFINITION 4.1. *Let $F: \{1, 0, -1\}^n \to \{1, 0, -1\}$, let $J$ be a nonempty subset of $\{1, \ldots, n\}$, and let $I$ be a subset of $J$. Then, with respect to $F$, $I$ is decisive for $x$ over $y$ within $J$ if and only if $F(D) = 1$ when $D_i = 1$ for all $i \in I$, $D_i = -1$ for all $i \in J - I$, and $D_i = 0$ for all $i \notin J$.*

That is, $I$ is decisive for $x$ over $y$ within $J$ if $x$ is elected when all $i \in I$ vote for $x$, all $i$ in $J$ but not $I$ vote for $y$, and all other voters abstain. A similar definition holds for $I$ decisive for $y$ over $x$ within $J$.

Suppose that $\#J = N > 0$. Then, under simple majority, every $I \subseteq J$ for which $N/2 < \#I \leq N$ is decisive within $J$. However, under weak majority, $I$ can be decisive within $J$ only if $\#I > n/2$. Thus, if $\#J \leq n/2$ then no $I \subseteq J$ is decisive within $J$ when $F$ is the weak majority social choice function.

The foregoing condition for $J$ decisive within $\{1, \ldots, n\}$ extends in an obvious way to $I$ decisive within $J$. This extension seems reasonable provided that we adopt the viewpoint that abstentions (indifferences) can be disregarded in determining the social choice. This point of view is shared by all representative systems, including simple and weighted majority, but it is not shared by weak majority. In Chapter 6 we shall distinguish between special majority social choice functions according to the effect of abstentions on the outcome of the vote.

We now state our general condition for the possibility of decisive majority coalitions. The condition will not presuppose that $F$ is dual, and it takes account of the possibility of nonessential voters (Definition 3.3). The dual of the condition (interchange $x$ and $y$) is implied by duality and the condition.

DEFINITION 4.2. *F satisfies the condition of decisive majority coalitions if and only if for every nonempty $J \subseteq \{1, \ldots, n\}$ that contains an essential $i$ and every integer $m$ for which $\#J/2 < m \le \#J$, there exists an $I \subseteq J$ such that $\#I = m$ and $I$ is decisive for $x$ over $y$ within $J$.*

The essential facts about the relationship of this condition to representative systems are summarized in the following theorem.

THEOREM 4.1. *Every representative system satisfies the condition of decisive majority coalitions. There are social choice functions that are monotonic, unanimous, dual and satisfy the condition of decisive majority coalitions, but which are not representative systems.*

Because it is efficient to use condition $RS$ of the next section in proving the first part of this theorem, we defer its proof to the next section. However, we can prepare for the proof and the introduction of $RS$ with an example.

EXAMPLE

Let $n = 5$ and consider the five potential preference profiles displayed in Figure 4.1. There is an obvious pattern to these profiles.

$i$

|  | 1 | 2 | 3 | 4 | 5 |
|---|---|---|---|---|---|
| $D^1$ | 1 | -1 | 1 | -1 | 1 |
| $D^2$ | 1 | 1 | -1 | 1 | -1 |
| $D^3$ | -1 | 1 | 1 | -1 | 1 |
| $D^4$ | 1 | -1 | 1 | 1 | -1 |
| $D^5$ | -1 | 1 | -1 | 1 | 1 |

FIGURE 4.1

Each has three $x$ votes and two $y$ votes, and each voter "votes" for $x$ three times and for $y$ twice in the five situations under consideration.

A key feature of the patterns in Figure 4.1 that may not be immediately obvious is that, for each column or voter, $D_i^k \ge -D_i^{k+1}$ for $k = 1, 2, 3, 4$, and $D_i^5 \ge -D_i^1$. This follows from the fact that the $-1$'s are not adjacent (or at the beginning and end) in any column. In fact, we have

$$D^1 > -D^2, D^2 > -D^3, D^3 > -D^4, D^4 > -D^5, D^5 > -D^1. \quad (4.1)$$

Another way to write this is $D^1 > -D^2 < D^3 > -D^4 < D^5 > -D^1$, which imparts a cyclic pattern to the figure.

Expression (4.1) makes a connection through $>$ between $D^1$ and its dual $-D^1$, or between any $D^k$ and its dual for that matter. For the moment, call $D$ and $D'$ adjacent if either $D > D'$ or $D' > D$, and call them connected within a subset $\mathfrak{D}'$ of $\mathfrak{D}$ if they are both in $\mathfrak{D}'$ and there is a finite sequence $D, E^1, \ldots, E^r, D'$ of elements in $\mathfrak{D}'$ such that each two contiguous elements in the sequence are adjacent. Then (4.1) shows that $D^1$ and $-D^1$ are connected within $\{D^1, -D^2, D^3, -D^4, D^5, -D^1\}$.

The point of this example for representative systems is that when (4.1) holds, when at least one of the $i$ in Figure 4.1 is essential, and when $F$ is a representative system, then it must be true that $F(D^k) = 1$ for at least one of the five $D^k$. In other words, we cannot have $F(D^k) \leq 0$ for all five $k$.

Stated another way, if $F$ is a representative system, then at least one of the five three-voter subsets of $\{1,2,3,4,5\}$ that arise from the figure— namely $\{1,3,5\}$, $\{1,2,4\}$, $\{2,3,5\}$, $\{1,3,4\}$, and $\{2,4,5\}$—must be decisive. These five subsets, determined by the $x$ votes in each $D^k$, are not the only three-voter subsets since there are 10 such subsets. The reason that the condition of decisive majority coalitions is *not* sufficient for representative majority (along with monotonicity, unanimity, duality) follows directly from this observation. This condition requires at least one of the 10 three-voter subsets to be decisive, but it does not require one of the noted five to be decisive.

To elaborate on this, let $F$ be defined on $\{1,0,-1\}^5$ by simple majority, except that $F(D^k) = F(-D^k) = 0$ for the five $D^k$ of Figure 4.1 and their duals. This $F$ is clearly monotonic, unanimous, and dual. Moreover, since $F(1,1,1,-1,-1) = 1$, it follows easily that it satisfies the condition of decisive majority coalitions. However, according to the claim made above, $F$ is not a representative system.

Thus, except for proving that one of the $F(D^k) = 1$ when $F$ is a representative system, we have just proved the latter half of Theorem 4.1.

## 4.2   A Condition for Representative Systems

Enough has been said in the preceding section to permit us to state the special condition for representative systems without further delay.

DEFINITION 4.3. $F: \mathfrak{D} \to \{1, 0, -1\}$ *satisfies* condition $RS$ *if and only if* $F(D^k) = 1$ *for some* $k \in \{1, \ldots, m\}$ *whenever $m$ is an odd positive integer,* $D^1 > -D^2$, $D^2 > -D^3$, $\ldots$, $D^{m-1} > -D^m$, $D^m > -D^1$, *and* $\Sigma_{k=1}^m D_i^k > 0$ *for some essential $i$.*

Because this condition and monotonicity imply the condition of decisive majority coalitions (see the end of this section), the intuitive aspects of the coalitions condition apply also to condition $RS$. The essential way that $RS$ goes beyond the coalitions condition has already been brought out in the preceding example. Not only does it require decisive majority coalitions in the same subsets as specified in the coalitions condition, but it requires decisiveness in certain "cyclic" subsets of $\mathfrak{D}$ that are not covered under the former condition.

There are, as one might expect, other ways to phrase condition $RS$. One of these, which hinges on the notion of connectedness within $F^*(0)$, is developed further in the next section.

Before we prove the necessity of $RS$ and the first part of Theorem 4.1, we shall comment on some of the structural aspects of the condition.

SOME FEATURES OF $RS$

For $m = 1$, condition $RS$ implies that if $D > 0$ (so that $D > -D$) and if $D_i > 0$ for some essential $i$ then $F(D) = 1$. Thus, if every $i$ is essential, then the $m = 1$ part of $RS$ along with duality implies that $F$ is strongly unanimous. Even when some $i$ are not essential, a slight variation of Theorem 3.6 shows that the conclusions of that theorem hold (the product of representative systems) when $F$ is monotonic, unanimous, dual, and satisfies the $m = 1$ part of condition $RS$. The effect on the product form (3.11) for $F$ in Theorem 3.6 that results from allowing larger values of $m$ under condition $RS$ is a reduction in the number of representative systems whose product equals $F$. For sufficiently large $m$ we can reduce the product until it has only one function. In other words, the conditions of monotonicity, unanimity, duality, and $RS$ imply that $F$ is a representative system. This is proved in the next section.

The hypothesis ($D^1 > -D^2$, $D^2 > -D^3$, $\ldots$, $D^m > -D^1$) of $RS$ requires that $D_i^{k-1} = D_i^{k+1} = 1$ when $D_i^k = -1$, and that $D_i^{k-1} \geq 0$ and $D_i^{k+1} \geq 0$ when $D_i^k = 0$. (Here $0 \to m$ and $m + 1 \to 1$ for the superscripts.) An example of an acceptable $(D_i^1, \ldots, D_i^m)$ with $m = 7$ is $(0, 1, 1, -1, 1, 0, 0)$.

Note also that ($D^1 > -D^2$, $D^2 > -D^3$, $\ldots$, $D^m > -D^1$) implies that $\Sigma_{k=1}^m D^k > 0$, so that $\Sigma_k D_i^k \geq 0$ for all $i$ and $\Sigma_k D_i^k > 0$ for some $i$. The reason that condition $RS$ states explicitly that $\Sigma_k D_i^k > 0$ for some *essential $i$* arises from the possibility that $D_i^k = 0$ for all $k$ and every essential $i$. In this case duality requires $F(D^k) = 0$ for every $k$. For example, suppose that $n = 2$ with $i = 1$ essential and $i = 2$ not essential. With $m = 1$ and $D^1 = (0,1)$, all hypotheses of condition $RS$ hold except for the final essentiality condition. Duality requires $F(D^1) = 0$.

The other major structural feature of condition $RS$ is that $m$ be odd. The obvious reason for this is that the condition is not necessary when $m$ is allowed to be even. Thus, suppose that $n = 3$ and $F(D) = (D_2,(2D_1,D_2,D_3))$. Take $m = 2$ with $D^1 = (1,-1,1)$ and $D^2 = (-1,1,0)$. Then $D^1 > -D^2$, $D^2 > -D^1$ and $D_3^1 + D_3^2 > 0$ so that all hypotheses except for $m$ odd are satisfied. The given representative system $F$ yields $F(D^1) = F(D^2) = 0$, so that $F(D^k) = 1$ for no $k \in \{1, \ldots ,m\}$.

The difference between $m$ even and odd can be illustrated graphically, as in Figure 4.2. A line from a higher point $D$ to a lower point $D'$

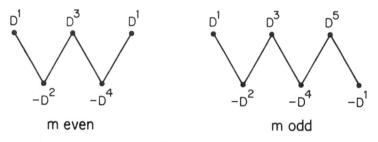

FIGURE 4.2

shows that $D > D'$. In the even case we see that $D^1 > -D^2, \ldots ,$ $D^m > -D^1$ does not imply that $D^1$ and its dual $-D^1$ are connected, as this term was defined following (4.1). But when $m$ is odd, $D^1$ and $-D^1$ are connected, as is evident from the diagram on the right.

The critical use of odd $m$ in the following theorem occurs in the chain of implications which leads to $F_r(D^k) = 0$ under the supposition of the proof.

THE NECESSITY OF RS

THEOREM 4.2. *Every representative system satisfies condition RS.*

*Proof.* Let $F$ be a representative system. In accord with Definition 3.2 we can write $F$ as

$$F = \mathrm{s}(F_1, F_2, \ldots ,F_R) \qquad (4.2)$$

where each $F_r$ is also a representative system.

Assume that the hypotheses of condition $RS$ hold, but suppose that its conclusion fails so that

$$F(D^k) \leq 0 \qquad \text{for} \qquad k = 1, \ldots, m. \qquad (4.3)$$

We shall use (4.2) to show that this is impossible.

For each $k$ from 1 to $m$ let

$$k^+ = \#\{r : F_r(D^k) = 1 \text{ in } (4.2)\}$$
$$k^- = \#\{r : F_r(D^k) = -1 \text{ in } (4.2)\}.$$

By (4.2) and (4.3), $k^+ \leq k^-$ for each $k$. Moreover, if $F_r(D^k) = -1$ then (with $m + 1 \to 1$) monotonicity, duality and $D^k > -D^{k+1}$ imply that $F_r(D^{k+1}) = 1$. Therefore $1^+ \leq 1^- \leq 2^+ \leq 2^- \leq \cdots \leq m^+ \leq m^- \leq 1^+$ so that, in fact,

$$1^+ = 1^- = 2^+ = 2^- = \cdots = m^+ = m^-.$$

Hence $F(D^k) = 0$ for all $k$.

Suppose that $F_r(D^k) = -1$. Then monotonicity, duality and $D^{k-1} > -D^k$ imply that $F_r(D^{k-1}) = 1$. Therefore

$$F_r(D^1) = -1 \Rightarrow F_r(D^2) = 1 \qquad \text{(by preceding paragraph)}$$
$$\Rightarrow F_r(D^3) = -1 \qquad \text{(this paragraph and } 2^+ = 3^-)$$
$$\Rightarrow F_r(D^4) = 1 \qquad \text{(by preceding paragraph)}$$
$$\vdots$$
$$\Rightarrow F_r(D^m) = -1 \qquad (\textit{since } m \textit{ is odd})$$
$$\Rightarrow F_r(D^1) = 1 \qquad \text{(preceding paragraph)},$$

which yields a contradiction. Hence $F_r(D^1) \geq 0$ for all $r$, and therefore $1^- = 0$. Consequently,

$$k^+ = k^- = 0 \qquad \text{for} \qquad k = 1, \ldots, m,$$

and $F_r(D^k) = 0$ for all $r$ and $k$.

Now each $F_r$ can be treated in precisely the same way that we treated $F$. That is, $F_r$ can be written as $F_r = s(F_{r1}, \ldots, F_{rT})$ with each $F_{rt}$ a representative system. $F_r(D^k) = 0$ for all $k$ takes the place of (4.3) and, by the analysis just completed, we conclude that $F_{rt}(D^k) = 0$ for all $t$ and $k$.

For definiteness let $i = 1$ be essential with $\Sigma_k D_1^k > 0$ by the hypotheses of $RS$. Since $F$ is built up in a finite number of steps from the projections $S_i$ for which $S_i(D) = D_i$, we eventually arrive at the conclusion that $S_1(D^k) = 0$ for all $k$. (Since 1 is essential, $S_1$ must be used in

**45**

the recursive construction of $F$.) But since $\Sigma D_1^k > 0$ we must have $S_1(D^k) = 1$ for some $k$, and we have thus arrived at the desired contradiction of (4.3). ◆

We conclude this section by noting that monotonicity and $RS$ imply the condition of decisive majority coalitions. This conclusion then serves to prove the first part of Theorem 4.1 by the following implications: $F \in \mathfrak{R} \Rightarrow F$ is monotonic and satisfies condition $RS$ (just proved) $\Rightarrow F$ satisfies the condition of decisive majority coalitions.

THEOREM 4.3. *If $F$ is monotonic and satisfies condition $RS$ then $F$ satisfies the condition of decisive majority coalitions.*

*Proof.* It will suffice to prove that condition $RS$ implies that there is an $I \subseteq J$ that is decisive for $x$ over $y$ within $J$ when $\#J$ is odd and contains an essential $i$ and when $m = (\#J + 1)/2$ so that $\#I = m$. The rest of the coalitions condition then follows easily from monotonicity.

Given an odd positive integer $\#J = N \leq n$, construct $D^1, D^2, \ldots, D^N$ in the manner of Figure 4.1, assuming without loss of generality that some voter in $\{1, \ldots, N\}$ is essential. The leading diagonal of this matrix and the diagonal immediately below the leading diagonal are filled in with 1's. The other diagonals alternate sign, as in Figure 4.1. $D_i^k = 0$ for $i > N$. It follows that $D^1, \ldots, D^N$ satisfy the hypotheses of condition $RS$ with $\Sigma_k D_i^k = 1$ for each $i \leq N$. Hence, by condition $RS$, $F(D^k) = 1$ for some $k \in \{1, \ldots, N\}$. Regardless of which $k$ this might be, its $D^k$ has one more 1 than $-1$, and $I = \{i : i \in \{1, \ldots, N\}$ and $D_i^k = 1\}$ with $\#I = (N + 1)/2$ is decisive for $x$ over $y$ within $J$. ◆

## 4.3 NECESSARY AND SUFFICIENT CONDITIONS

Section 3.4 shows that a monotonic, unanimous, and dual social choice function $F \in \mathfrak{M}$ fails to be a representative system only when $F^*(0)$ lacks an appropriate structure. The clue to the structure required for $F^*(0)$ has already appeared in the Fundamental Theorem for Representative Systems and in Corollary 3.2. We proceed to explore this clue.

First, a word about nonessential voters is in order. If $i$ is not essential then he has no effect on $F$. We shall therefore ignore all $D_i$ for nonessential $i$ and, for definiteness, assume that each $i \in \{1, \ldots, n\}$ is essential. Unanimity and duality assure us that $n \geq 1$. $\mathfrak{D}$ will be taken to be $\{1, 0, -1\}^n$. A representative system for $\mathfrak{D}$ can of course be extended in the obvious way to be a representative system defined on all preference profiles (including nonessential $i$). The properties for $F$ hold also on the restricted domain $\mathfrak{D}$ for essential voters, as can be seen by fixing each $D_j$ for nonessential $j > n$ at $D_j = 0$ throughout.

Under this convention let

$$\mathfrak{D}^0 = \{D : D \in \mathfrak{D}, F(D) = 0 \quad \text{and} \quad D \neq 0\}.$$

If $\mathfrak{D}^0 = \emptyset$ then $F \in \mathfrak{M}$ is a representative system according to Corollary 3.1. Henceforth assume that $\mathfrak{D}^0 \neq \emptyset$. Then, according to Corollary 3.2, $F \in \mathfrak{M}$ is a representative system if $\mathfrak{D}^0$ can be partitioned into dual subsets $\mathcal{E}$ and $-\mathcal{E}$ such that

$$D, D' \in \mathcal{E} \Rightarrow D_i > -D'_i \quad \text{for some} \quad i \in \{1, \ldots, n\} \quad (4.4)$$
$$D, D' \in -\mathcal{E} \Rightarrow D_i > -D'_i \quad \text{for some} \quad i \in \{1, \ldots, n\}. \quad (4.5)$$

These expressions are the same as (3.5), and constitute the clue referred to above.

Suppose that $D^1, D^2 \in \mathfrak{D}^0$ and $D^1 > D^2$. Suppose further that $D^1 \in \mathcal{E}$ and $D^2 \in -\mathcal{E}$. Then $-D^1 \in -\mathcal{E}$. Now with $D = D^2$ and $D' = -D^1$, (4.5) requires that $D_i^2 > -(-D_i^1) = D_i^1$ for some $i \in \{1, \ldots, n\}$. But this is false since $D^1 > D^2$ by hypothesis. Therefore, in order to satisfy (4.4) and (4.5) it is necessary to have both $D$ and $D'$ in either $\mathcal{E}$ or $-\mathcal{E}$ when $D > D'$.

Conversely, suppose that $D > D'$ and $D, D' \in \mathfrak{D}^0 \Rightarrow D, D' \in \mathcal{E}$ or $D, D' \in -\mathcal{E}$. Let $D^1$ and $D^2$ be any elements in $\mathcal{E}$. Then it is false that $D^1 < -D^2$, for this would require $-D^2 \in \mathcal{E}$, contrary to $\mathcal{E} \cap (-\mathcal{E}) = \emptyset$ since $-D^2$ is already in $-\mathcal{E}$. Moreover, $D^1 = -D^2$ is false since $\mathcal{E} \cap (-\mathcal{E}) = \emptyset$. Therefore $D_i^1 > -D_i^2$ for some $i$, and we have proved

LEMMA 4.1. *With $F \in \mathfrak{M}$ and $\mathfrak{D}^0 \neq \emptyset$, there is a partition of $\mathfrak{D}^0$ into dual subsets $\mathcal{E}$ and $-\mathcal{E}$ that satisfy (4.4) and (4.5) if and only if there is a partition of $\mathfrak{D}^0$ into dual subsets $\mathcal{E}$ and $-\mathcal{E}$ such that*

$$D > D' \quad \text{and} \quad D, D' \in \mathfrak{D}^0 \Rightarrow D, D' \in \mathcal{E} \quad \text{or} \quad D, D' \in -\mathcal{E}. \quad (4.6)$$

The ability to partition $\mathfrak{D}^0$ in either of the equivalent ways indicated by this lemma could be stated as an "acceptable" alternative to condition $RS$. Before using $RS$ we shall establish yet another way of viewing (4.6). This is done in the graph-theoretic terms used in the paragraph that follows (4.1).

Call $D, D' \in \mathfrak{D}^0$ *adjacent* if and only if either $D > D'$ or $D' > D$. We shall say that $D$ and $D'$ are *connected* if and only if there is a sequence $D, E^1, \ldots, E^r, D'$ of elements in $\mathfrak{D}^0$ such that each two contiguous elements in the sequence are adjacent. Such a sequence is a *path* from $D$ to $D'$.

Suppose that (4.6) holds with $\mathcal{E} \cup (-\mathcal{E}) = \mathfrak{D}^0$ and $\mathcal{E} \cap (-\mathcal{E}) = \emptyset$. Then if $D \in \mathcal{E}$ and $D' \in -\mathcal{E}$, there is no path from $D$ to $D'$, since such a path would require $D^1 > D^2$ or $D^2 > D^1$ for some $D^1 \in \mathcal{E}$ and

$D^2 \in -\mathcal{E}$, contrary to (4.6). Hence, (4.6) implies that no pair of dual elements in $\mathfrak{D}^0$ is connected.

Conversely, suppose that $D$ and $D'$ are not connected when $D = -D'$. Let $T_1, \ldots, T_K$ be the connected components of $\mathfrak{D}^0$. That is, $\{T_1, \ldots, T_K\}$ partitions $\mathfrak{D}^0$ with $D$, $D'$ in the same $T_k$ if and only if they are connected. By duality and the fact that $D > D'$ if and only if $-D' > -D$, $T \in \{T_1, \ldots, T_K\} \Rightarrow -T \in \{T_1, \ldots, T_K\}$. We can therefore group half the $T_k$ in one group and their duals in another group and let $\mathcal{E}$ be the union of the $T_k$ in the first group and let $-\mathcal{E}$ be the union of the $T_k$ in the second group. Then (4.6) will hold. Thus we have proved Lemma 4.2.

LEMMA 4.2. *Expression* (4.6) *holds for some dual partition* $\{\mathcal{E}, -\mathcal{E}\}$ *of* $\mathfrak{D}^0$ *if and only if*

$$D \in \mathfrak{D}^0 \Rightarrow D \text{ and } -D \text{ are not connected.} \qquad (4.7)$$

Expression (4.7) is of course another possible alternative for condition $RS$ since (4.7) and $F \in \mathfrak{M}$ imply that $F$ is a representative system. We shall now show that $F \in \mathfrak{M}$ and condition $RS$ imply (4.7). In view of Corollary 3.2, Lemmas 4.1 and 4.2, and Theorem 4.2, this will complete the proof of Theorem 4.4.

THEOREM 4.4. $F : \mathfrak{D} \to \{1, 0, -1\}$ *is a representative system if and only if it is monotonic, unanimous, dual, and satisfies condition RS.*

*Proof.* Under the conventions and definitions of this section we are to prove that $F \in \mathfrak{M}$ and $RS \Rightarrow$ (4.7). To the contrary, suppose that the hypotheses hold and that $D^1 \in \mathfrak{D}^0$ and $D^1$ and $-D^1$ are connected. Consider a shortest path from $D^1$ to $-D^1$. Such a path will exhibit no transitivities under $>$ and it will yield the form

$$D^1 > D^2, D^3 > D^2, D^3 > D^4, D^5 > D^4, \ldots, D^{r-1} > D^{r-2}, D^{r-1} > D^r \qquad (4.8)$$

or else $(D^2 > D^1, D^2 > D^3, D^4 > D^3, \ldots, D^{r-2} > D^{r-1}, D^r > D^{r-1})$, which is essentially the same as (4.8) since it is $(-D^1 > -D^2, -D^3 > -D^2, \ldots, -D^{r-1} > -D^r)$, with $r$ even and either $-D^1 = D^r$ or $-D^1 = D^{r-1}$. (In the latter case disregard $D^r$.)

Suppose first that $-D^1 = D^r$ in (4.8). We then get

$$D^1 > D^2, -D^2 > -D^3, D^3 > D^4, \ldots,$$
$$-D^{r-2} > -D^{r-1}, D^{r-1} > -D^1$$

which contains an odd number $r - 1$ of $D^k$ and satisfies the other hypotheses of condition $RS$ with $D^1, D^2, \ldots, D^m$ there replaced by $D^1, -D^2, D^3, -D^4, \ldots, -D^{r-2}, D^{r-1}$ in the present case. Condition

$RS$ and duality then imply that $F(D^k) \neq 0$ for one of the $D^k$ in (4.8). But this contradicts the supposition that the elements in (4.8) are all from $\mathfrak{D}^0$, and it therefore contradicts the initial supposition that $D^1$ and $-D^1$ are connected.

Suppose then that $-D^1 = D^{r-1}$ in (4.8). Then, since $D^1 > D^2$ and $D^1 > D^{r-2}$ imply $-D^{r-2} > D^2$, (4.8) reduces to

$$-D^{r-2} > D^2, \ -D^2 > -D^3, \ D^3 > D^4, \ \ldots, \ D^{r-3} > D^{r-2}$$

which again has an odd number $r-3$ of $D^k$ and which, as before, leads to a contradiction. ◆

THE NONDICTATORSHIP CONDITION

As we have seen, the nondictatorship condition stated after Definition 3.2 (there is no $i$ such that $F(D) = D_i$ whenever $D_i \neq 0$) has had no bearing on our analysis. Except for small values of $n$ (especially $n = 1$), it appears to be a quite reasonable condition. In practice, of course, many groups are dominated by de facto dictators regardless of the particular voting procedures that are used by these groups, but this is not the place to go on about group dynamics.

To incorporate the nondictatorship condition back into Murakami's notion of representative system, $F$ may be called a *proper representative system* if and only if $F$ is not dictatorial and is a representative system. When $n = 1$, there is clearly no proper representative system. When $n = 2$, there is exactly one proper representative system, namely the simple majority social choice function. In general, $F$ is a proper representative system if and only if it is monotonic, unanimous, dual, nondictatorial, and satisfies condition $RS$. This is obvious from Theorem 4.4.

# CHAPTER 5

# Weighted Voting and Anonymous
# Choice Functions

WEIGHTED MAJORITY social choice functions are an important subclass of representative systems. They have the form $F = \mathbf{s}(\rho_1 S_1, \ldots, \rho_n S_n)$ where $S_i(D) = D_i$ and $\rho > \mathbf{0}$, and are characterized by monotonicity, unanimity, and an extension of duality called strong duality. We shall comment on the fact that the $\rho_i$ weights may not accurately reflect the voting power of the individuals in the group.

The anonymity condition characterizes the one-man one-vote doctrine. Following a general characterization of monotonic, dual, and anonymous social choice functions, we shall give necessary and sufficient conditions for two special members of this class, simple and weak majority social choice functions.

May's theorem (1952) says that $F$ is a simple majority social choice function if and only if it is strongly monotonic, dual, and anonymous. A second set of conditions for simple majority replaces anonymity by weak nonreversibility, which says that if $x$ would win in one situation and if a second situation is like the first except that one $x$-voter abstains, then $y$ will not be the unique winner in the second situation.

A stronger condition of nonreversibility is used in the theorem for weak majority.

## 5.1 WEIGHTED MAJORITY

At the end of section 2.1 we defined weighted majority social choice functions in terms of hyperplanes through the origin $\mathbf{0}$ of $Re^n$. We shall make this our general definition.

DEFINITION 5.1. $F: \mathfrak{D} \to \{1, 0, -1\}$ *is a* weighted majority social choice function *if and only if there is a $\rho > \mathbf{0}$ such that*

$$F(D) = \mathbf{s}(\rho \cdot D) = \mathbf{s}(\rho_1 D_1, \ldots, \rho_n D_n) \qquad for\ all \qquad D \in \mathfrak{D}. \quad (5.1)$$

Thus, if $F$ is a weighted majority social choice function, then each voter has a nonnegative "weight" that he assigns to $x$ or to $y$ or to neither. The definition requires that at least one $\rho_i$ be positive, so that weighted majority social choice functions are unanimous. They are also monotonic ($\rho > \mathbf{0}$) and dual, since $\mathbf{s}(\rho \cdot D) = -\mathbf{s}(\rho \cdot (-D))$. Since $\rho_i = 0$ is allowed for some $i$, they are not necessarily strongly monotonic or strongly unanimous. However, they are strongly dual as we shall define this term shortly.

According to (5.1) and Definition 3.3, individual $i$ is essential if and only if $\rho_i > 0$. In effect, $\rho_i = 0$ can be used to identify ineligible voters.

Weighted majority social choice functions appear to arise most often under proportional representation, where each voter represents a portion of some resource (population, land, common stock, etc.) and has a vote whose weight is proportional in some way to the proportion of the resource that he represents. Needless to say, the question of how a person's voting weight $\rho_i$ should relate to his proportion of the resource can be very difficult and controversial. Involved with this question is the frequently-cited fact that an individual's power or voting effectiveness within a group need not be directly proportional to his $\rho_i$ weight. We shall comment further on this at the end of this section.

A SPECIAL CASE OF REPRESENTATIVE SYSTEMS

Weighted majority social choice functions can also be characterized in a simple way in terms of the recursive definition used for representative systems in section 3.2. As before, let $S_i(D) = D_i$ for each $i$, and let $\mathfrak{R}_1$ be the set of all functions $\mathbf{s}(F_1, \ldots ,F_K):\mathfrak{D} \to \{1,0,-1\}$ with $K$ any positive integer and $F_k \in \{S_1, \ldots ,S_n\}$ for each $k$.

Clearly, $F \in \mathfrak{R}_1$ if and only if there are nonnegative integers $\rho_1, \rho_2, \ldots , \rho_n$ at least one of which is positive such that $F(D) = \mathbf{s}(\rho_1 D_1, \ldots ,\rho_n D_n)$ for all $D \in \mathfrak{D}$. (Just let $\rho_i$ be the number of $F_k$ that equal $S_i$ in the foregoing definition for $\mathfrak{R}_1$.) This is precisely the same as (5.1) except for the integer condition. And since the $D_i$ values are rational it is not hard to show that, for any $\rho \in Re^n$, there is an integral $\rho' \in Re^n$ such that $\mathbf{s}(\rho \cdot D) = \mathbf{s}(\rho' \cdot D)$ for all $D \in \mathfrak{D}$. (This is obvious by small changes in the $\rho_i$, to make them rational, if $\rho \cdot D$ is never zero. If $\rho \cdot D = 0$ for some $D$, the elimination method for the solution of linear equations leads to the result.) Thus we have the following theorem.

THEOREM 5.1. $F:\mathfrak{D} \to \{1,0,-1\}$ *is a weighted majority social choice function if and only if* $F \in \mathfrak{R}_1$.

This shows that $\mathfrak{R}_1$ could be used as the definition of weighted majority, and that the weights in a weighted majority function can always be taken to be nonnegative integers.

STRONG DUALITY

By Definition 3.1, $F$ is dual if and only if $F(-D) = -F(D)$ for all $D \in \mathfrak{D}$. Equivalently, $F$ is dual if and only if, for all $D,D' \in \mathfrak{D}$,

$$D + D' = 0 \Rightarrow [F(D) = 1 \Leftrightarrow F(D') = -1]. \qquad (5.2)$$

For example, since $D + D' = 0 \Rightarrow D' = -D$, (5.2) shows that $F(D) = 1 \Rightarrow F(-D) = -1$, that $F(D) = -1 \Rightarrow F(-D) = 1$, and that $F(D) = 0 \Rightarrow F(-D) = 0$.

The condition of strong duality extends (5.2) by permitting more than two $D^k$ in the sum of (5.2).

DEFINITION 5.2. $F: \mathfrak{D} \to \{1, 0, -1\}$ *is strongly dual if and only if, for all $m > 1$ and all $D^1, \ldots, D^m \in \mathfrak{D}$,*

$$\Sigma_{k=1}^m D^k = 0 \Rightarrow [F(D^k) = 1 \quad \text{for some} \quad k \in \{1, \ldots, m\}$$
$$\text{if and only if} \quad F(D^j) = -1 \quad \text{for some} \quad j \in \{1, \ldots, m\}].$$
$$(5.3)$$

This says that when we consider a sequence $D^1, \ldots, D^m$ of possible situations that might arise in which each $i$ "votes" for $x$ the same number of times that he "votes" for $y$, so that $\Sigma_k D_i^k = 0$ for each $i$, then $x$ will win in at least one situation if and only if $y$ will win in at least one situation. For a simple example of this suppose that $n = 3$ with

$$\begin{aligned} D^1 &= (1, 1, 1) \\ D^2 &= (-1, 0, 0) \\ D^3 &= (0, -1, 0) \\ D^4 &= (0, 0, -1). \end{aligned} \quad (5.4)$$

Strong duality says that if $F(D^1) = 1$, then $F(D^k) = -1$ for some $k \in \{2, 3, 4\}$. Another example, with $n = 4$, is

$$\begin{aligned} D^1 &= (1, 1, -1, -1) \\ D^2 &= (-1, 0, 0, 1) \\ D^3 &= (0, -1, 1, 0). \end{aligned} \quad (5.5)$$

If $F(D^1) = -1$ then strong duality requires either $F(D^2) = 1$ or $F(D^3) = 1$. It also requires $F(D^1) = 0$ if both $F(D^2)$ and $F(D^3)$ equal zero.

An example of a representative system that is not strongly dual is the $n = 4$ system

$$((2D_1, D_2, D_3, D_4), (D_1, 2D_2, 2D_3), (D_1, 2D_2, 2D_4), (D_1, 2D_3, 2D_4))$$

of section 3.2. For this system the three $D^k$ in (5.5) have $F(D^1) = 1$, $F(D^2) = F(D^3) = 0$. Another example, with $n = 3$, is

$$((D_1, 2D_2), (2D_1, D_3), (D_2, 2D_3)),$$

since $F(1, -1, 0) = F(0, 1, -1) = F(-1, 0, 1) = -1$.

Weak majority illustrates a dual function that is not a representative system and is not strongly dual. The four $D^k$ in (5.4) have $F(D^1) = 1$ and $F(D^k) = 0$ for $k > 1$ when $F$ is the weak majority function of (3.12).

NECESSARY AND SUFFICIENT CONDITIONS

Strong duality is necessary for weighted majority, for suppose that $F$ satisfies (5.1) and $\Sigma_k D^k = \mathbf{0}$. Then $\Sigma_k \rho \cdot D^k = 0$, so that $\rho \cdot D^k > 0$ for some $k$ if and only if $\rho \cdot D^k < 0$ for another $k$. The following theorem notes that strong duality is also sufficient for weighted majority in the presence of monotonicity and unanimity.

THEOREM 5.2. $F: \mathfrak{D} \to \{1, 0, -1\}$ *is a weighted majority social choice function if and only if it is monotonic, unanimous and strongly dual.*

*Proof.* Assume that $F$ is monotonic, unanimous and strongly dual. Let $F^*(1) = \{D : F(D) = 1\}$. By unanimity, $F^*(1) \neq \emptyset$. Let $\mathcal{E}$ consist of one element from each dual pair $\{D, -D\}$ on which $F = 0$, but exclude $\mathbf{0}$ from $\mathcal{E}$.

Suppose there is no integral $\rho \in Re^n$ such that $\rho \cdot D > 0$ for all $D \in F^*(1)$ and $\rho \cdot D = 0$ for all $D \in \mathcal{E}$. Then, by Theorem 3.3 (Theorem of The Alternative), there are nonnegative integers $r_k$ at least one of which is positive that correspond to the $D^k \in F^*(1)$, and integers $r_k$ that correspond to the $D^k \in \mathcal{E}$ that satisfy $\Sigma_k r_k D_i^k = 0$ for each $i$. If $r_k$ is negative for a $D^k \in \mathcal{E}$ then we can replace $r_k$ by $-r_k$ and replace $D^k \in \mathcal{E}$ by its dual $-D^k$. In this way we obtain $r_k \geq 0$ for all $D^k \in F^*(1) \cup \mathcal{E}$. Using the $r_k$ to give multiplicities of the $D^k$, $\Sigma_k r_k D_i^k = 0$ implies that there is a sequence $D^1, D^2, \ldots, D^m$ with $m = \Sigma r_k$ such that $\Sigma_j D^j = \mathbf{0}$. If $m = 1$, this contradicts duality since it implies that $F(D^1) = 1$ and $D^1 = \mathbf{0}$. If $m > 1$, then strong duality is contradicted since $F(D^j) \geq 0$ for all $j$ and $F(D^j) = 1$ for at least one $j$ (since $r_k > 0$ for at least one $D^k$ in $F^*(1)$). Hence there is an integral $\rho$ that satisfies $\rho \cdot D > 0$ for all $D \in F^*(1)$, and $\rho \cdot D = 0$ for all $D \in \mathcal{E}$. Duality shows that $F$ is a weighted majority social choice function provided that $\rho > \mathbf{0}$.

Since $F(\mathbf{0}) = 0$ by duality, monotonicity shows that $\rho_i \geq 0$ for each $i$. Unanimity clearly requires $\Sigma \rho_i > 0$. ◆

VOTER EFFECTIVENESS

It should be clear from Definition 5.1 that any weighted majority social choice function is determined completely by certain equality and inequality relationships between sums of the $\rho_i$. The actual values of the $\rho_i$ that satisfy these relationships are of secondary importance. For example, for $n = 3$, $\rho_1 > \rho_2 > \rho_3 > 0$ and $\rho_2 + \rho_3 > \rho_1$ completely determine a weighted majority social choice function. Several $\rho$ vectors that characterize this particular function are $(4,3,2)$, $(11,9,3)$ and $(100,97,96)$. In terms of Definition 4.1, a weighted majority social choice function can be described by identifying all decisive majority coalitions (minimal coalitions will suffice) within nonempty subsets of $\{1, \ldots, n\}$. For example, the following statements describe $\rho_1 > \rho_2 > \rho_3 > 0$ and $\rho_2 + \rho_3 > \rho_1$: $\{1\}$ is decisive within $\{1,2\}$, $\{2\}$ is decisive within $\{2,3\}$, $\{3\}$ is decisive within $\{3\}$, and $\{2,3\}$ is decisive within $\{1,2,3\}$. Provided that such statements of decisiveness, when translated into $\rho_i$ inequalities (and equalities, in the case where neither $I$ nor $J - I$ is decisive within $J$), have a solution $\rho > 0$ that is unambiguous concerning the relationship between any "disjoint" pair in $\{\{\rho_1\}, \ldots, \{\rho_n\}, \{\rho_1 + \rho_2\}, \ldots, \{\rho_1 + \rho_2 + \cdots + \rho_n\}, 0\}$, they do indeed characterize a weighted majority social choice function.

From this it is clear that the $\rho_i$ values do not necessarily reflect the relative effectiveness of voters in the group. Such an effectiveness or "power" for each voter should depend, of course, at least on the ability of the voter to affect an outcome of the social decision by his vote, or on the decisive coalitions of which he is a member. Here we will define one measure of relative effectiveness based directly on an individual's ability to affect an outcome by his vote, and then comment on this definition and its implications for some weighted majority functions. The definition used is similar to one given by Banzhaf (1965).

Let $\mathfrak{D}^i$ denote all preference profiles of all voters except for voter $i$. That is, $\mathfrak{D}^i = \{(D_1, \ldots, D_{i-1}, D_{i+1}, \ldots, D_n): D_j \in \{1, 0, -1\}$ for all $j \neq i\}$. For $D^i \in \mathfrak{D}^i$ let $(D^i, 1)$ denote the $D$ that has $D^i$ for voters other than $i$, and $D_i = 1$. Similarly $(D^i, -1)$ is the $D$ given by $(D_1, \ldots, D_{i-1}, -1, D_{i+1}, \ldots, D_n)$. Given $D^i \in \mathfrak{D}^i$, voter $i$ can affect the outcome in this situation if and only if $F(D^i, 1) \neq F(D^i, -1)$. (This will be true for any monotonic $F$.) The unnormalized effectiveness $W_i$ of voter $i$ is then defined as the number of $D^i$ that voter $i$ can affect:

$$W_i = \#\{D^i : D^i \in \mathfrak{D}^i \text{ and } F(D^i, 1) \neq F(D^i, -1)\}.$$

The relative effectiveness of voter $i$ can then be taken as $w_i = W_i / \Sigma_i W_i$, so that $w_i \geq 0$ for all $i$ and $\Sigma w_i = 1$.

Several aspects of this definition, which might be viewed as short-comings, are: 1. it treats all potential $D$ equally, 2. it makes no distinction between an ability to completely change an outcome ($x$ to $y$, or $y$ to $x$) and an ability to only partially change an outcome ($x$ to a tie, or conversely), and 3. it takes no account of dynamic variables such as the ability of an individual to persuade other voters. For further discussion along these lines the reader is referred to Banzhaf's paper and the references in his footnote 31.

Finally, we note the effect of our definition of voter effectiveness on all weighted majority social choice functions for $n = 3$. By con-

TABLE 5.1
"Power" Distributions for $n = 3$ and $\rho_1 \geq \rho_2 \geq \rho_3$

| Characterization of Wtd. Majority | Voter 1 $100\ w_1$ | Voter 2 $100\ w_2$ | Voter 3 $100\ w_3$ |
|---|---|---|---|
| $\rho_1 > \rho_2 = \rho_3 = 0$ | 100 | 0 | 0 |
| $\rho_1 > \rho_2 > \rho_3 = 0$ | 75 | 25 | 0 |
| $\rho_1 > \rho_2 > \rho_3 > 0,\ \rho_1 > \rho_2 + \rho_3$ | 69 | 23 | 8 |
| $\rho_1 > \rho_2 = \rho_3 > 0,\ \rho_1 > \rho_2 + \rho_3$ | 60 | 20 | 20 |
| $\rho_1 > \rho_2 > \rho_3 > 0,\ \rho_1 = \rho_2 + \rho_3$ | 53 | 29 | 18 |
| $\rho_1 = \rho_2 > \rho_3 = 0$ | 50 | 50 | 0 |
| $\rho_1 > \rho_2 = \rho_3 > 0,\ \rho_1 = \rho_2 + \rho_3$ | 47 | 26 | 26 |
| $\rho_1 > \rho_2 > \rho_3 > 0,\ \rho_1 < \rho_2 + \rho_3$ | 47 | 33 | 20 |
| $\rho_1 = \rho_2 > \rho_3 > 0$ | 41 | 41 | 18 |
| $\rho_1 > \rho_2 = \rho_3 > 0,\ \rho_1 < \rho_2 + \rho_3$ | 41 | 29 | 29 |
| $\rho_1 = \rho_2 = \rho_3 > 0$ | 33 | 33 | 33 |

vention we take $\rho_1 \geq \rho_2 \geq \rho_3$ and list the eleven possible cases in descending order of the "power" of voter 1. The figures are accurate for the number of places shown.

For a sample calculation, consider the fifth row where $\rho_1 > \rho_2 > \rho_3 > 0$ and $\rho_1 = \rho_2 + \rho_3$. Each $\mathfrak{D}^i$ has $3^2 = 9$ elements. Since voter 1 can offset any combination of votes by 2 and 3 (at least up to a tie since $\rho_1 = \rho_2 + \rho_3$), $W_1 = 9$. When voter 1 abstains, voter 2 can affect anything that voter 3 does (3 cases of $D^2$), and voter 2 can also affect the outcome when voters 1 and 3 oppose each other (2 cases). Hence $W_2 = 5$. Finally, voter 3 is influential when both 1 and 2 abstain and when 1 and 2 oppose each other. Therefore, $W_3 = 3$. In summary, $w_1 = \frac{9}{17}$, $w_2 = \frac{5}{17}$, and $w_3 = \frac{3}{17}$.

## 5.2 Anonymity

For a given $n$, the simple majority social choice function $F(D) = s(D_1, \ldots, D_n)$ is the one weighted majority social choice function that gives equal "power" to each voter. The new condition that we shall use in characterizing simple majority is a direct reflection of the equal power or one-man one-vote doctrine. The two most common names for this condition are "equality" and "anonymity." It is also referred to as the egalitarian principle. We shall use "anonymity."

Definition 5.3. $F: \mathfrak{D} \to \{1, 0, -1\}$ is anonymous *if and only if, for all* $D \in \mathfrak{D}$, $F(D_1, \ldots, D_n) = F(D_{\sigma(1)}, \ldots, D_{\sigma(n)})$ *whenever* $\sigma$ *is a permutation on* $\{1, \ldots, n\}$.

This is equivalent to: $F(D) = F(D')$ when $D_i = D'_i$ for all but two voters $j$ and $k$ for which $D_j = D'_k$ and $D_k = D'_j$. A series of such two-voter interchanges will give a desired permutation.

What matters for any anonymous social choice function is not *who* votes for $x$ and $y$ but rather *how many* voters vote for $x$ and $y$. Unlike general weighted majorities, which require voters' "names on the ballots" so that the proper $\rho_i$ weights can be assigned, anonymous functions do not require "names on ballots." Thus, let

$$1(D) = \#\{i : D_i = 1\}$$
$$-1(D) = \#\{i : D_i = -1\}. \qquad (5.6)$$

Then any anonymous $F$ can be described by a function $f : \{(j,k) : j,k \in \{0,1, \ldots ,n\}$ and $j + k \leq n\} \to \{1,0,-1\}$ such that $F(D) = f(1(D),-1(D))$ for all $D \in \mathcal{D}$.

Anonymity is to voters as duality is to alternatives. Duality treats alternatives equally, whereas anonymity treats individual equally. Together, these conditions give conclusions (ii) and (iii) of the following lemma.

LEMMA 5.1. *Suppose that* $F : \mathcal{D} \to \{1,0,-1\}$ *is anonymous. Then, for all* $D,D' \in \mathcal{D}$,
    (i) $(1(D'),-1(D')) = (1(D),-1(D)) \Rightarrow F(D') = F(D)$.
*If, in addition, F is dual then, for all* $D,D' \in \mathcal{D}$,
    (ii) $(-1(D'),1(D')) = (1(D),-1(D)) \Rightarrow F(D') = -F(D)$,
    (iii) $1(D) = -1(D) \Rightarrow F(D) = 0$.

*Proof.* Conclusion (i) is an immediate consequence of anonymity. Conclusion (ii) is an easy consequence of duality and anonymity. For (iii), $1(D) = -1(D) \Rightarrow 1(D) = -1(D) = 1(-D) = -1(-D)$. Then $F(D) = F(-D)$ by (i) and $F(D) = -F(-D)$ by (ii), so that $F(D) = 0$. ◆

Lemma 5.1 suggests a simple way of representing any monotonic, dual, and anonymous social choice function. We now give such a representation, recalling that when $F$ is dual it is completely determined by $F^*(1)$. The largest integer that does not exceed $k$ is $[k]$.

THEOREM 5.3. *If* $F : \mathcal{D} \to \{1,0,-1\}$ *is monotonic, dual and anonymous then there are integers* $r(0), r(1), \ldots , r([n/2])$ *such that*

$$0 \leq r(0) \leq r(1) \leq \cdots \leq r([n/2]) \leq n, \qquad (5.7)$$
$$F^*(1) = \{D : -1(D) \leq n/2 \quad and \quad 1(D) > r(-1(D))\}. \qquad (5.8)$$

For simple majority, $(r(0),r(1), \ldots ,r([n/2])) = (0,1, \ldots ,[n/2])$, and for weak majority the $r$ vector is $([n/2], \ldots ,[n/2])$.

*Proof.* Let $F$ be monotonic, dual, and anonymous. Let $r(0)$ be the largest integer in $\{0, 1, \ldots, n\}$ for which $F(D) = 0$ when $-1(D) = 0$ and $1(D) \leq r(0)$. Since $F(0) = 0$, such a unique $r(0)$ exists. If $F(D) = 0$ for all $D$ that have $-1(D) = 0$, then $r(0) = n$. By monotonicity,

$$\{D: F(D) = 1 \text{ and } -1(D) = 0\} = \{D: -1(D) = 0 \text{ and } 1(D) > r(0)\}. \tag{5.9}$$

This set is empty if and only if $r(0) = n$. If $r(0) = n$, then $F(1, \ldots, 1) = 0$, so that $F^*(1) = \emptyset$ by monotonicity, and in this case we take $r(k) = n$ for each $k$. This satisfies (5.7) and (5.8).

To continue, suppose that $r(0) < n$. In this case we define $r(1)$ as the largest integer in $\{1, \ldots, n-1\}$ for which $F(D) = 0$ when $-1(D) = 1$ and $1(D) \leq r(1)$. Lemma 5.1 and monotonicity assure that $r(1)$ is well defined and that

$$\{D: F(D) = 1 \text{ and } -1(D) = 1\} = \{D: -1(D) = 1 \text{ and } 1(D) > r(1)\}. \tag{5.10}$$

Contrary to $r(1) \geq r(0)$ suppose that $r(1) < r(0) < n$. Then there is a $D$ with $-1(D) = 1$, $1(D) = r(1) + 1$ and $F(D) = 1$. Let $D' = D$ except for the one $D_i = -1$, which we replace by $D_i' = 0$. Then $-1(D') = 0$, $1(D') \leq r(0)$, and $F(D') = 1$ by monotonicity, contrary to (5.9). Hence $r(1) < r(0)$ must be false.

If, when $r(0) < n$, $r(1) = n - 1$, then (5.10) is empty and we take $r(k) = n - 1$ for $2 \leq k \leq [n/2]$, so that (5.7) holds. In this case (5.8) holds also, since, by monotonicity, $F(D) = 0$ whenever $1 \leq -1(D) \leq [n/2]$.

If $r(1) < n - 1$ we continue with $r(2)$ as in the paragraph of (5.10). The process continues in the obvious way either until $r(k) = n - k$ for some $k \leq [n/2]$, in which case we take $r(j) = n - k$ for $k \leq j \leq [n/2]$, or until we obtain $r([n/2]) = (n-1)/2$ for odd $n$. ◆

## 5.3 SIMPLE MAJORITY

In the rest of this chapter we concentrate on the two special types of monotonic, dual, and anonymous social choice functions that we identified following Theorem 5.3.

The following theorem, due to May (1952), follows directly from Lemma 5.1 (iii) and strong monotonicity. The conditions in the theorem are obviously necessary for simple majority.

**THEOREM 5.4.** $F: \mathcal{D} \to \{1, 0, -1\}$ *is a simple majority social choice function if and only if it is strongly monotonic, dual, and anonymous.*

## AN ALTERNATIVE AXIOMATIZATION

One of the necessary properties of simple majority social choice functions that was not used in Theorem 5.4 is a nonreversibility property. Suppose that $F$ is a simple majority social choice function and that $F(D) = 1$, so that $x$ wins under $D$ with $1(D) > -1(D)$. Suppose that $D'$ is the same as $D$ except that one voter who voted for $x$ in $D$ abstains in $D'$. Then $1(D') = 1(D) - 1$ and $-1(D') = -1(D)$, so that $1(D') \geq -1(D')$. This requires that $F(D') \geq 0$. Hence, under simple majority, the change by one voter from a vote for $x$ to an abstention cannot change the social choice from $x$ to $y$ although it may change the social choice from $x$ to a tie between $x$ and $y$.

DEFINITION 5.4. $F:\mathfrak{D} \to \{1,0,-1\}$ *is* weakly nonreversible *if and only if, for all* $D \in \mathfrak{D}$, *if* $D' = D$ *except that* $D_i' = 0$ *for one $i$ for which* $D_i = 1$, *then* $F(D) = 1 \Rightarrow F(D') \geq 0$.

The condition of weak nonreversibility is of at least passing interest since it allows us to characterize simple majority without making direct reference to anonymity.

THEOREM 5.5. $F:\mathfrak{D} \to \{1,0,-1\}$ *is a simple majority social choice function if and only if it is strongly monotonic, dual and weakly nonreversible.*

*Proof.* Necessity has been demonstrated. For sufficiency, assume that $F$ is strongly monotonic, dual, and weakly nonreversible. If $1(D) = -1(D) = 0$ then $D = \mathbf{0}$ so that $F(D) = 0$ by duality. Then, by strong monotonicity,

$$F(D) = 1 \quad \text{if} \quad 1(D) > -1(D) = 0$$
$$F(D) = -1 \quad \text{if} \quad -1(D) > 1(D) = 0.$$

Using induction on $m$, assume for $m \geq 0$ that
1. $F(D) = 0$    if    $1(D) = -1(D) = m$    (if $2m \leq n$)
2. $F(D) = 1$    if    $1(D) > -1(D) = m$    (if $2m + 1 \leq n$)
3. $F(D) = -1$    if    $-1(D) > 1(D) = m$    (if $2m + 1 \leq n$).

Suppose that $2(m + 1) \leq n$ and that $1(D) = -1(D) = m + 1$. Let

$$D' = D \quad \text{except for some } i \text{ where} \quad D_i = 1 \quad \text{and} \quad D_i' = 0$$
$$D^* = D \quad \text{except for some } j \text{ where} \quad D_j = -1 \quad \text{and} \quad D_j^* = 0.$$

Now $F(D^*) = 1$ by induction hypothesis 2, and $F(D') = -1$ by induction hypothesis 3. Weak nonreversibility and $F(D') = -1$ prohibit $F(D) = 1$. Similarly, the dual of weak nonreversibility and $F(D^*) = 1$ prohibit $F(D) = -1$. Therefore $F(D) = 0$. It then follows from strong monotonicity that 2 and 3 hold for $m + 1$ in place of $m$, so long as $2(m + 1) + 1 \leq n$. ◆

Shortly, in Part II, we will examine simple majority in detail for situations with many alternatives.

Bengt Hansson has noted (in correspondence) that weak nonreversibility is closely related to a condition which expresses the idea that "the effect is not greater than the cause," which we can write as follows: if $D = D'$ except that $D_i > D_i'$ for some $i$ then $D_i - D_i' \geq F(D) - F(D')$. It is easily seen that this condition is necessary for simple majority, and it implies weak nonreversibility since it requires $F(D') \geq 0$ when $D_i - D_i' = 1$ and $F(D) = 1$.

## 5.4  WEAK MAJORITY

If we use (5.6), the weak majority social choice function $F$ of (3.12) can be defined by

$$F(D) = 1 \Leftrightarrow 1(D) > n/2$$
$$F(D) = -1 \Leftrightarrow -1(D) > n/2.$$

Weak and simple majority share a lot in common. Both are monotonic, unanimous, dual, anonymous, and weakly nonreversible. The parting of the ways between these two functions arises because: 1. simple majority is strongly monotonic whereas weak majority is not, and 2. weak majority is strongly nonreversible whereas simple majority is not.

DEFINITION 5.5. $F: \mathfrak{D} \to \{1, 0, -1\}$ *is* strongly nonreversible *if and only if, for all* $D \in \mathfrak{D}$, *if* $D' = D$ *except that* $D_i' = 0$ *for one $i$ for which* $D_i = 1$, *then* $F(D) \geq 0 \Rightarrow F(D') \geq 0$.

The only difference between this definition and Definition 5.4 is that $F(D) = 1$ in 5.4 has been replaced by $F(D) \geq 0$. Thus, strong nonreversibility says that if $x$ and $y$ tie under $D$, and if one $x$ voter in $D$ changes to abstention in $D'$, then $x$ and $y$ will still tie under $D'$ (assuming monotonicity). Strong nonreversibility, which is clearly necessary for weak majority, is felt by some to be the most vulnerable aspect of weak majority.

Related to this, weak majority is often felt to be inferior to simple majority because of its greater propensity for ties. In practice, a special majority function, which is closely related to weak majority but does not permit ties, is sometimes used when a challenger $x$ is put against the status quo $y$ for a vote. This special majority takes $F(D) = 1 \Leftrightarrow 1(D) > n/2$, and $F(D) = -1$ otherwise. Thus, the challenger wins if and only if it obtains more than half of the possible

**59**

votes. Otherwise the status quo stays in effect. This example of "non-minority rule" will be examined further in the next chapter.

In order to characterize weak majority we need one more condition that holds also for simple majority. This condition is part of strong monotonicity. It says that if there are no abstentions in $D$, and if $D'$ is obtained from $D$ by one voter changing his vote from $y$ to $x$, then $x$ will be the choice under $D'$ if $x$ beats or ties $y$ under $D$. A slightly different form of this condition is stated in the following theorem.

THEOREM 5.6. $F:\mathfrak{D} \to \{1,0,-1\}$ *is a weak majority social choice function if and only if it is monotonic, dual, anonymous, strongly non-reversible, and if* $F(D') = 1$ *whenever* $F(D) \geq 0$, $D' > D$ *and* $D_i D'_i \neq 0$ *for each* $i$.

*Proof.* The conditions are easily seen to be necessary for weak majority. Assume henceforth that they hold.

By Lemma 5.1 (iii), $1(D) = -1(D) \Rightarrow F(D) = 0$. Monotonicity and strong nonreversibility then imply that $-1(D) \leq n/2 \Rightarrow F(D) \geq 0$. Lemma 5.1 (ii) then says that $1(D) \leq n/2 \Rightarrow F(D) \leq 0$.

If $n$ is even let $1(D^\circ) = -1(D^\circ) = n/2$ with $F(D^\circ) = 0$. Anonymity and the final condition of the theorem then imply

$$F(D) = 1 \quad \text{if} \quad 1(D) > n/2 \quad \text{and} \quad D_i \neq 0 \text{ for each } i.$$

From this and monotonicity, $1(D) > n/2 \Rightarrow F(D) = 1$. Duality then yields $F(D) = -1$ whenever $-1(D) > n/2$.

For $n$ odd let $1(D^\circ) = -1(D^\circ) + 1$ with all $D_i^\circ \neq 0$, and let $D' = D^\circ$ except that $D'_i = -1$ for one $i$ for which $D_i^\circ = 1$. Then $1(D') + 1 = -1(D')$. The second paragraph of this proof gives $F(D^\circ) \geq 0$ and $F(D') \leq 0$. If in fact $F(D') = 0$ then $F(D^\circ) = 1$ by anonymity and the final condition of the theorem. But $F(D^\circ) = 1 \Rightarrow F(D') = -1$ by Lemma 5.1 (ii), which contradicts $F(D') = 0$. Therefore, $F(D') = -1$, and $F(D^\circ) = 1$ by Lemma 5.1 (ii). Monotonicity and anonymity then imply that $F(D) = 1$ whenever $1(D) > n/2$. Duality yields $F(D) = -1$ whenever $-1(D) > n/2$. ◆

# CHAPTER 6

# Strong Decisiveness and Special Majorities

THUS FAR the special social choice functions that we have discussed satisfy the condition of duality. In this chapter we shall consider strongly decisive functions, which never permit a tie between $x$ and $y$. Since these cannot be dual (which requires $F(0) = 0$), this chapter is also concerned with nondual social choice functions.

The first section discusses the conditions of decisiveness and then characterizes social choice functions that are monotonic, strongly decisive, and anonymous. This characterization is similar to that of Theorem 5.3 for monotonic, dual, and anonymous functions. A weak duality condition, which is compatible with strong decisiveness, is shown to lead to a social choice function that agrees with simple majority when the latter does not yield a tie.

The second half of the chapter focuses on two types of strongly decisive special majority social choice functions. These are: 1. the absolute special majority, in which an abstention counts as a vote for the status quo, and 2. the relative special majority, under which the challenger wins if and only if it receives a certain percentage of the votes that are actually cast.

## 6.1 STRONGLY DECISIVE SOCIAL CHOICE FUNCTIONS

A possible virtue of some social choice functions is their avoidance of ties. Indeed, as we have remarked before, it is obvious that a tie result does not resolve the issue before the group. When ties are permitted by a social choice function, the practical procedure for breaking the deadlock—whether by coin flip, chairman's duty, a new ballot (which may well differ from the first since the voters have additional information to act on), or by some other means—is not part of the function. In some cases, however, it may be possible to alter the function to reflect the tie-breaking procedure.

A simple example will illustrate this. Let $n = 3$ and suppose that the group uses simple majority, written as $F = \mathbf{s}(S_1, S_2, S_3)$. If a tie occurs, then voter 1 breaks the tie by his vote, provided that $D_1 \neq 0$. If voter 1 abstains, then voter 2 breaks the tie, provided that $D_2 \neq 0$. If both 1 and 2 abstain, then a tie occurs if and only if 3 abstains. This tie-breaking procedure, when combined with $F$, can be written as $F' = \mathbf{s}(3F, 2S_1, S_2)$. It can also be written in the weighted form

$F' = \mathbf{s}(4S_1,3S_2,2S_3)$ whose voter "powers" $w_i$ are approximately .47, .33, and .20, by Table 5.1, for the three voters respectively.

But even $F'$ does not resolve the issue when all three voters abstain or are indifferent. If they are in fact indifferent then it should not matter to any of them which of $x$ and $y$ is implemented. Therefore, from the viewpoint of the *voters*, it would not matter if $x$ were designated as the choice when $D = 0$. This can be incorporated into the choice function by taking $F'' = \mathbf{s}(2F',1)$ or, equivalently, by writing $F'' = \mathbf{s}(8S_1,6S_2,4S_3,1)$.

In this example the weighted majority function $F'$ is weakly decisive and $F''$ is strongly decisive. $F^*(0) = \{D:F(D) = 0\}$.

DEFINITION 6.1. $F:\mathfrak{D} \to \{1,0,-1\}$ *is* decisive *if and only if* $D \neq \mathbf{0} \Rightarrow F(D) \neq 0$. *It is* weakly decisive *if* $F^*(0) = \{\mathbf{0}\}$, *and* strongly decisive *if* $F^*(0) = \emptyset$.

Thus, a decisive social choice function is either weakly decisive or strongly decisive, and not both. In logic, weak decisiveness and strong decisiveness are contrary conditions. They are not contradictories, since a social choice function need not be either weakly or strongly decisive.

Similarly, since duality implies $F(0) = 0$, duality and strong decisiveness are contrary conditions: if $F$ is dual then it is not strongly decisive; if $F$ is strongly decisive then it is not dual; and $F$ may be neither dual nor strongly decisive.

We have already seen in Corollary 3.1 that every weakly decisive social choice function that is monotonic and dual is a representative system. This is implied also by Theorem 3.5, since every monotonic and decisive function is strongly monotonic.

Clearly, since strong decisiveness and duality are contrary conditions, $F$ cannot be a representative system when it is strongly decisive. Since the remainder of this chapter concentrates on strongly decisive functions, duality will play no role except in comparisons and in a modified form called "weak duality" that is compatible with strong decisiveness.

## STRONG DECISIVENESS AND ANONYMITY

Continuing along the lines developed in the latter part of the preceding chapter, this chapter will maintain the emphasis on anonymity. When this condition is joined by monotonicity and strong decisiveness, the following correspondent of Theorem 5.3 results.

THEOREM 6.1. *If* $F:\mathcal{D} \to \{1,0,-1\}$ *is monotonic, strongly decisive and anonymous then there are integers* $s(0), s(1), \ldots, s(n)$ *such that*

$$0 \leq s(0) \leq s(1) \leq \cdots \leq s(n) \leq n + 1, \tag{6.1}$$
$$F^*(1) = \{D : 1(D) \geq s(-1(D))\}. \tag{6.2}$$

We will recall that $1(D) = \#\{i : D_i = 1\}$ and $-1(D) = \#\{i : D_i = -1\}$, and that $F^*(1)$ completely determines $F$ when $F$ is strongly decisive since $F^*(-1)$ is then the complement of $F^*(1)$ in $\mathcal{D}$. Unanimity has not been used in the theorem. If unanimity does not hold, then either $F^*(1) = \mathcal{D}$, in which case we take $s(k) = 0$ for each $k$, or $F^*(1) = \emptyset$, in which case $s(k) = n + 1$ for each $k$.

The comparison between Theorems 5.3 and 6.1 can be illustrated visually by $F$ arrays for the two cases. Since $F(D)$ depends only on $1(D)$ and $-1(D)$ when $F$ is anonymous, it will suffice to identify $F$ for each $(1(D), -1(D))$ for which $-1(D) + 1(D) \leq n$. Figure 6.1

1(D)

| | | 0 | 1 | 2 | 3 | 4 | 5 | 6 | 7 | s(k) |
|---|---|---|---|---|---|---|---|---|---|---|
| | 0 | -1 | 1 | 1 | 1 | 1 | 1 | 1 | 1 | 1 |
| | 1 | -1 | -1 | -1 | 1 | 1 | 1 | 1 | | 3 |
| | 2 | 1 | 1 | -1 | 1 | 1 | 1 | | | 3 |
| -1(D) | 3 | -1 | -1 | -1 | 1 | 1 | | | | 3 |
| | 4 | -1 | -1 | -1 | 1 | | | | | 3 |
| | 5 | -1 | -1 | -1 | | | | | | 3 |
| | 6 | -1 | -1 | | | | | | | 3 |
| | 7 | -1 | | | | | | | | 3 |

FIGURE 6.1. Monotonic, dual, anonymous

shows an $F$ for Theorem 5.3, and Figure 6.2 shows an $F$ for Theorem 6.1. Since $F$ is monotonic in each case, the entries must not decrease from left to right across any row, and must not increase from top to bottom down any column. In both figures, $n = 7$.

Duality for Figure 6.1 requires zeros in the main diagonal, and the array must satisfy $a_{jk} + a_{kj} = 0$ for each $j$, $k$ with $j + k \leq n$. No $-1$'s can appear above the main diagonal, and no 1's can appear below the main diagonal. Since only half of the displayed array is

1(D)

|        |      | 0  | 1  | 2  | 3 | 4 | 5 | 6 | 7 | r(k) |
|--------|------|----|----|----|---|---|---|---|---|------|
|        | 0    | 0  | 0  | 0  | 1 | 1 | 1 | 1 | 1 | 2    |
|        | 1    | 0  | 0  | 0  | 0 | 1 | 1 | 1 |   | 3    |
|        | 2    | 0  | 0  | 0  | 0 | 1 | 1 |   |   | 3    |
| -1(D)  | 3    | -1 | 0  | 0  | 0 | 0 |   |   |   | 4    |
|        | 4    | -1 | -1 | -1 | 0 |   |   |   |   |      |
|        | 5    | -1 | -1 | -1 |   |   |   |   |   |      |
|        | 6    | -1 | -1 |    |   |   |   |   |   |      |
|        | 7    | -1 |    |    |   |   |   |   |   |      |

FIGURE 6.2. Monotonic, strongly decisive, anonymous

needed to specify the dual $F$, it is completely determined by the $r(k)$ for $k = 0, 1, \ldots , [n/2]$ as described in Theorem 5.3.

Appropriate $s(k)$ for an $F$ satisfying the conditions of Theorem 6.1 are shown on Figure 6.2. The first five $s(k)$ must be as shown. The last three can be any numbers that satisfy $3 \leq s(5) \leq s(6) \leq s(7) \leq 8$. If there is a 1 in row $k$ ($k = 0,1, \ldots$) of the $F$ array then, according to (6.2), $s(k)$ must be the column number $(0,1, \ldots)$ for the first column that has a 1 in the row. If a row has no 1 then $s(k)$ must exceed $n - k$ so that $\{D: -1(D) = k \text{ and } 1(D) \geq k\} = \emptyset$ for (6.2). Monotonicity guarantees that $s(k)$ can be chosen in this way so as to satisfy (6.1).

WEAK DUALITY

Strong duality, Definition 5.2, extends duality. That is, it implies duality, but not conversely. We now define a condition that is implied by duality but does not imply duality.

DEFINITION 6.2. $F: \mathfrak{D} \to \{1, 0, -1\}$ *is* weakly dual *if and only if, for all* $D \in \mathfrak{D}$, $1(D) \neq -1(D) \Rightarrow F(-D) = -F(D)$.

For an anonymous function that is representable in the manner of Figure 6.1 or 6.2, weak duality says that duality applies to all symmetric pairs that are not on the main diagonal. If $F$ is strongly decisive as well as weakly dual then, in such an array, $a_{jk} = -a_{kj} \neq 0$ for all $j \neq k$ with $j + k \leq n$. Finally, if $F$ is monotonic also, then $F(D) = 1$ for all $D$ above the main diagonal and $F(D) = -1$ for all $D$ below the main diagonal. In this case the elements along the main diagonal can have any sequence of values in $\{1, -1\}$. These facts are summarized in Theorem 6.2.

THEOREM 6.2. *Suppose that* $F: \mathfrak{D} \to \{1, 0, -1\}$ *is monotonic, strongly decisive, anonymous, and weakly dual. Then* $F(D) = s(D_1, D_2, \ldots, D_n)$ *for all $D$ for which* $\mathbf{1}(D) \neq -\mathbf{1}(D)$, *and, for each* $k \in \{0, 1, \ldots, [n/2]\}$, *all $D$ with* $\mathbf{1}(D) = -\mathbf{1}(D) = k$ *have the same $F(D)$ value, which can be either 1 or* $-1$.

This says that every $F$ that satisfies the conditions of the theorem agrees with simple majority except when $\mathbf{1}(D) = -\mathbf{1}(D)$. With $t = [n/2] + 1$, there are exactly $2^t$ such functions (for the given $n$) according to the $2^t$ ways that $1$'s and $-1$'s can be placed along the main diagonal in a figure like Figure 6.2. When only $1$'s are placed on the main diagonal, the function is representable as $F = s(2s(D_1, D_2, \ldots, D_n), 1)$.

## 6.2  SPECIAL MAJORITIES

A very important class of social choice functions that are strongly decisive and are not generally weakly dual is the class of special majority functions. These arise most often in practice when a challenger, whom we shall suppose is $x$, requires something more than a simple majority to displace the status quo $y$.

Special majorities occur in many forms. A famous example involves changing the Constitution of the United States of America. An amendment to the Constitution requires ratification by $\frac{3}{4}$ of the state legislatures (38 of 50) before it becomes law, assuming of course that the amendment has been passed by Congress. This can be expressed by $F(D) = 1$ if and only if $\mathbf{1}(D) \geq (\frac{3}{4})n$, and $F(D) = -1$ otherwise, where $n = 50$ and $D_i$ represents the vote of state $i$. This function treats states (the "individuals" in this case) equally, despite differences in population. Since nine of the 50 states have more than half the population, a constitutional amendment could be ratified by states which contain less than half of the population, unlikely as this may be. Any amendment to change this or some other Constitution decision rule would of course require a $\frac{3}{4}$ majority of the states for ratification.

For another example, suppose that a government has a bicameral legislature, that the executive head of the government has the power of veto over the legislature, and that a $\frac{2}{3}$ majority is required in each house to override a veto. Given a veto, the social choice function from that point on can be represented by $s(F_1, F_2, -1)$, where $F_1$ and $F_2$ are $\frac{2}{3}$ special majority social choice functions for the two houses.

**65**

## TWO TYPES OF SPECIAL MAJORITY FUNCTIONS

Besides differing in the percentage vote required to unseat the status quo, elementary special majority social choice functions differ in their interpretation of percentage, or in their treatment of abstentions. For example, "the challenger requires a two-thirds majority to win" might be interpreted in any of the following ways:

1. at least $\frac{2}{3}$ of all eligible voters must vote for $x$;

2. more than $\frac{2}{3}$ of all eligible voters must vote for $x$;

3. at least $\frac{2}{3}$ of all nonabstaining voters must vote for $x$;

4. at least $\frac{2}{3}$ of all nonabstainers within an assembled quorum of voters must vote for $x$;

5. more than $\frac{2}{3}$ of all assembled voters must vote for $x$.

In the rest of this chapter we shall deal only with two simple types of special majorities, namely absolute and relative. An absolute special $\frac{2}{3}$ majority requires $\frac{2}{3}$ (or more than $\frac{2}{3}$) of all voters to vote for $x$, as in cases 1 and 2 above. A relative special $\frac{2}{3}$ majority requires $\frac{2}{3}$ (or more than $\frac{2}{3}$) of all voters who actually vote (do not abstain) to vote for $x$, as in case 3 above.

DEFINITION 6.3. $F : \mathfrak{D} \to \{1, 0, -1\}$ *is an* absolute special majority social choice function *if and only if there is an* $\alpha \in (0, 1)$ *such that*

$$F(D) = \quad 1 \Leftrightarrow 1(D) > \alpha n \qquad (6.3)$$
$$F(D) = -1 \Leftrightarrow 1(D) \leq \alpha n. \qquad (6.4)$$

$F$ *is a* relative special majority social choice function *if and only if there is a number* $\beta \geq 0$ *such that*

$$F(D) = \quad 1 \Leftrightarrow 1(D) > \beta(-1(D)) \qquad (6.5)$$
$$F(D) = -1 \Leftrightarrow 1(D) \leq \beta(-1(D)). \qquad (6.6)$$

Abstentions count as votes for the status quo under absolute special majorities. In the relative case, abstentions affect the outcome only so far as they change the ratio between $x$ votes and $y$ votes. Thus, if $\beta = 2$ (that is, $x$ needs more than two-thirds of the votes cast to win), if $n = 9$, $1(D) = 6$ and $-1(D) = 3$, then $F(D) = -1$ by (6.6). But if one of the $x$ voters and one of the $y$ voters abstain, so that $1(D) = 5$ and $-1(D) = 2$, then $F(D) = 1$ by (6.5).

"Non-minority rule" is identified by $\alpha = \frac{1}{2}$. If $x$ needs at least two-thirds of all potential votes to win, then $\alpha$ is slightly less than $\frac{2}{3}$ (or equal to $\frac{2}{3}$ if $n$ is not divisible by 3). If $x$ needs all votes to win then $\alpha > (n - 1)/n$. If $x$ needs all votes cast to win then $\beta \geq n - 1$.

Our two forms of special majority have simple representations in the terms of Theorem 6.1. For an absolute special majority function we can take $s(0) = s(1) = \cdots = s(n)$. For a relative special majority, $s(k) = \beta'k$, with $\beta'$ slightly less than $\beta$, will suffice (until $\beta'k$ exceeds $n + 1$).

According to the definitions, each type of special majority social choice function is monotonic, unanimous, anonymous and strongly decisive. Two additional conditions will distinguish between the types.

## 6.3 SPECIAL CONDITIONS

The new condition for absolute special majority says that a vote for the status quo is equivalent to an abstention.

CONDITION A. *If $D = D'$ except for one $i$ where $D_i = 0$ and $D_i' = -1$ then $F(D) = F(D')$.*

THEOREM 6.3. *$F:\mathfrak{D} \to \{1,0,-1\}$ is an absolute special majority social choice function if and only if it is monotonic, unanimous, anonymous, strongly decisive and satisfies condition A.*

*Proof.* Anonymity and condition A imply that $F(D)$ is a function of $\mathbf{1}(D)$. Unanimity requires $F(D) = 1$ when $\mathbf{1}(D) = n$, and unanimity and condition A imply $F(D) = -1$ when $\mathbf{1}(D) = 0$. Monotonicity and strong decisiveness then show that there is a number $\alpha n$ between 0 and $n$ that satisfies (6.3) and (6.4). ◆

The special condition that we shall use for relative special majority combines an aspect of anonymity and the notion that what is significant for $F(D)$ is the ratio of $\mathbf{1}(D)$ to $-\mathbf{1}(D)$.

CONDITION B. *If $D^1, \ldots, D^m$ and $E^1, \ldots, E^r$ are sequences of elements from $\mathfrak{D}$ with $m \geq 1$ and $r \geq 1$, if*

$$\Sigma_{j=1}^r \mathbf{1}(E^j) = \Sigma_{k=1}^m \mathbf{1}(D^k) \tag{6.7}$$
$$\Sigma_{j=1}^r -\mathbf{1}(E^j) = \Sigma_{k=1}^m -\mathbf{1}(D^k), \tag{6.8}$$

*and if $F(D^k) \geq 0$ for $k = 1, \ldots, m$, then $F(E^j) \geq 0$ for some $j \in \{1, \ldots, r\}$.*

This says that if $x$ would beat or tie $y$ in each of the potential $D^k$ situations, and if the totality of $x$ ($y$) votes in all $E^j$ situations listed equals the totality of $x$ ($y$) votes in all $D^k$ situations, then $x$ must beat or tie $y$ in at least one of the $E^j$ situations. Since there is no restriction on $m$ and $r$ other than that they be positive integers, the viability of condition B depends critically on the notion that the ratio of $x$ to $y$ votes is significant. For example, if $n = 9$ and if $F$ is strongly decisive with $F(1,1,1,1,1,1,-1,-1,-1) = 1$, then at least one of $F(1,1,0,0,0,0,-1,0,0)$, $F(0,0,1,1,0,0,0,-1,0)$ and $F(0,0,0,0,1,1,0,0,-1)$

must equal 1. In fact, the hypotheses of the preceding sentence along with condition B require that $F(D) = 1$ whenever $1(D) = 2$ and $-1(D) = 1$, since with $D^1 = (1,1,1,1,1,1,-1,-1,-1)$, $m = 1$, $E^1 = E^2 = E^3 = D$, and $r = 3$, $F(D^1) = 1$ requires $F(D) = 1$.

Condition B holds for simple majority but does not generally hold for representative systems or for absolute special majorities. To prove that the condition is necessary for relative special majority, suppose that $F$ satisfies (6.5) and (6.6) for some $\beta \geq 0$, and suppose that the hypotheses of condition B hold for some $D^k$ and $E^j$. Then $F(D^k) = 1$ for each $D^k$ so that $\Sigma_k 1(D^k) > \beta \Sigma_k - 1(D^k)$. Expressions (6.7) and (6.8) then give $\Sigma_j 1(E^j) > \beta \Sigma_j - 1(E^j)$, so that $1(E^j) > \beta(-1(E^j))$ for some $j$, or $F(E^j) = 1$ by (6.5).

THEOREM 6.4. $F: \mathfrak{D} \to \{1, 0, -1\}$ *is a relative special majority social choice function if and only if it is unanimous, strongly decisive and satisfies* $F(0) = -1$ *and condition* B.

*Proof.* Let the specified conditions hold. According to unanimity and strong decisiveness, $\mathfrak{D}$ can be partitioned into two nonempty subsets $F^*(1)$ and $F^*(-1)$. The system that corresponds to (6.5) and (6.6) with $\beta = -\rho_2/\rho_1$ is

$$\rho_1 1(D) + \rho_2(-1(D)) > 0 \qquad \text{for all} \qquad D \in F^*(1) \qquad (6.9)$$
$$\rho_1 1(D) + \rho_2(-1(D)) \leq 0 \qquad \text{for all} \qquad D \in F^*(-1). \quad (6.10)$$

If this system has no integral $\rho$ solution then, by Theorem 3.2, there are nonnegative integers $r_k$, at least one of which is positive, and nonnegative integers $s_j$ such that

$$\Sigma r_k 1(D^k) = \Sigma s_j 1(E^j)$$
$$\Sigma r_k(-1(D^k)) = \Sigma s_j(-1(E^j))$$

where $F^*(1) = \{D^1, D^2, \ldots\}$ and $F^*(-1) = \{E^1, E^2, \ldots\}$. If $s_j > 0$ for some $j$ then condition B is contradicted. If $s_j = 0$ for all $j$ then $D^k = 0$ for all $k$ with $r_k > 0$ and, since there is at least one such $r_k$, we get $F(0) = 1$, a contradiction to $F(0) = -1$ as stated in the theorem. Hence there is a $\rho$ solution. Unanimity then gives $\rho_1 > 0$ by (6.9) and $\rho_2 \leq 0$ by (6.10), so that $\beta = -\rho_2/\rho_1 \geq 0$. ◆

# PART II

# SIMPLE MAJORITY SOCIAL CHOICE

Because simple majority is widely used in two-alternative situations and is often judged to be reasonable and equitable for making decisions, its applicability in multiple-alternative situations has been studied extensively. Condorcet (1785), a champion of simple majority, was well aware of the difficulty of extending the simple-majority idea. He observed, for example, that simple majorities could be intransitive, a case of which arises when $x$ beats $y$, $y$ beats $z$, and $z$ beats $x$. He suggests also that straightforward reasoning will lead any sensible person to the conclusion that the social choice ought to be the alternative that has a strict simple majority over every other alternative when such an alternative exists.

A primary purpose of this part of the book is to study the structures of individual preference orders that give rise to an alternative that has a simple majority over each other alternative. Later in Part II we shall examine Condorcet's position on the best alternative in such situations. The final chapter presents some explicit social choice functions whose binary parts agree with simple majority, including several that adhere to Condorcet's position and others that do not.

Many of the topics that are discussed in Part II foreshadow more general analyses presented in Part III.

# CHAPTER 7

# Binary Relations and Binary Choices

BECAUSE THE REST of our study deals with social choice from more than two alternatives, we shall require mathematical concepts that were not used in Part I. The first purpose of this chapter is to set forth the most basic of these concepts, namely binary relations. After discussing some general properties, such as asymmetry and transitivity, we shall examine four order relations that are used extensively in the sequel. Readers who are familiar with the theory of binary relations may wish to take note only of the terminology that will be used.

The specific introduction to Part II begins in section 7.3 with a brief look at interrelations among binary choices. We shall comment on the case where, given $D$, every nonempty finite subset of $X$ contains an alternative that beats or ties every other alternative in the subset on the basis of binary choice comparisons under $F$. Some differences between transitive individual indifference (weak orders) and intransitive individual indifference (strict partial orders) are illustrated with the use of Pareto dominance conditions.

The next chapter begins our detailed examination of the particulars of simple majority social choice.

## 7.1  BINARY RELATIONS

Because binary relations play a fundamental role in this and succeeding chapters of the book, we shall set forth at this time many of the definitions that will be used.

A *binary relation R on a set* $X$ is a subset of $X \times X$. Thus $R$ can range anywhere from the empty relation $\emptyset$ to the universal relation $X \times X$. When an ordered pair $(x,y)$ is in $R$, or $(x,y) \in R$, we shall often write $xRy$ and say that $x$ stands in the relation $R$ to $y$. When $(x,y) \notin R$, so that $x$ does not stand in the relation $R$ to $y$, we shall write not $xRy$. That is, not $xRy$ means that it is false that $xRy$. Clearly, for any binary relation $R$ on $X$, it is true for any $(x,y) \in X \times X$ that either $xRy$ or not $xRy$, and not both.

In section 2.1 we defined binary relations $=$, $>$, and $\geq$ on $Re^n$. Each of these relations has certain properties. For example, all are transitive, since $xRy$ and $yRz \Rightarrow xRz$ in each case. A number of other potential properties are presented in the following list. A binary relation $R$ on $X$ is

$$\textit{reflexive} \Leftrightarrow xRx \text{ for all } x \in X$$
$$\textit{irreflexive} \Leftrightarrow \text{not } xRx, \text{ for all } x \in X$$
$$\textit{symmetric} \Leftrightarrow xRy \Rightarrow yRx, \text{ for all } x,y \in X$$
$$\textit{asymmetric} \Leftrightarrow xRy \Rightarrow \text{not } yRx, \text{ for all } x,y \in X$$
$$\textit{antisymmetric} \Leftrightarrow xRy \text{ and } yRx \Rightarrow x = y, \text{ for all } x,y \in X$$
$$\textit{connected} \Leftrightarrow xRy \text{ or } yRx, \text{ for all } x,y \in X$$
$$\textit{weakly connected} \Leftrightarrow x \neq y \Rightarrow xRy \text{ or } yRx, \text{ for all } x,y \in X$$
$$\textit{transitive} \Leftrightarrow xRy \text{ and } yRz \Rightarrow xRz, \text{ for all } x,y,z \in X$$
$$\textit{negatively transitive} \Leftrightarrow \text{not } xRy \text{ and not } yRz \Rightarrow \text{not } xRz,$$
$$\text{for all } x,y,z \in X.$$

We shall look first at the four groupings suggested by the terms used. The use of $=$, $>$, and $\geq$ in the examples is for $Re^n$, as defined after (2.2).

First, both $=$ and $\geq$ are reflexive, and $>$ is irreflexive. Reflexivity and irreflexivity are contrary properties, but they are not contradictories since $R$ may be neither reflexive nor irreflexive when $\#X > 1$. If $R$ is a relation of "respects" on a set of people, and if some people respect themselves but others do not respect themselves, then $R$ is neither reflexive nor irreflexive.

Second, $=$ is symmetric, $>$ is asymmetric, and $\geq$ is antisymmetric since $x \geq y$ and $y \geq x \Rightarrow x = y$. In this particular case, it turns out that $=$ is also antisymmetric ($x = y$ and $y = x \Rightarrow x = y$), and so is $>$ since we can never have both $x > y$ and $y > x$. In fact, every asymmetric $R$ is trivially antisymmetric. There are of course antisymmetric relations that are not asymmetric, an example of which is $\geq$. Symmetry and asymmetry are contrary properties so long as $R \neq \emptyset$. If $R = \emptyset$ then $R$ is symmetric, asymmetric, and antisymmetric. Note also that every asymmetric relation is irreflexive.

Consistent with our use of "weak" and "strong" in Part I, every connected binary relation is weakly connected, but not conversely. (Sometimes "strongly connected" and "connected" are used instead of "connected" and "weakly connected," respectively. Connected relations are also referred to as "complete.") If $n > 1$, then no one of $=$, $>$, and $\geq$ is weakly connected. However, if $n = 1$, then $>$ is weakly connected and $\geq$ is connected, since $a \geq b$ or $b \geq a$ for any two real numbers $a$ and $b$. $R$ is connected if and only if it is weakly connected and reflexive.

We have already noted that each of $=$, $>$, and $\geq$ is transitive. However, none of these is negatively transitive if $n > 1$. For example, not $(1,3) > (0,5)$ and not $(0,5) > (1,2)$, but $(1,3) > (1,2)$. On the other hand, if $n = 1$, then both $>$ and $\geq$ are negatively transitive. This is easily seen by the above definition or by observing that negative transitivity is the same as

$$xRz \Rightarrow xRy \quad \text{or} \quad yRz, \quad \text{for all} \quad x,y,z \in X. \quad (7.1)$$

(Proof: The original definition says that not (not $xRz$) $\Rightarrow$ not (not $xRy$ and not $yRz$), which is just $xRz \Rightarrow xRy$ or $yRz$. The original definition then follows from (7.1) by contradictories.)

The following lemma states three simple interconnections among some of the foregoing properties. It is proved in detail only to illustrate some proof methods to readers who are not used to working with binary relations.

LEMMA 7.1. *The following implications hold for any binary relation on a set:*

a. *(transitivity & irreflexivity) $\Rightarrow$ asymmetry*
b. *(negative transitivity & asymmetry) $\Rightarrow$ transitivity*
c. *(transitivity & irreflexivity & weak connectedness) $\Rightarrow$ negative transitivity.*

*Proof:*

a. Suppose that $xRy$. If $yRx$ also, then $xRx$ by transitivity. But this contradicts irreflexive. Hence not $yRx$.

b. Suppose that $xRy$ and $yRz$. By (7.1), ($xRz$ or $zRy$), and not $zRy$ by asymmetry. Therefore $xRz$.

c. Suppose that not $xRy$ and not $yRz$. If either $x = y$ or $y = z$, then not $xRz$. If $x \neq y$ and $y \neq z$, then $yRx$ and $zRy$ by weak connectedness, and hence $zRx$ by transitivity. Asymmetry, by part (a), then implies not $xRz$. ◆

RESTRICTIONS, DUALS, AND COMPOSITIONS

If $R$ is a binary relation on $X$ and if $Y \subseteq X$ then $R \cap (Y \times Y) = \{(x,y) : xRy \text{ and } x,y \in Y\}$ is the *restriction of $R$ on $Y$.* An example of the use of restrictions in social choice arises in the condition of independence from infeasible alternatives. As we noted in Chapter 1, this says that the social choice shall not depend on preference data involving infeasible or unavailable alternatives. When each $D$ consists of an $n$-tuple of preference orders on $X$, so that $D = (>_1, \ldots, >_n)$, this condition is: $F(Y,D) = F(Y,D')$ whenever the restriction of $>_i$ on $Y$ equals the restriction of $>'_i$ on $Y$, for each $i \in \{1, \ldots, n\}$.

The *dual* or converse of a binary relation $R$ on $X$ is $R^* = \{(x,y) : (y,x) \in R\}$. That is, $xR^*y \Leftrightarrow yRx$. Thus the duals of $=$, $\geq$, and $>$ are $=$, $\leq$, and $<$, respectively. $R$ is symmetric if and only if $R = R^*$, and asymmetric if and only if $R \cap R^* = \emptyset$. In addition, $R$ is connected if and only if $R \cup R^* = X \times X$, the universal relation. The *dual* of an $n$-tuple $(R_1, \ldots, R_n)$ of binary relations is the $n$-tuple $(R_1^*, \ldots, R_n^*)$ of duals. This is consistent with our usage of calling $-D$ the dual of $D$ in Part I.

The *composition* of binary relations $R$ and $S$ on $X$, written here as $(R)(S)$, is defined by

$$(R)(S) = \{(x,z) : xRy \ \& \ ySz \text{ for some } y \in X\}.$$

That is, $x(R)(S)z$ if and only if there is a $y$ such that $xRySz$. Clearly, with $X = Re^n$, $(>)(>)=(>)$ and $(=)(\geq)=(\geq)$. It is not quite as obvious that, for any $n$, $(<)(>) = (Re^n)^2$. That is, for every $a,b \in Re^n$, there is a $c \in Re^n$ such that $a < c$ and $c > b$. Any $c$ larger than both $a$ and $b$ will do.

Transitivity is expressed in terms of composition by $(R)(R) \subseteq R$. With $R^c = \{(x,y) : (x,y) \in X \times X \text{ and } (x,y) \notin R\} = X \times X - R$, the *complement* of $R$ in $X \times X$, negative transitivity is given by $(R^c)(R^c) \subseteq R^c$. Composition is associative, so that $((R)(S))(T) = (R)((S)(T))$. The $m$-fold composition of $R$ with itself will be written as $(R)^m$. An important property of duals and complements is that the dual of the complement is the complement of the dual: $R^{c*} = R^{*c}$. Also, the dual of a composition is the composition of the duals in reverse order, thus: $((R)(S))^* = (S^*)(R^*)$.

## TRANSITIVE CLOSURE

The *transitive closure* $R^t$ of a binary relation $R$ on $X$ is $R^t = R \cup (R)^2 \cup (R)^3 \cup \cdots$, so that $xR^ty \Leftrightarrow xRy$ or $xRx_1Rx_2R \cdots Rx_mRy$ for some $x_1, x_2, \ldots, x_m \in X$. The transitive closure of $R$ is always transitive, since $x(R)^my$ and $y(R)^kz \Rightarrow x(R)^{m+k}z$. $R$ itself is transitive if and only if $R = R^t$.

If $R$ is reflexive, then $R \subseteq (R)^2 \subseteq (R)^3 \subseteq \cdots$, so that $R^t = (R)^m$ for some $m$ if $X$ is finite. If $R$ is irreflexive, then $R^t$ need not be irreflexive, for we might have $xRyRx$ (if $R$ is not asymmetric or antisymmetric) or $xRyRzRx$. In general, $R^t$ is irreflexive if and only if $R$ is irreflexive and there is no $R$ cycle $x_1Rx_2Rx_3R \cdots Rx_mRx_1$.

## 7.2 ORDER RELATIONS

Many of the binary relations that we will use arise in connection with individual preferences and binary social choices. Four of the order relations that will be used in this connection are listed in order of decreasing generality in the following definition. Each of these is asymmetric.

DEFINITION 7.1. *A binary relation R on X is a*

1. suborder $\Leftrightarrow R^t$ *is irreflexive,*
2. strict partial order $\Leftrightarrow R$ *is irreflexive and transitive,*
3. weak order $\Leftrightarrow R$ *is asymmetric and negatively transitive,*
4. linear order $\Leftrightarrow R$ *is irreflexive, transitive and weakly connected.*

One should have no difficulty in showing that ($R$ is a linear order) $\Rightarrow$ ($R$ is a weak order) $\Rightarrow$ ($R$ is a strict partial order) $\Rightarrow$ ($R$ is a suborder). Although the converse implications do not hold in general, each of the first three relations in the definition is included in some relation in each successor class. That is, if $R$ is a suborder, then there is a strict partial order $S$ ($S = R^t$ will suffice) such that $R \subseteq S$ (that is, $xRy \Rightarrow xSy$ for all $x,y \in X$); if $R$ is a strict partial order then there is a weak order $S$ such that $R \subseteq S$; if $R$ is a weak order then there is a linear order $S$ such that $R \subseteq S$. The second of these implications follows from Szpilrajn's theorem (1930), which says that every strict partial order is included in some linear order, and from the fact that a linear order is a weak order. The final implication also follows from this reasoning: a weak order is a strict partial order; a strict partial order is included in a linear order; therefore a weak order is included in a linear order.

### EQUIVALENCE RELATIONS AND INDIFFERENCE

Some of the differences among the four orders of Definition 7.1 can be brought out with the use of equivalence relations, compositions, and several derived relations.

An *equivalence* (or "equivalence relation") is a reflexive, symmetric, and transitive binary relation. The most common equivalence is the identity relation $=$ on a set. Another equivalence $E$ is obtained by taking $xEy \Leftrightarrow x,y \in X$, in which case $E = X \times X$, the universal relation.

An equivalence $E$ on $X$ partitions $X$ into a set of *equivalence classes* such that $xEy$ if and only if $x$ and $y$ are in the same equivalence class. Conversely, any partition of $X$ determines an equivalence $E$ on $X$ by taking $xEy$ if and only if $x$ and $y$ are in the same element of the partition. The set of equivalence classes of $X$ under $E$ is usually written as $X/E$, which is often called a quotient set. When $E$ is the identity relation, $X/E = \{\{x\}:x \in X\}$. When $E$ is the universal relation, $X/E = \{X\}$, the set whose only element is $X$.

Let $>$ be a binary relation on $X$. Using this relation we define several new relations as follows: for all $x,y \in X$,

$$x \sim y \Leftrightarrow \text{not } x > y \quad \& \quad \text{not } y > x, \tag{7.2}$$
$$x \geqslant y \Leftrightarrow x > y \quad \text{or} \quad x \sim y, \tag{7.3}$$
$$x \approx y \Leftrightarrow (x \sim z \Leftrightarrow y \sim z, \text{ for all } z \in X). \tag{7.4}$$

75

Using duals and complements, (7.2) is the same as $\sim = (> \cup >*)^c = >^c \cap >^{*c}$. (7.3) is $\geqslant \, = \, > \cup \sim$. When $>$ is viewed as a preference relation, with $x > y$ interpreted as "$x$ is preferred to $y$," $\sim$ is referred to as an indifference relation, and $\geqslant$ is a preference-or-indifference relation.

We shall now state a number of theorems that involve the relations of Definition 7.1 and those defined in the preceding paragraph. Like other assertions in this and the preceding section that are not proved here, the proofs are left to the reader as exercises. Many of these proofs are contained in Fishburn (1970, Chapter 2).

When we write a relation in a "strict" notation, such as $>$, $>_i$, $>$, or $>_0$, it will always be assumed, if it is not otherwise evident, that the relation is asymmetric. Given that $>$ is asymmetric, exactly one of $x > y$, $y > x$, and $x \sim y$ holds for each $(x,y) \in X \times X$, so that $\geqslant$ is connected. Moreover, $\sim$ is reflexive $(x \sim x)$ and symmetric $(x \sim y \Rightarrow y \sim x)$, and $\approx$ is reflexive, symmetric, and transitive, and is therefore an equivalence.

A difference between suborders and strict partial orders arises from the fact that if $>$ is a strict partial order then

$$(\approx)(>) \subseteq > \qquad \text{and} \qquad (>)(\approx) \subseteq >. \qquad (7.5)$$

That is, $((x \approx y \ \& \ y > z) \text{ or } (x > y \ \& \ y \approx z)) \Rightarrow x > z$. This can be false when $>$ is a suborder, for with $X = \{x,y,z\}$ and $x > y$, $y > z$ and $x \sim z$, we get $z \approx x$, $x > y$ and $y > z$ in violation of $(\approx)(>) \subseteq >$.

A familiar example of a strict partial order that is not a weak order is the strict inclusion relation $\subset$ on the set of subsets of a set with more than three elements. Another example is $>$ on $Re^2$.

When $>$ is a strict partial order, $\sim$ is not necessary transitive. In fact, a strict partial order $>$ is a weak order if and only if $\sim$ is transitive. Thus, if $>$ is a weak order then $\sim$ is transitive and is therefore an equivalence. The quotient set $X/\sim$ is referred to as the set of indifference classes when $>$ is a preference weak order. The following correspondent of (7.5) holds for all weak orders but not for all strict partial orders:

$$(\sim)(>) \subseteq > \qquad \text{and} \qquad (>)(\sim) \subseteq >. \qquad (7.6)$$

Moreover, when $>$ is a weak order, $\geqslant$ is connected and transitive. Such a $\geqslant$ is also referred to as a "weak order" or as a "complete preorder."

A weak order is a linear order if and only if $x \sim y \Leftrightarrow x = y$. The prime example of a linear order is $>$ on $Re$. Suppose that $X$ is a set of people and $x > y$ means that $x$ is heavier than $y$, with weight being reckoned to the nearest whole pound. Then $>$ is a linear order if no two people in $X$ weigh the same. Otherwise $>$ is a weak order, but not a linear order.

If $>$ on $X$ is a weak order then $>'$, defined on $X/\sim$ by $a >' b \Leftrightarrow x > y$ for some (and hence for all) $x \in a$ and $y \in b$, is a linear order.

The dual of any binary relation has the same properties as the original relation. Thus, the dual of a suborder is a suborder, the dual of a linear order is a linear order, and so forth.

NUMERICAL REPRESENTATIONS

Another way to express the differences among the four orders of Definition 7.1 is through numerical representations. The following theorem summarizes this for countable sets (either finite or denumerably infinite).

THEOREM 7.1. *Suppose that $X$ is countable, and that $>$ on $X$ is a binary relation. Then, for each case listed below, there is a real-valued function $u$ on $X$ that satisfies the displayed properties for all $x,y \in X$:*

1. $>$ *is a suborder* $\Leftrightarrow [x > y \Rightarrow u(x) > u(y)]$,
2. $>$ *is a strict partial order* $\Rightarrow [x > y \Rightarrow u(x) > u(y)$, *and* $x \approx y \Leftrightarrow u(x) = u(y)]$,
3. $>$ *is a weak order* $\Leftrightarrow [x > y \Leftrightarrow u(x) > u(y)]$,
4. $>$ *is a linear order* $\Leftrightarrow [x > y \Leftrightarrow u(x) > u(y)$, *and* $u(x) = u(y) \Rightarrow x = y]$.

The numerical representation for each of the last three cases is not generally valid for each of its predecessors. In the first two cases, $u(x) > u(y)$ does *not* indicate that $x > y$, although it does signify that $x \geqslant y$, for if $y > x$ then we must have $u(y) > u(x)$. In all cases, $u(x) \geq u(y) \Rightarrow x \geqslant y$. In the weak order case, the definition of $\sim$ insures that $x \sim y \Leftrightarrow u(x) = u(y)$, so that the indifference classes are identified by their different $u$ values. In the linear order case, no two distinct elements have the same $u$ value, and (as in the weak order case also) $>$ is completely determined by the $u$ values.

It should be evident that the $u$ values can be changed in drastic ways without affecting the validity of the representation. For example, if $x > y > z > w$, then $u$ values of $10^6$, 15.375, $-1$ and $-1.0001$ for $x$, $y$, $z$, $w$, respectively, are just as appropriate as $u$ values of 4, 3, 2, and 1. The latter are certainly easier to view.

The proofs that ensure the existence of $u$ functions as specified in Theorem 7.1 are not too difficult. First, with $X$ enumerated as $x_1$, $x_2$, $x_3$, . . . , $u(x) = \Sigma\{2^{-n} : x > x_n\}$ shows the existence of $u$ for case 4. The suborder representation then follows from the fact that a suborder can be embedded in a linear order ($R \subseteq S$, as after Definition 7.1). Case 2 follows from the fact that $>'$ on $X/\approx$ (defined in the

77

natural way) is a strict partial order when $>$ on $X$ is a strict partial order, and case 3 follows from the fact that $>'$ on $X/\sim$ is a linear order when $>$ on $X$ is a weak order.

DISPLAYS OF ORDERS

As noted above, suborders and strict partial orders are not generally uniquely determined by numerical representations as in Theorem 7.1. For suborders that are not also strict partial orders, it may be necessary to explicitly identify all pairs in $>$. One such suborder, on $X = \{a,b,c,d,e,f\}$, is

$$> = \{(a,b),(b,c),(c,d),(a,d),(b,e),(e,d),(f,e),(f,d)\}.$$

This can be displayed as in Figure 7.1, where $x > y$ if and only if there is a line *from x to y*. In graph-theoretic terms, a suborder on $X$ (usually

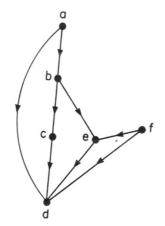

FIGURE 7.1. A suborder

taken to be finite) is a directed graph (i.e. irreflexive binary relation) with no cycles (i.e. $x_1 > x_2 > \cdots > x_m > x_1$ for no $x_1, \ldots, x_m \in X$).

A suborder can also be displayed by a 0-1 matrix, as in Figure 7.2, where there is a 1 in the cell for row $x$ and column $y$ if and only if $x > y$, and a zero otherwise.

Needless to say, *any* irreflexive binary relation can be displayed either in the form of Figure 7.1 (with no loops, but perhaps with cycles) or Figure 7.2 (with zeros on the main diagonal), at least when $X$ is finite.

Strict partial orders can be displayed more easily since they are transitive. Let $>$ be a strict partial order and call $>_1$ a *generator* of $>$

if and only if $>_1^t = >$. Then, if $X$ is finite, $>$ has a unique *minimal generator* $>_0$ defined by

$$>_0 = \{(x,y) : x > y \text{ and } x > z > y \text{ for no } z \in X\}.$$

It should be clear that $>_0$ generates $>$ and that every other generator of $>$ must include $>_0$. To identify a strict partial order it is only necessary to specify its minimal generator. The minimal generator can be displayed in the manner of Figure 7.1, or we can omit the arrows and agree that $x > y$ if and only if $x$ is above $y$ in the figure and there is a path of lines from $x$ to $y$ that always goes downward. For example, Figure 7.3 represents the strict partial order whose minimal generator

|   | a | b | c | d | e | f |
|---|---|---|---|---|---|---|
| a | 0 | 1 | 0 | 1 | 0 | 0 |
| b | 0 | 0 | 1 | 0 | 1 | 0 |
| c | 0 | 0 | 0 | 1 | 0 | 0 |
| d | 0 | 0 | 0 | 0 | 0 | 0 |
| e | 0 | 0 | 0 | 1 | 0 | 0 |
| f | 0 | 0 | 0 | 1 | 1 | 0 |

FIGURE 7.2. A 0–1 matrix for Figure 7.1

is $\{(a,b),(b,c),(c,d),(b,h),(e,g),(f,g),(g,d)\}$. The other elements in $>$ are $(a,c)$, $(a,d)$, $(a,h)$, $(b,d)$, $(e,d)$, and $(f,d)$.

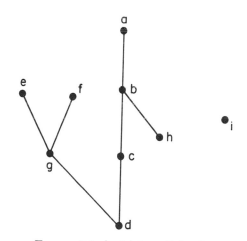

FIGURE 7.3. A strict partial order

In the sense of Figure 7.3, a linear order can be represented by points on a vertical line segment, with no two elements represented by the same point. A weak order can be displayed in a similar way with each point representing an indifference class. Of course, a horizontal line is also used to show this, with $x > y$ if and only if $x$ is to the right of $y$ on the line. In some of our displays we shall use the *reverse* orientation, as when we write

$$\text{Voter } i{:}x \ y \ z \ w \ r \ s \ t \qquad (7.7)$$

to mean that the preference order $>_i$ for the $i$th individual is linear with $x >_i y >_i \cdots >_i s >_i t$. A weak order in this notation may be written as

$$\text{Voter } i{:}x \ (y \ z) \ w \ (r \ s \ t), \qquad (7.8)$$

where the elements within parentheses are indifferent. That is, the foregoing display means that $x >_i y \sim_i z >_i w >_i r \sim_i s \sim_i t$. These may also be represented by appropriate $u$ values for the representations of Theorem 7.1, as follows:

|   | (7.7) | (7.8) |
|---|-------|-------|
| $x$ | 7 | 4 |
| $y$ | 6 | 3 |
| $z$ | 5 | 3 |
| $w$ | 4 | 2 |
| $r$ | 3 | 1 |
| $s$ | 2 | 1 |
| $t$ | 1 | 1 |

Another way to picture a weak order or linear order is by a Cartesian display of an appropriate numerical representation. Suppose that a university is considering changing its policy for the length of time an assistant professor can remain as an assistant professor. It is considering nine proposals, represented by $k = 1, 2, \ldots, 9$ in the following: "An individual hired as an assistant professor or promoted to the rank of assistant professor can remain in that category for $k$ years, and if at the end of $k$ years in that category he has not been promoted then his services with the university shall be terminated." A member of the faculty council decides to rank his preferences for the nine values of $k$ and eventually arrives at the order $5 > 4 > 3 > 6 > 7 > 8 > 2 > 9 > 1$, as displayed on Figure 7.4. This sort of unimodal or single-peaked preference pattern seems to arise in many situations where the alternatives correspond to a natural order of points on a line or continuum. We shall see later that such patterns play an important role in simple majority social choice.

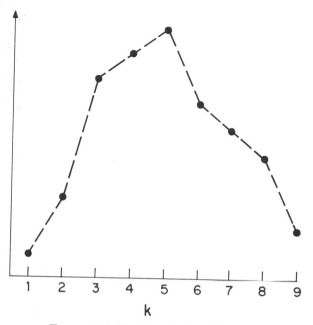

FIGURE 7.4. Single-peaked preferences

## 7.3 BINARY CHOICES

As noted in Chapter 1, a social choice function is a function $F$ from the Cartesian product $\mathfrak{X} \times \mathfrak{D}$ of a nonempty set $\mathfrak{X}$ of nonempty subsets of $X$ and a nonempty set $\mathfrak{D}$ of profiles of individuals' preference data on $X$, to the nonempty subsets of $X$, such that $F(Y,D) \subseteq Y$ for each $(Y,D) \in \mathfrak{X} \times \mathfrak{D}$.

In this part of the book we shall generally *assume that $\mathfrak{X}$ is the set of all nonempty subsets of $X$.* There are other cases of interest that we shall not look at here, for example when $\mathfrak{X} = \{Y : x_0 \in Y \text{ and } Y \subseteq X\}$ with $x_0$ the status quo, and when $\mathfrak{X}$ is the set of all finite subsets of $X$ in cases where $X$ is not finite.

We shall also *assume throughout Part II that $\mathfrak{D}$ is a set of n-tuples $D = (\succ_1, \ldots, \succ_n)$ of strict partial orders on $X$.* The binary relation $\succ_i$ is a preference relation for the $i$th individual. The indifference and preference-indifference relations defined from $\succ_i$ by (7.2) and (7.3) will be denoted by $\sim_i$ and $\succcurlyeq_i$, respectively. Some situations in which $\sim_i$ might not be transitive were mentioned in Chapter 1. In general, it is felt that intransitive individual indifference arises in situations where a series of indifferences, each of which seems reasonable, adds up to a sufficiently large difference to yield a definite preference between the first and last items in the series.

**81**

## BINARY CHOICES

Binary social choices arise from the two-element subsets of $X$. In writing $F(\{x,y\},D)$ one should keep in mind that this represents a situation where $x$ and $y$ are the only available or feasible alternatives in $X$.

For a given $D$, the binary part of $F$ is the restriction of $F$ to subsets of $X$ with no more than two elements. From this restriction we can define an asymmetric binary relation $F_D$ on $X$ as follows:

$$xF_Dy \Leftrightarrow x \neq y \quad \text{and} \quad F(\{x,y\},D) = \{x\}. \tag{7.9}$$

Thus $xF_Dy$ if and only if $x \neq y$ and $x$ is the unique social choice from $\{x,y\}$ when $D$ obtains. If $x \neq y$ and $F(\{x,y\},D) = \{x,y\}$, which indicates a tie, then not $xF_Dy$ and not $yF_Dx$.

The binary relation $F_D$ may or may not be transitive or have an irreflexive transitive closure. This will depend on the particular $D$ and the way that the binary social choices are determined by $F$ under $D$. For example, if binary choices are made by simple majority, then $F_D$ will be transitive for some $D$ and intransitive for other $D$ when $n > 1$ and $\#X > 2$.

Suppose that there is a $z \in Y$ that is never defeated in a binary comparison with any other $y \in Y$. That is, suppose that $z$ beats or ties each other $y \in Y$, given $D$ and $F$:

$$z \in \{x : x \in Y \text{ and } yF_Dx \text{ for no } y \in Y\}.$$

It may then seem reasonable to have $z \in F(Y,D)$ for each such $z$ and only such $z$, so that

$$F(Y,D) = \{x : x \in Y \text{ and } yF_Dx \text{ for no } y \in Y\}. \tag{7.10}$$

The following theorem specifies precisely when $F(Y,D)$ can be defined on the basis of binary social choices in the manner of (7.10), at least for finite $Y$.

THEOREM 7.2. *$F_D$ on $X$ is a suborder if and only if, for every nonempty finite $Y \subseteq X$,*

$$\{x : x \in Y \text{ and } yF_Dx \text{ for no } y \in Y\} \neq \emptyset. \tag{7.11}$$

*Proof.* If $Y$ is finite and (7.11) fails, so that for every $x \in Y$ there is an $x' \in Y$ such that $x'F_Dx$, then there must be $x_1F_Dx_2F_D \cdots F_Dx_mF_Dx_1$ with $x_1, \ldots, x_m \in Y$, and hence $F_D$ is not a suborder. Conversely, if $F_D$ is not a suborder, then $x_1F_Dx_2F_D \cdots F_Dx_mF_Dx_1$ for some $x_1$, $x_2$, $\ldots, x_m \in X$, and (7.11) then fails with $Y = \{x_1, x_2, \ldots, x_m\}$.◆

## PARETO DOMINANCE AND UNANIMITY

We now develop some notions which highlight the difference between transitive and intransitive individual indifference.

For given $D \in \mathfrak{D}$, we define binary relations of Pareto dominance and indifference as follows:

$$x \gg_D y \Leftrightarrow x \succ_i y \qquad \text{for all} \qquad \succ_i \text{ in } D,$$
$$x \succ_D y \Leftrightarrow x \succ_i y \qquad \text{for some} \qquad \succ_i \text{ in } D \text{ and } y \succ_i x \text{ for no}$$
$$\qquad \qquad \qquad \qquad \qquad \qquad \qquad \qquad \qquad \succ_i \text{ in } D, \quad (7.12)$$
$$x =_D y \Leftrightarrow x \sim_i y \qquad \text{for all} \qquad \succ_i \text{ in } D,$$
$$x \geq_D y \Leftrightarrow x \succ_D y \qquad \text{or} \qquad x =_D y.$$

If each $\succ_i$ is a strict partial order then $\gg_D$ is transitive and is therefore a strict partial order. But none of $\succ_D$, $=_D$, and $\geq_D$ need be transitive. For example, if $n = 3$, $X = \{x,y,z\}$, and $D = (\succ_1, \succ_2, \succ_3)$ is given by

$$\succ_1 = \{(x,y)\}, \ \succ_2 = \{(y,z)\}, \ \succ_3 = \{(z,x)\}, \qquad (7.13)$$

each of which is a strict partial order, then $x \succ_D y \succ_D z \succ_D x$, so that $\succ_D$ is not even a suborder. On the other hand, if each $\succ_i$ is a weak order, then every relation in (7.12) is transitive, and $=_D$ is an equivalence.

Strong unanimity and unanimity are defined for a general social choice function in a manner similar to the definitions for binary choices in section 2.3.

DEFINITION 7.2. *A social choice function* $F: \mathfrak{X} \times \mathfrak{D} \to \mathfrak{X}$ *is* unanimous *if and only if, for all* $x,y \in Y$, $Y \in \mathfrak{X}$ *and* $D \in \mathfrak{D}$,

$$x \gg_D y \qquad and \qquad x,y \in Y \Rightarrow y \notin F(Y,D), \qquad (7.14)$$

*and is* strongly unanimous *if and only if, for all cases,*

$$x \succ_D y \qquad and \qquad x,y \in Y \Rightarrow y \notin F(Y,D). \qquad (7.15)$$

The following lemma states the observations of the preceding paragraph in a slightly different way.

LEMMA 7.2. *Assume that $X$ is finite. If every $D \in \mathfrak{D}$ is an n-tuple of weak orders on $X$ then there are social choice functions $F: \mathfrak{X} \times \mathfrak{D} \to \mathfrak{X}$ that are strongly unanimous. If $\mathfrak{D}$ is the set of all n-tuples of strict partial orders on $X$ then there are social choice functions $F: \mathfrak{X} \times \mathfrak{D} \to \mathfrak{X}$ that are unanimous, but if $n \geq 3$ and $\#X \geq 3$ then no social choice function can be strongly unanimous.*

The final assertion follows from (7.13), where strong unanimity requires $y \notin F(\{x,y,z\},D)$ and similarly for $z$ and $x$, so that $F(\{x,y,z\},D) = \emptyset$. But this contradicts the definition of a social choice function.

ANOTHER PAIR OF CONDITIONS

To further illustrate the difference between weak orders and strict partial orders, we may consider the following binary conditions for $F$:

$$x \gg_D y \quad \text{and} \quad yF_Dz \Rightarrow xF_Dz \qquad (7.16)$$
$$x >_D y \quad \text{and} \quad yF_Dz \Rightarrow xF_Dz. \qquad (7.17)$$

Condition (7.16) is the same as $(\gg_D)(F_D) \subseteq F_D$, and it has the natural companion $(F_D)(\gg_D) \subseteq F_D$. Likewise, (7.17) is $(>_D)(F_D) \subseteq F_D$.

Both conditions seem like monotonicity conditions. The first says that if everyone prefers $x$ to $y$ and if $y$ beats $z$ in their binary choice comparison, then $x$ beats $z$ in *their* binary comparison. When every $>_i$ in $D$ is a strict partial order, the hypotheses of the condition say that $x >_i z$ when $y >_i z$, and $x \geqslant_i z$ when $y \sim_i z$. When every $>_i$ is a weak order, the hypotheses of (7.16) give $x >_i z$ whenever $y \geqslant_i z$. In any event, (7.16) seems like a rather reasonable condition.

On the other hand, although (7.17) seems fine when weak orders apply, it is generally unacceptable under strict partial orders. To argue this, let *binary unanimity* mean that (7.14) holds for all $Y$ with $\#Y = 2$: that is, $x \gg_D y \Rightarrow xF_Dy$.

LEMMA 7.3. *Suppose that* $(n \geq 2, \#X \geq 5)$ *or* $(n \geq 3, \#X \geq 4)$, $\mathcal{D}$ *is the set of all n-tuples of strict partial orders on* $X$, *and* $F$ *is a social choice function that satisfies* (7.17). *Then* $F$ *cannot satisfy binary unanimity.*

It will suffice to verify the lemma for $(n = 2, X = \{x,y,z,r,s\})$ and for $(n = 3, X = \{x,y,z,r\})$. For the $n = 2$ case let the minimal generators of $>_1$ and $>_2$ be $(x >_1 y, y >_1 z, r >_1 s)$ and $(x >_2 y, s >_2 x, z >_2 r)$. Then $x \gg_D y, y >_D z, z >_D r, r >_D s$ and $s >_D x$, which give $yF_Dy$ if both (7.17) and binary unanimity hold. But $yF_Dy$ contradicts (7.9). For the $n = 3$ case let the minimal generators for $D$ be $(x >_1 y, y >_1 z)$, $(x >_2 y, z >_2 r)$ and $(x >_3 y, r >_3 x)$. Then $x \gg_D y, y >_D z, z >_D r$ and $r >_D x$, which again give $yF_Dy$ if both (7.17) and binary unanimity hold.

We shall conclude this chapter with two theorems suggested by a theorem of Pattanaik (1968). Our theorems will use conditions (7.16) and (7.17) in the appropriate contexts along with the "Pareto optimal sets"

$$Y(\gg_D) = \{x : x \in Y \text{ and } y \gg_D x \text{ for no } y \in Y\}$$
$$Y(>_D) = \{x : x \in Y \text{ and } y >_D x \text{ for no } y \in Y\}.$$

The theorems show that, if we are interested in a particular $Y \subseteq X$, then $F_D$ does not have to be a suborder on all of $Y$ for there to be an alternative in $Y$ that beats or ties every other alternative in $Y$ under binary comparisons. In each case it may be noted that condition (7.16) or (7.17) holds if binary choices are made according to some one representative system, or if weak majority is used for the binary choices. First, the weak-order theorem.

THEOREM 7.3. *Suppose that $Y \subseteq X$ is finite, that each $>_i$ in D is a weak order, that the restriction of $F_D$ on $Y(>_D)$ is a suborder, and that (7.17) holds on Y. Then there is an alternative in $Y(>_D)$ that is in $\{x : x \in Y$ and $yF_Dx$ for no $y \in Y\}$.*

*Proof.* Assume that the conditions of the theorem hold. Then the weak-order assumption (which implies that $>_D$ is transitive) and finiteness imply that $Y(>_D) \neq \emptyset$. Then, by Theorem 7.2, there is a $z \in Y(>_D)$ such that $yF_Dz$ for no $y \in Y(>_D) - \{z\}$. That is, $z$ beats or ties each other alternative in $Y(>_D)$ on the basis of binary choice comparisons.

Suppose that $x \in Y - Y(>_D)$. Then, by the transitivity of $>_D$, finiteness and the definition of $Y(>_D)$, there is a $y \in Y(>_D)$ such that $y >_D x$. Then not $xF_Dz$ by (7.17), and therefore not $xF_Dz$ for every $x \in Y$.◆

The following theorem modifies Theorem 7.3 in an obvious way, and its proof is similar to the proof just given.

THEOREM 7.4. *Suppose that $Y \subseteq X$ is finite, that each $>_i$ in D is a strict partial order, that the restriction of $F_D$ on $Y(\gg_D)$ is a suborder, and that (7.16) holds on Y. Then there is an alternative in $Y(\gg_D)$ that is in $\{x : x \in Y$ and $yF_Dx$ for no $y \in Y\}$.*

# CHAPTER 8

# Simple Majority Social Choice

THIS CHAPTER begins our specific consideration of general social choice functions whose binary choices $F(\{x,y\},D)$ agree with simple majority. Conditions sufficient for $F$ to agree with simple majority in this way are presented in the first section.

We then go on to examine the binary relations $P_D$, $R_D$, and $I_D$ of strict simple majority, simple majority, and simple-majority ties, noting that any asymmetric binary relation on a finite set $X$ is equal to some $P_D$ on $X$ for an appropriate choice of $D$ and $n$.

As in section 7.3, the binary simple-majority relations are considered in compositions with Pareto dominance relations, both for individual weak orders (transitive indifference) and strict partial orders (intransitive indifference). General conditions for the existence of an alternative that has a simple majority over each other alternative are noted.

The final section discusses why one might be concerned about the existence of a "best" simple-majority alternative. In this setting, we shall examine two simple-majority voting procedures in which the alternatives are voted on in a definite order. The chapter concludes with a brief look at voter strategies in the two sequential voting procedures.

## 8.1 AGREEMENT WITH SIMPLE MAJORITY

The rest of Part II concentrates on social choice functions whose binary choices coincide with the simple majority decision rule. The binary part of a social choice function $F\colon \mathfrak{X} \times \mathfrak{D} \to \mathfrak{X}$ is fully determined by the indexed family $\{F_D\colon D \in \mathfrak{D}\}$ of binary relations $F_D$ on $X$ as defined by (7.9). We recall that $xF_Dy$ if and only if $x \neq y$ and $F(\{x,y\},D) = \{x\}$.

Correspondingly, for the simple majority decision rule for binary choices we define, for all $x,y \in X$,

$$xP_Dy \Leftrightarrow \#\{i\colon x >_i y\} > \#\{i\colon y >_i x\}. \tag{8.1}$$

For a given $D = (>_1, \ldots, >_n)$, $P_D$ is the asymmetric binary relation of *strict* simple majority.

DEFINITION 8.1. *A social choice function* $F\colon \mathfrak{X} \times \mathfrak{D} \to \mathfrak{X}$ *agrees with simple majority if and only if* $F_D = P_D$ *for every* $D \in \mathfrak{D}$.

One aspect of this definition that deserves special emphasis is that, when $F$ agrees with simple majority, the definition says absolutely nothing about the behavior of $F$ for subsets $Y \subseteq X$ that contain more than two alternatives. Although we shall be concerned with relationships between $F(Y,D)$ when $\#Y \geq 3$ and the restriction of $P_D$ on $Y$, Definition 8.1 avoids any mention of such relationships.

CONDITIONS FOR AGREEMENT

Another significant aspect of the definition is that, by assumption, $\mathfrak{X}$ is the set of all nonempty subsets of $X$. If $x \neq y$ and $\{x,y\}$ were not in $\mathfrak{X}$, then $F(\{x,y\},D)$ would not be defined, in which case neither $x F_D y$ nor $y F_D x$, regardless of the nature of $D$. Hence no such $F$ could agree with simple majority by our definition unless $\#\{i: x >_i y\} = \#\{i: y >_i x\}$ for every $D \in \mathfrak{D}$.

As specified in section 7.3, $\mathfrak{D}$ is presumed to be a nonempty subset of $n$-tuples of strict partial orders on $X$. Although agreement with simple majority does not place any restriction on $\mathfrak{D}$ when $\{x,y\} \in \mathfrak{X}$ for all $x,y \in X$, we shall generally suppose that every pair $\{x,y\}$ is *free* in $\mathfrak{D}$, by which we mean the following:

$x,y \in X$, $x \neq y$ and $\alpha_i \in \{\{(x,y)\}, \{(y,x)\}, \emptyset\}$ for $i = 1, \ldots,$
$n \Rightarrow$ there is a $D = (>_1, \ldots, >_n)$ in $\mathfrak{D}$ such that the restric-  (8.2)
tion of $>_i$ on $\{x,y\}$ equals $\alpha_i$ for $i = 1, \ldots, n$.

Thus a given $x,y \in X$ with $x \neq y$ is free in $\mathfrak{D}$ if and only if each possible $n$-tuple of individuals' preferences on $\{x,y\}$ appears in some $D \in \mathfrak{D}$. Later cases in which $\mathfrak{D}$ is restricted in some manner will always satisfy the condition that each pair of alternatives is free in $\mathfrak{D}$.

The notion of free pairs enters directly into the following theorem for agreement with simple majority.

THEOREM 8.1. *Suppose that $F: \mathfrak{X} \times \mathfrak{D} \to \mathfrak{X}$ is a social choice function and that, for all $x,y \in X$ and all $D = (>_1, \ldots, >_n)$, $D' = (>'_1, \ldots, >'_n)$ in $\mathfrak{D}$, and each $i \in \{1, \ldots, n\}$:*

(1) $x \neq y \Rightarrow \{x,y\}$ *is free in $\mathfrak{D}$,*
(2) $F(\{x,y\}, D) = \{x,y\}$ *if $x \sim_i y$ for every $i$,*
(3) *if $x \sim'_i y$ and $x >_i y$, and if the restriction of $>'_j$ on $\{x,y\}$ equals the restriction of $>_j$ on $\{x,y\}$ for each $j \neq i$, then $x F_D y \Leftrightarrow$ not $y F_{D'} x$.*
*Then $F$ agrees with simple majority.*

*Proof.* In view of condition (1), the proof of Theorem 5.5 shows that $F$ agrees with simple majority if (in terms of Part I) for any $x,y \in X$

with $x \neq y$, strong monotonicity, weak nonreversibility and its dual, and the part of duality given by $F(0) = 0$ hold. The $F(0) = 0$ condition is condition (2) of Theorem 8.1. Since $x$ and $y$ are not fixed in condition (3), but may not vary over $X$, the $\Rightarrow$ implication in the conclusion of condition (3) verifies weak nonreversibility and its dual (interchange $x$ and $y$).

To verify strong monotonicity we need to show that if $>_j'$ on $\{x,y\}$ equals $>_j$ on $\{x,y\}$ for all $j \neq i$, then

$$(\text{not } yF_{D'}x, \text{ and } (y >_i' x \ \& \ x \geqslant_i y) \text{ or } (x \sim_i' y \ \& \ x >_i y)) \Rightarrow xF_Dy. \quad (8.3)$$

The general form of strong monotonicity on $\{x,y\}$ then follows from sequences of single-component changes under condition (1). We shall consider cases for $i$ in (8.3).

a. $x \sim_i' y \ \& \ x >_i y$. Then $xF_Dy$ by condition (3).

b. $y >_i' x \ \& \ x \sim_i y$. If not $xF_Dy$ then $yF_{D'}x$ by condition (3), and this contradicts not $yF_{D'}x$ in the hypotheses of (8.3).

c. $y >_i' x \ \& \ x >_i y$. Let $D^0$ be like $D$ and $D'$ on $\{x,y\}$ for $j \neq i$, and take $y \sim_i^0 x$. Condition (1) implies the existence of such a $D^0$. By case (b), $xF_{D^0}y$, so that not $yF_{D^0}x$. Then, by condition (3) for $D$ and $D^0$, $xF_Dy$. ◆

As is frequently the case in theorems such as Theorem 8.1 that contain fairly weak structural conditions, it is possible to simultaneously strengthen a structural condition and weaken some other condition without affecting the conclusion of the theorem. The following variant of Theorem 8.1 illustrates this principle. Condition (1) has been strengthened (more structure is assumed for $\mathfrak{D}$), and (3) has been weakened. The proof of the theorem is left as an exercise.

THEOREM 8.2. *Suppose that* $F: \mathfrak{X} \times \mathfrak{D} \to \mathfrak{X}$ *is a social choice function and that, for all* $x,y \in X$ *and* $D,D' \in \mathfrak{D}$ *and each* $i \in \{1, \ldots ,n\}$:

(1') $\mathfrak{D} = A_1 \times A_2 \times \cdots \times A_n$, *where each* $A_i$ *is a set of strict partial orders on* $X$ *(which can differ for different* $i$*) such that each distinct pair of alternatives is free in* $A_i$,

(2') $F(\{x,y\},D) = \{x,y\}$ *if* $x \sim_i y$ *for every* $i$,

(3') *if* $x \sim_i' y$ *and* $x >_i y$, *and if* $>_j' = >_j$ *for each* $j \neq i$, *then* $xF_Dy \Leftrightarrow \text{not } yF_{D'}x$.

*Then* $F$ *agrees with simple majority.*

It should be noted that (3') requires $>_j' = >_j$ on all of $X$, and not just on $\{x,y\}$. However, as in condition (3) of Theorem 8.1, condition (3') does not require any specific relationships between $>_i'$ and $>_i$ outside of $\{x,y\}$.

## 8.2 SIMPLE MAJORITY RELATIONS

Along with the binary dominance relations of (7.12) and the strict simple majority relation $P_D$ of (8.1), we shall use the following:

$$xI_Dy \Leftrightarrow \#\{i:x >_i y\} = \#\{i:y >_i x\}$$
$$xR_Dy \Leftrightarrow \#\{i:x >_i y\} \geq \#\{i:y >_i x\}, \tag{8.4}$$

so that $xI_Dy$ if and only if $x$ and $y$ tie under simple majority, and $xR_Dy$ if and only if $x$ beats or ties $y$ under simple majority. Clearly, $I_D$ and $R_D$ can be defined from $P_D$ in the way that we defined $\sim$ and $\geqslant$ from $>$:

$$xI_Dy \Leftrightarrow \text{not } xP_Dy \text{ and not } yP_Dx$$
$$xR_Dy \Leftrightarrow xP_Dy \text{ or } xI_Dy.$$

We shall say that $x$ *has a strict simple majority over* $y$ if and only if $xP_Dy$, and that $x$ *has a simple majority over* $y$ if and only if $xR_Dy$. In particular, it should be noted that $y$ can have a simple majority over $x$ when $x$ has a simple majority over $y$, in which case $xI_Dy$.

To illustrate the relation $P_D$ with simple examples, suppose that there are three voters and four alternatives $x$, $y$, $z$, $w$ with each voter having a linear preference order on $X$ as follows:

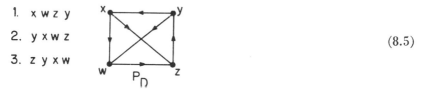

1. x w z y
2. y x w z
3. z y x w

$$\tag{8.5}$$

For example, $x >_1 w >_1 z >_1 y$ for voter 1. The directed graph for strict simple majority is as indicated. $P_D$ is not a suborder because it contains cycles such as $xP_DzP_DyP_Dx$, $wP_DzP_DyP_Dw$, and $xP_DwP_DzP_DyP_Dx$. Harary, Norman, and Cartwright (1965, pp. 313–314) provide an interesting context for this situation, in which a faculty committee of three is to decide whether to spend an alumnus' gift of \$100,000 on athletic scholarships ($x$), a botanical garden ($y$), a faculty club ($z$), or a parking structure ($w$).

In (8.5) there is no alternative that has a simple majority over each other alternative. In contrast to this, the following situation with $n = 4$ and $X = \{x,y,z,w,v\}$ has a linear $P_D$ in the order $x\ y\ z\ w\ v$.

1. $x\ y\ z\ v\ w$
2. $x\ z\ w\ v\ y$
3. $x\ y\ w\ v\ z$
4. $y\ z\ w\ v\ x$.

$$\tag{8.6}$$

Our third example comes from an actual situation. Two neighborhood church congregations decided to join together to form a new congregation. Robert Elwood, who was kind enough to share his data with me, chaired a committee that was responsible for guiding the selection of a name for the new congregation. After long deliberation, his committee submitted five names (here denoted $A$, $B$, $C$, $D$, $E$) to the combined membership. Ballots were distributed, and each member who wished to vote was instructed to rank the five names from most preferred to least preferred (ties prohibited). One hundred and seventy-five members responded. Of the 120 possible linear preference orders, 56 appeared on the ballots. The most frequent of these ($ACBDE$) appeared on 30 ballots. The next most frequent ($BDCAE$) was on 11 ballots. The analysis of simple majority comparisons is shown in Figure 8.1, where the ordered pair in row $x$ and column $y$

|   | B | C | D | E |
|---|---|---|---|---|
| A | (99,76) | (118,57) | (118,57) | (138,37) |
| B | - - - - - - | (88,87) | (134,41) | (147,28) |
| C | - - - - - - - - - - - | (106,69) | (139,36) |
| D | - - - - - - - - - - - - - - - - - - - - | (133,42) |

FIGURE 8.1. Simple majority with $n = 175$

gives the number of voters who preferred $x$ to $y$ and then the number who preferred $y$ to $x$. It is clear from the figure that $P_D$ is linear ($ABCDE$) and that $A$ had a significant strict simple majority over each of the other names. The only close comparison was $B$ versus $C$, where a change by one voter could have caused $P_D$ to be $ACBDE$ (still linear). Despite the fact that $A$ had a significant majority in each comparison, less than half the voters had $A$ listed first. The number of first-place votes for $(A,B,C,D,E)$ was $(76,60,15,13,11)$.

We shall now show that every asymmetric binary relation on a finite $X$ coincides with some strict simple majority relation $P_D$ for an appropriate choice of $D$.

McGARVEY'S THEOREM

Let $P$ be any asymmetric binary relation on a finite set $X$. Then there is some $n$ for which an $n$-tuple $D$ of strict partial orders on $X$ gives $P = P_D$, for if $P \neq \emptyset$ it will suffice to assign an $>_i$ to each $(x,y) \in P$ such that $x >_i y$ and $a \sim_i b$ whenever $\{a,b\} \neq \{x,y\}$. The following theorem, due to McGarvey (1953), shows that the conclusion of $P = P_D$ holds even when each $>_i$ is required to be a linear order.

THEOREM 8.3. *Suppose that $P$ is an asymmetric binary relation on a finite set $X$. Then for some $n > 0$ there is an n-tuple $D$ of linear orders on $X$ such that $P_D = P$.*

*Proof.* Let $X = \{x_1, \ldots, x_m\}$. If $P = \emptyset$, let $D$ consist of the two linear orders $x_1x_2 \cdots x_m$ and $x_m \cdots x_2x_1$. Then $P_D = \emptyset$. Suppose then that $P \neq \emptyset$. For each $(x,y) \in P$, assign linear orders $xya_1 \cdots a_{m-2}$ and $a_{m-2} \cdots a_1xy$, where $\{a_1, \ldots, a_{m-2}\} = X - \{x,y\}$. For these two orders, $x$ beats $y$, but every other pair is tied under simple majority. With $\#P = k$, let $D$ be a $2k$-tuple of linear orders constructed in this way, with two orders for each $(x,y) \in P$. Then $P_D = P.$ ◆

As McGarvey points out, it is not always necessary to have $n = 2(\#P)$ linear orders in order to make $P_D = P$. For example, if $P$ is a linear order then $n = 1$ in the theorem will do. For a somewhat more complicated example, one can show that, when

$$P = \{(x,y),(y,z),(z,w),(w,y)\},$$

the smallest $n$ that will suffice in the theorem is $n = 6$. If $n < 6$ then this $P$ equals no $P_D$ obtained from a $D$ composed of $n$ linear orders.

Stearns (1959) shows that, when $\#X$ is odd, some $n \leq \#X + 1$ will serve in Theorem 8.3, and that some $n \leq \#X + 2$ will do when $\#X$ is even. In the preceding example with $\#X = 4$ we required $n = 6$, or $n = \#X + 2$, which agrees with Stearns' theorem.

## 8.3 "Best" Simple Majority Alternatives

Having seen that simple majority can give rise to any asymmetric $P_D$ for sufficiently large $n$ compared to $\#X$, we shall now begin our examination of conditions that lead to the existence of an alternative that has a simple majority over each other alternative. A first step along these lines can be made within the setting of the theory of section 7.3. To preface this discussion we shall first consider combinations of the binary relations of (7.12) and the simple majority relations $P_D$, $I_D$, and $R_D$. Once again we shall point out some differences between transitive and intransitive individual indifference. Our first lemma is concerned with transitive indifference.

LEMMA 8.1. *If every* $\succ_i$ *in* $D = (\succ_1, \ldots, \succ_n)$ *is a weak order on* $X$ *then, for all* $x,y,z \in X$:

    a. $x =_D y$ & $y =_D z \Rightarrow x =_D z$,
    b. $x \geq_D y$ & $yR_Dz \Rightarrow xR_Dz$, *and* $(R_D)(\geq_D) \subseteq R_D$ *also*,
    c. $x \geq_D y$ & $yP_Dz \Rightarrow xP_Dz$, *and* $(P_D)(\geq_D) \subseteq P_D$ *also*,
    d. $x =_D y$ & $yI_Dz \Rightarrow xI_Dz$, *and* $(I_D)(=_D) \subseteq I_D$ *also*,

*but it is not necessarily true that* $x \gg_D y$ & $yI_Dz \Rightarrow xP_Dz$.

*Proof.* For the final assertion, suppose that $D$ consists of the two linear orders $xyz$ and $zxy$. Then $x \gg_D y$ and $yI_Dz$, but $xP_Dz$ is false since $xI_Dz$. Conclusion (a) is immediate from transitive indifference since $x =_D y$ & $y =_D z \Leftrightarrow (x \sim_i y$ & $y \sim_i z$ for all $i) \Rightarrow (x \sim_i z$ for all $i) \Leftrightarrow x =_D z$. Given $x \geq_D y$ & $yR_Dz$ as in (b), we have $x \geq_i y$ for all $i$, and $\#\{i:y >_i z\} \geq \#\{i:z >_i y\}$, whence, since $y >_i z \Rightarrow x >_i z$ and $z >_i x \Rightarrow z >_i y$ by weak orders,

$$\#\{i:x >_i z\} \geq \#\{i:y >_i z\} \geq \#\{i:z >_i y\} \geq \#\{i:z >_i x\}.$$

The first and last terms give $xR_Dz$, the conclusion of (b). Part (c) is proved similarly with $>$ in the middle of the foregoing chain of inequalities, and (d) is a direct consequence of (b) and the fact that $vI_Dw \Leftrightarrow vR_Dw$ & $wR_Dv$. ◆

The weak order lemma compares with the following lemma which allows individual indifference to be intransitive.

**LEMMA 8.2.** *If every $>_i$ in $D = (>_1, \ldots, >_n)$ is a strict partial order on $X$ then, for all $x,y,z \in X$:*

e. $x \gg_D y$ & $yR_Dz \Rightarrow xR_Dz$, and $(R_D)(\gg_D) \subseteq R_D$ also,
f. $x \gg_D y$ & $yP_Dz \Rightarrow xP_Dz$, and $(P_D)(\gg_D) \subseteq P_D$ also,

*but each of* (a) *through* (d) *in Lemma 8.1 may be false.*

The proofs of (e) and (f) are similar to the preceding proofs of (b) and (c). With $n = 1$ and $X = \{x,y,z\}$, the single strict partial order $> = \{(z,x)\}$ shows that (a), (b), and (d) can fail, and $> = \{(y,z)\}$ shows that (c) can fail.

### BEST SIMPLE MAJORITY SUBSETS

Using $P_D$ and $R_D$, we now define functions $P$ and $R$ on $\mathcal{X} \times \mathcal{D}$ as follows:

$$P(Y,D) = \{x:x \in Y \text{ and } xP_Dy \text{ for all } y \in Y - \{x\}\} \quad (8.7)$$
$$R(Y,D) = \{x:x \in Y \text{ and } xR_Dy \text{ for all } y \in Y\}$$
$$= \{x:x \in Y \text{ and } yP_Dx \text{ for no } y \in Y\}. \quad (8.8)$$

For a given $(Y,D)$, $P(Y,D)$ is the set of all alternatives in $Y$ that have a strict simple majority over every other alternative in $Y$ on the basis of $D$, and $R(Y,D)$ is the set of alternatives in $Y$ that have a simple majority over each other alternative in $Y$.

For a given $(Y,D)$ it should be clear that $P(Y,D)$ is either empty or contains a single alternative, that $P(Y,D) \subseteq R(Y,D)$, and that $x,y \in R(Y,D) \Rightarrow xI_Dy$. In addition, if $n$ is odd and if each $>_i$ in $D$ is linear then ties between distinct elements cannot arise and therefore $P(Y,D) = R(Y,D)$.

Henceforth we shall be principally interested in those cases for which $R(Y,D) \neq \emptyset$.

According to Theorem 7.2, $R(Y,D) \neq \emptyset$ for all finite nonempty $Y \subseteq X$ and a fixed $D \in \mathfrak{D}$ if and only if $P_D$ on $X$ is a suborder. In this connection it may be of some interest to note that $(xP_Dy$ & $yP_Dz \Rightarrow xP_Dz)$ for all $x,y,z \in X$ implies that $P_D$ is a suborder (obvious, since then $P_D$ is a strict partial order), but that $(xP_Dy$ & $yP_Dz \Rightarrow xR_Dz)$ for all $x,y,z \in X$ does not imply that $P_D$ is a suborder, even when each $\succ_i$ in $D$ is linear. To prove the latter statement, take $n = 4$ with the following linear orders on $X = \{x,y,z,w\}$:

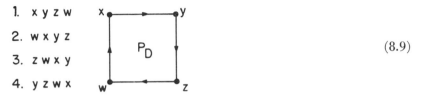

1. x y z w

2. w x y z

3. z w x y

4. y z w x

$$(8.9)$$

The four orders are obtained by the cyclic permutations of $xyzw$: each is obtained from its predecessor by moving the final term in the order to the head of the order. $P_D$, as shown in (8.9), satisfies the condition $uP_Dv$ & $vP_Dt \Rightarrow uR_Dt$, but $P_D$ is clearly not a suborder.

When $F$ agrees with simple majority, (7.17) follows immediately from Lemma 8.1(c) under weak orders, and (7.16) follows from Lemma 8.2(f). These lemmas and Theorems 7.3 and 7.4 give rise to the following corollary.

THEOREM 8.4. *Suppose that $Y \subseteq X$ is finite. Then, if each $\succ_i$ in $D$ is a weak order, $R(Y,D) \neq \emptyset$ if the restriction of $P_D$ on $Y(\succ_D) = \{x : x \in Y$ and $y \succ_D x$ for no $y \in Y\}$ is a suborder. And, if each $\succ_i$ in $D$ is a strict partial order, then $R(Y,D) \neq \emptyset$ if the restriction of $P_D$ on $Y(\gg_D) = \{x : x \in Y$ and $y \gg_D x$ for no $y \in Y\}$ is a suborder.*

A somewhat different and, in a sense, more general result for $R(Y,D) \neq \emptyset$ is suggested by Lemma 6 in Sen and Pattanaik (1969). A slight generalization of their lemma is Theorem 8.5.

THEOREM 8.5. *Suppose that $Y \subseteq X$ is finite. Then, if each $\succ_i$ in $D$ is a weak order, $R(Y,D) = R(Y(\succ_D),D)$. And, if each $\succ_i$ in $D$ is a strict partial order then $R(Y,D) = R(Y(\gg_D),D)$, and it may be true that $R(Y,D) \neq R(Y(\succ_D),D)$.*

By the definitions, $Y(\succ_D) \subseteq Y(\gg_D)$ and we can surely have $Y(\succ_D) \subset Y(\gg_D)$ when all $\succ_i$ are weak orders. Nevertheless, Theorem 8.5 implies that $R(Y(\succ_D),D) = R(Y(\gg_D),D)$ when each $\succ_i$ in $D$ is a weak order, since every weak order is also a strict partial order. On the other hand, the final statement in the theorem says that it is

**93**

possible to have $R(Y(>_D),D) \neq R(Y(\gg_D),D)$ when strict partial orders apply. To prove this, let $n = 3$ and $X = \{x,y,z\}$ with $>_1$ the linear order $xyz$ and $>_2 = >_3 = \{(z,x)\}$. Then

$$X(>_D) = \{x\} \quad \text{and} \quad R(X(>_D),D) = \{x\}$$
$$X(\gg_D) = X \quad \text{and} \quad R(X(\gg_D),D) = \emptyset.$$

Since $Y(>_D) \subseteq Y(\gg_D)$, it should be clear in general that $R(Y(\gg_D),D) \subseteq R(Y(>_D),D)$, for if $xR_Dy$ for every $y \in Y(\gg_D)$ then surely $xR_Dy$ for every $y \in Y(>_D)$.

*Proof of Theorem* 8.5. Suppose first that each $>_i$ in $D$ is a weak order. If $x \in R(Y(>_D),D)$ then the proof of Theorem 7.3 shows that $x \in R(Y,D)$. Conversely, if $x \in R(Y,D)$ then $yP_Dx$ for no $y \in Y$, so that $y >_D x$ for no $y \in Y$, and hence $x \in Y(>_D)$. Then, since $Y(>_D) \subseteq Y$, $x \in R(Y(>_D),D)$. The proof that $R(Y,D) = R(Y(\gg_D),D)$ under strict partial orders is similar. The preceding example proves the final assertion. ◆

PROPORTIONS WITH $R(X,D) = \emptyset$

Given that $n$ is an odd positive integer, that $\#X = m$, and that $\mathfrak{D}$ is the set of all $(m!)^n$ $n$-tuples of linear orders on $X$, let $p(n,m)$ be the fraction of $\mathfrak{D}$ on which $P(X,D) = R(X,D) = \emptyset$. That is,

$$p(n,m) = \#\{D : D \in \mathfrak{D} \ \& \ R(X,D) = \emptyset\}/(m!)^n.$$

A number of investigators have computed $p(n,m)$ for various values of $n$ and $m$, either precisely or by computer simulation. Exact (though complex) analytical expressions for $p(n,m)$ under the given conditions have been obtained by DeMeyer and Plott (1970), Niemi and Weisberg (1968) and Garman and Kamien (1968). Some interesting related material is presented by May (1971).

Figure 8.2 presents $p(n,m)$ for a number of values of $n$ and $m$. The entries with asterisks are estimates obtained by computer simulation by Campbell and Tullock (1965). The other entries are accurate to the number of places shown and are from Garman and Kamien (1968) with the exception of the exact 1.000 limits from May (1971). The limits for $\sup\{p(n,m) : n = 3,5,7, \ldots\}$ are given by Garman and Kamien and by Niemi and Weisberg (1968).

Although it may be tempting to view $p(n,m)$ as the probability that $R(X,D) = \emptyset$ given $\#X = m$, $n$ odd, and linear orders, this viewpoint requires special assumptions whose warrantability is questionable in many situations. Apart from things such as persuasion, agreements, and coalitions, there are many situations in which there is reason to believe that $R(Y,D)$ will almost surely not be empty for the $D$ that will actually obtain. The prime motivator for such a belief is the case

|          | n |  |  |  |  |  |  |
|----------|-------|-------|-------|-------|-------|-----|-------|
|          | 3     | 5     | 7     | 9     | 11    | ... | limit |
| 3        | .056  | .069  | .075  | .078  | .080  | ... | .088  |
| 4        | .111  | .139  | .150  | .156  | .160  | ... | .176  |
| m = #X    5 | .160 | .200  | .215  | .230* | .251* | ... | .251  |
| 6        | .202  | .255* | .258* | .284* | .294* | ... | .315  |
| 7        | .239* | .299* | .305* | .342* | .343* | ... | .369  |
| .        | .     | .     | .     | .     | .     |     | .     |
| .        | .     | .     | .     | .     | .     |     | .     |
| .        | .     | .     | .     | .     | .     |     | .     |
| limit    | 1.000 | 1.000 | 1.000 | 1.000 | 1.000 | ... | 1.000 |

FIGURE 8.2. $p(n,m)$. Entries marked * are estimates

of single-peaked preferences, which will be examined in detail in the next chapter.

## 8.4 SEQUENTIAL VOTING AND VOTER STRATEGY

Before getting deeper into our study of conditions that ensure $R(Y,D) \neq \emptyset$, we shall comment on why one might be concerned about the existence of an alternative that has a simple majority over each other alternative.

One reason for concern arises from the position that $x$ is a satisfactory social alternative only if $x \in R(Y,D)$. When $R(Y,D) = \emptyset$, this position holds that every alternative is socially unsatisfactory, and that the group is therefore forced to select an unsatisfactory alternative.

A related reason is that, whereas there may be widespread agreement that $F(Y,D)$ be a subset of $R(Y,D)$ when $R(Y,D) \neq \emptyset$, there may nevertheless be widespread disagreement about how to choose a feasible alternative when $R(Y,D)$ is empty. A rather large number of procedures have been proposed for this case, but none of these, as far as we are aware, is generally felt to be completely satisfactory.

Perhaps the main pragmatic reason for concern about whether $R(Y,D)$ is empty arises from voting procedures that make a choice solely on the basis of simple-majority votes regardless of whether $R(Y,D)$ is empty. We are thinking here of procedures that are widely used because of their efficiency, especially when voters are assembled together, and which take votes on the alternatives in $Y$ in a definite order. This order may be prescribed before the voting begins, or it may be determined progressively as the voting proceeds. We shall com-

**95**

ment on two such procedures, the first of which is more efficient (may require fewer ballots) than the second, but perhaps less satisfactory in other ways.

## TWO SEQUENTIAL VOTING PROCEDURES

Given that the $m$ alternatives in $Y$ will be voted on in the order $x_1 x_2 \cdots x_m$, the first procedure takes a simple-majority vote on $x_1$. If the votes for $x_1$ exceed (or perhaps equal) those against $x_1$, then $x_1$ is elected without further balloting. Otherwise, $x_1$ is discarded, and a similar vote is taken on $x_2$. If none of $x_1$, $x_2$, . . . , $x_{m-2}$ carries a majority, then $x_{m-1}$ or $x_m$ is elected on the final vote.

Suppose that individuals vote according to their preferences in the following way. When a vote is taken on $x_j$, individual $i$ votes for $x_j$ if and only if $x_j \succcurlyeq_i x_k$ for all $k > j$. Then, even if $P(Y,D) \neq \emptyset$, the elected alternative might not be the one in $P(Y,D)$. Suppose, for example, that $n = 3$ and $Y = \{x,y,z\}$ with the following linear orders:

1. $z \ x \ y$
2. $x \ z \ y$ $\qquad\qquad x P_D z P_D y \ \& \ x P_D y.$ $\qquad\qquad$ (8.10)
3. $y \ x \ z$

Then $P_D$ is a linear order with $P(Y,D) = \{x\}$. However, if $x$ is voted on first, then, under the foregoing supposition, it will not be elected since individuals 1 and 3 vote against $x$ and only 2 votes for $x$. For either $xyz$ or $xzy$ as the order of voting, $z$ will win.

The second procedure attempts to correct this apparent defect. In it, the first simple-majority vote is between $x_1$ and $x_2$. The winner of this vote then goes against $x_3$ in a second simple-majority vote. The winner of the second vote is then put against $x_4$ in a third vote, and so on up to the final alternative, $x_m$.

Suppose that individuals vote their preferences in the second procedure, so that $i$ votes for $x_j$ over $x_k$ if and only if $x_j >_i x_k$. If $P(Y,D) \neq \emptyset$ then, *regardless of the order in which the alternatives are voted on,* the element in $P(Y,D)$ will be elected: for this alternative will win the first vote in which it appears and will then win each succeeding vote. In addition, if $P_D$ is a weak order (or, equivalently, if $R_D$ is transitive) then, regardless of how simple-majority ties are resolved and regardless of the voting order, an $x \in R(Y,D)$ will be elected. If the procedure is modified slightly to explore ties further (among later alternatives) then an $x \in R(Y,D)$ will be elected when $R(Y,D) \neq \emptyset$.

However, if $R(Y,D)$ is empty, then strange things can happen under the second procedure. Consider, for example, the situation of (8.5). If the voting order is $xyzw$, then $w$ will be elected. However, *every* voter prefers $x$ to $w$ and therefore unanimity, as in (7.14), is violated. Other voting orders for (8.5) will of course select other alternatives: of the 24 orders, $x$ wins under 6, $y$ wins under 10, $z$ wins under 6 and $w$ wins under 2.

Thus, for those cases where $R(Y,D) = \emptyset$, this procedure may be quite unsatisfactory, and it suggests the need for an alternate procedure that may be less efficient but which takes greater cognizance of the full complexities of $D$. On the other hand, an awareness of structures for $D$ that assure $R(Y,D) \neq \emptyset$, and an awareness of the types of situations in which these structures are likely to obtain, may be useful information either for individual voting situations or for the design of "efficient" voting procedures that do not lead to obviously undesirable social choices.

VOTER STRATEGY

Although we have generally spoken of individual votes as if they agree with preferences, both throughout Part I and in the preceding paragraphs, this should be regarded as an aid to discourse that is not literally true in many situations. Indeed, voters may have very good reasons for voting contrary to some of their "actual preferences." For example, an individual's voting behavior may depend not only on his own preferences but also on things such as: 1. the particular voting procedure that is used, 2. his beliefs about other voters' preferences and their voting strategies, and 3. the opportunity to make intervoter deals before and/or during the course of the balloting. A small sample of the sizable literature on these subjects is the books by Buchanan and Tullock (1962) and Farquharson (1969), and the articles by Harsanyi (1966) and Wilson (1969).

Although voter strategy is not a main subject of this book, the preceding discussion of sequential voting seems inadequate without at least a few words on strategy. We therefore conclude this section with some brief remarks on aspects 1 and 2 in the preceding paragraph.

Let us suppose first that, as before, voters vote their preferences, but that they have some influence on the order of voting. Consider (8.10) under the first sequential procedure and assume that each voter knows the preferences of the others. The only real question at stake here is which alternative will be voted on first: if $x$ is first then $z$ will win; if either $y$ or $z$ is first then $x$ will win. Hence voter 1 would like to have $x$ first, and voter 2 would like to have $z$ first. Since $y$ can win under no order, voter 3 would like to have either $y$ or $z$ first. If a simple plurality vote is used to determine which alternative is voted on first, then voters 2 and 3 can force $z$ to be first, in which case $x$ will be elected.

It is sometimes suggested that an individual will do best under the second sequential procedure if his favorite alternatives come late in the voting order, since then they (or it) will have to beat fewer other alternatives in order to win. Although this may be a reasonable suggestion, it is not in general an optimal individual strategy. Consider, for example, the voting order $zwyx$ for (8.5), and recall that $x >_1 w >_1 z >_1 y$, for voter 1. Under the given voting order, which has the most preferred alternative for voter 1 last, voting according to preferences will elect $y$, which is voter 1's least preferred alternative. Or suppose that voter 1 can specify the voting order in another situation where his preference order is $x_1 x_2 x_3 x_4$. Would he do best to make $x_4 x_3 x_2 x_1$ the voting order? Surely not, if he has good reason to believe that $\{(x_1,x_3),(x_2,x_1),(x_2,x_3),(x_3,x_4),(x_4,x_2)\} \subseteq P_D$, for then the voting order $x_4 x_3 x_2 x_1$ would make $x_2$ the winner, whereas the order $x_4 x_2 x_3 x_1$ would make $x_1$ the winner.

Consider now a fixed voting order and suppose no longer that the voters vote according to their preferences. With the order $xyz$ for (8.10) under the first procedure, voter 3 can do best by voting for $x$ on the first ballot, for then his second choice ($x$) will be elected. Voter 2 will also vote for $x$ on the first ballot, since he has nothing to gain by voting otherwise, since if $x$ does not win on the first ballot then his second choice ($z$) will surely win on the second ballot between $y$ and $z$.

Suppose next that the voting order $xyz$ is used in (8.10) under the second sequential procedure. As in the preceding paragraph, voter 2 has nothing to gain by voting contrary to his preferences. However, if voter 1 votes for $y$ instead of his preferred $x$ on the first ballot, and if voters 2 and 3 vote "straight," then $y$ will win the first ballot and $z$ will then beat $y$ on the second ballot, thus giving voter 1 his first choice ($z$) instead of his second choice ($x$) when all voters vote straight. However, voter 3 can foil voter 1's strategy by voting for $x$ instead of $y$ on the first ballot. In fact, if voter 3 knows the preferences of the other two voters, then he should vote for $x$ on the first ballot. This will insure the election of $x$ on the first ballot, and thus the election of $x$ over $z$ on the second ballot, so that he gets his second choice ($x$) regardless of how voter 1 votes.

This example shows that, even when $P_D$ is a linear order, a consideration of voting strategies in the second procedure is not an idle exercise.

For our final example, suppose each voter knows the other voters' preferences in the following situation:

1. $x \; y \; z$
2. $z \; x \; y$                      $x P_D y P_D z P_D x.$
3. $y \; z \; x$

Suppose also that the second procedure is used. If the voting order is $(xy)z$, then $z$ wins the second vote if $x$ wins the first, and $y$ wins the second if $y$ wins the first. Therefore, either $y$ or $z$ wins. Hence, on the first ballot, 1 will vote for $y$, 2 will vote for $x$, and 3 will vote for $y$, so that $y$ wins. Similarly, if the voting order $(xz)y$ is used, then $x$ will win; and if $(yz)x$ is used, $z$ will win. Hence, in this situation, no voter will want his most preferred alternative to be last in the voting order, for if voter 1's favorite $(x)$ is last then his least preferred alternative $(z)$ will win; if voter 2's favorite $(z)$ is last then his least preferred $(y)$ will win; and if voter 3's favorite $(y)$ is last then his least preferred $(x)$ will win.

# CHAPTER 9

## Single-Peaked Preferences

THIS CHAPTER begins a study of specific types of structures for $D$ that assure a nonempty $R(Y,D)$ for finite $Y$, where $R(Y,D)$ is the subset of $Y$ in which each alternative has a simple majority over every other alternative in $Y$. We shall concentrate here on the widespread case of single-peaked preferences.

Our general definition for single-peaked preferences permits intransitive individual indifference and does not require $X$ to be finite. A characterization of single-peaked preferences is then given for the case where $X$ is finite. It says, approximately, that the alternatives in $X$ can be ordered along a line so that, as we go from left to right on the line, an individual's preference increases up to an indifference plateau or peak, and then decreases after we pass the plateau.

It is then proved that the strict simple majority relation $P_D$ is transitive when $(X,D)$ is single peaked. When $X$ is finite, we show that there is a simple method, based on the end points of the individuals' indifference plateaus, for determining $R(X,D)$.

### 9.1 SINGLE-PEAKED PREFERENCES

Suppose that every individual in a group has the same preference order on $X$. Then $P_D$ must be the same order. Since the common order is presumed to be a strict partial order, it follows from Theorem 7.2 and (8.8) that $R(Y,D) \neq \emptyset$ for every finite $Y \subseteq X$, and this is true regardless of the size of the group.

For another example, suppose that each individual's preference order on $X$ is a weak order and that, for all $x,y \in X$, if any individual prefers $x$ to $y$ then no other individual prefers $y$ to $x$, although others may be indifferent between $x$ and $y$. Then, as can readily be shown, $P_D$ is the weak order on $X$ defined by $xP_Dy \Leftrightarrow x \succ_i y$ for some $i$. Here again $R(Y,D) \neq \emptyset$ for every finite $Y \subseteq X$, and this is true regardless of the size of the group.

Although these examples are simple, they illustrate the approach that will be used in the next few chapters. Our general concern will be to identify subsets of individual preference orders on $X$, each of which has the following property:

> if each individual in the group has one of the orders in the subset then, regardless of the size of the group or the number (9.1) of individuals that have each order in the subset, $R(Y,D) \neq \emptyset$ for every finite $Y \subseteq X$.

As in the foregoing examples, we shall be concerned with conditions on individual preference orders which imply (9.1) for each subset of orders that satisfies the conditions.

This chapter is devoted to what may be the most common of the types of situations that give rise to subsets of orders that satisfy (9.1). It is the case of single-peaked preferences. In approximate terms, this means that the alternatives can be ordered along a line in such a way that, as we pass from left to right along the line, each individual's preference increases up to a peak or to an indifference plateau, and then decreases thereafter. Figure 9.1 illustrates this for three indi-

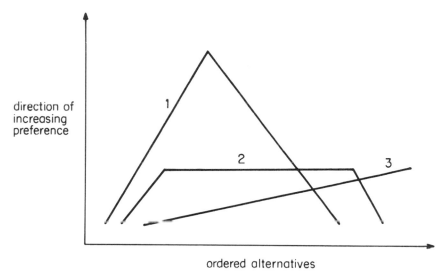

ordered alternatives

FIGURE 9.1. Single-peaked preferences

viduals. Individual 1 has a unique peak point, individual 2 exhibits an indifference plateau that contains more than one alternative, and individual 3's preferences continue to increase indefinitely or until the right-most of the ordered alternatives is reached. A natural situation for single-peaked preferences is given in Figure 7.4, for the question of allowable years of service as an untenured assistant professor. Other situations in which single-peaked preferences would be likely to obtain can easily be conceived.

A GENERAL DEFINITION

We shall now examine a general definition of single-peaked preferences.

101

DEFINITION 9.1. *Let* $D = (>_1, \ldots , >_n)$ *be an n-tuple of strict partial orders on a nonempty set* $X$. *Then* $(X,D)$ *is* single peaked *if and only if there is a linear order* $<_0$ *on* $X$ *such that, for each* $i \in \{1, \ldots ,n\}$, *there are disjoint subsets* $A_i$, $B_i$ *and* $C_i$ (*one or two of which can be empty*) *of* $X$ *such that*

(1)  $A_i \cup B_i \cup C_i = X$
(2)  $(x,y) \in A_i \times B_i \cup B_i \times C_i \cup A_i \times C_i \Rightarrow x <_0 y$
(3a) $x,y \in A_i$ *and* $x <_0 y \Rightarrow y >_i x$
(3b) $x,y \in B_i \Rightarrow x \sim_i y$
(3c) $x,y \in C_i$ *and* $y <_0 x \Rightarrow y >_i x$
(4)  $(x,y) \in (A_i \cup C_i) \times B_i \Rightarrow y \gtrsim_i x$
(5)  $x <_0 y <_0 z$ *and* $x \sim_i y$ *and* $y \sim_i z \Rightarrow x \sim_i z$.

Although this looks complicated, it is easy to interpret. In terms of $<_0$, (2) says that $A_i$ is to the left of $B_i$ and $C_i$, and $C_i$ is to the right of $A_i$ and $B_i$. If $B_i$ is not empty, then (when $B_i$ is as large as possible) it is the *indifference plateau* of individual $i$: (3b) says that all alternatives in $B_i$ are indifferent to each other, and (4) says that no alternative to the left or right of $B_i$ is preferred to an alternative in $B_i$. Condition (3a) requires the restriction of $>_i$ on $A_i$ to be a linear order, with preference strictly increasing left to right along $A_i$; condition (3c) requires the restriction of $>_i$ on $C_i$ to be a linear order, with preference strictly decreasing left to right along $C_i$.

Condition (5) is clearly redundant if each $>_i$ is a weak order. For the general case, (5) requires transitive indifference when the middle member $y$ of the transitivity hypothesis $x \sim_i y \sim_i z$ is between the other two elements in the $<_0$ order, as $x <_0 y <_0 z$ or $z <_0 y <_0 x$.

Given $x <_0 y <_0 z$, intransitive indifferences can arise in several ways. For example, $x \sim_i z \sim_i y$ and $y >_i x$ can occur with

$$x \text{ and } y \text{ in } A_i, z \text{ in } B_i \cup C_i;$$
$$x \text{ in } A_i, y \text{ and } z \text{ in } B_i \cup C_i.$$

If $x \in A_i$, $z \in B_i$ and $x \sim_i z$, then (5) requires $x$ to be indifferent to each element in $B_i$ to the right of $z$.

If $X$ is infinite, it may be necessary to have $B_i = \emptyset$ when neither $A_i$ nor $C_i$ is empty. This is illustrated on Figure 9.2, where $X = [0,1) \cup (1,2]$, consisting of all $0 \leq x \leq 2$ except for $x = 1$.

WHEN $X$ IS FINITE

On the other hand, if $X$ is finite and if preferences are single peaked, then it is always possible to have $B_i$ nonempty for each $i$. In terms of the following theorem, we can take $B_i = \{x : a_i \leq_0 x \leq_0 b_i\}$, where $x \leq_0 y$ if and only if $x <_0 y$ or $x = y$.

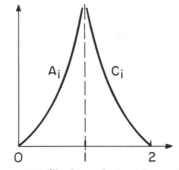

FIGURE 9.2. Single-peaked with no plateau

THEOREM 9.1. *Let $D = (\succ_1, \ldots, \succ_n)$ be an n-tuple of strict partial orders on a nonempty finite set $X$. Then $(X,D)$ is single peaked if and only if there is a linear order $<_0$ on $X$ such that, for each $i \in \{1, \ldots, n\}$, there are unique $a_i, b_i \in X$ with $a_i \leq_0 b_i$ such that*

(a) $x <_0 y \leq_0 a_i \Rightarrow y \succ_i x$
(b) $a_i \leq_0 x \leq_0 b_i$ and $a_i \leq_0 y \leq_0 b_i \Rightarrow x \sim_i y$
(c) $b_i \leq_0 y <_0 x \Rightarrow y \succ_i x$
(d) $(x <_0 a_i$ or $b_i <_0 x)$ and $a_i \leq_0 y \leq_0 b_i \Rightarrow y \succ\!\!\!\!\succ_i x$
(e) $x <_0 y <_0 z$ and $x \sim_i y$ and $y \sim_i z \Rightarrow x \sim_i z$.

Although we have kept (b) and (d) separate for ease in interpretation, they could be combined under the following condition: $x \in X$ and $a_i \leq_0 y \leq_0 b_i \Rightarrow y \succ\!\!\!\!\succ_i x$. Condition (a) says that preference increases up to $a_i$, and (c) says that it decreases after $b_i$. This does not prevent some $x <_0 a_i$ from being indifferent to some $y$ such that $a_i <_0 y \leq_0 b_i$.

*Proof of Theorem* 9.1. Suppose first that (a) through (e) hold for each $i$. Define $A_i = \{x : x <_0 a_i\}$, $B_i = \{x : a_i \leq_0 x \leq_0 b_i\}$ and $C_i = \{x : b_i <_0 x\}$. Then the conditions of Definition 9.1 hold, and therefore $(X,D)$ is single peaked.

Conversely, suppose that $X$ is finite and $(X,D)$ is single peaked as in Definition 9.1. Given $A_i$, $B_i$, and $C_i$, if $B_i \neq \emptyset$ then take the last element from $A_i$ and add it to $B_i$ if and only if it is indifferent to the first element in $B_i$, and take the first element in $C_i$ and add it to $B_i$ if and only if it is indifferent to the last element in $B_i$. Then (a) through (e) hold for the modified $A_i$, $B_i$, $C_i$ with $a_i$ the first element in this $B_i$ and $b_i$ the last element in $B_i$. Suppose next that $B_i$, as given, is empty. If $A_i = \emptyset$ also, take $a_i = b_i =$ first element in $(X, <_0)$; and if $C_i = \emptyset$ also, take $a_i = b_i =$ last element in $(X, <_0)$.

**103**

Then (a) through (e) hold. Finally, with $B_i = \emptyset$, suppose that neither $A_i$ nor $C_i$ is empty. Let $z$ be the last element in $A_i$, and let $w$ be the first element in $C_i$. Then (1) if $z >_i w$ take $a_i = b_i = z$, (2) if $w >_i z$ take $a_i = b_i = w$, and (3) if $z \sim_i w$ take $a_i = z$ and $b_i = w$. Again, (a) through (e) hold. Thus, $a_i, b_i$ exist for all $i$ and, in view of (a) through (e), they are unique. ◆

Under weak orders and finite $X$, the characterization of Theorem 9.1 is the same as the definition of single-peaked preferences in Chapter V of Black (1958).

## 9.2 Transitivity of Strict Majority

Suppose that $(X,D)$ is single peaked with $<_0$ an appropriate linear order on $X$. Suppose further that $x <_0 y <_0 z$. Then precisely 10 of the 19 possible individual preference orders on $\{x,y,z\}$ are admissible under these conditions. One of these is $> = \emptyset$ on $\{x,y,z\}$, or $\{x \sim y, y \sim z, x \sim z\}$. The other nine admissible orders are shown in Figure 9.3. It is easily verified that each of these can arise when $x <_0 y <_0 z$. The final two cases, 8 and 9, are the only ones with intransitive indifference.

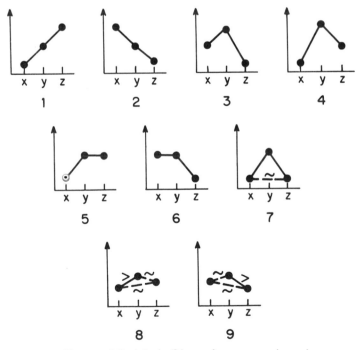

FIGURE 9.3. Admissible preferences on $\{x,y,z\}$

The nine orders of Figure 9.3 are shown on the left of Table 9.1. The nine orders that are not allowed under single-peaked preferences are numbered 10 through 18. Under $x <_0 y <_0 z$ you should verify that none of these can arise when $(X,D)$ is single peaked. We shall use the right part of the table later in this section, after we prove the following theorem and discuss a generalizing corollary.

TABLE 9.1

$x <_0 y <_0 z$

| Admissible Orders | Inadmissible Orders | Orders | Frequencies | Cycle |
|---|---|---|---|---|
| 1. $z \succ y \succ x$ | 10. $x \succ z \succ y$ | (1,3,10) | [1,1,1] | $xzyx$ |
| 2. $x \succ y \succ z$ | 11. $z \succ x \succ y$ | (2,4,11) | [1,1,1] | $xyzx$ |
| 3. $y \succ x \succ z$ | 12. $z \succ (x \sim y)$ | (2,4,12) | [2,1,2] | $xyzx$ |
| 4. $y \succ z \succ x$ | 13. $(x \sim z) \succ y$ | (2,4,13) | [1,2,2] | $xyzx$ |
| 5. $(y \sim z) \succ x$ | 14. $x \succ (y \sim z)$ | (1,3,14) | [2,1,2] | $xzyx$ |
| 6. $(x \sim y) \succ z$ | 15. $z \sim x \succ y \sim z$ | (4,15) | [1,2] | $xyzx$ |
| 7. $y \succ (x \sim z)$ | 16. $y \sim x \succ z \sim y$ | (1,16) | [1,2] | $xzyx$ |
| 8. $z \sim y \succ x \sim z$ | 17. $y \sim z \succ x \sim y$ | (2,17) | [1,2] | $xyzx$ |
| 9. $x \sim y \succ z \sim x$ | 18. $x \sim z \succ y \sim x$ | (3,18) | [1,2] | $xzyx$ |

THEOREM 9.2. *Suppose that each* $\succ_i$ *in* $D = (\succ_1, \ldots, \succ_n)$ *is a strict partial order and that* $(X,D)$ *is single peaked. Then:*

(1) $P_D$ *on* $X$ *is a strict partial order;*

(2) *if each* $\succ_i$ *is a weak order, if n is odd, and if* $(x \sim_i y$ *and* $y \sim_i z)$ *never holds when* $x <_0 y <_0 z$, *then* $P_D$ *is a weak order;*

(3) *if each* $\succ_i$ *is a linear order and if n is odd then* $P_D$ *is a linear order.*

An obvious corollary of Theorem 9.2 is:

COROLLARY 9.1. *If* $(X,D)$ *is single peaked then* $R(Y,D) \neq \emptyset$ *for every finite* $Y \subseteq X$.

*Proof of the theorem.* If $\#X \leq 2$ then the theorem is obvious. Henceforth assume that $X$ has more than two elements. Let $\{x,y,z\}$ be an arbitrary triple in $X$ and suppose for definiteness that $x <_0 y <_0 z$. Under the initial hypotheses of the theorem let $n_k$ be the number of individuals whose preference order on $\{x,y,z\}$ is order $k$ of Table 9.1, for $k = 1, \ldots, 9$. If some individuals are indifferent on $\{x,y,z\}$ then $n_1 + \cdots + n_9 < n$. Otherwise $n_1 + \cdots + n_9 = n$.

From Table 9.1 it is easily seen that

$$xP_D y \Leftrightarrow n_2 > n_1 + n_3 + n_4 + n_5 + n_7 + n_8 \qquad (9.2)$$
$$yP_D z \Leftrightarrow n_2 + n_3 + n_4 + n_6 + n_7 + n_9 > n_1 \qquad (9.3)$$
$$xP_D z \Leftrightarrow n_2 + n_3 + n_6 > n_1 + n_4 + n_5, \qquad (9.4)$$

from which it is clear that (using duals where indicated)

| | | |
|---|---|---|
| $xP_D y \Rightarrow xP_D z$, | and therefore | $xP_D y$ & $yP_D z \Rightarrow xP_D z$; |
| $xP_D z \Rightarrow yP_D z$, | and therefore | $yP_D x$ & $xP_D z \Rightarrow yP_D z$; |
| $zP_D x \Rightarrow yP_D x$, | and therefore | $yP_D z$ & $zP_D x \Rightarrow yP_D x$; |
| $zP_D y \Rightarrow zP_D x$, | and therefore | $zP_D y$ & $yP_D x \Rightarrow zP_D x$. |

The other two hypotheses for transitivity lead to contradictions, for by adding inequalities we get $xP_D z$ & $zP_D y \Rightarrow 0 > 2n_4 + n_5 + n_7 + n_9$, and $zP_D x$ & $xP_D y \Rightarrow 0 > 2n_3 + n_6 + n_7 + n_8$. Since $\{x,y,z\}$ is an arbitrary triple in $X$, this proves that $P_D$ is transitive and the proof of Theorem 9.2 (1) is complete.

Under the hypotheses of (2) it will suffice to prove that $I_D$ is transitive, for this and (1) imply that $P_D$ is a weak order. Since each $>_i$ is assumed to be a weak order, $n_8 = n_9 = 0$. Moreover, since each indifference plateau has no more than two points, $n = n_1 + n_2 + \cdots + n_7$. Suppose first that $xI_D y$ and $yI_D z$. Then equality in (9.2) and (9.3) implies $n_3 = n_4 = n_5 = n_6 = n_7 = 0$, so that $n_1 = n_2$ and therefore $n = n_1 + n_2 = 2n_1$. But this requires $n$ to be even, thus contradicting the $n$-odd hypothesis of (2). Therefore, when $x <_0 y <_0 z$, $xI_D y$ & $yI_D z$ is false under (2). Suppose next that $yI_D z$ & $zI_D x$. Then equality in (9.3) and (9.4) implies that $2n_4 + n_5 + n_7 = 0$ so that $n_4 = n_5 = n_7 = 0$, and hence that $n_1 = n_2 + n_3 + n_6$, so that $n = 2n_1$, which again is even. Hence $yI_D z$ & $zI_D x$ is false. Similarly, $yI_D x$ & $xI_D z$ is false under (2) when $x <_0 y <_0 z$, and the proof of (2) is complete.

Theorem 9.2 (3) follows immediately from (1) since the hypotheses in (3) imply that $P_D$ is weakly connected. ◆

The proof of the transitivity of $P_D$ used here requires only an examination of an arbitrary triple in $X$, for if $P_D$ is transitive on each triple then it is transitive. In the next chapter we shall use the triples approach to uncover other preference sets that ensure a transitive $P_D$. For the present we shall note only the following fact along this line.

COROLLARY 9.2. *If* $(\{x,y,z\},D)$ *is single peaked for each* $\{x,y,z\} \subseteq X$ *then* $P_D$ *on* $X$ *is a strict partial order.*

This corollary is in fact a more general result than Theorem 9.2 (1), for if $(X,D)$ is single peaked then each $(\{x,y,z\},D)$ is necessarily single peaked. However, if each $(\{x,y,z\},D)$ is single peaked, then it may be false that $(X,D)$ is single peaked. To prove this, let $X = \{x,y,z,w\}$ and let each $>$ in $D$ be the weak order $x(yzw)$, or $x > (y \sim z \sim w)$. Then $(X,D)$ is not single peaked, for any linear order $<_0$ on $X$ will require at least two indifferent elements to be on one side of the "peak" $x$. However, each triple is single peaked: $y <_0 x <_0 z$ shows this for $\{x,y,z\}$, $y <_0 x <_0 w$ serves for $\{x,y,w\}$, $z <_0 x <_0 w$ serves for $\{x,z,w\}$, and any linear order will do for $\{y,z,w\}$.

### INADMISSIBLE ORDERS

Another question of interest in connection with this analysis is whether any of the inadmissible orders in Table 9.1 can be joined to the collection of admissible orders without damaging the conclusion that $P_D$ on the triple is transitive. If this were true then we might be able to relax the definition of single peakedness (for example, by allowing indifference between distinct alternatives in $A_i$) without losing the desired conclusion of the transitivity of $P_D$. The following lemma shows that, generally speaking, we cannot do this.

LEMMA 9.1. *Suppose that $n \geq 5$ and that $>$ on $\{x,y,z\}$ is any one of the inadmissible orders in Table 9.1. Then there is an n-tuple $D$ of strict partial orders on $X$ such that the only inadmissible order in $D$ is $>$ and such that $P_D$ on $\{x,y,z\}$ is not a suborder.*

*Proof.* To the right of each inadmissible order in Table 9.1, in the "orders" column, we have listed a trio or a pair of orders on $\{x,y,z\}$. The only inadmissible order in this trio or pair is the order to its immediate left: the other orders are from the first column. The "frequencies" column states the number of individuals in our construction of $D$ who have the corresponding order in the "orders" column. Thus, for inadmissible order 14, the frequencies [2,1,2] for (1,3,14) mean that two individuals have order 1, one individual has order 3, and two individuals have order 14. All other individuals are given the admissible empty order $\emptyset$ on $\{x,y,z\}$. The final column of Table 9.1 shows the $P_D$ cycle for the constructed $D$. In the case of [2,1,2] for (1,3,14) we get $xP_DzP_DyP_Dx$, or $xzyx$ for short. Each of the other cases gives the indicated $P_D$ cycle. ◆

### 9.3 A LOCATION THEOREM

One of the nicest aspects of single-peaked preferences is the ease with which we can locate $R(X,D)$ when $X$ is finite. If we have a satisfactory $<_0$ on $X$ and know $a_i$, $b_i$ of Theorem 9.1 for each $i$, then the set of all alternatives that have a simple majority over each other alternative is located by the simple method described in the following theorem.

**107**

THEOREM 9.3. *Suppose that $X$ is finite and that $(X,D)$ is single peaked, with $<_0$ and the $a_i$ and $b_i$ $(i = 1, \ldots, n)$ as displayed in Theorem 9.1. Let $c_1, c_2, \ldots, c_{2n}$ be a rearrangement of the sequence $a_1, \ldots, a_n, b_1, \ldots, b_n$ in such a way that $c_1 \leq_0 c_2 \leq_0 \cdots \leq_0 c_{2n}$. Then*

$$R(X,D) = \{x : c_n \leq_0 x \leq_0 c_{n+1}\}. \qquad (9.5)$$

*Proof.* Suppose first that $x <_0 y \leq_0 c_n$, with $y$ to the immediate right of $x$ under $<_0$. That is, $x <_0 z <_0 y$ for no $z \in X$. With $r + s + t = n$, let $r = \#\{i : x \sim_i y\}$, $s = \#\{i : x >_i y\}$, and $t = \#\{i : y >_i x\}$. For each of the indifferent individuals, we must have $a_i \leq_0 x$ and $y \leq_0 b_i$, for suppose for example that $x <_0 a_i$. Then, since $y$ is immediately to the right of $x$, $x <_0 y \leq_0 a_i$, and $x \sim_i y$ would contradict (a) of Theorem 9.1. Similarly, if $x >_i y$ then $a_i \leq_0 x$ and $b_i \leq_0 x$; and if $y >_i x$ then $y \leq_0 a_i$ and $y \leq_0 b_i$. Therefore, $r + 2s$ of the terms in $a_1, \ldots, a_n, b_1, \ldots, b_n$ are $\leq_0 x$, and $r + 2t$ of these terms are to the right of $x$. Now since $c_1 \leq_0 \cdots \leq_0 c_n \leq_0 \cdots \leq_0 c_{2n}$ and since $x <_0 c_n$, it must be true that $r + 2s < r + 2t$, or that $s < t$, which means that $yP_Dx$. By the transitivity of $P_D$, as in Theorem 9.2 (1), it follows that $x <_0 c_n \Rightarrow c_nP_Dx$. And by a similar proof with $c_{n+1} \leq_0 y <_0 x$ and $x, y$ adjacent in $(X, <_0)$, it follows that $c_{n+1} <_0 x \Rightarrow c_{n+1}P_Dx$.

If $c_n = c_{n+1}$, then clearly $R(X,D) = P(X,D) = \{c_n\}$. Henceforth, assume that $c_n <_0 c_{n+1}$, and suppose that $c_n \leq_0 x <_0 y \leq_0 c_{n+1}$. Again let $r = \#\{i : x \sim_i y\}$, $s = \#\{i : x >_i y\}$, and $t = \#\{i : y >_i x\}$. Since $c_n \leq_0 x <_0 y \leq_0 c_{n+1}$, no $a_i$ or $b_i$ is between $x$ and $y$. It then follows that $a_i \leq_0 x$ and $y \leq_0 b_i$ for the indifferent individuals, that $a_i \leq_0 b_i \leq_0 x$ for the $x >_i y$ individuals $(s)$, and that $y \leq_0 a_i \leq_0 b_i$ for the $y >_i x$ individuals $(t)$. Therefore, $r + 2s$ of the $a_i, b_i$ are $\leq_0 x$, and $r + 2t$ of the $a_i, b_i$ are to the right of $x$. Since $c_1 \leq_0 \cdots \leq_0 c_n \leq_0 x <_0 c_{n+1} \leq_0 \cdots \leq_0 c_{2n}$, this requires $r + 2s = r + 2t$, or $s = t$, so that $xI_Dy$.

Now suppose that $x <_0 c_n \leq_0 y \leq_0 c_{n+1}$ and $xP_Dy$. Then, since $c_nP_Dx$ by the first paragraph of this proof, the transitivity of $P_D$ implies $c_nP_Dy$, which contradicts $c_nI_Dy$ as just derived. Hence $yR_Dx$. Similarly, $yR_Dx$ if $c_n \leq_0 y \leq_0 c_{n+1} <_0 x$. In summary, we have

$$
\begin{array}{llll}
c_nP_Dx & \text{if} & x <_0 c_n & \\
c_{n+1}P_Dx & \text{if} & c_{n+1} <_0 x & \\
xI_Dy & \text{if} & c_n \leq_0 x \leq_0 c_{n+1} & \text{and} \quad c_n \leq_0 y \leq_0 c_{n+1} \\
yR_Dx & \text{if} & c_n \leq_0 y \leq_0 c_{n+1} & \text{and} \quad (x <_0 c_n \text{ or } c_{n+1} <_0 x).
\end{array}
$$

Therefore $R(X,D) = \{x : c_n \leq_0 x \leq_0 c_{n+1}\}$. ◆

If $Y$ is a proper subset of $X$, then of course we will have to recompute $a_i$ and $b_i$ as appropriate to $Y$ before we can specify $R(Y,D)$ in the manner of the theorem.

Theorem 9.3 gives rise to several corollaries when additional restrictions are placed on the $>_i$. The following result, obtained by Black (1948), is an example.

COROLLARY 9.3. *Suppose that $X$ is finite and $(X,D)$ is single peaked with $a_i = b_i$ for each $i$, so that each indifference plateau contains a single point. Let the $a_i$ be arranged so that $a_1 \leq_0 a_2 \leq_0 \cdots \leq_0 a_n$. Then*

$$R(X,D) = P(X,D) = \{a_{(n+1)/2}\} \qquad if \qquad n \ is \ odd,$$
$$R(X,D) = \{x : a_{n/2} \leq_0 x \leq_0 a_{1+n/2}\} \qquad if \qquad n \ is \ even.$$

When $n$ is odd in the corollary, the median peak, $a_{(n+1)/2}$, has a strict simple majority over each other alternative. A similar result holds for even $n$ if $a_{n/2} = a_{1+n/2}$, but if $a_{n/2} <_0 a_{1+n/2}$ then a range of "best" simple-majority alternatives is obtained.

## 9.4 VOTING ON VOTING RULES

An interesting use of the notion of single-peaked preferences with simple majorities arises in some contexts where a group must decide on the voting rule that they will use in certain situations. Suppose, for the sake of illustration, that the group is writing a constitution. One of the factors they must specify is the size of a vote for a constitutional amendment that is required before the amendment becomes law. Let us suppose that they agree to use an absolute special majority social choice function, as specified in Definition 6.3, for this purpose. To complete the specification of this rule, they need to decide the number $k$ of votes ($1 \leq k \leq n$) that an amendment must obtain before it becomes law.

Different individuals may prefer different $k$ values, but in any event it seems reasonable to suppose that, with $j <_0 k \Leftrightarrow j < k$, the preference orders on $X = \{1, \ldots, n\}$ for the individuals will be single peaked. For example, for $n = 9$, the preference order for one person might be the order shown in Figure 7.4.

Our analysis of single-peaked preferences shows that at least one of the $k$ values will have a simple majority over every other $k$ value. And if $n$ is odd and each person has a unique favorite (peak), then, by Corollary 9.3, there will be a $k^* \in \{1, \ldots, n\}$ that has a strict simple majority over every other $k$. In such a case, it does not seem unreasonable to take $k^*$ as the value that is written into the constitution.

A value of $k^*$ chosen in this way might differ significantly from $n/2$. For example, if about half the voters favor a $k \geq 2n/3$ and the other half favor a $k < 2n/3$ then the chosen rule will be close to a two-thirds absolute special majority rule.

**109**

Suppose in fact that a $k^*$ in the vicinity of $2n/3$ is approved. Then, although this was determined by simple majority, it can no longer be changed by a strict simple majority. For, according to the $k^*$ rule, if a member of the group makes a motion to amend the constitution by changing $k$ from $k^*$ to $k'$, then $k'$ requires the approval of two-thirds of the group. Indeed, as time passes, more than half the group may come to prefer $k'$ to $k^*$, but if less than two-thirds of the members have this preference then $k^*$ will remain in effect.

# CHAPTER 10

# Guarantees and Triples

In the preceding chapter we saw that $P_D$ is transitive when $(X,D)$ is single peaked, regardless of the size of $D$ or the particular mix of single-peaked preference orders that appear in $D$. In this chapter we shall continue our investigation of sets of preference orders that guarantee a certain result, such as transitivity of strict simple majority. A set $S$ of preference orders guarantees a certain result when every $D$ whose orders are all in $S$ yields this result.

The first section discusses the general guarantee concept and shows that, except for one case, conditions that guarantee a specified property can be stated in terms of preferences on three-element subsets of $X$. The exception is for conditions that guarantee that $P_D$ is a suborder when orders in $S$ are allowed to exhibit intransitive indifference. For reasons explained in section 10.1, we shall not characterize all $S$ that guarantee a suborder.

However, sections 10.2 and 10.3 develop and verify a characterization of all sets of strict partial orders on a triple $\{x,y,z\}$ that guarantee a suborder on the triple. In doing this we shall illustrate a general method that can be used to uncover conditions that guarantee a certain result. The results for suborders on a triple will be used in Chapter 11, which presents conditions for transitive strict simple majority and transitive simple majority.

## 10.1 UNIVERSAL GUARANTEES

In pursuing conditions on individual preference orders that yield results like (9.1), we shall first set forth some general definitions. As shown later in this section, notable simplifications arise when all preference orders are weak orders.

DEFINITION 10.1. *Let $S$ be a nonempty set of strict partial orders on $X$. Then $S$ guarantees*

(1) a suborder
(2) transitivity (*or* a strict partial order)
(3) a weak order
(4) a linear order

**111**

*if and only if, for every $n > 0$ and every $D \in S^n$,*

(1) $P_D$ *on* $X$ *is a suborder*
(2) $P_D$ *on* $X$ *is transitive*
(3) $P_D$ *on* $X$ *is a weak order*
(4) $P_D$ *on* $X$ *is a linear order.*

This is obviously a four-part definition. Because our primary interest is in nonempty $R(Y,D)$ for finite $Y \subseteq X$, part (1) is of primary concern. Part (2) also will be used extensively, and (3) will receive some attention. Part (4) is included mainly to show how restrictive the notion of "guarantee" can be, for $S$ guarantees a linear order if and only if $S$ contains only one element, which is itself a linear order. For example, to guarantee a linear order, $S$ cannot contain any nonlinear order, for then a nonlinear $P_D$ would be obtained under $n = 1$. And if $S$ contains more than one linear order, then there must be $x,y \in X$ such that $x > y$ for one order and $y > x$ for another, and with $n = 2$ we can get $xI_Dy$.

As in Definition 7.4, the concepts in Definition 10.1 have been arranged in a hierarchical order. Clearly ($S$ guarantees a linear order) $\Rightarrow$ ($S$ guarantees a weak order) $\Rightarrow$ ($S$ guarantees a strict partial order) $\Rightarrow$ ($S$ guarantees a suborder). Although the reverse implications are generally false, we shall observe later in this section that, when every order in $S$ is a weak order, ($S$ guarantees a suborder) $\Rightarrow$ ($S$ guarantees transitivity).

The emphasis of Definition 10.1 is the universality of the guarantee notion which requires every $P_D$ for all $D \in S \cup S^2 \cup S^3 \cup \cdots$ to have certain properties. For example, to show that $S$ does not guarantee transitivity, it is sufficient to identify one $D$ composed of orders in $S$ for which $xP_DyP_DzP_Dx$ for some $x,y,z \in X$.

The effect on different $n$ is nicely shown with $X = \{x,y,z\}$ and the familiar set $S = \{xyz,zxy,yzx\}$ of three linear orders on $X$. For part (1) of the definition we note that,

for $n = 2$, $D \in S^2 \Rightarrow P_D$ is a suborder
for $n = 3$, $P_D$ is not a suborder for $D = (xyz,zxy,yzx)$
for $n = 4$, $D \in S^4 \Rightarrow P_D$ is a suborder
for $n \geq 5$, $P_D$ is not a suborder for some $D \in S^n$.

The result for $n = 4$ may seem surprising in view of $n = 3$. The main reason that $P_D$ is a suborder when $D \in S^4$ is that the indifferent order $\emptyset$ is not in $S$, so that $D$ must have one of the orders in $S$ in more than one position. This $S$ does not of course guarantee a suborder. But when $S$ does guarantee a suborder, it is immaterial whether $\emptyset$ is in $S$ unless $S = \{\emptyset\}$, for if $\emptyset \notin S$ then $S$ guarantees a suborder if and only if $S \cup \{\emptyset\}$ guarantees a suborder.

OTHER CONDITIONS

It should be noted that there are various conditions on individual preferences that imply a suborder (or transitivity, etc.) that cannot be included under our guarantee definition because of restrictions that they impose on the size of the group or on the numbers of orders that can appear in various combinations in an "allowable" $D$. We illustrate this with two examples.

Let $<_0$ be a linear order on $X$ and let $S$ be the set of all linear orders on $X$ that satisfy the single-peaked conditions of Definition 9.1. Then $S$ guarantees transitivity, as in Theorem 9.2 (1). And, as we noted in Theorem 9.2 (3), $P_D$ must be a linear order if $n$ is odd. However, if $\#X > 1$, then $S$ does not guarantee a linear order, for $n = 2$ will give a satisfactory violation of the general linearity of $P_D$.

For the second example let $X = \{x,y,z\}$ and let $S$ be the set of strict partial orders on $X$ for which

$$x > y \qquad \text{and} \qquad (x > z \text{ or } z > y). \tag{S}$$

There are exactly five orders that satisfy this condition, namely $xyz$, $x(yz)$, $xzy$, $(xz)y$ and $zxy$, and it is easily verified that $S$ guarantees transitivity. $S$ does not guarantee a weak order in view of $D = (xyz,zxy)$. Now suppose we generalize the foregoing condition by letting $T$ be the set of strict partial orders on $X$ for which

$$x > y \qquad \text{and} \qquad (x > y \text{ or } x > z \text{ or } z > y). \tag{T}$$

In addition to the five orders in $S$, this allows five more orders, namely $(xy)z$, $z(xy)$, $z \sim x > y \sim z$, $y \sim x > z \sim y$, and $x \sim z > y \sim x$, the last three of which exhibit intransitive indifference. As we shall note later (see VI in Table 10.1), $T$ guarantees a suborder. However, it does not guarantee transitivity, since $P_D$ is not transitive for $D = (y \sim x > z \sim y, x \sim z > y \sim x)$, which gives $xP_Dz$, $zP_Dy$ and $xI_Dy$.

On the other hand, consider the set of all $D$ such that (a) $D \in T \cup T^2 \cup T^3 \cup \cdots$ and (b) $x > y$ for at least one order in $D$. It can be shown that $P_D$ is transitive for *every* such $D$, and therefore it might be said that (a) and (b) guarantee transitivity. However, conditions (a) and (b) cannot be stated in a manner appropriate for Definition 10.1 since (b) requires that some order in a proper subset of $T$ must appear in each "acceptable" $D$.

TRIPLES

Since case (4) of Definition 10.1 is trivial, we shall not comment further on it. In each of the other cases, with one exception, guaranteeing conditions on $S$ can be stated in terms of individual preferences on triples. A *triple*, in the sense used here, is a three-element subset of $X$.

The lone exception to our triples rule is for $S$ guaranteeing a suborder when $S$ is allowed to contain strict partial orders that are not weak orders.

To develop these ideas further, we shall use the following definition.

DEFINITION 10.2. *Let $Y$ be any nonempty subset of $X$ and let $Q \in \{a$ suborder, a strict partial order, a weak order$\}$. Then $S$ guarantees $Q$ on $Y$ if and only if, for every $n > 0$ and every $D \in S^n$, the restriction of $P_D$ on $Y$ is $Q$.*

Since any $S$ guarantees $Q$ when $\#X < 3$, and since the defining properties for strict partial orders and weak orders deal with subsets of $X$ with no more than three elements, the following lemma is obvious.

LEMMA 10.1. *$S$ guarantees transitivity (rsp., a weak order) if and only if $S$ guarantees transitivity (rsp., a weak order) on each triple in $X$.*

If $S$ guarantees a suborder, then it must guarantee a suborder on each triple. However, the converse is false when $\#X > 3$. For example, let $\{x,y,z,w\} \subseteq X$ with

$$S = \{\{(x,y),(z,w)\},\{(y,z),(w,x)\}\},$$

consisting of two strict partial orders, each of which exhibits intransitive indifference. It is easily seen that $S$ guarantees a suborder on each triple. However, with $D = (\{(x,y),(z,w)\},\{(y,z),(w,x)\}) \in S^2$, $P_D$ on $X$ is not a suborder since $xP_DyP_DzP_DwP_Dx$.

As shown by the following lemma, this negative result depends crucially on intransitive indifference.

LEMMA 10.2. *If every $\succ\, \in S$ is a weak order and if $S$ guarantees a suborder on a triple, then $S$ guarantees transitivity on the triple.*

*Proof.* To the contrary, suppose that each $\succ\, \in S$ is a weak order, that $S$ guarantees a suborder on $\{x,y,z\}$, and that $S$ does not guarantee transitivity on $\{x,y,z\}$. Then there is an $n$ and $D \in S^n$ such that, for example, $xP_Dy$ & $yP_Dz$ & $xI_Dz$. If $x \sim z$ for every $\succ\, \in S$ then, by the weak order hypothesis, $x \succ y \Leftrightarrow z \succ y$ and $y \succ x \Leftrightarrow y \succ z$ for every $\succ\, \in S$. But then $xP_Dy \Leftrightarrow zP_Dy$, which contradicts the assumed $xP_Dy$ & $yP_Dz$. Therefore, since $xI_Dz$, $z \succ x$ for some $\succ\, \in S$. Let $\succ'$ be such an order, and form $D' \in S^{2n+1}$ as follows:

$$D' = (D,D,\succ').$$

Clearly, $xP_{D'}yP_{D'}zP_{D'}x$, which contradicts the hypothesis that $S$ guarantees a suborder on $\{x,y,z\}$. ◆

114

We hasten to add that if $S$ guarantees transitivity on a triple then $S$ does not necessarily guarantee a weak order on the triple, even when all $> \in S$ are linear. This is shown with $S = \{xzy, yxz\}$. If $D$ has $xzy$ in $r$ positions and $yxz$ in $s$ positions then $r > s \Rightarrow P_{D'} = xzy$, $s > r \Rightarrow P_D = yxz$, and $r = s \Rightarrow yI_DxP_DzI_Dy$, in which case $P_D$ is not a weak order.

The following theorem follows immediately from Lemma 10.2 and other preceding observations.

THEOREM 10.1. *If every $> \in S$ is a weak order, then $S$ guarantees a suborder if and only if $S$ guarantees transitivity on each triple in $X$.*

This theorem greatly simplifies the development of a general set of conditions that characterize all $S$ for which $S$ guarantees a suborder when it is presumed that all individual preference orders are weak orders. Such a set of conditions, stated in terms of preference orders on triples, have been given by Sen and Pattanaik (1969, Theorem V). A similar characterization, for guaranteeing transitivity when intransitive indifference is allowed, is given by Inada (1970) and Fishburn (1970b). These conditions, along with results of Inada (1969) and others for guaranteeing weak orders, will be presented in the next chapter.

The rest of this chapter develops a set of conditions that characterize all sets of strict partial orders on a triple $\{x,y,z\}$ that guarantee a suborder on the triple. Some of the results in the next chapter will then follow from this characterization with very little additional effort.

As we have seen, the conditions that describe all sets of strict partial orders on a triple that guarantee a suborder on a triple cannot characterize all $S$ that guarantee a suborder when $\#X > 3$. Indeed, suppose that $X = \{x_1, \ldots, x_m\}$ and $S = \{\{(x_1,x_2)\},\{(x_1,x_3)\}, \ldots, \{(x_{m-1},x_m)\},\{(x_m,x_1)\}\}$, consisting of $m$ strict partial orders. Then $S$ guarantees a suborder on *every* proper subset of $X$, but $S$ does not guarantee a suborder on $X$. Hence conditions for a finite $X$ that characterize all $S$ that guarantee suborders must explicitly consider all elements in $X$ simultaneously. Because such a characterization, if it could be obtained, would almost surely be incomprehensibly complex, we shall not pursue it further.

## 10.2 SUBORDERS ON TRIPLES

Throughout the rest of this chapter we shall work with a triple $\{x,y,z\}$. Our goal is to characterize or describe, in some reasonable way, all nonempty sets of strict partial orders on $\{x,y,z\}$ that guarantee a

**115**

suborder on $\{x,y,z\}$. Since there are 19 different strict partial orders on $\{x,y,z\}$, as described in section 9.2, there are $2^{19} - 1$ nonempty subsets $S$ of strict partial orders. Since it would be impractical to list all of these that guarantee a suborder, we shall need to find a more efficient way of doing things. To aid in this, the following special definitions will be used.

DEFINITION 10.3. *A* SET *is any nonempty subset of strict partial orders on* $\{x,y,z\}$. *A* SET $S$ *is:*

good $\Leftrightarrow$ $S$ *guarantees a suborder*
bad $\Leftrightarrow$ $S$ *does not guarantee a suborder*
GOOD $\Leftrightarrow$ $S$ *is a good* SET *that is not properly included in another good* SET (that is, a GOOD SET *is a maximal good* SET)
BAD $\Leftrightarrow$ $S$ *is a bad* SET *that does not properly include another bad* SET (that is, a BAD SET *is a minimal bad* SET).

One way of characterizing all good SETS is as follows:

$S$ is good if and only if there is no BAD SET included in $S$.

Later we shall list all BAD SETS, noting that there are exactly 100 of these and that none of them contains more than three orders. However, by itself this would be a rather dry exercise since it would not tell us very much about the nature of good SETS.

The opposite approach is to seek out the GOOD SETS, noting that

$S$ is good if and only if $S$ is included in some GOOD SET.

There are exactly 28 GOOD SETS (each of which contains the empty order $\emptyset$ on $\{x,y,z\}$). The smallest GOOD SET has five orders, and the largest contains 11 of the 19 possible orders.

Although we shall proceed with the GOOD-SETS approach, again it would not be very revealing to simply list the 28 GOOD SETS. The approach we shall use is to systematically search for GOOD SETS by a method to be described shortly. The method reveals that the 28 GOOD SETS fall into seven natural categories. Each of the seven categories is easily described by a set of conditions on the nonempty orders that are permitted under the category. One example of such a set of conditions is given by expression (T) in the preceding section. This (T), which describes one of the GOOD SETS that contains 11 orders, is a member of category VI. Another category, which is category VII below, includes the GOOD SETS that are single peaked. Since it can be observed that no GOOD SET is included in some other GOOD SET (by Definition 10.3), the seven categories are independent in the sense

**116**

that a GOOD SET can fall under exactly one category, and this is true for each category.

THE SEVEN INDEPENDENT CATEGORIES

For the purposes of this section we have listed the 18 nonempty strict partial orders on $\{x,y,z\}$ at the top of Table 10.1 according to the number of indifferent pairs in the order. Intransitive indifference arises in the final six orders, numbered 13 through 18. Because of the change in purpose, the numbering in Table 10.1 is *not* the same as that in Table 9.1.

TABLE 10.1

NONEMPTY ORDERS AND SEVEN CATEGORIES

THE 18 NONEMPTY ORDERS ON $\{x,y,z\}$

| No indifference | Single indifference | Double indifference |
|---|---|---|
| 1. $x \succ y \succ z$ | 7. $(x \sim y) \succ z$ | 13. $z \sim x \succ y \sim z$ |
| 2. $x \succ z \succ y$ | 8. $z \succ (x \sim y)$ | 14. $z \sim y \succ x \sim z$ |
| 3. $y \succ x \succ z$ | 9. $(x \sim z) \succ y$ | 15. $y \sim x \succ z \sim y$ |
| 4. $y \succ z \succ x$ | 10. $y \succ (x \sim z)$ | 16. $y \sim z \succ x \sim y$ |
| 5. $z \succ x \succ y$ | 11. $(y \sim z) \succ x$ | 17. $x \sim y \succ z \sim x$ |
| 6. $z \succ y \succ x$ | 12. $x \succ (y \sim z)$ | 18. $x \sim z \succ y \sim x$ |

THE SEVEN CATEGORIES

| Representative | GOOD SETS:<br>Nonempty orders | Characterization |
|---|---|---|
| I. $a = b$ | 7, 8, 15, 16, 17, 18 | $x \sim y$ |
| II. $a + c = b + d$ | 2, 3, 4, 5, 9, 10, 15, 16 | $(y \succ x \,\&\, y \succ z)$ or $(x \succ y \,\&\, z \succ y)$ or $(x \sim y \,\&\, y \sim z)$ |
| III. $a + c + e =$<br>$\quad b + d + f$ | 7, 8, 9, 10, 11, 12 | exactly one $\sim$ |
| IV. $u + e = d + f \,\&$<br>$\quad c + e = b + f$ | 1, 6, 9, 10 | $x \succ y \succ z$ or $(x \sim z) \succ y$ or their duals |
| V. $a \geq b \,\&\, d \geq c$ | 2, 5, 8, 9, 12, 13, 15, 16, 18 | $x \succsim y \,\&\, z \succsim y$ |
| VI. $a \geq b \,\&\, f \geq c$<br>$\quad \& \, d \geq e$ | 1, 2, 5, 7, 8, 9, 12, 13, 15, 18 | $x \succsim y \,\&\, (x \succ y$ or $x \succ z$ or $z \succ y)$ |
| VII. $c \geq f \geq a \,\&$<br>$\quad b \geq e \geq d$ | 1, 3, 4, 6, 7, 10, 11, 14, 17 | $y \succ x$ or $y \succ z$ |

To understand our procedure observe first that $S$ is good if and only if both $xP_D y P_D z P_D x$ and $xP_D z P_D y P_D x$ are false for every $D \in S \cup S^2 \cup S^3 \cup \cdots$, and that $S$ is bad if and only if there is a $D \in \cup S^n$ such that $xP_D y P_D z P_D x$ or $xP_D z P_D y P_D x$.

117

Now let $D$ denote a generic $n$-tuple of strict partial orders on $\{x,y,z\}$ and let $a$, $b$, $c$, $d$, $e$ and $f$ be, respectively, the number of components in $D$ for which $x > y$, $y > x$, $y > z$, $z > y$, $z > x$, and $x > z$. Then $P_D$ is not a suborder if and only if

$$(a > b \ \& \ c > d \ \& \ e > f) \quad \text{or} \quad (b > a \ \& \ d > c \ \& \ f > e), \quad (10.1)$$

where these represent $xP_DyP_DzP_Dx$ and $xP_DzP_DyP_Dx$, respectively. Clearly, $S$ *is good if and only if* (10.1) *is false for every* $D \in \cup \ S^n$.

Because of this we shall look for general expressions in $a$, $b$, $\ldots$ , $f$ that violate (10.1). Specifically, we shall identify seven categories of expressions, such that any statement within a category violates (10.1). In doing this it should be noted that we are dealing only with the algebraic inequalities of (10.1). Nothing is being said at this point about orders on $\{x,y,z\}$.

The seven categories divide into four based on equality relations and three based on inequalities. We consider the equality categories first.

Category I. This category contains the following three expressions:

$$a = b, \quad c = d, \quad e = f.$$

It is obvious that each of these causes both expressions in (10.1) to be false. Note that, for (10.1) to fail, we must negate both expressions: not [(. . .) or (. . .)] $\Leftrightarrow$ not (. . .) & not (. . .).

Category II. The second category also contains three expressions:

$$a + c = b + d, \quad a + e = b + f, \quad c + e = d + f.$$

Any one of these violates (10.1).

Category III. This category contains the single expression:

$$a + b + c = d + e + f.$$

Category IV. This is the most complex of the equality categories. Like I and II it has three expressions:

$$\begin{aligned} a + e = d + f \quad & \& \quad c + e = b + f, \\ a + c = d + f \quad & \& \quad c + e = b + d, \\ a + c = b + f \quad & \& \quad a + e = b + d. \end{aligned}$$

To show that the first of these violates (10.1), simply add its two parts to get $a + c + 2e = b + d + 2f$.

118

Category V. Each of the inequality categories has six expressions. Three of these six are the duals of the other three. For each case we list the dual pairs on the same line. For the simplest inequality category, we have:

$$a \geq b \,\&\, d \geq c \qquad b \geq a \,\&\, c \geq d$$
$$a \geq b \,\&\, f \geq e \qquad b \geq a \,\&\, e \geq f$$
$$c \geq d \,\&\, f \geq e \qquad d \geq c \,\&\, e \geq f.$$

Each of these six expressions clearly violates (10.1).

Category VI. The six expressions of this category are:

$$a \geq b \,\&\, f \geq c \,\&\, d \geq e \qquad b \geq a \,\&\, c \geq f \,\&\, e \geq d$$
$$c \geq d \,\&\, f \geq a \,\&\, b \geq e \qquad d \geq c \,\&\, a \geq f \,\&\, e \geq b$$
$$e \geq f \,\&\, d \geq a \,\&\, b \geq c \qquad f \geq e \,\&\, a \geq d \,\&\, c \geq b.$$

Consider the first of these. $a \geq b$ contradicts the second part of (10.1). Then $f \geq c \,\&\, d \geq e$, along with $c > d$ implies $f > e$, so that the first part of (10.1) cannot hold.

Category VII. Our final category is composed of:

$$c \geq f \geq a \,\&\, b \geq e \geq d \qquad a \geq f \geq c \,\&\, d \geq e \geq b$$
$$a \geq d \geq e \,\&\, f \geq c \geq b \qquad e \geq d \geq a \,\&\, b \geq c \geq f$$
$$c \geq b \geq e \,\&\, f \geq a \geq d \qquad e \geq b \geq c \,\&\, d \geq a \geq f.$$

Again, take the first of these. If $a > b$ then $f > e$, so that the first part of (10.1) fails. If $d > c$ then $e > f$, so that the second part fails also.

It will be noted that the seven categories contain a total of 28 expressions. Each of these 28 expressions corresponds to one of the 28 GOOD SETS. A representative expression from each category and its corresponding GOOD SET of orders is shown in the lower part of Table 10.1. (Only nonempty orders are shown: the empty order is a member of every GOOD SET.) The expressions listed above that are not in the table are obtainable from the representatives in the table by obvious substitutions of letters in $\{a, b, \ldots, f\}$ and by taking duals in the inequality categories.

### THE IDENTIFICATION OF GOOD SETS

To remove the element of mystery from the foregoing description, we now show how a GOOD SET is obtained from an expression in any category.

For a generic $D$, let $n_k$ be the number of components in $D$ that contain order $k$ as given on the top of Table 10.1. Then,

$$
\begin{array}{lll}
(x > y) & a = n_1 + n_2 + n_5 + n_9 + n_{12} + n_{13} & \\
(y > x) & b = n_3 + n_4 + n_6 + n_{10} + n_{11} + n_{14} & \\
(y > z) & c = n_1 + n_3 + n_4 + n_7 + n_{10} + n_{17} & \\
(z > y) & d = n_2 + n_5 + n_6 + n_8 + n_9 + n_{18} & (10.2) \\
(z > x) & e = n_4 + n_5 + n_6 + n_8 + n_{11} + n_{16} & \\
(x > z) & f = n_1 + n_2 + n_3 + n_7 + n_{12} + n_{15} &
\end{array}
$$

We have seen that any one of our categorical expressions guarantees the failure of (10.1). For any one of these expressions we now determine the minimal set of $n_k$ such that, when each of these is set equal to zero, the given expression must be true regardless of the (nonnegative) values of the other $n_k$. The orders for the $n_k$ that must be set equal to zero to guarantee the expression are precisely those that are inadmissible for the expression. Those that remain, along with the empty order, constitute the GOOD SET that corresponds to the categorical expression. We shall illustrate this with the representatives of categories I, IV, and VII in Table 10.1.

For category I we have $a = b$. Substitution from (10.2) gives $n_1 + n_2 + n_5 + n_9 + n_{12} + n_{13} = n_3 + n_4 + n_6 + n_{10} + n_{11} + n_{14}$. To guarantee $a = b$ we must therefore set all of these $n_k$ equal to zero. This leaves the nonempty orders 7, 8, 15, 16, 17, and 18, as shown on Table 10.1 alongside $a = b$. The $n_k$ for these six $k$ can have any values without affecting the $a = b$ expression.

Our representative expression for category IV is $a + e = d + f$ & $c + e = b + f$. For $a + e = d + f$, (10.2) requires

$$ n_4 + n_5 + n_{11} + n_{13} + n_{16} = n_2 + n_3 + n_7 + n_{15} + n_{18}, $$

after cancellation of $n_k$ that appear on both sides of the equality with equal coefficients. Similarly, $c + e = b + f$ gives $n_4 + n_5 + n_8 + n_{16} + n_{17} = n_2 + n_3 + n_{12} + n_{14} + n_{15}$. To guarantee the given expression, every $n_k$ in these two equalities is set equal to zero. This leaves us with the four nonempty orders 1, 6, 9, and 10 as shown in the table.

For category VII we have $c \geq f \geq a$ & $b \geq e \geq d$. Taking $c \geq f$ first, substitution from (10.2) gives $n_4 + n_{10} + n_{17} \geq n_2 + n_5 + n_{15}$ after cancellation. Thus $n_2 = n_5 = n_{15} = 0$ assures $c \geq f$. Taking $f \geq a$, $b \geq e$, and $e \geq d$ in like manner, we are left with orders 1, 3, 4, 6, 7, 10, 11, 14, and 17 whose $n_k$ do not have to be set equal to zero to guarantee the categorical expression.

CHARACTERIZATIONS

To complete the description of Table 10.1, we shall now characterize each of the representatives and their corresponding orders (GOOD SETS) in terms of conditions on preferences. This is done by identifying the properties that are common to all nonempty orders in the GOOD SET and which hold for no nonempty order that is not in the GOOD SET.

For example, $x \sim y$ for each of orders 7, 8, 15, 16, 17, and 18 for the category I representative $a = b$, and $x \sim y$ holds for no other nonempty order. We could have determined this from $a = b$ alone, since this is the same as $xI_{D}y$: to guarantee $xI_{D}y$ we admit only those orders for which $x \sim y$. However, other categories are not as obvious as category I in this sense, with the exception of category V: $a \geq b$ & $d \geq c$ corresponds to $xR_{D}y$ & $zR_{D}y$, which is guaranteed by $x \geqslant y$ & $z \geqslant y$ for all orders.

For another instance, consider category VI. By looking back through the upper part of Table 10.1 we find that $x \geqslant y$ & ($x > y$ or $x > z$ or $z > y$) for each of the nonempty orders listed for the representative of this category. None of the other orders satisfies this description.

The only one of the categories whose characterization is not simpler than what amounts to a listing of the orders in a GOOD SET is category IV. This is the smallest GOOD SET, and there appears to be no simple property that summarizes its four nonempty orders while excluding all others.

We shall now discuss the characterizations more fully, and simultaneously define terms that will be used in the main theorem that results from our analysis. The first sentence in each of the next seven paragraphs is to be regarded as a definition.

*S is in category* **I** *if and only if there are two elements in* $\{x,y,z\}$, *say x and y, such that* $x \sim y$ *for all* $> \in S$. The other two cases, with $x \sim z$, and with $y \sim z$, correspond to the categorical expressions $c = d$ and $e = f$. An $S$ in category I is sometimes described by the phrase "limited agreement," since every individual in such a case is indifferent between the same two alternatives.

*S is in category* **II** *if and only if there is an alternative in* $\{x,y,z\}$, *say y, such that* ($y > x$ & $y > z$) *or* ($x > y$ & $z > y$) *or* ($x \sim y$ & $y \sim z$) *for each* $> \in S$. In the given case the "chosen" alternative $y$ is either preferred to the other two, or less preferred than the other two, or indifferent to the other two alternatives for each $> \in S$. The other two specific cases for $S$ in category II are ($z > x$ & $z > y$) or ($x > z$ & $y > z$) or ($x \sim z$ & $z \sim y$), and ($x > y$ & $x > z$) or ($y > x$ & $z > x$) or ($y \sim x$ & $x \sim z$), which correspond to the "choice" of $z$ and $x$ respectively.

121

*S is in category* **III** *if and only if each nonempty* $>\ \in S$ *has exactly one indifference pair.* This has been referred to as a condition of "single indifference."

*S is in category* **IV** *if and only if the three elements in* $\{x,y,z\}$ *can be placed in an order, say xyz, such that every nonempty* $>\ \in S$ *is in* $\{xyz,zyx,(xz)y,y(xz)\}$, where as usual $(xz)y$ means $(x \sim z) > y$. Because the displayed set contains two orders and their duals, this case is sometimes referred to as "antagonistic preferences." Because of the duals aspect, the other five orders on $\{x,y,z\}$ give rise to only two more GOOD SETS.

*S is in category* **V** *if and only if there is an alternative in* $\{x,y,z\}$, *say y, such that either* $(x \geqslant y \ \& \ z \geqslant y)$ *for all* $>$ *in S or else* $(y \geqslant x \ \& \ y \geqslant z)$ *for all* $>\ \in S$. Because this requires one alternative to be at least as preferred as each of the other two in each order (or, dually, not preferred to either of the other two in each order) it is another case of "limited agreement."

*S is in category* **VI** *if and only if the three elements in* $\{x,y,z\}$ *can be placed in an order, say xyz, such that* $x \geqslant y \ \& \ (x > y$ *or* $x > z$ *or* $z > y)$ *for each nonempty* $>\ \in S$. Here the six different orders do give rise to six different GOOD SETS. This is also a case of "limited agreement."

*S is in category* **VII** *if and only if there is an alternative in* $\{x,y,z\}$, *say y, such that either* $(y > x$ *or* $y > z)$ *for every nonempty* $>\ \in S$ *or else* $(x > y$ *or* $z > y)$ *for every nonempty* $>\ \in S$. The first of these, $(y > x$ *or* $y > z)$, is a case of single-peaked preferences under the order $x <_0 y <_0 z$. The second, $(x > y$ *or* $z > y)$, is the dual of the first, and is referred to as "single-caved" or "single-troughed" preferences. A general picture of single-troughed preferences can be obtained by looking at Figure 9.1 or 9.2 or 9.3 upside down.

The categories can be summarized in several ways. One of these follows.

SUMMARY DEFINITION. *S is in one of categories* **I** *through* **VII** *if and only if there is an alternative in* $\{x,y,z\}$, *say y, such that every nonempty* $>\ \in S$ *satisfies one and the same of the following ten expressions:*

I. $x \sim z$

II. $(y > x$ *and* $y > z)$ *or* $(x > y$ *and* $z > y)$ *or* $(x \sim y$ *and* $y \sim z)$

III. $(x \sim y) > z$ *or* $z > (x \sim y)$ *or* $(x \sim z) > y$ *or* $y > (x \sim z)$ *or* $(y \sim z) > x$ *or* $x > (y \sim z)$

IV. $x > y > z$ *or* $z > y > x$ *or* $(x \sim z) > y$ *or* $y > (x \sim z)$

V. $y \geqslant x$ *and* $y \geqslant z$

V. $x \geqslant y$ *and* $z \geqslant y$

VI. $x \geqslant z$ *and* $(x > z$ *or* $x > y$ *or* $y > z)$

VI. $z \geqslant x$ *and* $(z > x$ *or* $z > y$ *or* $y > x)$
VII. $y > x$ *or* $y > z$
VII. $x > y$ *or* $z > y$.

It must be remarked that some of our categories seem rather artificial in terms of actual situations that might give rise to such SETS. The most natural cases appear to be the single-peaked half of category VII. An exercise of some interest is to think of a situation that is naturally single troughed. Some of the limited-agreement cases (I, V, VI) could arise under certain natural circumstances. A category II case might obtain when one of the alternatives, say $y$, is the kind of candidate that will either be violently liked or violently disliked by each voter, or when $y$ is quite dissimilar from $x$ and $z$ with these two the same except for minor details.

THE THEOREM

The foregoing definitions and analysis suggest the following theorem.

THEOREM 10.2. *A set $S$ of strict partial orders on $\{x,y,z\}$ guarantees a suborder on $\{x,y,z\}$ if and only if $S$ is in at least one of categories I through VII.*

We have already proved the "if" part of this theorem, for our categories were developed in such a way that any $S$ in any category is a good SET.

In the next section we shall outline the proof of the "only if" part of the theorem by showing that if $S$ is in none of the seven categories then $S$ must include a BAD SET and must therefore be bad. Among other things, this will show that the 28 SETS developed for our 28 categorical expressions are indeed GOOD SETS and are the only GOOD SETS. This means that there are no other categorical expressions that give a violation of (10.1) and are independent (in terms of good SETS) of the 28 given above.

## 10.3 BAD SETS

As stated before, there are 100 minimal SETS (i.e. BAD SETS) that do not guarantee a suborder on $\{x,y,z\}$. These are listed in Table 10.2, from $\{1,4,5\}$, $\{1,4,8\}$, . . . , to $\{13,16,17\}$ and $\{14,15,18\}$. All but six of the BAD SETS are three-order SETS. The six two-order BAD SETS are

$$\{1,16\}, \{2,14\}, \{3,18\}, \{4,13\}, \{5,17\}, \{6,15\} \qquad (10.3)$$

**123**

## TABLE 10.2
### ALL BAD SETS

| 1 | VIOLATION OF TRANS. | SUB-ORDER | 2 | 3 | 4 | 5 | 6 |
|---|---|---|---|---|---|---|---|
| 4, 5 | [1,1,1] | [1,1,1] | 3, 6 | 6, 9 | 5, 7 | 7, 10 | 7, 9 |
| 4, 8 | [1,1,1] | [2,1,2] | 3, 8 | 6, 12 | 5, 12 | 7, 11 | 7, 12 |
| 4, 9 | [1,1,1] | [1,2,2] | 3, 11 | 8, 9 | 7, 9 | 7, 16 | 7, 18 |
| 5, 10 | [1,1,1] | [1,2,2] | 6, 7 | 8, 12 | 7, 18 | 10, 12 | 9, 17 |
| 5, 11 | [1,1,1] | [2,1,2] | 6, 10 | 8, 15 | 8, 12 | 10, 13 | 10, 12 |
| 8, 10 | [2,2,1] | [3,4,2] | 7, 11 | 9, 11 | 8, 15 | 11, 15 | 10, 13 |
| 8, 11 | [2,1,1] | [3,2,2] | 7, 16 | 9, 14 | 9, 12 | 12, 14 | 12, 14 |
| 8, 17 | [1,2,1] | [1,2,2] | 8, 10 | 11, 13 | 9, 17 | 14, 15 | 13, 17 |
| 9, 11 | [2,1,2] | [2,3,4] | 8, 17 | 12, 16 | 12, 16 | 17 | 15 |
| 9, 14 | [0,1,2] | [1,2,4] | 10, 11 | 13, 16 | 15, 18 | | |
| 10, 18 | [0,1,2] | [1,2,4] | 10, 18 | 18 | 13 | | |
| 11, 13 | [0,1,2] | [1,2,2] | 11, 15 | | | | |
| 14, 18 | [0,1,1] | [1,2,2] | 16, 17 | | | | |
| 16 | [1,1] | [1,2] | 14 | | | | |

| 7 | | | 8 | 9 | 10 | 11 | 12 |
|---|---|---|---|---|---|---|---|
| 9, 14 | [0,1,2] | [1,2,3] | 9, 17 | 11, 15 | 11, 13 | 13, 17 | 14, 18 |
| 9, 16 | [1,0,2] | [2,1,3] | 10, 13 | 11, 17 | 12, 16 | 15, 18 | 16, 17 |
| 10, 18 | [0,1,2] | [1,1,3] | 10, 15 | 12, 14 | 12, 18 | | |
| 11, 13 | [0,1,2] | [1,2,3] | 11, 15 | 16, 17 | 13, 16 | | |
| 11, 18 | [1,0,2] | [2,1,3] | 12, 14 | | 15, 18 | | |
| 12, 16 | [0,1,2] | [1,1,3] | 12, 17 | | | | |
| 13, 16 | [0,1,1] | [1,1,2] | 13, 17 | | | | |
| 14, 18 | [0,1,1] | [1,1,2] | 14, 15 | | | | |

| 13 | | | 14 | | | | |
|---|---|---|---|---|---|---|---|
| 16, 17 | [1,1,0] | [1,1,1] | 15, 18 | | | | |

which are obtainable from each other by permutations on $\{x,y,z\}$. It is easily seen that there are no other two-order BAD SETS so that, if each of the three-order SETS in the table is bad, then it is BAD. To verify that each of these is bad it will suffice to show a violation of a suborder for each of the SETS that contain 1, or 7, or 13 as the order with smallest identifying number. The reason for this is that all other SETS in Table 10.2 can be obtained from these (in the first column of the table) by permutations on $\{x,y,z\}$.

124

The second and third columns of the table show, respectively, frequencies of the corresponding orders that will give a violation of transitivity and of a suborder. For example, for the SET $\{1,4,8\}$, let $D = (1,4,8)$. Then $yP_D z$, $zP_D x$ and $xI_D y$, so that $P_D$ is not transitive. And with $D = (1,1,4,8,8)$, corresponding to [2,1,2], we get $xP_D yP_D zP_D x$, so that $P_D$ is not a suborder for this $D$.

As a consequence of this analysis, which has little to do with Theorem 10.2 except to verify that each SET in Table 10.2 is BAD, we have the following lemma.

LEMMA 10.3. *If S does not guarantee a suborder on $\{x,y,z\}$ then there is a $D \in S^n$ for some $n \leq 9$ for which $P_D$ on $\{x,y,z\}$ is not a suborder, and 9 is the smallest number that will serve this purpose.*

*Proof.* The necessity proof given later in this section will show that all BAD SETS are indeed listed in Table 10.2. The "Violation of suborder" column shows that an $n \leq 9$ will always suffice to obtain a $D \in S^n$ for which $P_D$ is not a suborder when $S$ is bad.

Consider the BAD SET $\{1,0,10\}$, or $\{xyz, z(xy), y(xz)\}$, each order in which happens to be a weak order. With $n_1$, $n_8$ and $n_{10}$ the number of times these orders are in $D$, we need

$$n_1 + n_{10} > n_8 > n_1 > n_{10} \qquad \text{for} \qquad yP_D zP_D xP_D y,$$

and the smallest values of $n_1$, $n_8$ and $n_{10}$ that can produce this are 3, 4, and 2, respectively. ($yP_D xP_D zP_D y$ is impossible to obtain with the three orders.) Hence the smallest $n$ that will do is $n = 9$. ◆

NECESSITY PROOF OF THEOREM 10.2

Henceforth in this section *a* BET *is any* SET *that violates* (is in none of) *categories* I *through* VII. Our task is to show that every BET is bad. We shall show that every BET includes a SET in Table 10.2, which will verify that Table 10.2 includes all BAD SETS.

To violate category III (single indifference) a BET must contain at least one of orders 1 through 6 (no indifference) or at least one of orders 13 through 18 (double indifference). For this reason, we shall divide all BETS into three disjoint classes. Class A BETS contain none of orders 13 through 18. Class B BETS contain none of 1–6. Class C BETS contain at least one order from 1–6 *and* at least one order from 13–18. Without loss in generality we shall always assume that order 1 is in a class A BET and in a class C BET, and that order 13 is in a class B BET. All other BETS arise from these under the five nonidentify permutations on $\{x,y,z\}$.

To be as explicit as possible in this proof, all alleged GOOD SETS (obtained as in the bottom of Table 10.1) that contain order 1 or order 13 are listed for future reference. The empty set is omitted from each.

I. {9,10,13,14,17,18}, {11,12,13,14,15,16}.
II. {1,3,5,6,7,8,13,14}, {1,2,4,6,11,12,17,18}.
IV. {1,6,9,10}.
V. {2,5,8,9,12,13,15,16,18}, {1,2,7,9,12,13,15,17,18}, {5,6,8,9,11,13,14,16,18}, {1,3,7,10,12,13,14,15,17}.
VI. {1,2,5,7,8,9,12,13,15,18}, {1,2,3,7,9,10,12,13,15,17}, {1,3,4,7,10,11,12,14,15,17}, {2,5,6,8,9,11,12,13,16,18}.
VII. {1,3,4,6,7,10,11,14,17}, {1,2,5,6,8,9,12,13,18}, {1,2,3,5,7,9,12,13,15}, {1,2,3,4,7,10,12,15,17}.

## CLASS A BETS

These contain 1 and none of 13–18. To violate all categories, a class A BET must contain an order in {2,3, . . . ,12} that is *not* in each of the above listed SETS that includes order 1. There are twelve such SETS. Taking complements of these, a class A BET must contain at least one order from each of the following lines:

| | | |
|---|---|---|
| L1. | 2, 4, 9, 10, 11, 12 | from II |
| L2. | 3, 5, 7, 8, 9, 10 | II |
| L3. | 2, 3, 4, 5, 7, 8, 11, 12 | IV |
| L4. | 3, 4, 5, 6, 8, 10, 11 | V |
| L5. | 2, 4, 5, 6, 8, 9, 11 | V |
| L6. | 3, 4, 6, 10, 11 | VI |
| L7. | 4, 5, 6, 8, 11 | VI |
| L8. | 2, 5, 6, 8, 9 | VI |
| L9. | 2, 5, 8, 9, 12 | VII |
| L10. | 3, 4, 7, 10, 11 | VII |
| L11. | 4, 6, 8, 10, 11 | VII |
| L12. | 5, 6, 8, 9, 11 | VII. |

Suppose first that the BET contains 4 or 11. Then, by the first column of Table 10.2, if {5,8,9} ∩ BET ≠ ∅, the BET is bad. Henceforth in this paragraph assume that {5,8,9} ∩ BET = ∅. Then, by L2,

the BET must contain 3 or 7 or 10.

Suppose now that 11 ∈ BET. Then, by L8 and L9, the BET must contain 2 or 6 and 2 or 12. Since {2,3,11}, {2,7,11}, {2,10,11}, {3,6,12}, {6,7,12}, and {6,10,12} are in Table 10.2, every BET that contains 11 is bad. Dispense with 11 and assume that 4 ∈ BET. Then L12 requires 6 ∈ BET, and L9 requires 2 or 12 in the BET. Since {2,3,6}, {2,6,7},

{2,6,10}, {3,6,12}, {6,7,12}, and {6,10,12} are in Table 10.2, each BET that contains 4 is bad. We can therefore dispense with both 4 and 11 in the rest of the proof for class A BETS.

Suppose next that the BET contains 5 or 8. If it contains 10 also then it is bad, so assume henceforth in this paragraph that $10 \notin$ BET. Then, by L1,

the BET must contain 2 or 9 or 12.

Suppose now that $8 \in$ BET. Then, by L6 and L10, the BET must contain 3 or 6 and 3 or 7. Since {2,3,8}, {3,8,9}, {3,8,12}, {2,6,7}, {6,7,9}, and {6,7,12} are in Table 10.2, each BET that contains 8 is bad. Dispense with 8 and assume that $5 \in$ BET. Then L11 requires $6 \in$ BET and L10 requires 3 or 7 in the BET. Since Table 10.2 includes {2,3,6}, {3,6,9}, {3,6,12}, {2,6,7}, {6,7,9}, and {6,7,12}, all BETS that contain 5 are bad.

Dispensing with 5 and 8 along with 4 and 11, and observing that, by L7, the BET must then include 6, we assume henceforth that $6 \in$ BET. This leaves the following reductions of our lines:

L1. 2, 9, 10, 12
L2. 3, 7, 9, 10
L3. 2, 3, 7, 12
L9. 2, 9, 12
L10. 3, 7, 10.

First, take $7 \in$ BET. If either 9 or 12 is in the BET then it is bad by Table 10.2. If neither 9 nor 12 is in the BET then it must contain 2, by L9, and is therefore bad since {2,6,7} is in Table 10.2. Henceforth assume that $7 \notin$ BET. Take $2 \in$ BET. Then if $10 \in$ BET also, the BET is bad since {2,6,10} is in Table 10.2, and if $10 \notin$ BET then $3 \in$ BET by L10 and {2,3,6} is in Table 10.2. Henceforth assume that $2 \notin$ BET. If $3 \in$ BET, then, by L9, 9 or 12 must be in the BET, and since {3,6,9} and {3,6,12} are in Table 10.2 the BET is bad. Deleting 3, L3 and L10 require 12 and 10 to be in the BET, and since {6,10,12} is in Table 10.2, the BET is bad.

CLASS B BETS

Class B BETS contain 13 and none of 1–6. Using the same procedure that was used for class A BETS, each class B BET must contain an order from each of the following lines:

| | | |
|---|---|---|
| L1. 7, 8, 11, 12, 15, 16 | from I | |
| L2. 7, 8, 9, 10, 17, 18 | I | |
| L3. 9, 10, 11, 12, 15, 16, 17, 18 | II | |
| L4. 7, 10, 11, 14, 17 | V | |

| | | |
|---|---|---|
| L5. | 8, 10, 11, 14, 16 | V |
| L6. | 7, 10, 12, 15, 17 | V |
| L7. | 8, 9, 11, 16, 18 | V |
| L8. | 10, 11, 14, 16, 17 | VI |
| L9. | 8, 11, 14, 16, 18 | VI |
| L10. | 7, 10, 14, 15, 17 | VI |
| L11. | 7, 10, 11, 14, 15, 16, 17 | VII |
| L12. | 8, 10, 11, 14, 16, 17, 18 | VII. |

Suppose first that $\{10,17\} \cap$ BET $\neq \emptyset$. By Table 10.2, any such BET that contains 8, 11 or 16 is bad. Henceforth in this paragraph, assume that $\{8,11,16\} \cap$ BET $= \emptyset$. By L1,

the BET must contain 7 or 12 or 15.

Take $10 \in$ BET. Since L7 and L9 require 9 or 18 and 14 or 18, respectively, and since $\{7,10,18\}$, $\{10,12,18\}$, $\{10,15,18\}$, $\{7,9,14\}$, $\{9,12,14\}$, and $\{9,14,15\}$ are in Table 10.2, every BET with 10 is bad. Henceforth assume that $10 \notin$ BET. Then take $17 \in$ BET. This requires $14 \in$ BET by L5, and either 9 or 18 in the BET by L7. Since $\{7,9,14\}$, $\{9,12,14\}$, $\{9,14,15\}$, $\{7,14,18\}$, $\{12,14,18\}$ and $\{14,15,18\}$ are in Table 10.2, each class B BET that contains 17 is bad. Henceforth assume that $17 \notin$ BET.

Suppose next that $\{11,16\} \cap$ BET $\neq \emptyset$. If $7 \in$ BET then the BET is bad. Henceforth in this paragraph, assume that $7 \notin$ BET. Then, by L2,

the BET must contain 8 or 9 or 18.

Take $11 \in$ BET. Then L6 and L10 require 12 or 15 and 14 or 15. Since $\{8,12,14\}$, $\{9,12,14\}$, $\{12,14,18\}$, $\{8,11,15\}$, $\{9,11,15\}$ and $\{11,15,18\}$ are in Table 10.2, each BET with 11 is bad. Henceforth assume that $11 \notin$ BET. Then take $16 \in$ BET. This requires $14 \in$ BET by L4, and either 12 or 15 by L6. Since $\{8,12,14\}$, $\{9,12,14\}$, $\{12,14,18\}$, $\{8,14,15\}$, $\{9,14,15\}$, and $\{14,15,18\}$ are in Table 10.2, all class B BETS with 16 are bad.

Thus all class B BETS with 10 or 11 or 16 or 17 are bad. Deleting these and observing by L8 that a BET must then contain 14, our lines reduce to

| | |
|---|---|
| L1. | 7, 8, 12, 15 |
| L2. | 7, 8, 9, 18 |
| L3. | 9, 12, 15, 18 |
| L6. | 7, 12, 15 |
| L7. | 8, 9, 18. |

First, take $12 \in$ BET. If either 8, 9, or 18 is in the BET then it is bad since {8,12,14}, {9,12,14}, and {12,14,18} are in Table 10.2. If {8,9,18} $\cap$ BET = $\emptyset$ then L7 is contradicted. Hence any BET with 12 is bad. Henceforth assume that $12 \notin$ BET. Take $18 \in$ BET. L6 requires 7 or 15, and {7,14,18} and {14,15,18} are in Table 10.2. Hence all BETS with 18 are bad. Henceforth assume that $18 \notin$ BET. If $9 \in$ BET then, since L6 requires 7 or 15, and {7,9,14} and {9,14,15} are in Table 10.2, the BET is bad. Henceforth assume that $9 \notin$ BET. Then L3 and L7 require 15 and 8 to be in the BET, and since {8,14,15} is in Table 10.2, all class B BETS that contain 14 are bad.

CLASS C BETS

These BETS contain order 1 and one of 13 through 18. Since {1,16} is in Table 10.2, assume henceforth that $16 \notin$ BET. Proceeding as before, we first pair up 1 and 13 and show that any BET that contains both is bad. Order 13 is then deleted from further consideration. The process is repeated with 1 and 14, with 1 and 18, with 1 and 15, and finally with 1 and 17.

We shall detail only the proof for 1 and 13. Since {4,13} is in Table 10.2, 4 as well as 16 is deleted from further consideration. Taking complements of sets displayed earlier in this section that contain both 1 and 13, we require an order from each of the following lines to be in any BET that contains 1 and 13, and neither 4 nor 16.

| | | |
|---|---|---|
| L1. | 2, 9, 10, 11, 12, 15, 17, 18 | from II |
| L2. | 3, 5, 6, 8, 10, 11, 14 | V |
| L3. | 2, 5, 6, 8, 9, 11, 18 | V |
| L4. | 3, 6, 10, 11, 14, 17 | VI |
| L5. | 5, 6, 8, 11, 14, 18 | VI |
| L6. | 3, 7, 10, 11, 14, 15, 17 | VII |
| L7. | 6, 8, 10, 11, 14, 17, 18 | VII. |

Since {1,11,13} is in Table 10.2, 11 is deleted from further consideration. Suppose next that $6 \in$ BET. Only L1 and L6 do not have 6. Since {6,15}, {6,10,13}, and {6,13,17} are BAD SETS, we dispense with 15, 10, and 17 and consider the reductions of L1 and L6:

$$\{2,9,12,18\} \qquad \text{and} \qquad \{3,7,14\}.$$

If $2 \in$ BET then the BET is bad since {2,3,6}, {2,6,7}, and {2,14} are in Table 10.2. If $9 \in$ BET, then it is bad since {3,6,9}, {6,7,9}, and {1,9,14} are in Table 10.2. Likewise for 12 and for 18. Hence every class C BET that contains 6 as well as 1 and 13 is bad.

Henceforth assume that $6 \notin$ BET. Take $10 \in$ BET. Since {1,5,10}, {1,8,10}, and {1,10,18} are in Table 10.2, we dispense with 5, 8 and 18.

**129**

Then L5 requires $14 \in$ BET and L3 requires 2 or 9. Since $\{2,14\}$ and $\{1,9,14\}$ are in Table 10.2, such a BET is bad.

Henceforth assume that $10 \notin$ BET. Take $14 \in$ BET. Since $\{2,14\}$, $\{1,9,14\}$, and $\{1,14,18\}$ are in Table 10.2, we dispense with 2, 9, and 18. From L3 and L1 we require one order from each of

$$\{5,8\} \qquad \text{and} \qquad \{12,15,17\}.$$

Since $\{5,12,14\}$, $\{5,14,15\}$, $\{5,17\}$, $\{8,12,14\}$, $\{8,14,15\}$ and $\{8,13,17\}$ are in Table 10.2, each BET with 14 is bad.

Deleting 14, the reductions we have made in our lines leave the following:

L1. 2, 9, 12, 15, 17, 18
L2. 3, 5, 8
L3. 2, 5, 8, 9, 18
L4. 3, 17
L5. 5, 8, 18
L6. 3, 7, 15, 17
L7. 8, 17, 18.

Suppose $17 \in$ BET. Since $\{5,17\}$ and $\{1,8,17\}$ are in Table 10.2, we dispense with 5 and 8. This leaves 3 from L2 and 18 from L5. Since $\{3,18\}$ is in Table 10.2, all BETs with 17 are bad.

Deleting 17, L4 requires $3 \in$ BET, and L7 requires one of 8 and 18. We can dispense with 18 since $\{3,18\}$ is in Table 10.2. Thus $8 \in$ BET. With L1 we then have $\{2,3,8\}$, $\{3,8,9\}$, $\{3,8,12\}$, $\{3,8,15\}$, and $\{3,18\}$ in Table 10.2. Hence every BET with 3 is bad. This exhausts L4, and we have completed our proof that every BET that includes $\{1,13\}$ is bad.

# CHAPTER 11

# Transitive Majorities

THIS CHAPTER concludes our present discussion of conditions on triples that guarantee a specified result. We shall first identify all conditions that guarantee transitivity of strict simple majority. Section 11.2 then shows what happens to these conditions when all individual preference orders are presumed to be weak orders, and it goes on to specify all conditions that guarantee a weak order.

Two specializations of the guarantee notion are examined in the third section. The first involves "oddly guarantees," which look only at profiles $D$ that have an odd number of nonempty components. The second involves "odd-guarantees," which look only at profiles that have an odd number of nonempty weak order components.

The main theorems are summarized in Table 11.1 in the final section, and it may prove helpful to examine this table before reading further. Category representatives are listed at the bottom of the table, which includes four new categories that are developed in the chapter.

As far as we are aware, Theorem 11.1 was first proved by Inada (1970); Corollary 11.2 was first proved by Sen and Pattanaik (1969); and Theorems 11.2 and 11.4 were first established by Inada (1969).

## 11.1 CONDITIONS THAT GUARANTEE TRANSITIVITY

In examining sets of orders that guarantee transitivity it will suffice, as noted in Lemma 10.1, to consider an arbitrary triple $\{x,y,z\} \subseteq X$. In this section we shall characterize all sets of strict partial orders on a triple that guarantee transitivity. Recall that, by Definition 10.1, we are here talking about the transitivity of strict simple majority. The transitivity of simple majority $(R)$ will be examined in sections 11.2 and 11.3.

As in section 10.2 we shall let $a$, $b$, $c$, $d$, $e$, and $f$ denote the number of orders in a generic $D$ for which $x > y$, $y > x$, $y > z$, $z > y$, $z > x$, and $x > z$, respectively. Then $S$ does not guarantee transitivity on $\{x,y,z\}$ if and only if one of the following six expressions holds for some $D \in \cup S^n$:

$$
\begin{array}{ll}
(a \geq b \ \& \ c > d \ \& \ e > f) & (b \geq a \ \& \ d > c \ \& \ f > e) \\
(a > b \ \& \ c \geq d \ \& \ e > f) & (b > a \ \& \ d \geq c \ \& \ f > e) \quad (11.1) \\
(a > b \ \& \ c > d \ \& \ e \geq f) & (b > a \ \& \ d > c \ \& \ f \geq e).
\end{array}
$$

In other words, $S$ guarantees transitivity if and only if all six expressions in (11.1) are violated for every $D \in \cup S^n$. An examination of the seven categories of section 10.2 shows that the categorical expressions for categories II, III, IV, and VII guarantee a violation of all of (11.1). The representatives of these categories from Table 10.1 are:

II. $a + c = b + d$
III. $a + c + e = b + d + f$
IV. $a + e = d + f$ and $c + e = b + f$
VII. $c \geq f \geq a$ and $b \geq e \geq d$.

Hence, the sets of orders in these categories guarantee transitivity. Clearly, neither category I $(a = b)$ nor category V $(a \geq b$ and $d \geq c)$ guarantees a complete violation of (11.1). This leaves only category VI with representative

$$a \geq b \quad \& \quad f \geq c \quad \& \quad d \geq e. \tag{11.2}$$

This violates all expressions in (11.1) except for $(b \geq a \ \& \ d > c \ \& \ f > e)$, which holds and does not contradict (11.2) only when $a = b$, $d > c$, and $f > e$. Thus, if we replace the categorical expression (11.2) for VI by

VI'. $f \geq c \ \& \ d \geq e \ \& \ (a > b$ or $(a = b \ \& $ not $(d > c \ \& \ f > e))$

then all expressions in (11.1) are violated. Referring to Table 10.1, the nonempty orders allowed for VI are 1, 2, 5, 7, 8, 9, 12, 13, 15, and 18. Any subset of these guarantees $f \geq c \ \& \ d \geq e \ \& \ a \geq b$, so we need only worry about the possibility of $a = b \ \& \ d > c \ \& \ f > e$. The only way to ensure $a = b$ is when all orders with $x \succ y$ are absent, which leaves only orders 7, 8, 15, and 18. Given only these four, both $d > c$ and $f > e$ hold if and only if $n_7 + n_{15} > n_8$ and $n_8 + n_{18} > n_7$. Hence, to guarantee not $(d > c \ \& \ f > e)$ in this case we set $n_{15} = n_{18} = 0$, for then we cannot have both $n_7 > n_8$ and $n_8 > n_7$. Deleting orders 15 and 18 from the list for VI, we are left with the following orders which guarantee VI':

VI'. 1, 2, 5, 7, 8, 9, 12, 13.

Checking the top of Table 10.1 for the common properties of these orders which no other nonempty orders possess, we see that the representative for VI' is characterized by

VI'. $x \succcurlyeq y$ for each order, and $x \succ y$ if $\sim$ is not transitive.

Thus we shall say that a set $S$ of orders on $\{x,y,z\}$ *is in category* VI' *if and only if the elements in $\{x,y,z\}$ can be placed in an order,* *say xyz, such that $x \geqslant y$ for each $> \in S$, and $x > y$ for each $> \in S$ for which $\sim$ on $\{x,y,z\}$ is not transitive.*

THEOREM 11.1. *A set $S$ of strict partial orders on a triple $\{x,y,z\}$ guarantees transitivity on the triple if and only if $S$ is in at least one of categories* II, III, IV, VI′, *and* VII.

*Proof.* Since we already know that any $S$ in any one of the categories guarantees transitivity, it is only necessary to verify that $S$ does not guarantee transitivity when it violates all of categories II, III, IV, VI′, and VII. Now if $S$ violates all seven of our original categories, then $S$ does not guarantee a suborder, and hence it does not guarantee transitivity. (See Theorem 10.2.) Thus we need only consider the case where $S$ violates all of II, III, IV, VI′, and VII, and where $S$ is in at least one of categories I, V, and VI. For future reference we note here some two-element SETS that guarantee a suborder but do not guarantee transitivity:

$$\{8,15\}, \{12,16\}, \{13,16\}, \{15,18\}, \{7,18\}. \tag{11.3}$$

Suppose first that $S$ is in category V, and suppose for definiteness that $x \geqslant y$ and $z \geqslant y$ for all orders in $S$. To violate VII ($x > y$ or $z > y$) we need order 15 or 16; to violate VII ($z > x$ or $z > y$) we need 12 or 13 or 15; and to violate VII ($x > y$ or $x > z$) we need 8 or 16 or 18 in $S$. The only way to have an element from each of $\{15,16\}$, $\{12,13,15\}$, and $\{8,16,18\}$ in $S$ and not to have one of the SETS in (11.3) included in $S$ is to have both 15 and 16 in $S$. But to violate category II ($y > x$ & $y > z$ or $x > y$ & $z > y$ or $x \sim y$ & $y \sim z$) we need one of 8, 12, 13, and 18 in $S$, and each of these adjoined to $\{15,16\}$ gives a SET in Table 10.2. Hence, if $S$ is in category V but not in category II or VII, then $S$ cannot guarantee transitivity.

Suppose next that $S$ is in category I with $x \sim y$ for all orders in $S$, and that $S$ is not in category V. Then $S$ must contain an order for each of the following four cases:

$z > y$    ($>$ must be 8 or 18)
$y > z$    ($>$ must be 7 or 17)
$x > z$    ($>$ must be 7 or 15)
$z > x$    ($>$ must be 8 or 16).

Moreover, to violate III (single indifference), $S$ must contain one of 15, 16, 17, and 18. (Recall that none of 1–6 and 13 and 14 have $x \sim y$.) If order 15 is in $S$, then since 8 or 18 is in $S$ by $z > y$ above, and since $\{8,15\}$ and $\{15,18\}$ are in (11.3), $S$ does not guarantee transitivity. Orders 16, 17, and 18 are handled in similar fashion.

Finally, suppose that $S$ is in category VI with $x \geqslant y$ and ($x > y$ or $x > z$ or $z > y$) for each nonempty order in $S$. Since VI' is presumed to be violated by $S$, $S$ must contain 15 or 18. Also, violation of VII ($x > y$ or $z > y$) requires 7 or 15, and violation of VII ($x > y$ or $x > z$) requires 8 or 18. Since each combination of an order from each of $\{15,18\}$, $\{7,15\}$, and $\{8,18\}$ gives a pair in (11.3), $S$ does not guarantee transitivity. ◆

Theorem 11.1 and Lemma 10.1 have the following immediate corollary.

COROLLARY 11.1. *S guarantees transitivity if and only if, for each triple $\{x,y,z\} \subseteq X$, the set of restrictions on the triple of the orders in S is in at least one of categories II, III, IV, VI', and VII.*

This clearly does not require the restrictions of the orders in $S$ on different triples to be in the same category. For example, with $X = \{x,y,z,w,t\}$ and

$$S = \{w(xt)yz,(zt)yxw,(xz)(ty)w,w(ty)(xz)\},$$

$\{y,z,w\}$ is in categories II, IV, and VII; $\{z,w,t\}$ is in categories II and VII; and each of the other eight triples is in one category: $\{x,y,w\}$, $\{x,z,w\}$, and $\{x,w,t\}$ are in II; $\{x,z,t\}$ is in III; $\{x,y,z\}$ is in IV; $\{x,y,t\}$, $\{y,z,t\}$, and $\{y,w,t\}$ are in VI'. According to the corollary, $P_D$ is transitive for every $D \in S \cup S^2 \cup S^3 \cup \cdots$.

Using the "Violation of trans." column of Table 10.2 and the observation that the sets in (11.3) do not require an $n > 3$ to obtain a $P_D$ that is not transitive, we have the following correspondent of Lemma 10.3 in section 10.3.

LEMMA 11.1. *If S does not guarantee transitivity on X then there is a $D \in S^n$ for some $n \leq 5$ for which $P_D$ on X is not transitive, and 5 is the smallest number that will serve this purpose.*

The simple proof of this is left to the reader.


## 11.2  INDIVIDUAL WEAK ORDERS

In this section we shall first note the effect on Theorems 10.2 and 11.1 when all orders in $S$ are presumed to be weak orders, in which case $S$ guarantees a suborder on $X$ if and only if $S$ guarantees transitivity on $X$ according to Theorem 10.1. We shall then characterize all $S$ that guarantee a weak order, as defined by Definition 10.1.

### INDIVIDUAL WEAK ORDERS AND TRANSITIVE STRICT MAJORITY

Suppose that every order in $S$ is a weak order. Then categories VI $(x \geqslant y \ \& \ (x > y \text{ or } x > z \text{ or } z > y))$ and VI' $(x \geqslant y, \text{ and } x > y \text{ if } \sim$ is not transitive on $\{x,y,z\})$ reduce to the same thing, namely $x \geqslant y$, which includes category I $(x \sim y)$, and category V $(x \geqslant y \ \& \ z \geqslant y)$ is included in category VII $(x > y \text{ or } z > y$ for every nonempty order on $\{x,y,z\})$. Thus the categories of Theorems 10.2 and 11.1 reduce to those specified in the following corollary.

COROLLARY 11.2. *A set $S$ of weak orders on a triple $\{x,y,z\}$ guarantees a suborder (or, equivalently, transitivity) on the triple if and only if $S$ is in at least one of categories* II, III, IV, VI', *and* VII.

### WEAK ORDERS THAT GUARANTEE A WEAK ORDER

Definition 10.1 stated that $S$ guarantees a weak order if and only if $P_D$ is a weak order for every $D \in \cup S^n$. Clearly, $S$ can guarantee a weak order only if all $> \ \in S$ are weak orders. Hence, we need only consider orders 1 through 12 of Table 10.1 for this case.

Similar to (11.1), $S$ guarantees a weak order on the triple $\{x,y,z\}$ if and only if every one of the following six expressions is violated for every $D \in \cup S^n$:

$$
\begin{aligned}
&(a \geq b \ \& \ c \geq d \ \& \ e > f) \qquad (b \geq a \ \& \ d \geq c \ \& \ f > e) \\
&(a \geq b \ \& \ c > d \ \& \ c \geq f) \qquad (b \geq a \ \& \ d > c \ \& \ f \geq e) \qquad (11.4) \\
&(a > b \ \& \ c \geq d \ \& \ e \geq f) \qquad (b > a \ \& \ d \geq c \ \& \ f \geq e).
\end{aligned}
$$

Each of these constitutes a violation of the transitivity of simple majority. For example, the first says that $x R_D y \ \& \ y R_D z \ \& \ z P_D x$, so that $R_D$ is not transitive. If all expressions in (11.4) fail for a given $D$ then $R_D$ is transitive and therefore $P_D$ is a weak order.

Of the categorical expressions used before, both those in III $(a + c + e = b + d + f)$ and IV $(a + e = d + f \ \& \ c + e = b + f)$ guarantee a violation of all of (11.4). Although it is not immediately obvious, I and V also guarantee violations of (11.4) under weak orders. For example, consider $a = b$ in category I. To ensure this, we must have $x \sim y$ for all orders in $S$, or $a = b = 0$. Now under weak orders and $x \sim y$, $x P_D z \Leftrightarrow y P_D z$, and $z P_D x \Leftrightarrow z P_D y$, which can be stated as $c > d \Leftrightarrow f > e$, and $d > c \Leftrightarrow e > f$, which are seen to violate all expressions in (11.4) when $a = b$. Of course, category I in this case is subsumed under category III (single indifference), so that I does not have to be listed explicitly.

**135**

Consider V, with representative $a \geq b$ & $d \geq c$, which is characterized by $x \geqslant y$ & $z \geqslant y$, requiring $b = c = 0$. If both $a > 0$ and $d > 0$ then $a > b$ and $d > c$, so that all expressions in (11.4) are violated. If $a = 0$ and $d > 0$ then, since each order in $S$ is presumed to be a weak order, $e > f = 0$, which is the same as saying that ($x \sim y$ for all $>$ and $z \geqslant y$ for all $>$ and $z > y$ for some $>$) $\Rightarrow$ ($z \geqslant x$ for all $>$ and $z > x$ for some $>$). It is easily seen that ($a = b = 0$, $d > c = 0$, $e > f = 0$) violates all expressions in (11.4). Similarly, if $a > 0$ and $d = 0$ then (11.4) is violated, and if $a = 0$ and $d = 0$ then $e = f = 0$ so that V reduces to the case where each order in $S$ is empty.

Under weak orders, a typical representative in category V, namely $a \geq b$ & $d \geq c$, admits the following nonempty weak orders from Table 10.1:

V. 2, 5, 8, 9, 12.    ($x \geqslant y$ & $z \geqslant y$).

Although none of the other categories (II, VI, VII) guarantees a violation of (11.4), a modification of VI under weak orders does violate (11.4). A typical representative of this modification is

VI*. $a \geq b$, and $d + f > c + e$ if $a > b$.

The only expressions in (11.4) that might hold for this are ($b \geq a$ & $d \geq c$ & $f > e$) and ($b \geq a$ & $d > c$ & $f \geq e$). However, to guarantee $a \geq b$ we need to have $b = 0$ (or $x \geqslant y$ for all orders) and hence $a = b = 0$ if $b \geq a$. Then under $a = b = 0$ and weak orders, $c > d \Leftrightarrow f > e$, and $d > c \Leftrightarrow e > f$ as before, so that the two remaining possibilities from (11.4) are contradicted. As can easily be verified, the weak orders admitted under the above representative of VI* and their characterization are

VI*. 2, 7, 8, 9, 12. ($x \geqslant y$, and $x > z > y$ if $>$ is linear).

This differs from the display for V above only in the second order listed (5 or 7).

We shall say that a set of orders on $\{x,y,z\}$ *is in category* VI* *if and only if there is a distinct pair* $u,v \in \{x,y,z\}$ *such that* $u \geqslant v$ *for all orders in the set and, with* $w$ *the other element in* $\{x,y,z\}$, $u > w > v$ *for every order that is linear on* $\{x,y,z\}$.

THEOREM 11.2. *A set $S$ of weak orders on a triple $\{x,y,z\}$ guarantees a weak order on the triple if and only if $S$ is in at least one of categories III, IV, V, and VI\*.*

*Proof.* It remains only to show that each SET of weak orders on $\{x,y,z\}$ that is in none of categories III, IV, V, and VI* does not guarantee a weak order on the triple. For future reference we list all minimal

SETS of weak orders that do not guarantee a weak order. All these can be obtained from the four for order 1 by permutations on $\{x,y,z\}$.

$$
\begin{array}{llllll}
\{1,4\} & \{2,3\} & \{3,6\} & \{4,5\} & \{5,7\} & \{6,7\} \\
\{1,5\} & \{2,6\} & \{3,8\} & \{4,9\} & \{5,10\} & \{6,12\} \\
\{1,8\} & \{2,10\} & \{3,9\} & \{4,12\} & & \\
\{1,11\} & \{2,11\} & & & &
\end{array}
\qquad (11.5)
$$

Since one of orders 1 through 6 must be in the SET to violate III (single indifference), we assume for definiteness that order 1 is in the SET. Taking complements of allowable orders for the cases of the other categories whose allowable orders include 1, we see that a violating SET with order 1 must include an order from each of the following lines.

L1.  2, 3, 4, 5, 7, 8, 11, 12      IV ($xyz$ or $(xz)y$ or duals)
L2.  2, 4, 5, 6, 8, 9, 11      V ($x \geqslant z\ \&\ y \geqslant z$)
L3.  3, 4, 5, 6, 8, 10, 11      V ($x \geqslant y\ \&\ x \geqslant z$)
L4.  2, 3, 4, 5, 6, 8, 11      VI* ($x \geqslant z\ \&\ x > y > z$ if linear).

If either 4, 5, 8, or 11 is in the SET then the first column of (11.5) applies to show that the SET does not guarantee a weak order. Henceforth delete 4, 5, 8, and 11. If $2 \in$ SET then L3 requires 3, 6, or 10, and $\{2,3\}$, $\{2,6\}$, and $\{2,10\}$ are in (11.5). Delete 2. If $3 \in$ SET then L2 requires 6 or 9, and $\{3,6\}$ and $\{3,9\}$ are in (11.5). Delete 3. If $6 \in$ SET then L1 requires 7 or 12, and $\{6,7\}$ and $\{6,12\}$ are in (11.5). Since the deletion of 6 exhausts L4, the proof is complete. ◆

It is easily seen that when $D = (j,k)$ for any set $\{j,k\}$ in (11.5), then $P_D$ is not a weak order. Hence we have the following correspondent of Lemmas 10.3 and 11.1.

LEMMA 11.2. *If $S$ does not guarantee a weak order on $X$ then there is a $D \in S^n$ for some $n \leq 2$ for which $P_D$ on $X$ is not a weak order, and 2 is the smallest number that will serve this purpose.*

## 11.3  ODD NUMBERS OF VOTERS

The notion of guarantees has been specialized in two ways that involve odd numbers of voters. The first of these specializations is identified by the following definition.

DEFINITION 11.1. *Let $S$ be a nonempty set of strict partial orders on a triple $\{x,y,z\}$. Then $S$ oddly guarantees*

   (1) a suborder
   (2) transitivity
   (3) a weak order

*if and only if, for every n > 0 and every D ∈ S<sup>n</sup> for which the number of nonempty components in D is odd,*

(1) $P_D$ *on* {x,y,z} *is a suborder*
(2) $P_D$ *on* {x,y,z} *is transitive*
(3) $P_D$ *on* {x,y,z} *is a weak order.*

The second specialization involves an odd number of voters with nonempty weak orders but, like Definition 11.1, it permits strict partial orders in S that are not also weak orders.

DEFINITION 11.2. *Let S be a nonempty set of strict partial orders on* {x,y,z} *that contains a nonempty weak order. Then S odd-guarantees*

(1) a suborder
(2) transitivity
(3) a weak order

*if and only if, for every n > 0 and D ∈ S<sup>n</sup> for which the number of nonempty weak order components is odd,*

(1) $P_D$ *on* {x,y,z} *is a suborder*
(2) $P_D$ *on* {x,y,z} *is transitive*
(3) $P_D$ *on* {x,y,z} *is a weak order.*

Note that odd-guarantee is defined only for the case where S contains a nonempty weak order in accord with the last part of the definition. If all orders in S are weak orders then, except for the case where S contains only the empty weak order, Definitions 11.1 and 11.2 are equivalent.

ODDLY GUARANTEES

We note first that the oddly guarantees notion does not affect the suborder or transitivity cases.

THEOREM 11.3. *Suppose that S is a nonempty set of strict partial orders on* {x,y,z}. *Then S oddly guarantees a suborder if and only if S guarantees a suborder; and S oddly guarantees transitivity if and only if S guarantees transitivity.*

*Proof.* The "if" assertions follow from the definitions. For the suborder "only if" part, suppose that S does not guarantee a suborder, with $D ∈ S^n$ and $xP_DyP_DzP_Dx$. Let $D' = (D,D,\succ)$ where $\succ \neq \emptyset$ and $\succ \in S$. Then $D'$ has an odd number of nonempty components and $P_{D'}$ is not a suborder. For the transitivity "only if" part, suppose that S does not guarantee transitivity, with $D ∈ S^n$ and $xP_DyP_DzR_Dx$. If $zP_Dx$ then the preceding proof applies. Assume henceforth that $zI_Dx$. Then, if $x \sim z$ for all orders in S, $P_{D'}$ is not transitive when $D'$ is defined as before; and if $x \sim z$ is false for some order in $S$ then we can define $D'$ as before with $> \neq \emptyset$, $> \in S$ and either $x \sim z$ or $z > x$, in which case $P_{D'}$ is not transitive. ◆

Naturally, the conclusion of Theorem 11.3 holds if all orders in $S$ are required to be weak orders.

In contrast to Theorem 11.3, the weak order guarantee case is affected by the odd condition of Definition 11.1, as is seen by comparing the categories in the following theorem to those (III, IV, V, VI*) of Theorem 11.2.

THEOREM 11.4. *A set $S$ of weak orders on a triple $\{x,y,z\}$ oddly guarantees a weak order if and only if $S$ is in at least one of categories* II, III, IV, VI', *and* VII.

*Proof.* Suppose first that $S$ is in none of categories II, III, IV, VI', and VII. Since these are the categories used in Corollary 11.2, $S$ does not guarantee a suborder. Then, by Theorem 11.3, $S$ does not oddly guarantee a suborder and hence cannot oddly guarantee a weak order.

In view of Corollary 11.2, the proof is complete if we can show that, if $S$ does not oddly guarantee a weak order, then $S$ does not guarantee transitivity. Hence suppose that $S$ does not oddly guarantee a weak order, with $D \subset S^n$ such that each component of $D$ is nonempty, $n$ is odd, and, to violate negative transitivity, $xP_D y$, $zR_D x$, and $yR_D z$. If either $R_D$ is $P_D$ then $S$ does not guarantee transitivity. Henceforth suppose $xP_D y$, $zI_D x$, and $yI_D z$. If $S$ contains an order for which $z > x$ & $y \geqslant z$ or $y > z$ & $z \geqslant x$, then $D' = (D,D,>)$ shows that $S$ does not guarantee transitivity. If there is no such order in $S$ then, for each component of $D$, $z > x \Rightarrow z > y$ and $y > z \Rightarrow x > z$, and therefore $z \geqslant x \Rightarrow z > y$. Now, since $n$ is odd, $zI_D x$ requires $x \sim z$ for at least one component in $D$, with the number of components with $x > z$ equal to the number with $z > x$. But then the number with $z \geqslant x$ exceeds the number with $x > z$ and hence, in view of $z \geqslant x \Rightarrow z > y$, we must have $zP_D y$, contrary to $yI_D z$. Hence when $xP_D y$, $zI_D x$ and $yI_D z$ hold, $z > x$ & $y \geqslant z$ or $y > z$ & $z \geqslant x$ for some order in $S$. ◆

ODD GUARANTEES

Two new specializations of categories V and VI, characterized by:

V°. $x \geqslant y$ & $z \geqslant y$, and $(x > y$ & $z > y$ if $\sim$ is transitive),
VI°. $x \geqslant y$ & $(x > y$ or $x > z$ or $z > y)$ & $(x > y$ if $\sim$ is transitive),

are needed for our main result for odd-guarantees. We shall say that a set $S$ of orders on $\{x,y,z\}$ *is in category* V° *if and only if there is an alternative in $\{x,y,z\}$, say $y$, such that either $x \geqslant y$ & $z \geqslant y$ & $(x > y$ & $z > y$ if $\sim$ is transitive) for all nonempty $>$ in $S$, or else $y \geqslant x$ & $y \geqslant z$*

& $(y > x$ & $y > z$ if $\sim$ is transitive) for all nonempty $>$ in $S$. A set $S$ of orders on $\{x,y,z\}$ is in category VI° if and only if there is a distinct pair $u,v \in \{x,y,z\}$ such that $u \geqslant v$ for all $>$ in $S$ and, with $w = \{x,y,z\} - \{u,v\}$, $(u > v$ or $u > w$ or $w > v)$ & $(u > v$ if $\sim$ is transitive) for every nonempty order in $S$.

THEOREM 11.5. *Suppose that $S$ is a set of strict partial orders on $\{x,y,z\}$ and $S$ contains a nonempty weak order. Then:*

a. *$S$ odd-guarantees a suborder if and only if $S$ guarantees a suborder;*
b. *$S$ odd-guarantees transitivity if and only if $S$ odd-guarantees a weak order, and $S$ odd-guarantees a weak order if and only if $S$ is in at least one of categories II, III, IV, V°, VI°, VI', and VII.*

*Proof.* We assume throughout that $S$ contains a nonempty weak order. Part (a) follows from the fact that if $S$ does not guarantee a suborder then a $D'$ with components in $S$ can be constructed to show that $S$ does not odd-guarantee a suborder.

To prove part (b) we note first that each of the categories in part (b) odd-guarantees a weak order when $S$ contains a nonempty weak order. This is immediate from Theorem 11.2 for categories III and IV, since these categories permit no strict partial orders that are not also weak orders. The other five categories are examined in the next five paragraphs. Since each of II, VI', and VII guarantees transitivity (Theorem 11.1), it is only necessary to show that $I_D$ is transitive for each of these when $D$ has an odd number of nonempty weak order components.

Category II. Using the representative for category II in Table 10.1, we have admissible orders 2, 3, 4, 5, 9, 10, 15, 16 with

$$xI_Dy \Leftrightarrow n_2 + n_5 + n_9 = n_3 + n_4 + n_{10}$$
$$yI_Dz \Leftrightarrow n_3 + n_4 + n_{10} = n_2 + n_5 + n_9.$$

Hence if either of these holds then $D$ must have an even number of nonempty weak order components, violating the odd hypothesis. It follows that $I_D$ must be transitive (trivially) when the odd hypothesis holds.

Category VI'. Using the representative of category VI' that precedes Theorem 11.1, orders 1, 2, 5, 7, 8, 9, 12, and 13 are allowed with

$$xI_Dy \Leftrightarrow n_1 + n_2 + n_5 + n_9 + n_{12} + n_{13} = 0$$
$$yI_Dz \Leftrightarrow n_1 + n_7 = n_2 + n_5 + n_8 + n_9$$
$$xI_Dz \Leftrightarrow n_5 + n_8 = n_1 + n_2 + n_7 + n_{12}.$$

Each of the transitivity hypotheses $uI_Dv$ & $vI_Dw$, with $\{u,v,w\} = \{x,y,z\}$, implies that the number of nonempty weak order components in $D$ is even.

140

Category VII. The representative for category VII in Table 10.1 allows the orders 1, 3, 4, 6, 7, 10, 11, 14, and 17 with

$$xI_Dy \Leftrightarrow n_1 = n_3 + n_4 + n_6 + n_{10} + n_{11} + n_{14}$$
$$yI_Dz \Leftrightarrow n_1 + n_3 + n_4 + n_7 + n_{10} + n_{17} = n_6$$
$$xI_Dz \Leftrightarrow n_4 + n_6 + n_{11} = n_1 + n_3 + n_7.$$

Once again each of the transitivity hypotheses violates the odd condition for the number of nonempty weak order components.

Category V°. The representative $x \geqslant y$ & $z \geqslant y$ and ($x > y$ & $z > y$ if $\sim$ is transitive) for category V° allows the nonempty orders 2, 5, 9, 13, 15, 16, and 18 from Table 10.1. Since one of 2, 5, and 9 must be in $D$ for the odd hypothesis, both $xP_Dy$ and $zP_Dy$ hold, from which it follows that $P_D$ and $I_D$ are transitive.

Category VI°. The representative $x \geqslant y$ & ($x > y$ or $x > z$ or $z > y$) & ($x > y$ if $\sim$ is transitive) for category VI° allows the nonempty orders 1, 2, 5, 9, 12, 13, 15, and 18 in $S$. The odd hypothesis requires at least one of 1, 2, 5, 9, and 12 in $D$, and therefore $xP_Dy$. Transitivity of $P_D$ is then violated if and only if ($yP_Dz$ & not $xP_Dz$) or ($zP_Dx$ & not $zP_Dy$). With

$$yP_Dz \Leftrightarrow n_1 > n_2 + n_5 + n_9 + n_{18}$$
$$zP_Dx \Leftrightarrow n_5 > n_1 + n_2 + n_{12} + n_{15},$$

either of the ways to violate transitivity of $P_D$ gives $0 > 2n_2 + n_9 + n_{12} + n_{15} + n_{18}$, which is impossible. The only way to violate transitivity of $I_D$ is to have $xI_Dz$ & $zI_Dy$, in which case $0 = 2n_1 + n_9 + n_{12} + n_{15} + n_{18}$, or $n_2 = n_9 = n_{12} = n_{15} = n_{18} = 0$. But then $yI_Dz$ requires $n_1 = n_5$, which gives an even number of nonempty weak order components in $D$.

Thus if $S$ is in at least one of categories II, III, IV, V°, VI°, VI′, and VII, then $S$ odd-guarantees a weak order. It follows from this and from Theorem 11.1 that

$S$ guarantees transitivity or $S$ is in category V° or VI° $\Rightarrow$ $S$ odd-guarantees a weak order $\Rightarrow$ $S$ odd-guarantees transitivity.

To complete the proof of Theorem 11.5(b), we shall prove that if $S$ does not guarantee transitivity and is not in category V° or VI° then $S$ does not odd-guarantee transitivity.

Begin by assuming that $S$ does not guarantee transitivity. For definiteness, suppose there is a $D \in S^n$ such that

$$xP_Dz, \quad zP_Dy \quad \text{and} \quad yR_Dx. \tag{11.6}$$

If $y > x$ for some order in $S$ then $D' = (D, D, >)$ shows that $S$ does not guarantee a suborder and hence, by Theorem 11.5(a), that $S$ does not odd-guarantee a suborder, so that $S$ does not odd-guarantee transitivity. Hence, given (11.6), $S$ does not odd-guarantee transitivity when $y > x$ for some $>$ in $S$.

Thus, we need only consider further the case where (11.6) holds and $x \geqslant y$ for all $>$ in $S$, which gives

$$x \geqslant y \text{ for all } > \text{ in } S, xP_Dz, zP_Dy \text{ and } xI_Dy.$$

Suppose $x \sim y$ for some nonempty weak order in $S$. Then $D' = (D,D,>)$ shows that $S$ does not odd-guarantee transitivity. Hence we need only consider further the case where

$$x \geqslant y \text{ for all } > \text{ in } S, x > y \text{ every nonempty weak order in } S,$$
$$xP_Dz, zP_Dy \text{ and } xI_Dy.$$

These conditions allow the following ten nonempty orders.

| | |
|---|---|
| 1. $xyz$ | 13. $z \sim x > y \sim z$ |
| 2. $xzy$ | 15. $y \sim x > z \sim y$ |
| 5. $zxy$ | 16. $y \sim z > x \sim y$ |
| 9. $(xz)y$ | 17. $x \sim y > z \sim x$ |
| 12. $x(yz)$ | 18. $x \sim z > y \sim x$. |

Now suppose that $S$ is in neither of categories V° and VI°. Then $S$ must contain 16 or 17 to violate VI°, it must contain 1 or 12 or 17 to violate V° in the form $[x \geqslant y \& z \geqslant y$ and $(x > y \& z > y$ if $\sim$ is transitive$)]$, and it must contain 5 or 9 or 16 to violate V° in the form $[x \geqslant y \& x \geqslant z \& (x > y \& x > z$ if $\sim$ is transitive$)]$.

Suppose first that both 16 and 17 are in $S$. Then, since one of 1, 2, 5, 9, and 12 must be in $S$ (a nonempty weak order), $D =$ (one of 1, 2, 5, 9 and 12; 16, 16, 17, 17) gives $xPy$, $yPz$, and $zPx$, so that $S$ does not odd-guarantee transitivity.

Suppose next that 16 is in $S$. Then, for V° to fail, one of 1 and 12 must be in $S$ if 17 is not. But $D = (1,16,16)$ and $D = (12,16,16)$ give $xPy \& yPz \& zPx$ and $xPy \& yIz \& zPx$, respectively, and in neither case is $P$ transitive. Similar results obtain if 17 is in $S$ and either 5 or 9 is in $S$.

Hence if $S$ does not guarantee transitivity and is in neither category V° nor VI°, then $S$ does not odd-guarantee transitivity. ◆

## WEAK ORDERS

Our final theorem summarizes the odd-guarantee aspects when every order in $S$ is a weak order.

142

THEOREM 11.6. *Suppose that S is a set of weak orders on $\{x,y,z\}$ and S contains a nonempty order. Then the following four statements are equivalent:*

a. *S guarantees a suborder,*
b. *S odd-guarantees a suborder,*
c. *S odd-guarantees transitivity,*
d. *S odd-guarantees a weak order.*

*Proof.* Immediate from Definitions 11.1, 11.2, and Theorems 11.3 and 11.4. ◆

## 11.4 SUMMARY

The main theorems for guarantees on a triple $\{x,y,z\}$ are summarized in Table 11.1. In all the cases considered, only four distinctly different sets of categories have been used. The appropriate theorem (T) or corollary (C) from the text is noted in the "Text" column.

TABLE 11.1

A SET OF ORDERS GIVES THE RESULT IF AND ONLY IF THE SET IS IN ONE OF THE CATEGORIES. FOR THE ODD-GUARANTEE CASES THE SET IS PRESUMED TO CONTAIN A NONEMPTY WEAK ORDER

| RESULT ON A TRIPLE $\{x,y,z\}$ | TEXT | CATEGORIES |
|---|---|---|
| Guarantees a Suborder | T 10.2 | |
| Oddly Guarantees a Suborder | T 11.3 | I, II, III, IV, V, VI, VII |
| Odd-Guarantees a Suborder | T 11.5 | |
| Guarantees Transitivity | T 11.1 | |
| Oddly Guarantees Transitivity | T 11.3 | |
| When all orders are weak orders: | | |
|   Guarantees a Suborder | C 11.2 | |
|   Guarantees Transitivity | C 11.2 | |
|   Oddly Guarantees a Suborder | T 11.3 | II, III, IV, VI', VII |
|   Oddly Guarantees Transitivity | T 11.3 | |
|   Oddly Guarantees a Weak Order | T 11.4 | |
|   Odd-Guarantees a Suborder | T 11.6 | |
|   Odd-Guarantees Transitivity | T 11.6 | |
|   Odd-Guarantees a Weak Order | T 11.6 | |
| Guarantees a Weak Order (with all orders weak orders) | T 11.2 | III, IV, V, VI* |
| Odd-Guarantees Transitivity | | |
| Odd-Guarantees a Weak Order | T 11.5 | II, III, IV, V°, VI°, VI', VII |

  I. $x \sim y$

 II. $(y > x \,\& \, y > z)$ or $(x > y \,\& \, z > y)$ or $(x \sim y \,\& \, y \sim z)$

III. $(x \sim y) > z$ or $z > (x \sim y)$ or $(x \sim z) > y$ or $y > (x \sim z)$ or $(y \sim z) >$ $x$ or $x > (y \sim z)$

 IV. $x > y > z$ or $z > y > x$ or $(x \sim z) > y$ or $y > (x \sim z)$

  V. $x \geqslant y \,\& \, z \geqslant y$

V°. $x \geqslant y \,\& \, z \geqslant y$ and $(x > y \,\& \, z > y$ if $\sim$ is transitive)

 VI. $x \geqslant y \,\& \, (x > y$ or $x > z$ or $z > y)$

VI°. $x \geqslant y \,\& \, (x > y$ or $x > z$ or $z > y) \,\& \, (x > y$ if $\sim$ is transitive)

VI′. $x \geqslant y \,\& \, (x > y$ if $\sim$ is not transitive)

VI*. $x \geqslant y \,\& \, (x > z > y$ if $>$ is linear)

VII. $y > x$ or $y > z$

Representatives of the categories are given in the lower part of the table. All other characterizations for the categories can be obtained by permutations on $\{x,y,z\}$ and, in the cases of V through VII, by taking the duals of the displayed expressions. Thus $(x \sim z$ for all orders) falls in category I, and $(x > z$ or $y > z$ for each nonempty order) is in category VII.

# CHAPTER 12

# Condorcet Conditions

THUS FAR in Part II we have concentrated on conditions for $D$ which imply that some alternative in finite $Y$ has a simple majority over every other alternative in $Y$. In this chapter we shall maintain the focus on nonempty $R(Y,D)$ as defined by (8.8), but instead of worrying about $D$ that give $R(Y,D) \neq \emptyset$ we shall examine the position that says that an element in $R(Y,D)$ should be the social choice when this subset of $Y$ is not empty. We shall not argue that this is an untenable position, nor shall we conclude that it is the only sensible position. Our purpose rather is to point out some of the aspects of the case that show why the question of whether an $x \in R(Y,D)$ should be the social choice when $R(Y,D)$ is not empty is by no means an idle question.

The next chapter, which concludes Part II, is a natural continuation of the present chapter. In it we shall examine a number of social choice functions that agree with simple majority (Definition 8.1), including some that give $F(Y,D) = P(Y,D)$ when $P(Y,D) \neq \emptyset$ and some that do not.

The material in both chapters foreshadows a number of topics that will be covered in more general form in Part III.

## 12.1 THE CONDORCET CONDITIONS

In the preceding chapters we have seen that if $X$ is finite and if $\mathfrak{D}$ is restricted in certain ways then a social choice function $F: \mathfrak{X} \times \mathfrak{D} \to \mathfrak{X}$ can be fully defined by $F(Y,D) = R(Y,D)$ for all $(Y,D) \in \mathfrak{X} \times \mathfrak{D}$. We shall now examine the more general situation in which there may be $D$ for which $R(Y,D) = \emptyset$. *Unless stated otherwise, we shall assume that $n \geq 2$, that $X$ is finite and has more than two alternatives, and that $\mathfrak{D}$ is the set of all n-tuples of strict partial orders on $X$.*

A major fascination of some social choice theorists has been the question of how $F(Y,D)$ ought to be defined when $R(Y,D) = \emptyset$. Although we shall not propose a definitive answer this interesting and perhaps perplexing question, it will be examined at length in the next chapter.

First, however, we shall begin with a more basic question: If one of the feasible alternatives has a simple majority (perhaps strict) over each of the others, should such an alternative be the social choice? An even more basic question relates to the appropriateness of simple majority when only two feasible alternatives are involved, but this will not be at issue here. Our frame of reference in the succeeding discussion will be the types of situations in which simple majority seems reasonable for binary social choices.

## THREE CONDORCET CONDITIONS

Because Condorcet (1785) was a strong proponent of the position that an alternative with a strict simple majority over each other alternative should be the social choice, his name is frequently linked with this position. Our purpose in this section will be to examine three versions of the "Condorcet criterion."

DEFINITION 12.1. *A social choice function* $F: \mathfrak{X} \times \mathfrak{D} \to \mathfrak{X}$ *satisfies the*

(1) weak Condorcet condition
(2) Condorcet condition
(3) strong Condorcet condition

*if and only if, for all* $(Y,D) \in \mathfrak{X} \times \mathfrak{D}$,

(1) $F(Y,D) = P(Y,D)$ *whenever* $P(Y,D) \neq \emptyset$
(2) $F(Y,D) \subseteq R(Y,D)$ *whenever* $R(Y,D) \neq \emptyset$
(3) $F(Y,D) = R(Y,D)$ *whenever* $R(Y,D) \neq \emptyset$.

Thus, $F$ is *weakly* Condorcet when it specifies the social choice as the unique alternative that has a strict simple majority over the other feasible alternatives whenever such an alternative exists. If $P(Y,D) = \emptyset$ and $R(Y,D) \neq \emptyset$, then a weak Condorcet function does not necessarily include any $x \in R(Y,D)$ in $F(Y,D)$, but this is required if $F$ satisfies the Condorcet condition (2). Moreover, when there is an alternative that has a simple majority over each other feasible alternative then (2) does not permit $F(Y,D)$ to contain an alternative that is defeated under simple majority by another feasible alternative. The strong Condorcet condition requires $F(Y,D)$ to contain all alternatives in $R(Y,D)$ and no others when $R(Y,D)$ is not empty. In keeping with our previous usage of "weak" and "strong," a strong Condorcet function is a Condorcet function, and a Condorcet function is a weak Condorcet function.

In passing, we note another condition that is similar to those in the definition. It is: $F(Y,D) \cap R(Y,D) \neq \emptyset$ whenever $R(Y,D) \neq \emptyset$. This is implied by (2) and (3), but it neither implies nor is implied by (1).

## THE WEAK CONDORCET CONDITION

To illustrate some aspects of the weak Condorcet condition, and therefore of (2) and (3) as well, consider the case where $X = \{x,y,a,b,c\}$

and $n = 5$ and each individual preference order is linear. We imagine two situations as follows:

Situation 1: $D$ obtains and $P_D$ is a linear order with $x P_D y P_D a P_D b$ $P_D c$.

Situation 2: $D'$ obtains and, in $D'$, $x$ has two first-place votes, one second-place vote, one fourth, and one fifth; $y$ has two first-place votes, two second-place votes, and one third.

Given only the simple-majority information about $D$ in situation 1, it seems quite reasonable to take $F(X,D) = \{x\}$. And given only the positional information of situation 2, it seems reasonable to take $F(X,D') = \{y\}$. (In situation 2, the best positional array for a third alternative would be one first-place vote, two seconds, and two thirds. Compare this to the positional array for $y$.)

The interesting fact about situations 1 and 2 is that they may be one and the same situation with $D = D'$ as follows:

1. $x\ y\ a\ b\ c$
2. $y\ a\ c\ b\ x$
3. $c\ x\ y\ a\ b$ $\hspace{4cm}$ (12.1)
4. $x\ y\ b\ c\ a$
5. $y\ b\ a\ x\ c$.

Although this might raise a question in some minds about the universal acceptability of the weak Condorcet condition, Condorcet used a similar example, reproduced by Black (1958, pp. 176–177), to argue against a positional approach. Specifically, Condorcet wished to demonstrate a deficiency in the "method of marks," set forth several years earlier by Borda (1781) in a paper that has been translated and commented on by de Grazia (1953). Under linear orders for the individuals, Borda essentially proposed that, with $m$ alternatives, the highest-ranked (most preferred) alternative in each order be assigned a mark of $m - 1$, the next highest a mark of $m - 2$, and so on down to the least preferred, which is assigned a mark of 0. The marks obtained by each alternative are then added over the voters, and the alternative with the largest total is declared the winner.

In (12.1), the total marks for $x$, $y$, $a$, $b$, $c$, are 12, 16, 8, 7, 7, respectively, so that $y$ wins under this method. Furthermore, as Condorcet observed for his example, if instead of $m - 1 > m - 2 \cdots > 1 > 0$ for the marks from best to worst we use numbers $a_1, \ldots, a_m$ that satisfy $a_1 > a_2 > \cdots > a_m$, then $y$ will still beat $x$ under a simple summation procedure. For $y$'s total score will then be $2a_1 + 2a_2 + a_3$,

147

and $x$'s total score will be $2a_1 + a_2 + a_4 + a_5$, and $2a_1 + 2a_2 + a_3 > 2a_1 + a_2 + a_4 + a_5$ when $a_1 > a_2 > a_3 > a_4 > a_5$.

Because Condorcet took simple majority as the norm (when it applies), he "proved" by his example that Borda's procedure, or any simple modification of it as indicated in the preceding paragraph, can lead to a "wrong" result.

The point at issue here, as suggested by the descriptions of situations 1 and 2 above, is the kind of information in $D$ that is to be taken into account in determining the social choice. The weak Condorcet condition is essentially based on binary comparisons within each order. If in the comparison between $x$ and $y$, $x > y$ in some order, then only this fact and not the number of other feasible alternatives that are ranked between $x$ and $y$ is taken into account. In a positional procedure, on the other hand, the crucial information is the positions of $x$ and $y$ in each order, not just whether $x > y$ or $y > x$.

A REDUCTION CONDITION AND INDEPENDENCE

To further illustrate a difference between these two viewpoints, we state a condition that is somewhat weaker than one suggested by Condorcet. Arrow (1963, p. 27) also mentions the following condition informally. It is not used in his analysis.

DEFINITION 12.2. *A social choice function $F: \mathfrak{X} \times \mathfrak{D} \to \mathfrak{X}$ satisfies the* reduction condition *if and only if, for all $(Y,D) \in \mathfrak{X} \times \mathfrak{D}$,*

$$F(Y,D) = F(Y - \{y\},D) \text{ whenever } y \in Y \text{ and } x \gg_D y$$
$$\text{for some } x \in Y.$$

Suppose that $x,y \in Y$ and $x \gg_D y$, so that $x >_i y$ for all $i$. Then the reduction condition says that $y$ is not in $F(Y,D)$. However, this is not new since unanimity (Definition 7.2) already covers it. The reduction condition goes beyond unanimity by requiring the choice set from $Y$ under $D$ to be precisely the same as the choice set from $Y - \{y\}$ under $D$.

The force of the reduction condition comes into play when it is used along with the condition of independence from infeasible alternatives, which we have discussed in Chapter 1 and section 7.1. For present and future reference we shall give a formal definition of this condition.

DEFINITION 12.3. *A social choice function $F: \mathfrak{X} \times \mathfrak{D} \to \mathfrak{X}$ satisfies the* condition of independence from infeasible alternatives *if and only if, for all $(Y,D) \in \mathfrak{X} \times \mathfrak{D}$,*

$$F(Y,D) = F(Y,D') \text{ whenever the restriction of } >_i \text{ on } Y$$
$$\text{equals the restriction of } >'_i \text{ on } Y$$
$$\text{for each } i \in \{1, \ldots ,n\}.$$

This is Arrow's Condition 3 (1963, p. 27), which he refers to as "the independence of irrelevant alternatives." As noted before, this says that the social choice shall in no way depend on preferences that involve infeasible or unavailable alternatives.

Now under the condition of independence from infeasible alternatives, the reduction condition says that we must completely ignore $y$ and the individual preferences that involve $y$ when making a choice from $Y$, provided that $x \gg_D y$ for some $x \in Y$. Thus, when both conditions are used, a feasible but dominated ($\gg_D$) alternative receives the same treatment as infeasible or unavailable alternatives.

Since $P(Y,D) = P(Y - \{y\},D)$ whenever $y \in Y$ and $x \gg_D y$ for some $x \in Y$, the reduction condition is wholly compatible with the weak Condorcet condition. This does not say that every $F$ that satisfies the weak Condorcet condition also satisfies the reduction condition, for the weak Condorcet condition says nothing about the behavior of $F$ when $P(Y,D) = \emptyset$. It does say, however, that, for any $X$ and $n$, there are $F$'s that satisfy both conditions. For example, any $F$ that satisfies unanimity, the weak Condorcet condition, and has $F(Y,D)$ as a unit subset of $Y$ for all cases, also satisfies the reduction condition.

On the other hand, the Borda method of marks does not satisfy the reduction condition. For (12.1), this method gives $F(\{x,y,a,b,c\},D) = \{y\}$. However, $y \gg_D a$ and $y \gg_D b$ in (12.1) and therefore, under the reduction condition we get $F(\{x,y,a,b,c\},D) = F(\{x,y,c\},D)$. But if only $x$, $y$ and $c$ are treated as feasible, then (12.1) reduces to

1. $x$ $y$ $c$
2. $y$ $c$ $x$
3. $c$ $x$ $y$
4. $x$ $y$ $c$
5. $y$ $x$ $c$

in which case the method of marks gives $F(\{x,y,c\},D) = \{x,y\}$. In this reduced case each of $x$ and $y$ has two first-place votes, two seconds, and one third.

In order not to convey a wrong impression here, it should also be pointed out that the Pareto dominance in (12.1) is not essential for the kind of oddity expressed by situations 1 and 2. For example, if the third individual order is changed from $cxyab$ to $cxaby$ then strict simple majority is still linear ($xyabc$), no alternative is dominated ($\gg_D$) by another, and

$x$ has two first-place votes, one 2nd, one 4th, one 5th;
$y$ has two first-place votes, two 2nd's and one 5th.

A further illustration of the Condorcet versus positional approach is provided by an example used by C. L. Dodgson (Lewis Carroll), which is made available by Black (1958) in his reprintings of several of Dodgson's pamphlets on election procedures. This example is interesting in that it brings out a position of a serious student of election procedures who later changed his mind. The example, which is on page 216 in Black's book, has $\#X = 4$ and $n = 11$ with $D$ as follows:

| | | |
|---|---|---|
| 3 voters: | $b\ a\ c\ d$ | 6 have $b$ first and |
| 3 voters: | $b\ a\ d\ c$ | 5 have $b$ last; |
| 3 voters: | $a\ c\ d\ b$ | 5 have $a$ first and |
| 2 voters: | $a\ d\ c\ b$. | 6 have $a$ second. |

Dodgson used this to argue against the single-vote plurality method when one candidate ($b$ here) has an absolute majority (since 6 of 11 have $b$ first). Noting the positions of $a$ and $b$ in the orders, Dodgson concludes that "There seems to be no doubt that $a$ ought to be elected; and yet, by the above Method, $b$ would win." He did not explicitly mention that $a \gg_D c$ and $a \gg_D d$, which of course brings the reduction condition into play, but this dominance is somewhat beside the point as far as his position is concerned.

In later writings [see pp. 222–234 in Black (1958)] Dodgson rejects his former position and becomes an advocate of the weak Condorcet condition which, in the above example, would make $b$ the winner.

In concluding this section we present a theorem suggested by Bengt Hansson and Peter Gärdenfors which shows that the weak Condorcet condition is incompatible with another condition that we shall call the strong independence condition.

DEFINITION 12.4. *A social choice function* $F\colon \mathfrak{X} \times \mathfrak{D} \to \mathfrak{X}$ *satisfies the* strong independence condition *if and only if, for all* $(Y,D) \in \mathfrak{X} \times \mathfrak{D}$,

$$x \in F(Y,D) \Rightarrow x \in F(Y,D') \qquad \begin{array}{l} \textit{whenever } x >_i y \Leftrightarrow x >'_i y \\ \textit{and } y >_i x \Leftrightarrow y >'_i x \textit{ for} \\ \textit{all } y \in Y - \{x\}. \end{array}$$

This condition implies the condition of independence from infeasible alternatives, for if the restriction of $D$ on $Y$ equals the restriction of $D'$ on $Y$ then the "whenever" conditional of strong independence holds for all $x \in Y$ and therefore $F(Y,D) \subseteq F(Y,D')$ and $F(Y,D') \subseteq F(Y,D)$.

To illustrate the incompatibility of strong independence with Borda's method and to simultaneously point out a potential weakness in the strong independence condition, I have chosen the following example with $n = 4$ and $X = \{x,y,z,w\}$:

|        D        |       D'        |
|-----------------|-----------------|
| 1. $z$ $y$ $w$ $x$ | 1. $z$ $y$ $w$ $x$ |
| 2. $y$ $z$ $x$ $w$ | 2. $z$ $y$ $x$ $w$ |
| 3. $x$ $w$ $z$ $y$ | 3. $x$ $z$ $w$ $y$ |
| 4. $x$ $w$ $y$ $z$ | 4. $x$ $w$ $y$ $z$ |

Suppose Borda's method is used with *any* set of marks $a_1 > a_2 > a_3 > a_4$ for the most preferred through least preferred alternative for each voter. Then $F(X,D) = \{x\}$ and $F(X,D') = \{z\}$. This violates strong independence since, in going from $D$ to $D'$, no change has been made in the preferences of $x$ relative to each other alternative, and $x \in F(X,D)$ but $x \notin F(X,D')$. The example has been structured so that the reduction condition plays no part ($u \gg_D v$ or $u \gg_{D'} v$ never holds). Moreover, the unique choices made by any Borda method ($a_1 > a_2 > a_3 > a_4$) seem rather reasonable in view of the structures of $D$ and $D'$.

That strong independence is incompatible also with the weak Condorcet condition is brought out by the following theorem of Hansson and Gärdenfors.

THEOREM 12.1. *Suppose that $n \geq 3$, $\#X \geq 3$ and $\mathfrak{D}$ includes all n-tuples of weak orders on $X$. Then there is no social choice function $F: \mathfrak{X} \times \mathfrak{D} \to \mathfrak{X}$ that satisfies both the weak Condorcet condition and the strong independence condition.*

*Proof.* Contrary to the theorem, suppose that $n \geq 3$, $\#X \geq 3$, and both the weak Condorcet condition and the strong independence condition hold. Since the latter implies independence from infeasible alternatives, it will suffice to work with an arbitrary triple $Y = \{x,y,z\}$ in $X$. In addition, we shall work with three voters since if $n > 3$, all but three voters can be assigned the empty preference order throughout the proof.

We begin with the familiar cyclic majority profile $D = (xyz,zxy,yzx)$. Suppose first that $x \in F(Y,D)$. Then, with $D' = (xyz,zxy,zyx)$, strong independence requires $x \in F(Y,D')$. But this conflicts with weak Condorcet, which requires $F(Y,D') = \{z\}$. Therefore $x \notin F(Y,D)$. By the symmetry of $D$, a similar result obtains if we suppose either $y \in F(Y,D)$ or $z \in F(Y,D)$. Hence $F(Y,D) = \emptyset$, which contradicts the definition of a social choice function. ◆

A variation of this proof shows that if $F$ satisfies the reduction condition and strong independence then with $(n = 3, \#X \geq 3)$ it cannot agree with simple majority. For with $D = (xyz,zxy,yzx)$, $x \in F(Y,D)$ and the strong independence condition imply that $x \in F(Y,(xzy,zxy,zyx))$. The reduction condition and independence then give $x \in F(\{x,z\},(xz,zx,zx))$, which does not agree with simple majority. A similar conclusion holds if we begin with $y \in F(Y,D)$ or $z \in F(Y,D)$.

Several other versions of the independence condition are discussed by Hansson (1972) and Blau (1971).

## 12.2 THE STRONG CONDORCET CONDITION

With $Y(\gg_D) = \{x : x \in Y \text{ and } y \gg_D x \text{ for no } y \in Y\}$, we know from Theorem 8.5 that $R(Y,D) = R(Y(\gg_D),D)$. Therefore the reduction condition of the preceding section is compatible with the Condorcet and strong Condorcet conditions as well as with the weak Condorcet condition. However, there are other conditions that are compatible with the weak Condorcet condition but incompatible with the strong condition. We shall comment on several of these in the rest of this chapter, both for the purpose of illustrating some differences between the weak and strong conditions, and to indicate that there may be reasons for rejecting the strong condition even when the weak condition is judged to be acceptable.

One simple condition that is compatible with the weak Condorcet condition but not the Condorcet or strong Condorcet condition is (with $x \geq_D y \Leftrightarrow x \succcurlyeq_i y$ for all $i$):

$$\text{if } x \geq_D y, \ x \in Y \text{ and } y \in F(Y,D), \text{ then } x \in F(Y,D). \quad (12.2)$$

If $P(Y,D) = \{y\}$ then $x \geq_D y$ for no $x \neq y$, and therefore this condition is consistent with weak Condorcet. However, with $X = \{x,y,z\}$ and $D = (\{(z,x)\},\{(y,z)\})$, we get $x \geq_D y$ and $R(Y,D) = \{y\}$, which shows that (12.2) is incompatible with the Condorcet condition. As in some of our earlier examples, intransitive indifference is vital to this conclusion. If we restrict $\mathfrak{D}$ to be a set of $n$-tuples of weak orders on $X$, it then follows from Lemma 8.1 that (12.2) is compatible with the strong Condorcet condition.

### PAIRED DOMINANCE

We shall now consider a condition that can fail only when $F(Y,D)$ contains more than one alternative for some $(Y,D)$, and which therefore is easily seen to be compatible with the Condorcet condition as well as the weak Condorcet and reduction conditions. This new condition is designed along the lines of (12.2), but it does not use $\geq_D$ or $>_D$

directly. Instead, it uses a kind of paired dominance relation $\succ_D$ that is a binary relation on $X \times X$:

$(x,x^*) \succ_D (y,y^*) \Leftrightarrow x, x^*, y$ and $y^*$ are all different and, for each $\succ$
in $D$, either $(x \succ y \ \& \ x^* \succcurlyeq y^*)$
or $(x \succcurlyeq y \ \& \ x^* \succ y^*)$ or $(x \succ y^* \ \& \ x^* \succcurlyeq y)$
or $(x \succcurlyeq y^* \ \& \ x^* \succ y)$.

Thus $(x,x^*) \succ_D (y,y^*)$ if and only if all four alternatives are different and each individual prefers one of $x,x^*$ to one of $y,y^*$, and does not prefer the other one of $y,y^*$ to the other one of $x,x^*$.

The condition that we shall use with $\succ_D$ is:

$$\text{if } (x,x^*) \succ_D (y,y^*), \text{ if } x,x^* \in Y \text{ and if} \atop y,y^* \in F(Y,D), \text{ then } x \text{ or } x^* \text{ is in } F(Y,D). \tag{12.3}$$

This condition prohibits the possibility that neither $x$ nor $x^*$ is in the choice set when both $y$ and $y^*$ are in the choice set and $(x,x^*) \succ_D (y,y^*)$, and it may thus seem like a fairly reasonable condition.

If $\mathfrak{D}$ is confined to $n$-tuples of weak orders then (12.3) is compatible with strong Condorcet since $(x,x^*) \succ_D (y,y^*) \Rightarrow xP_Dy$ or $xP_Dy^*$ or $x^*P_Dy$ or $x^*P_Dy^*$, so that we cannot have both $y$ and $y^*$ in $R(Y,D)$ when $(x,x^*) \succ_D (y,y^*)$ and $x,x^* \in Y$.

Therefore, as with (12.2), an example which shows the incompatibility of (12.3) and strong Condorcet requires a $D$ that exhibits intransitive indifference. One such $D$ with $X = \{x,x^*,y,y^*,z\}$ and $n = 4$ is given by the following four strict partial orders on $X$:

1. $y^* \succ x \succ y$     and     $z \succ x^*$
2. $y^* \succ x^* \succ y$     and     $y^* \succ z$
3. $y \succ x \succ y^*$     and     $y \succ z$
4. $y \succ x^* \succ y^*$     and     $z \succ x$.

Alternatives $y$ and $y^*$ tie or beat each other alternative on the basis of simple majority, and each of $x$, $x^*$, and $z$ is beaten by another alternative. Therefore $R(X,D) = \{y,y^*\}$. Moreover, $(x,x^*) \succ_D (y,y^*)$. Therefore, if the strong Condorcet condition holds then (12.3) must fail.

An interesting aspect of this example is that, although $(x,x^*) \succ_D (y,y^*)$, it is true also that $(y,y^*) \succ_D (x,x^*)$. Therefore $\succ_D$ is not asymmetric for the given $X$. This raises several questions that we leave as exercises for the reader: 1. Is $\succ_D$ asymmetric when $\mathfrak{D}$ is a set of $n$-tuples of weak orders? 2. Is it possible to construct an example in which $(x,x^*) \succ_D (y,y^*)$, $y,y^* \in R(Y,D)$, $x,x^* \in Y$ and neither $x$ nor $x^*$ is in $R(Y,D)$, and it is false that $(y,y^*) \succ_D (x,x^*)$?

## PAIRED DOMINANCE WITH WEAK ORDERS

In concluding this section we shall show that a strong version of (12.3) conflicts with the strong Condorcet condition when $\mathcal{D}$ is assumed to be the set of all $n$-tuples of weak orders on $X$. Let

$$(x,x^*) \geqslant_D (y,y^*) \leftrightarrow x, x^*, y \text{ and } y^* \text{ are all different}$$
$$\text{and, for each} > \text{in } D, \text{ either}$$
$$(x \geqslant y \ \& \ x^* \geqslant y^*) \text{ or } (x \geqslant y^* \ \& \ x^* \geqslant y).$$

Our strong version of (12.3) is:

$$\text{if } (x,x^*) \geqslant_D (y,y^*), \text{ if } x,x^* \in Y \text{ and if } y,y^* \in F(Y,D), \text{ then}$$
$$x \text{ or } x^* \text{ is in } F(Y,D). \quad (12.4)$$

Under weak orders, $(x \geqslant y \ \& \ x^* \geqslant y^*)$ implies that $x^* > y$ when $y^* > x$ and that $x > y^*$ when $y > x^*$. It follows that $(x,x^*) \geqslant_D (y,y^*) \Rightarrow xR_Dy$ or $xR_Dy^*$ or $x^*R_Dy$ or $x^*R_Dy^*$ when every $>$ in $D$ is a weak order. Moreover, if there is a strict relation $>$ in any of the individual statements that yield $(x,x^*) \geqslant_D (y,y^*)$, then $xP_Dy$ or $xP_Dy^*$ or $x^*P_Dy$ or $x^*P_Dy^*$. Therefore, to obtain an example where $(x,x^*) \geqslant_D (y,y^*)$, $y,y^* \in R(Y,D)$ and neither $x$ nor $x^*$ is in $R(Y,D)$, we require $(x \sim y \ \& \ x^* \sim y^*)$ or $(x \sim y^* \ \& \ x^* \sim y)$ for each weak order in $D$. With $X = \{x,x^*,y,y^*,z,w\}$ and $n = 4$, the following case satisfies this requirement.

1. $(xy)z(x^*y^*w)$
2. $(x^*yz)w(xy^*)$
3. $(xy^*w)z(x^*y)$
4. $(x^*y^*)w(xyz)$.

Recall that the notation here means that $>_1$ is a weak order with $x \sim_1 y >_1 z >_1 x^* \sim_1 y^* \sim_1 w$. An examination of the given $D$ shows that $R(X,D) = \{y,y^*\}$ and that $(x,x^*) \geqslant_D (y,y^*)$. Therefore (12.4) must fail if the strong Condorcet condition holds.

We shall go one step further in this case and prove that this example is the smallest example that shows the incompatibility of (12.4) and strong Condorcet under weak orders.

THEOREM 12.2. *Let $\mathcal{D}$ be the set of all $n$-tuples of weak orders on $X$. There is a social choice function $F: \mathcal{X} \times \mathcal{D} \to \mathcal{X}$ that satisfies both the strong Condorcet condition and (12.4) if and only if either $\#X < 6$ or $n < 4$.*

*Proof.* With both $\#X \geq 6$ and $n \geq 4$, the preceding example shows that we can construct a $D$ with weak orders such that there is no social choice function that satisfies both (12.4) and the strong Condorcet condition. We now show that such an example exists only if both $\#X \geq 6$ and $n \geq 4$.

To contradict the combination of (12.4) and the strong Condorcet condition we require distinct $x,x^*,y,y^*$ such that $y,y^* \in R(X,D)$, $(x,x^*) \succcurlyeq_D (y,y^*)$, and $\{x,x^*\} \cap R(X,D) = \emptyset$. We have already noted that this requires $(x \sim y$ & $x^* \sim y^*)$ or $(x \sim y^*$ & $x^* \sim y)$ for each weak order in $D$. Suppose one of $y,y^*$ has a strict simple majority over one of $x,x^*$; say $yP_Dx$. It follows easily then that $x^*P_Dy^*$, contrary to $y^* \in R(X,D)$. Hence we must have $aI_Db$ when $a \in \{x,x^*\}$ and $b \in \{y,y^*\}$. Now partition the $n$ weak orders in $D$ according to the following five exclusive and exhaustive cases:

$n_1$ of $n$    have    $(xy)(x^*y^*)$
$n_2$ of $n$    have    $(x^*y^*)(xy)$
$n_3$ of $n$    have    $(xy^*)(x^*y)$
$n_4$ of $n$    have    $(x^*y)(xy^*)$
$n_5$ of $n$    have    $(xx^*yy^*)$        (all four indifferent).

The $aI_Db$ analysis shows that $n_1 = n_2 = n_3 = n_4$. If $n_1 = 0$ then $n_5 = n$ and thus $x,x^* \in R(X,D)$ if $y,y^* \in R(X,D)$, contrary to what we need. Hence $n_1 > 0$ and therefore $n \geq 4$. Moreover, $xI_Dx^*$.

To have $\{x,x^*\} \cap R(X,D) = \emptyset$ we require at least one more alternative, say $z$. Suppose $zP_Dx$ and $zP_Dx^*$, which with $\#X = 5$ is the only way to get $\{x,x^*\} \cap R(X,D) = \emptyset$. Using the five cases of the preceding paragraph, it is obvious that, wherever $z$ is ranked, it will be preferred to the same number of elements in $\{x,x^*\}$ as in $\{y,y^*\}$, and less preferred than the same number of elements in $\{x,x^*\}$ as in $\{y,y^*\}$. It follows that either $zP_Dy$ or $zP_Dy^*$, which contradicts $y,y^* \in R(X,D)$. Therefore $\#X = 5$ will not do, and we need $\#X \geq 6$ to obtain the desired example. ◆

An explicit example of an $F$ that satisfies both (12.4) and the strong Condorcet condition when $\#X < 6$ or $n < 4$ is the strong Condorcet function that has $F(Y,D) = Y(>_D)$ whenever $R(Y,D) = \emptyset$.

## 12.3 STRONG MONOTONICITY

To note another aspect of the strong Condorcet condition we now introduce the "strong" part of a generalized version of strong monotonicity as defined for two-alternative situations in Definition 2.3. Our new condition says that if $x,y \in F(Y,D)$ and if $D'$ is like $D$ in all respects except that, for some $i$, $x$ increases in preference with respect to some other alternative in $Y$, then $x \in F(Y,D)$ and $y \notin F(Y,D)$.

**155**

Suppose that $x,y \in Y$ and that $D = D'$ except that, for some $i$, $>_i$ on $X - \{x\}$ equals $>'_i$ on $X - \{x\}$, $x >_i z \Rightarrow$ $x >'_i z$ and $x \sim_i z \Rightarrow x \geqslant'_i z$ for all $z \in X - \{x\}$, and there $\quad$ (12.5) is a $z \in Y$ for which either $(x \sim_i z \,\&\, x >'_i z)$ or $(z >_i x \,\&\, x \geqslant'_i z)$. Then $x \in F(Y,D')$ and $y \notin F(Y,D')$ if $x,y \in F(Y,D)$ and $x \neq y$.

Because this prevents a large number of social-choice ties and therefore pushes $F$ in the direction of decisiveness, it might be looked on favorably. However, because it allows $y$ to be deleted from the choice set when there is only a minimal change in individual preferences that may not alter the preferences between $x$ and $y$, some people will regard it as too strong.

One example which shows the incompatibility of (12.5) and strong Condorcet is given by $\#X = n = 4$ and

1. $x\ y\ z\ w$
2. $y\ x\ w\ z$
3. $z\ x\ y\ w$ $\quad\quad\quad\quad\quad\quad\quad\quad\quad\quad\quad\quad\quad$ (12.6)
4. $w\ y\ z\ x.$

$R(X,D) = \{x,y\}$. If order 3 is changed to $xzyw$ in $D'$, then $R(X,D') = \{x,y\}$. Hence both (12.5) and strong Condorcet can not hold, for $F(X,D) = \{x,y\}$ and (12.5) imply that $F(X,D') = \{x\}$.

### REDUCTION AND SIMPLE-MAJORITY AGREEMENT

A simpler example for incompatibility is

$$D = (xyz,yzx) \quad \text{with } n = 2$$
$$D' = (xyz,yxz) \quad \text{and } \#X = 3.$$

The strong Condorcet condition requires $R(X,D) = R(X,D') = \{x,y\}$, but if $F(X,D) = \{x,y\}$ and (12.5) holds then $F(X,D') = \{x\}$.

This example exhibits dominance since $y \gg_D z$ and $y \gg_{D'} z$. If the reduction condition is used we obtain

$$F(X,D) = F(\{x,y\},D)$$
$$F(X,D') = F(\{x,y\},D').$$

Furthermore, if we assume only that $F$ agrees with simple majority (Definition 8.1) and do not necessarily subscribe to the entire strong Condorcet condition, then

$$F(X,D) = F(X,D') = \{x,y\}.$$

Since this conflicts with (12.5), we observe the following result.

THEOREM 12.3. *Let* $\mathfrak{D}$ *be the set of all n-tuples of weak orders on* $X$. *Then if* $\#X \geq 3$ *and* $n \geq 2$ *there is no social choice function* $F: \mathfrak{X} \times \mathfrak{D} \rightarrow$ $\mathfrak{X}$ *that satisfies* (12.5), *the reduction condition and also agrees with simple majority.*

*Proof.* If $\#X > 3$ let $w$ represent all alternatives other than $x$, $y$, $z$. $D = (xyzw,\ yzxw,\ (xy)(zw)$ for each $i > 2)$ and $D' = (xyzw,\ yxzw,\ (xy)(zw)$ for each $i > 2)$. Then reduction and simple majority agreement give $F(X,D) = F(X,D') = \{x,y\}$, but $F(X,D) = \{x,y\}$ and (12.5) require $F(X,D') = \{x\}$. ◆

## 12.4  DUALITY

According to Definition 3.1, binary duality holds with $X = \{x,y\}$ if and only if, when $D^*$ is the dual of $D$,

$$F(\{x,y\},D) \cap F(\{x,y\},D^*) \in \{\emptyset,\{x,y\}\}. \tag{12.7}$$

Clearly, this says that $F(\{x,y\},D) = \{x\} \Leftrightarrow F(\{x,y\},D^*) = \{y\}$, and that $F(\{x,y\},D) = \{x,y\} \Leftrightarrow F(\{x,y\},D^*) = \{x,y\}$.

There are several ways to generalize this condition to situations where $\#X \geq 3$. One of these generalizations, based on permutations on $X$, is called neutrality. Neutrality says in effect that the social choice function shall not have a built-in bias or favoritism for one or more alternatives. We shall consider it further in section 13.1.

Another generalization of binary duality, which we shall simply refer to as duality, is defined in the manner of (12.7) as follows.

DEFINITION 12.5. *A social choice function* $F: \mathfrak{X} \times \mathfrak{D} \rightarrow \mathfrak{X}$ *is* dual *if and only if, for all* $Y \in \mathfrak{X}$ *and* $D \in \mathfrak{D}$, *if* $D^*$ *is the dual of* $D$ (i.e., $\succ_i^*$ *is the dual of* $\succ_i$ *for each* $i$), *then*

$$F(Y,D) \cap F(Y,D^*) \in \{\emptyset,Y\}. \tag{12.8}$$

In a very rough sense, duality says that if we turn all individual orders in $D$ upside down, then $F(Y,D)$ will be turned upside down. More precisely, if we view the choice set $F(Y,D)$ as dividing $Y$ into satisfactory alternatives (those in $F(Y,D)$) and unsatisfactory alternatives (those in $Y$ but not in $F(Y,D)$), and if $F(Y,D)$ is a proper subset of $Y$, then the operation of duality on $D$ will make each satisfactory alternative unsatisfactory and it will make at least one originally unsatisfactory alternative satisfactory. The exception to this is when $F(Y,D) = Y$, in which case no change is caused in the choice set by taking duals.

In the direct terms of (12.8), duality says that the choice sets $F(Y,D)$

**157**

and $F(Y,D^*)$ can contain an alternative in common only when each set contains all alternatives in $Y$.

Since $P_{D^*}$ is the dual of $P_D$, it is clear that duality and the weak Condorcet condition are compatible, for if $x$ beats every other alternative in $Y$ under $D$, then $x$ will be beaten by every other alternative in $Y$ under $D^*$. However, duality is incompatible with both the Condorcet and the strong Condorcet conditions.

To show this, it is only necessary to take $X = \{x,y,z,w\}$ with a $D$ that has $xI_Dy$, $xI_Dz$, $xI_Dw$, and the strict majority cycle $yP_DzP_DwP_Dy$ on $\{y,z,w\}$. Then $R(X,D) = \{x\} = R(X,D^*)$, which clearly violates (12.8) if the social choice function agrees with the Condorcet condition. An example of such a $D$ is obtained with $n = 3$ and the weak orders

$$\begin{array}{llr}
1.\ y(xz)w & 1.^*\ w(xz)y & \\
2.\ w(xy)z & 2.^*\ z(xy)w & (12.9) \\
3.\ z(xw)y & 3.^*\ y(xw)z. &
\end{array}$$

This analysis might well be considered as an indictment against duality rather than against the Condorcet condition, since in the example just given it may seem reasonable to many people to take $x$ as the social choice in both the initial situation and its dual.

# CHAPTER 13

# From Borda to Dodgson

WHEN THERE ARE more than two alternatives in $X$, it is possible to define a number of different social choice functions that agree with simple majority. The purpose of this chapter is to examine some of these.

All the functions that we shall present here share a number of properties. They are all unanimous, independent of infeasible alternatives, and agree with simple majority. Moreover, they satisfy natural generalizations of the binary conditions of monotonicity, duality (the neutrality generalization), and anonymity.

Section 13.2 discusses functions that do not satisfy the weak Condorcet condition, with special emphasis on Borda's function. Section 13.3 goes on to discuss three functions that satisfy the weak Condorcet condition. Two of these are based on positional information when $P(Y,D) = \emptyset$. The other one determines $F(Y,D)$ using only the information given by $P_D$.

As in the preceding chapter, we shall assume that $X$ is finite and that $\mathfrak{D}$ is the set of all $n$-tuples of strict partial orders on $X$, unless specified otherwise in context. $\mathfrak{X}$ is the set of all nonempty subsets of $X$.

## 13.1 CONDITIONS FOR SOCIAL CHOICE FUNCTIONS

All explicit social choice functions discussed in later sections of this chapter agree with simple majority. That is, when $x,y \in X$ and $x \neq y$, $F(\{x,y\},D) = \{x\}$ if and only if $x$ has a strict simple majority over $y$, or $xP_Dy$. If $xI_Dy$ then $F(\{x,y\},D) = \{x,y\}$.

The functions that we shall examine divide into two exclusive classes, according to whether they satisfy the weak Condorcet condition of Definition 12.1. We shall refer to those that satisfy this condition as *Condorcet social choice functions*, even though they might not satisfy the strong Condorcet condition or the Condorcet condition (2) of Definition 12.1. Functions that do not satisfy the weak Condorcet condition will be referred to as *non-Condorcet social choice functions*. The functions in this class that we shall present are based on a positional approach and will be discussed in the next section. The Condorcet functions are in section 13.3.

Whether Condorcet or not, all social choice functions defined later have a number of properties in common in addition to their agreement with simple majority. These conditions are all generalizations of the binary conditions for simple majority employed in section 5.3. Two of these have already been defined in Part II, namely unanimity (Definition 7.2) and independence from infeasible alternatives (Definition 12.3). The latter was not used explicitly in Part I since we dealt there with only two-alternative situations. For such situations the independence condition is implicit in the definition of a social choice function.

The purpose of this section is to set forth the other properties that are shared by the functions considered later. These are generalizations of monotonicity, duality, and anonymity.

MONOTONICITY

Following the lead of Definition 2.1, monotonicity for the general case says that if $x \in F(Y,D)$ $[x \notin F(Y,D)]$ and if $D'$ is like $D$ except perhaps that $x$ increases $[x$ decreases] in one or more of the individual preference orders in going from $D$ to $D'$, then $x \in F(Y,D')$ $[x \notin F(Y,D')]$.

DEFINITION 13.1. *A social choice function* $F: \mathfrak{X} \times \mathfrak{D} \to \mathfrak{X}$ *is* monotonic *if and only if, for all* $Y \in \mathfrak{X}$ *and* $D, D' \in \mathfrak{D}$, *and for any* $i \in \{1, \ldots, n\}$, *if* $>_j = >'_j$ *for all* $j \neq i$, *if* $>_i$ *on* $X - \{x\}$ *equals* $>'_i$ *on* $X - \{x\}$, *and if*:

(1) $x >_i z \Rightarrow x >'_i z$ *and* $x \sim_i z \Rightarrow x \succcurlyeq'_i z$ *for all* $z \in X - \{x\}$, *and if* $x \in F(Y,D)$, *then* $x \in F(Y,D')$;

(2) $z >_i x \Rightarrow z >'_i x$ *and* $z \sim_i x \Rightarrow z \succcurlyeq'_i x$ *for all* $z \in X - \{x\}$, *and if* $x \notin F(Y,D)$, *then* $x \notin F(Y,D')$.

Under independence, $X - \{x\}$ in the definition reduces to $Y - \{x\}$, and $>_j = >'_j$ reduces to $>_j = >'_j$ on $Y$.

There are several forms of strong monotonicity that add things to monotonicity. One of these, which holds for no function considered later since it is incompatible with the conditions of independence from infeasible alternatives and simple majority agreement, says that if the hypotheses of monotonicity (1) hold and if $(x \sim_i z \,\&\, x >'_i z)$ or $(z >_i x \,\&\, x \succcurlyeq'_i z)$ for some $z \in X$, and if $y \in F(Y,D)$ and $y \neq x$, then $x \in F(Y,D')$ and $y \notin F(Y,D')$. A weaker form of strong monotonicity, that holds for some later functions but not for others, is stated as (12.5). A still weaker form is obtained from (12.5) by requiring an actual inversion of preference between $x$ and $y$ before $y$ must be deleted from the choice set.

NEUTRALITY

Binary duality was written one way in (12.7). A different way of expressing this is as follows:

if $\sigma$ is a permutation on $\{x,y\}$ and if, for each $i$, $x >_i y \Leftrightarrow \sigma(x) >_i^\sigma \sigma(y)$ and $y >_i x \Leftrightarrow \sigma(y) >_i^\sigma \sigma(x)$, then $x \in F(\{x,y\},D) \Leftrightarrow \sigma(x) \in F(\{x,y\},D^\sigma)$, and $y \in F(\{x,y\},D) \Leftrightarrow \sigma(y) \in F(\{x,y\},D^\sigma)$.

Since there are only two permutations on $\{x,y\}$, namely the identity permutation $\{\sigma(x) = x,\ \sigma(y) = y\}$ and the permutation $\{\sigma(x) = y,\ \sigma(y) = x\}$, this is easily seen to be equivalent to (12.7).

For any permutation $\sigma$ on $X$ we take $\sigma Z = \{\sigma(x) : x \in Z\}$ for any nonempty $Z \subseteq X$. The neutrality generalization of binary duality is defined as follows.

DEFINITION 13.2. *A social choice function* $F : \mathfrak{X} \times \mathfrak{D} \to \mathfrak{X}$ *is* neutral *if and only if, for all* $Y \in \mathfrak{X}$ *and* $D \in \mathfrak{D}$, *and any permutation* $\sigma$ *on* $X$, *if* $x >_i y \Leftrightarrow \sigma(x) >_i^\sigma \sigma(y)$ *for all* $x,y \in X$ *and all* $i \in \{1, \ldots, n\}$, *then*

$$F(\sigma Y, D^\sigma) = \sigma F(Y,D). \qquad (13.1)$$

This preserves the interpretation of binary duality stated after Definition 3.1, since it prohibits the social choice function from having a built-in bias for one or more alternatives. Under neutrality, the only change caused is a uniform "re-labeling" of the alternatives. For example, if $x,y \in Y$ and $F(Y,D) = \{x\}$, and if $D'$ is obtained from $D$ by interchanging $x$ and $y$ in every individual order, then neutrality requires $F(Y,D') = \{y\}$.

For a second example, suppose that $D = (xyz,yzx)$ and

$$F(\{x,y,z\},D) = \{x,y\}.$$

Then, with $\sigma(x) = y$, $\sigma(y) = z$ and $\sigma(z) = x$, $D^\sigma = (yzx,zxy)$ and $\sigma F(\{x,y,z\},D) = \{y,z\}$. Neutrality requires that $F(\{x,y,z\},D^\sigma) = \{y,z\}$.

Suppose that $X = \{x,y,z,w\}$, $Y = \{x,y,w\}$, $D = (xyzw,xwyz,wzyx)$, and let $\sigma(x) = y$, $\sigma(y) = z$, $\sigma(z) = x$ and $\sigma(w) = w$. Then $D^\sigma = (yzxw,ywzx,wxzy)$. If $F(\{x,y,w\},D) = \{x\}$ then neutrality implies that

$$F(\sigma\{x,y,w\},D^\sigma) = F(\{y,z,w\},D^\sigma) = \sigma F(\{x,y,w\},D)$$
$$= \sigma\{x\} = \{y\}.$$

Since $x P_D y \Leftrightarrow \sigma(x) P_{D^\sigma} \sigma(y)$, and therefore $\sigma R(Y,D) = R(\sigma Y, D^\sigma)$, neutrality is compatible with the strong Condorcet condition of Definition 12.1 (3).

ANONYMITY

The binary anonymity condition of Definition 5.3 generalizes immediately to the following.

DEFINITION 13.3. *A social choice function* $F : \mathfrak{X} \times \mathfrak{D} \to \mathfrak{X}$ *is* anonymous *if and only if, for all* $Y \in \mathfrak{X}$ *and* $D \in \mathfrak{D}$, *and any permutation* $\sigma$ *on* $\{1, \ldots, n\}$,

$$F(Y,(>_1, \ldots, >_n)) = F(Y,(>_{\sigma(1)}, \ldots, >_{\sigma(n)})). \qquad (13.2)$$

As in the binary case, this is designed to treat voters equally. It plays the same role for voters that neutrality (but *not* duality as in Definition 12.5) plays for alternatives.

In the ensuing sections, all social choice functions that we shall consider are unanimous, independent of infeasible alternatives, monotonic, neutral, anonymous, and they all agree with simple majority.

## 13.2  NON-CONDORCET FUNCTIONS

We shall begin with the plurality social choice function because it is a good example of a commonly used function that is widely felt by social choice theorists to be generally unsatisfactory, despite the often-accepted conditions that it satisfies that were stated in the preceding paragraph. These conditions do not of course give a complete characterization of plurality or of any other function considered here. With

$$p(x,Y,D) = \#\{i : y >_i x \text{ for no } y \in Y\},$$

the *plurality social choice function* is defined by

$$F(Y,D) = \{x : x \in Y \text{ and } p(x,Y,D) \geq p(y,Y,D) \text{ for all } y \in Y\}.$$

When every $>$ in $D$ is linear, $p(x,Y,D)$ for $x \in Y$ is the number of first-place votes for $x$ within $Y$, and $F(Y,D)$ contains the alternatives in $Y$ with the most first-place votes within $Y$.

It is easily checked that the conditions in the final paragraph of section 13.1 hold for plurality, and that it satisfies the reduction condition of Definition 12.2. In general, plurality is neither weakly Condorcet nor dual (Definition 12.5), as is shown by the following linear-orders example for five voters and $\#X = 4$.

1. $x\ y\ w\ z$
2. $x\ y\ z\ w$
3. $y\ w\ z\ x$
4. $z\ y\ w\ x$
5. $w\ y\ z\ x.$

Here $yP_D t$ for all $t \neq y$, but plurality takes $F(X,D) = \{x\}$ since $x$ has more first-place votes than any other alternative. Duality is violated since $F(X,D) = F(X,D^*) = \{x\}$.

Arguments against plurality are usually based on its failure to satisfy the weak Condorcet condition or on a positional viewpoint. Both apply to the foregoing example. For the positional viewpoint we note that $y$ has one first-place vote and four second-place votes, whereas $x$ has two first-place votes but three fourth-place votes.

A second example where both arguments apply is obtained with $X = \{x,y,z\}$ and the following $D$ for a 100-member group:

34 voters have $xyz$
33 voters have $yzx$
33 voters have $zyx$.

Plurality selects $x$. Weak Condorcet selects $y$, which has a 67 to 33 majority over $z$ and a 66 to 34 majority over $x$. The positional argument notes that $x$ has 34 first-place votes and 66 third-place votes, whereas $y$ has 33 first-place votes, 67 second-place votes, and no third-place votes. A typical positional argument would also favor $z$ over $x$ in this case.

### THE BORDA FUNCTION

A positional summation procedure, applicable when individual orders are linear, was described after (12.1). A generalization of this procedure of Borda (1781) that can deal with weak orders is mentioned by Black (1958, p. 62) and Luce and Raiffa (1957, p. 358). Their generalization will be referred to as the Borda social choice function. To define it we first define

$$r_i(x,Y,D) = \#\{y:y \in Y \text{ and } x >_i y\} - \#\{y:y \in Y \text{ and } y >_i x\},$$

so that $r_i(x,Y,D)$ is the number of alternatives in $Y$ that individual $i$ has less preferred than $x$, minus the number of alternatives in $Y$ that individual $i$ prefers to $x$. The total number of binary comparisons in $D$ that involve $x$ and an element in $Y$ and in which $x$ is preferred, minus the total binary comparisons that involve $x$ and an element in $Y$ and in which $x$ is less preferred, is therefore

$$r(x,Y,D) = \Sigma_{i=1}^{n} r_i(x,Y,D).$$

The *Borda social choice function* is then defined by

$$F(Y,D) = \{x:x \in Y \text{ and } r(x,Y,D) \geq r(y,Y,D) \text{ for all } y \in Y\}. \quad (13.3)$$

Before looking at various conditions for the Borda social choice function, we shall first note some aspects of the individual numerical representations $r_i$ as defined above. In doing this we shall presume that we are working with a fixed $Y$, and we consider only the alternatives in $Y$.

Suppose first that each $>_i$ on $Y$ is linear. If $\#Y = m$ and $>_i$ is the linear order $x_1 x_2 \cdots x_m$ on $Y$ then the $r_i$ values for $x_1, x_2, \ldots, x_m$

**163**

are, respectively, $m - 1, m - 3, m - 5, \ldots, -m + 3$, and $-m + 1$. For example, with $m = 5$ the ranking values are 4, 2, 0, $-2$, $-4$. Since these are equally spaced, we can just as well use ranking values of 4, 3, 2, 1, 0 for $m = 5$, or of $m - 1, m - 2, \ldots, 1, 0$ for the general case, and this will cause no change in (13.3). To be more specific, the change from $m - 1, m - 3, \ldots, -m + 1$ to $m - 1, m - 2, \ldots, 0$ causes a change from $r(x, Y, D)$ to $\frac{1}{2}r(x, Y, D) +$ constant, in taking sums over $i$. Hence, under linear orders, (13.3) is equivalent to the procedure described after (12.1).

Suppose next that each $>_i$ on $Y$ is a weak order, and consider the following Borda-type procedure. Assign preliminary values of $m - 1$, $m - 2, \ldots, 0$ to the $m$ alternatives in $Y$ for a given order so that these values agree with the linear Borda assignment for some linear order that includes the weak order. The final ranking value for an alternative $x$ for the given weak order equals the average of the preliminary values for the alternatives in that order that are indifferent to $x$. Thus $a$, $b$, $c$, $d$, $e$ for the weak order $(ab)c(de)$ would get final ranking values of 3.5, 3.5, 2, 0.5, 0.5. Sums of these values are then used to determine $F(Y, D)$. Now it is easily seen that if $s_i(x, Y, D)$ is the final ranking value for alternative $x$ and the order $>_i$, then $s_i(x, Y, D) = \frac{1}{2}r_i(x, Y, D) +$ constant for each $x \in Y$. It follows that this procedure is equivalent (under weak orders) to (13.3).

Continuing with weak orders, suppose that $Y = \{a, b, c, d, e\}$. The following three weak orders, the first of which is linear, have the $r_i$ values shown for $a$, $b$, $c$, $d$, $e$.

| | | |
|---|---|---|
| 1. | $abcde$ | 4, 2, 0, $-2$, $-4$ |
| 2. | $(ab)c(de)$ | 3, 3, 0, $-3$, $-3$ |
| 3. | $a(bcde)$ | 4, $-1$, $-1$, $-1$, $-1$. |

It is clear from this that $r_i$ does not maintain equal differences between adjacent indifference sets over the several orders. These differences for the three orders are respectively 2, 3, and 5. A modification of the Borda procedure requires these differences to be equal, in which case the following ranking values could apply:

| | | |
|---|---|---|
| 1. | $abcde$ | 4, 2, 0, $-2$, $-4$ |
| 2. | $(ab)c(de)$ | 2, 2, 0, $-2$, $-2$ |
| 3. | $a(bcde)$ | 2, 0, 0, 0, 0. |

Ranking values of 4, 3, 2, 1, 0 and 2, 2, 1, 0, 0 and 1, 0, 0, 0, 0 would lead to the same result under the modified procedure.

A curiosity of this modified equal-spacing procedure that makes it somewhat suspect is noted by two related seven-voter examples with $X = \{x, y, z, w\}$.

|       I       |              |       II      |              |
| :-----------: | :----------: | :-----------: | :----------: |
| 4 voters.     | $(xyz)w$     | 4 voters.     | $x(yzw)$     |
| 1 voter.      | $wxyz$       | 1 voter.      | $yzwx$       |
| 1 voter.      | $wxzy$       | 1 voter.      | $ywzx$       |
| 1 voter.      | $wyzx$       | 1 voter.      | $zwyx$       |

In each case the individual orders are weak orders and $P_D$ is a linear order with $xP_DyP_DzP_Dw$, so that a Condorcet function picks $x$ in each. The Borda function also selects $x$ in each case, as one can easily verify. However, in case I, the modified Borda selects $w$, which is not only the lowest alternative in the $P_D$ order but also has the smallest regular Borda total. And, in case II, the alternative with the smallest modified Borda total is $x$, which has the largest regular Borda total and is at the top of the $P_D$ order.

The $r_i$ for the Borda procedure need not give equal adjacent intervals within the same weak order either, as is shown by $(ab)(cd)e$ with ranks 3, 3, $-1$, $-1$, $-4$, where the intervals from 3 to $-1$ and from $-1$ to $-4$ are not of equal length.

With weak orders, it should be clear that for all $x,y \in Y$, $r_i(x,Y,D) > r_i(y,Y,D) \Leftrightarrow x >_i y$, so that $r_i$ faithfully preserves the preference order on $Y$. However, as we noted in connection with Theorem 7.1, it is not possible to have an $\Leftrightarrow$ numerical representation for $>_i$ when $>_i$ is a strict partial order for which $\sim_i$ is not transitive. As described in Theorem 7.1 (2), the "best" general numerical representation that can be obtained for strict partial orders is given by a real-valued function $u_i$ that satisfies

$$x >_i y \Rightarrow u_i(x) > u_i(y)$$
$$x \approx_i y \Leftrightarrow u_i(x) = u_i(y)$$

where $x \approx_i y$ if and only if ($x \sim_i z \Leftrightarrow y \sim_i z$, for all $z \in Y$). (Since we are taking $Y$ as fixed, and defining $\approx_i$ with respect to $Y$, $\approx_i$ may change as $Y$ changes. For example, we could have $x,y \in Y \cap Y'$, with $x \approx_i y$ for $Y$ but not $x \approx_i y$ for $Y'$.) With respect to $Y$, it is easily seen that for a strict partial order $>_i$ on $Y$,

$$x >_i y \Rightarrow r_i(x,Y,D) > r_i(y,Y,D)$$
$$x \approx_i y \Rightarrow r_i(x,Y,D) = r_i(y,Y,D).$$

The first of these follows from transitivity (if $y >_i z$ then $x >_i z$, and if $z >_i x$ then $z >_i y$), and the second follows from (7.5), which says that $y >_i z \Leftrightarrow x >_i z$ and $z >_i x \Leftrightarrow z >_i y$ whenever $x \approx_i y$.

With $Y = \{x,y,z,w\}$, the strict partial order $>_i = \{(x,z),(y,w)\}$ has

**165**

$r_i$ values of 1, 1, $-1$, $-1$ for $x$, $y$, $z$, $w$. This shows that we can have $r_i(x,Y,D) = r_i(y,Y,D)$ when it is not true that $x \approx_i y$. However, this possibility might not cause any grave concern since, at least in the example given, it seems reasonable to assign the same "rank" to $x$ and $y$.

## CONDITIONS FOR THE BORDA FUNCTION

It is easily seen that the Borda function (13.3) satisfies the conditions in the final paragraph of section 13.1. Moreover, it satisfies the version of strong monotonicity in (12.5), and it is dual (Definition 12.5). Duality would fail for the Borda function if and only if for some $x \in Y$, $x \in F(Y,D)$ and $x \in F(Y,D^*)$ and $F(Y,D) \neq Y$. Since $r(x,Y,D) = -r(x,Y,D^*)$, and since $\Sigma_Y r(y,Y,D) = 0$, $x \in F(Y,D) \cap F(Y,D^*)$ would require $r(y,Y,D) = r(y,Y,D^*) = 0$ for all $y \in Y$, in which case $F(Y,D) = F(Y,D^*) = Y$.

As we have noted in section 12.1, the Borda function is not weakly Condorcet and it does not satisfy the reduction condition of Definition 12.2. There is of course a modification of the Borda method that does satisfy the reduction condition. It is obtained by first deleting all alternatives from $Y$ that are dominated ($\gg_D$) by some other alternative in $Y$, and then applying the Borda procedure given above to $Y(\gg_D)$ instead of to $Y$. As we noted in section 12.1, by changing order 3 in (12.1) to $cxaby$, this modification of the Borda procedure still does not satisfy the weak Condorcet condition.

The analysis of section 12.1 suggests a positional condition that holds for the Borda function, but which is not generally satisfied by Condorcet social choice functions. I will refer to this as the condition of permuted dominance. It will be defined only for situations where each $\succ_i$ on $Y$ is a linear order. It is based on the following relation.

$x(Y,D)y \Leftrightarrow x,y \in Y$, each $\succ_i$ on $Y$ is linear, and there is a permutation $\sigma$ on $\{1,2, \ldots ,n\}$ such that $r_i(x,Y,D) \geq r_{\sigma(i)}(y,Y,D)$ for $i = 1, \ldots , n$, and $r_i(x,Y,D) > r_{\sigma(i)}(y,Y,D)$ for at least one $i \in \{1, \ldots ,n\}$.

Thus, under positions within the linear orders $\succ_i$ on $Y$, $x(Y,D)y$ if and only if

  (1) the number of first-place votes for $x$ is as great as the number of first-place votes for $y$,
  (2) the number of first and second-place votes for $x$ is as great as the number of first and second-place votes for $y$,
  (3) the number of first and second and third-place votes for $x$ is as great as the number of first and second and third-place votes for $y$,

and so forth, with "as great as" replaced by "greater than" in at least one of (1), (2), (3), . . . .

A specific example of this was stated before (12.1) by situation 2, where $y(Y,D')x$.

DEFINITION 13.4. *A social choice function* $F: \mathfrak{X} \times \mathfrak{D} \to \mathfrak{X}$ *satisfies the* condition of permuted dominance *if and only if, for all* $Y \in \mathfrak{X}$ *and* $D \in \mathfrak{D}$, *if the restriction of every* $>_i$ *on* $Y$ *is linear and*

$$if \quad x(Y,D)y, \quad then \quad y \notin F(Y,D).$$

If every $>_i$ on $Y$ is linear and if $x(Y,D)y$, then it is clear from the definition of $x(Y,D)y$ that $r(x,Y,D) > r(y,Y,D)$. Hence the Borda social choice function satisfies the condition of permuted dominance. Example (12.1) shows that this condition does not generally hold for Condorcet social choice functions.

REDUCTION AND PERMUTED DOMINANCE

The reduction condition is based on the usual dominance $\gg_D$, whereas permuted dominance is based on interindividual positional information. An interesting incompatibility between these conditions is brought out by the following lemma, which says nothing directly about Condorcet and Borda functions, but which indicates in a more general way the conflicting philosophies of the two positions.

LEMMA 13.1. *Suppose that* $F: \mathfrak{X} \times \mathfrak{D} \to \mathfrak{X}$ *is a social choice function,* *that* $\mathfrak{D}$ *contains all n-tuples of linear orders on* $X$ *but need not contain any* *other n-tuple of strict partial orders on* $X$, *and that* $n \geq 4$ *and* $\#X \geq 4$. *Then* $F$ *does not satisfy both the reduction condition and the condition of* *permuted dominance.*

*Proof.* Let the hypotheses of the lemma hold. If $\#X > 4$, let $w$ denote all but four alternatives $(x,y,a,b)$, arranged in a linear order. Consider $n = 4$ first, with $D$ as follows:

1. $x \ a \ y \ b \ w$
2. $x \ a \ y \ b \ w$
3. $y \ b \ x \ a \ w$
4. $y \ x \ a \ b \ w.$

Take $Y = \{x,y,a,b\}$, and suppose that both the reduction and permuted dominance conditions hold. Since $x \gg_D a$ and $y \gg_D b$, the reduction condition implies that neither $a$ nor $b$ is in $F(Y,D)$, and that $F(Y,D)$ $= F(Y - \{a\},D) = F(Y - \{b\},D) = F(Y - \{a,b\},D) = F(\{x,y\},D).$

**167**

Since $x(Y,D)y$, permuted dominance says that $y \notin F(Y,D)$. Moreover, since $y(Y - \{a\},D)x$, as is seen by deleting $a$ to give

1. $x \; y \; b$
2. $x \; y \; b$
3. $y \; b \; x$
4. $y \; x \; b,$

$x \notin F(Y - \{a\},D)$ and therefore $x \notin F(Y,D)$. But then no one of $a$, $b$, $y$, and $x$ is in $F(Y,D)$, contradicting the definition of a social choice function. ⸳

If $n$ is even and greater than four, we simply add the orders $xyabw$ and $yxabw$ in equal proportions to the original list of four orders.

Suppose next that $n = 5$. Taking $w$ at the bottom of every linear order, let the rest of $D$ be

1. $x \; a \; y \; b$
2. $x \; a \; y \; b$
3. $y \; b \; x \; a$
4. $y \; b \; x \; a$
5. $b \; x \; y \; a.$

Then $x(Y,D)y$, $x(Y,D)b$ and $x \gg_D a$ so that, if both reduction and permuted dominance hold, then $F(Y,D) = \{x\}$ and $F(Y,D) = F(Y - \{a\},D)$. But $y(Y - \{a\},D)x$, so that $x \notin F(Y,D)$. Hence $F(Y,D) = \emptyset$, a contradiction.

If $n$ is odd and greater than five, add the orders $xyabw$ and $yxabw$ in equal proportions to the preceding list. This will not affect the conclusion. ◆

QUESTIONS ABOUT SUMS

Several questions naturally arise when one suggests that a choice set be determined by summing individual rankings or utilities as in (13.3). One question asks whether any such procedure is applicable. Another asks how the individual utilities ought to be specified or determined, given that some summation procedure might be applicable.

As could be expected, there are many opinions on these questions. A number of these lie outside the present situational context in which we presume that simple majority is felt to be appropriate for the binary choices in $F$.

Within this situational context, persons who like the Condorcet position will be likely to reject a summation procedure, at least when it is suggested that the choice set be based solely on utility sums. Those who favor a summation or positional approach may feel that something like the Borda function should be used, especially if they agree to conditions such as anonymity and neutrality. But "something like a Borda function" leaves open a huge number of specific possibilities, some of which were mentioned earlier in this section and in section 12.1, and it is quite possible that different ones of these might seem appropriate for different types of situations.

The Condorcet position also leads to a wide variety of specific choice functions since the weak Condorcet condition does not say anything about the choice set when $P(Y,D)$ is empty. We now consider some of these.

## 13.3 CONDORCET FUNCTIONS

The Condorcet social choice functions divide rather naturally into those that base $F(Y,D)$ solely on $P_D$, and those that do not. We shall consider one function in the former category and two in the latter. Other Condorcet functions may occur to you as you read this section.

Our first function, which is suggested by Black (1958, p. 66), takes $F(Y,D) = P(Y,D)$ if $P(Y,D) \neq \emptyset$, and if $P(Y,D) = \emptyset$ then $F(Y,D)$ is determined by the Borda function of (13.3). I shall refer to this mixed Condorcet-positional function as *Black's function*. There are obviously many modifications of this procedure, and we shall not discuss these here.

To illustrate Black's function, suppose first that $n = 5$, $X = \{x,y,z,w\}$ and $D$ is given by the linear orders

1. $x\ y\ z\ w$
2. $w\ x\ y\ z$
3. $w\ x\ y\ z$
4. $y\ z\ x\ w$
5. $y\ z\ x\ w$.

Then $P_D$ is linear with $xP_DyP_DzP_Dw$, so that every $F(Y,D)$ for Black's function is determined by the weak Condorcet condition.

Now let $D'$ be obtained from $D$ by changing order 2 ($wxyz$) to $wzxy$. Then $P_{D'}$ is given by the directed graph of Figure 13.1. This shows that Black's function is determined by $P(Y,D')$ except for $X$ and $\{x,y,z\}$, for which the Borda function gives $F(X,D') = F(\{x,y,z\},D') = \{y\}$. Although the change in order 2 did not change the order or adjacency of $x$ and $y$, Black's function gives $F(X,D) = \{x\}$ and $F(X,D') = \{y\}$.

One can readily verify that Black's function is strongly monotonic in the sense of (12.5), and dual (Definition 12.5). It does not satisfy the reduction condition, although an obvious modification does.

**169**

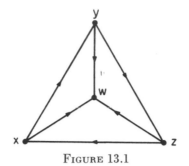

FIGURE 13.1

COPELAND'S FUNCTION

The second Condorcet social choice function that we shall examine bases $F(Y,D)$ solely on $P_D$. Since it has been suggested by Copeland (1950) [or see Goodman (1954)] as a "reasonable" method of determining social choices, we shall refer to it as *Copeland's function.* Let

$$s(x,Y,D) = \#\{y:y \in Y \text{ and } xP_Dy\} - \#\{y:y \in Y \text{ and } yP_Dx\},$$

so that $s(x,Y,D)$ is the number of alternatives in $Y$ that $x$ has a strict simple majority over, minus the number of alternatives in $Y$ that have strict simple majorities over $x$. Copeland's function then takes

$$F(Y,D) = \{x:x \in Y \text{ and } s(x,Y,D) \geq s(y,Y,D) \text{ for all } y \in Y\}. \quad (13.4)$$

When $n$ is odd and all $n$-tuples in $\mathcal{D}$ are $n$-tuples of linear orders, there is an equivalent way of looking at Copeland's function. If $P(Y,D) \neq \emptyset$, take $F(Y,D) = P(Y,D)$. If $P(Y,D) = \emptyset$ and if $P(Y - \{x\},D) \neq \emptyset$ for some $x \in Y$, take $F(Y,D) = \cup_{x \in Y}P(Y - \{x\},D)$. If this union is empty, take $F(Y,D) = \cup_{x,y \in Y}P(Y - \{x,y\},D)$ unless this new union is empty, and continue in the obvious way until a nonempty union is obtained. Under linear orders and odd $n$, this $F$ is identical to Copeland's function.

Although Copeland's function obviously satisfies the weak Condorcet condition, it does not satisfy the Condorcet condition, as is shown by the following $D$ on $Y = \{x,y,a,b,c\}$ with $n = 4$:

1. $x\ y\ a\ b\ c$
2. $x\ y\ b\ a\ c$
3. $c\ b\ a\ x\ y$
4. $y\ a\ c\ b\ x.$

For this example, $R(Y,D) = \{x\}$. However, the $s$ values of $x$, $y$, $a$, $b$, $c$ are 1, 2, 0, $-1$, $-2$ respectively, so that the Copeland function selects $y$. The Borda and Black functions also select $y$.

An interesting comparison between the Copeland and Borda functions is given by the following nine-voter $D$:

$$
\begin{array}{lll}
4 \text{ voters.} & y\ x\ a\ c\ b \\
3 \text{ voters.} & b\ c\ y\ a\ x & (13.5) \\
2 \text{ voters.} & x\ a\ b\ c\ y.
\end{array}
$$

$P(Y,D) = \emptyset$, with $P_D$ as shown in Figure 13.2. The $s$ value at each point in the figure is obtained by subtracting the number of lines

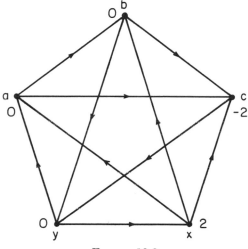

FIGURE 13.2

directed into the point from the number of lines directed away from the point. Since $x$ has the largest $s$ value, Copeland's function selects $x$. On the other hand, the Borda function chooses $y$. Thus the winner ($x$) based solely on simple majority comparisons loses by a 7 to 2 majority to the winner ($y$) determined by a positional approach.

A COMPUTER COMPARISON

Although our examples are designed to "bring out the worst" in various methods and to highlight the differences between methods, there may be some question about how really different several functions might be. For example, we may suspect that the Borda and Copeland functions will yield the same choice set in a large percentage of possible cases.

To examine this suspicion, a computer was programmed to compare the Borda and Copeland functions. For each $(n,m)$ pair with $m = \#X$, the computer generated, by uniformly distributed random numbers, 1000 $n$-tuples of linear orders on $X$, and determined $F(X,D)$ for each $n$-tuple according to the two functions. Table 13.1 shows the

TABLE 13.1

NUMBER OF CASES OUT OF 1000 CASES (FOR EACH $n,m$) WHERE THE BORDA AND COPELAND FUNCTIONS HAD A COMMON ALTER-NATIVE IN THEIR CHOICE SETS

|  |  | $m = \#X$ | | | | | | |
|---|---|---|---|---|---|---|---|---|
|  |  | 3 | 4 | 5 | 6 | 7 | 8 | 9 |
|  | 3 | 1000 | 979 | 945 | 940 | 918 | 920 | 892 |
|  | 5 | 991 | 964 | 944 | 926 | 898 | 880 | 865 |
|  | 7 | 983 | 952 | 933 | 909 | 894 | 876 | 865 |
|  | 9 | 974 | 947 | 915 | 914 | 862 | 886 | 861 |
| $n$ | 11 | 962 | 941 | 915 | 905 | 884 | 855 | 857 |
|  | 13 | 962 | 941 | 910 | 902 | 889 | 879 | 842 |
|  | 15 | 964 | 931 | 914 | 890 | 890 | 867 | 850 |
|  | 17 | 942 | 924 | 898 | 868 | 867 | 856 | 838 |
|  | 19 | 950 | 922 | 894 | 876 | 883 | 863 | 844 |
|  | 21 | 946 | 914 | 888 | 865 | 865 | 866 | 840 |

number of cases for each $(n,m)$ pair for which the choice sets for the two functions had an element in common. Generally speaking, the number of cases with a nonempty intersection for the two choice sets decreases as either $n$ or $m$ increases. The smallest percentage agreement obtained was 83.8 percent for $(n,m) = (17,9)$.

For $m = 3$, about 85 percent of the cases enumerated in column 1 of the table had *identical* choice sets for the two functions. At the other extreme, for $m = 9$, about 70 percent of the cases enumerated in the final column had identical choice sets. Moreover, these percentages did not vary significantly for changes in $n$. For example, of the 892 agreeing cases for $(n,m) = (3,9)$, 648, or about 73 percent, had identical choice sets. For $(n,m) = (21,9)$, 584, or about 70 percent of the 840 agreeing cases, had identical choice sets.

DODGSON'S INVERSION METHOD

To simplify the discussion of our final function we shall assume henceforth that $\mathfrak{D}$ is the set of all $n$-tuples of *linear* orders on $X$.

Our final function is based on C. L. Dodgson's idea of taking inversions in the orders in $D$, and will therefore be referred to as *Dodgson's function*. Let $L_1$ and $L_2$ be two linear orders on $X$. In going from $L_1$ to $L_2$ an *inversion* occurs whenever, for any $x,y \in X$, $xL_1y$ and $yL_2x$. The total number of inversions equals the number of ordered pairs $(x,y) \in X^2$ for which $xL_1y$ and $yL_2x$. For example, if $L_1$ is *abcxy* and $L_2$ is $axbcy$, then two inversions are involved: from $bx$ to $xb$ and from $cx$ to $xc$.

Given $(Y,D)$ let $t(x,Y,D)$ be the fewest number of inversions required in the linear restrictions of the $>_i$ on $Y$ so that we obtain a $D'$ for which $P(Y,D') = \{x\}$. Then Dodgson's function is defined by

$$F(Y,D) = \{x : x \in Y \text{ and } t(x,Y,D) \leq t(y,Y,D) \text{ for all } y \in Y\}.$$

If $P(Y,D) \neq \emptyset$ then $t(P(Y,D),Y,D) = 0$ and $F(Y,D) = P(Y,D)$. Therefore Dodgson's function is a Condorcet social choice function.

For (13.5), the least number of inversions that will cause $x$ to have a strict simple majority over each other alternative is three. These three inversions interchange $y$ and $x$ in three of the first four orders in (13.5). Hence $t(x,Y,D) = 3$. Similarly, $t(y,Y,D) = 2$ (change one of the $bcyax$ orders to $ybcax$). Since the inversions required for each of $a$, $b$ and $c$ exceed two, Dodgson's function selects $y$ in (13.5). This is also the Borda and Black selection, but it differs from the Copeland result $(x)$.

Because Dodgson's function does not rely solely on $P_D$ for its computation, it joins Black's function in the category of Condorcet social choice functions that are not based solely on $P_D$. However, since Dodgson's function is based on strict simple majorities under inversion, it appears to be intermediate between the Black and Copeland functions.

Our final example shows that each of the three functions defined in this section can give a different result in the same situation. Let $n = 3$, $\#X = 9$, with $D$ as follows:

1. $a\ z\ c\ y\ x\ b\ f\ e\ d$
2. $x\ d\ b\ a\ e\ f\ y\ z\ c$
3. $y\ z\ b\ x\ c\ a\ e\ d\ f.$

We might suppose that a three-man board of commissioners, composed of a Democrat, a Republican, and an Independent, is charged with selecting one of nine land-use plans for a certain area within their domain. Alternative $x$ represents the parkland proposal, $y$ stands for the airport plan, $z$ is a residential development scheme, and the other six alternatives refer to other proposals. The overall preferences of the commissioners are given by $D$. As one can easily verify, Black's function selects the parkland proposal, Copeland's function selects the airport plan, and Dodgson's function picks the residential development scheme.

# SOCIAL CHOICE FUNCTIONS

HAVING CONSIDERED numerous aspects of multiple-alternative social choice theory in the simple-majority setting, we proceed to look at these aspects, and others, in a more general way.

Part III begins with a classification of conditions for social choice functions. The classification includes structural, existential, intraprofile, and interprofile categories. The categories are then related to a number of topics, including the transitivity of binary choices, Arrow's impossibility theorem and close relatives, and social choice functions that are defined in terms of sums of individual utilities.

The final chapter discusses the use of lotteries to make social choices. If a group decides to use a lottery, an alternative is then chosen "at random" according to the chances or probabilities specified by the lottery. The chapter includes an analysis of simple majorities in the lottery context.

# CHAPTER 14

# Conditions for Social Choice

ALTHOUGH OUR FOCUS thus far has been on special types of situations, it should be clear that most of the conditions for social choice functions that we have used apply, either as stated or in modified form, to a general study of social choice functions. To impart a degree of organization to our general study we shall begin Part III by sorting the many conditions into a few easily recognized classes. It is hoped that this classification will help the reader to better understand and interrelate the various topical divisions of this book and related studies.

It has long been recognized that the isolation of specific conditions facilitates a deeper analysis of social choice procedures. This analytic approach is complemented by the synthetic approach, which considers various combinations of conditions. In some cases a combination of conditions will serve to characterize a certain set of social choice functions, and such a combination may imply other conditions. In other cases, the conditions in a certain combination will be mutually incompatible, thus giving rise to an "impossibility theorem." Theorems of this sort are useful in illustrating conflicting philosophies about "reasonable" choice procedures. An example is Lemma 13.1. Others are noted in Chapter 16.

Both the analytic and synthetic approaches have been used extensively in Parts I and II, and they will continue to play an important role in the rest of the book. Our first general synthetic investigation of Part III comes in sections 14.3 and 14.4, where we shall generalize the analysis of single-peaked and triple conditions of Chapters 9 through 11 along the lines developed by Murakami (1968, pp. 124 129), Sen and Pattanaik (1969), and Pattanaik (1970).

## 14.1 A CLASSIFICATION OF CONDITIONS

To provide an initial overview and summary, the classification that will be used here is set forth in Table 14.1. As can be seen, the conditions have been divided into three major classes. The third class, which is the most extensive, has been divided into two main subclasses, each of which is further divided into two parts. We shall return to these in the next section.

## STRUCTURAL CONDITIONS

The first class, here referred to as the class of structural conditions, deals with the structure of the sets on which $F$ is defined. These conditions provide the prerequisites for a proper definition of a social choice function, serving to identify the domain on which $F$ is to be defined.

TABLE 14.1

A CLASSIFICATION OF CONDITIONS

A. *Structural.* Nature of sets on which $F$ is defined.
   Examples. $X$ is finite and $\#X \geq 3$; $\mathfrak{X}$ is the set of all nonempty subsets of $X$; $n$ is an integer and $n \geq 2$; $\mathfrak{D}$ is the set of all $n$-tuples of strict partial orders on $X$.
B. *Existential.* Conditions on $F$ that use existential qualifiers.
   Examples. Condition of decisive majority coalitions (Def. 4.2); Nondictatorship conditions; Every voter is essential.
C. *Universal.* Conditions on $F$ that don't use existential qualifiers. They are to apply for all applicable structural configurations.
   1. *Intraprofile.* Consider one $D$ at a time.
      1a. *Active.* Involve specific conditions on contents of $D$. Examples. Unanimity (Def. 7.2); Reduction (Def. 12.2), Permuted Dominance (Def. 13.4); Decisiveness (Def. 6.1).
      1b. *Passive.* Don't say anything about contents of $D$. Examples. $F_D$ is transitive; $F(Y,D) \subseteq \{x : x \in Y \text{ and } y \, F_D \, x \text{ for no } y \in Y\}$ when $\{x : \ldots\} \neq \emptyset$.
   2. *Interprofile.* Consider more than one $D$ at a time.
      2a. *Two-profile.* Monotonicity (Def. 13.1); Duality (Def. 12.4); Neutrality (Def. 13.2); Anonymity (Def. 13.3); Independence (Def. 12.3).
      2b. *Multiprofile.* Representative system condition (Def. 4.3); Strong duality (Def. 5.2); Condition B of section 6.3.

As we have noted before, three sets need to be specified for the definition of $F$: the set $\mathfrak{X}$ of potentially feasible sets of social alternatives; the set of voters or individuals; and $\mathfrak{D}$, the set of admissible data points that describe potential preference profiles. With $X$ the universal set of alternatives, we require at the minimum that $X$ be nonempty. In specific cases we may wish to further restrict $X$, by conditions such as finiteness or $\#X \geq 3$.

Likewise, a minimum restriction for $\mathfrak{X}$ is that it contain only nonempty subsets of $X$ and not be empty. Some other conditions for $\mathfrak{X}$ are: $\mathfrak{X}$ contains every finite subset of $X$; for every $x \in X$ there is a $Y \in \mathfrak{X}$ such that $x \in Y$; if $Y, Z \in \mathfrak{X}$ then $Y \cup Z \in \mathfrak{X}$; $\mathfrak{X} \cup \{\emptyset\}$ is a Boolean algebra with unit $X$. The last of these means that $X \in \mathfrak{X}$ and that $\mathfrak{X} \cup \{\emptyset\}$ is closed under complementations (if $Y \in \mathfrak{X}$ then $X - Y \in \mathfrak{X} \cup \{\emptyset\}$) and finite unions (if $Y,Z \in \mathfrak{X}$ then $Y \cup Z \in \mathfrak{X}$).

In almost all cases we assume for obvious reasons that the number of individuals is a positive integer. To have an explicitly social situation we can specify that $n \geq 2$. On occasion one might indulge in the fantasy of supposing that the number of voters is infinite, in which case $D \in \mathfrak{D}$ can be viewed in a general way as a function that assigns a preference order to each individual in the infinite set.

Throughout Part III we shall continue to suppose that $\mathfrak{D}$ is a non-empty set of $n$-tuples of strict partial orders on $X$. (The general view of $D$ just mentioned can be used regardless of the size of the set of voters; it is equivalent to the $n$-tuple specification in the finite case.)

Some conditions for $\mathfrak{D}$ place restrictions on individual orders that do not limit acceptable mixes of orders in any further way. An example of such a condition is: each component of every $D \in \mathfrak{D}$ is a weak order on $X$. Other conditions for $\mathfrak{D}$ are interindividual conditions which generally prohibit $\mathfrak{D}$ from being written as a Cartesian product of $n$ sets of orders. An example is: $\mathfrak{D}$ is the set of all $n$-tuples of strict partial orders on $X$ for which $(X,D)$ is single peaked.

When we deal with expected utilities in the final chapter, additional conditions will be specified for the individual preference orders.

SOCIAL CHOICE FUNCTIONS

For our general definition, let $\mathcal{P}(X)$ be the power set of $X$, or the set of all subsets of $X$.

DEFINITION 14.1. $F : \mathfrak{X} \times \mathfrak{D} \to \mathcal{P}(X)$ *is a* social choice function *if and only if* $\mathfrak{X}$ *is a nonempty set of nonempty subsets of a nonempty set* $\mathfrak{X}$, $\mathfrak{D}$ *is a nonempty set, and* $F(Y,D)$ *is a nonempty subset of* $Y$ *for each* $(Y,D) \in \mathfrak{X} \times \mathfrak{D}$.

Throughout Part II we used $\mathfrak{X}$ in place of $\mathcal{P}(X)$ since we assumed that $\mathfrak{X}$ contained all nonempty subsets of $X$. However, if $\mathfrak{X}$ is restricted in some way, we leave open the possibility that a choice set may not itself be a feasible set in $\mathfrak{X}$ although it must be a subset of a feasible set. The many conditions for social choice functions that were presented in Part II modify in an obvious way under the general definition.

The general definition of a social choice function obviously imposes certain minimal conditions on the behavior of $F$, namely $\emptyset \neq F(Y,D) \subseteq Y$. Some writers omit the nonempty feature of $F(Y,D)$ from the definition and use a separate condition (sometimes referred to as "decisiveness," which should not be confused with decisiveness as defined in Definition 6.1) to specify that $F(Y,D)$ must not be empty.

**179**

All conditions in the existential and universal classes restrict the allowable behavior of $F$ in some way. The existential conditions are based primarily on existential qualifiers ("there exists . . ."), although they may also use universal qualifiers ("for all . . ."). The universal conditions either do not use existential qualifiers in any way, or else they use such qualifiers in a secondary manner. Although this allows some question about the appropriate classification of a few conditions, the examples that we shall use should clarify the general intention of the two classes.

Most existential conditions definitely assert the existence of certain elements in the sets used to structure the definition of $F$ and may themselves impose structural conditions. A case in point is the following nonimposition condition:

there is a $Y \in \mathfrak{X}$ and $D,D' \in \mathfrak{D}$ such that $F(Y,D) \neq F(Y,D')$.

This requires some $Y$ in $\mathfrak{X}$ to contain at least two alternatives, and it implies that $\mathfrak{D}$ has more than one element. A related condition, which also has no universal qualifiers, is an essentiality condition:

there is an $i \in \{1, \ldots ,n\}$, a $Y \in \mathfrak{X}$ and $D,D' \in \mathfrak{D}$ such that $D_j = D'_j$ for all $j \neq i$ and $F(Y,D) \neq F(Y,D')$.

This clearly implies the preceding nonimposition condition, and it requires the presence of a pair of elements in $\mathfrak{D}$ that differ in only one component.

Many of the conditions here referred to as existential can be viewed as negations of simple universal conditions. For example, if $F$ is *constant* means that $F(Y,D) = F(Y,D')$ for all $(Y,D)$, $(Y,D') \in \mathfrak{X} \times \mathfrak{D}$, then the nonimposition condition given above says that $F$ is not constant. The condition of constancy is a universal interprofile condition: its negation is an existential condition since it requires the presence of certain elements with specified properties.

An existential condition with a universal qualifier is the following nondictatorship condition:

for every $i \in \{1, \ldots ,n\}$ there are $x^i,y^i \in X$ and $D^i \in \mathfrak{D}$ such that $x^i >_i^i y^i$ and $y^i \in F(\{x^i,y^i\},D^i)$.

This can also be stated in the familiar form: "if $i \in \{1, \ldots ,n\}$ then there exist $x^i,y^i \in X$ . . . ."

The final condition that we shall use as an example of an existential condition does not definitely assert the existence of certain elements because its first universal would never apply if there were no essential voter. It is the condition of decisive majority coalitions given by Definition 4.2 with $X = \{x,y\}$:

for every nonempty $J \subseteq \{1, \ldots ,n\}$ that contains an essential $i$ and for every integer $m$ for which $\#J/2 < m \leq \#J$, there exists an $I \subseteq J$ such that $\#I = m$ and $I$ is decisive for $x$ over $y$ within $J$.

The existential conditions are somewhat less plentiful than the universal conditions that we shall now examine.

## 14.2 UNIVERSAL CONDITIONS

Universal conditions are usually written in either the form "if such-and-such hold, then $F$ has such-and-such properties" or "for all things that satisfy such-and-such, $F$ has such-and-such properties." Our subdivisions of this class depend on the number of elements in $\mathfrak{D}$ that are involved in each $F$ statement and, in one case, on whether anything specific is supposed about the element in $\mathfrak{D}$ that appears in the condition.

The main division of universal conditions depends on whether more than one $D$ is actively involved in the statement of the condition. Those with only one $D$ are called intraprofile conditions; the others are interprofile conditions. Both subclasses are very important.

### INTRAPROFILE CONDITIONS

The intraprofile conditions further divide in a natural way into conditions which assume certain specific properties for the components of $D$, and those that do not. We refer to the former as active intraprofile conditions; the latter are passive intraprofile conditions since they say nothing about the contents of $D$.

Three active intraprofile conditions are decisiveness (Definition 6.1), unanimity, and reduction:

if $D \neq (0,0, \ldots ,0)$ then $F(D) \neq 0$;
if $x,y \in Y$, if $Y \in \mathfrak{X}$, if $D \in \mathfrak{D}$, and if $x \gg_D y$, then $y \notin F(Y,D)$;
if $x,y \in Y$, if $Y \in \mathfrak{X}$ and $Y - \{y\} \in \mathfrak{X}$, if $D \in \mathfrak{D}$, and if $x \gg_D y$, then $F(Y,D) = F(Y - \{y\},D)$.

Another active intraprofile condition is the condition of permuted dominance in Definition 13.4. In the next section we shall discuss some other active intraprofile conditions that are closely related to independence, neutrality, and some of the other interprofile conditions.

**181**

Within the two-alternative context of Part I, the strong decisiveness condition (if $D \in \mathfrak{D}$ then $F(D) \neq 0$) is a passive intraprofile condition although its decisive counterpart as noted above is active. Like strong decisiveness, the other passive conditions make categorical assertions about $F$ for a generic $D \in \mathfrak{D}$, regardless of the specific nature of $D$. Assuming that $\mathfrak{X}$ contains all two-element subsets of $\mathfrak{X}$ so that $F_D$ as in (7.9) is conceptually well defined, the following are samples of passive intraprofile conditions:

if $D \in \mathfrak{D}$, then $F_D$ is a suborder;
if $D \in \mathfrak{D}$, then $F_D$ is a weak order;
if $D \in \mathfrak{D}$ and $Y \in \mathfrak{X}$ and if $\{x : x \in Y$ and $y F_D x$ for no $y \in Y\}$ is a unit subset of $Y$, then $F(Y,D)$ equals this unit subset.

Another passive condition that we have not explicitly considered thus far is:

if $D \in \mathfrak{D}$, if $Y,Z \in \mathfrak{X}$ and if $Y \subseteq Z$ and $Y \cap F(Z,D) \neq \emptyset$ then $Y \cap F(Z,D) \subseteq F(Y,D)$.

This says that, if $Y$ is a subset of $Z$ and if the choice set from $Z$ under $D$ contains at least one element in $Y$, then each such element must be in the choice set from $Y$ under $D$. We shall examine this and related passive intraprofile conditions in the next chapter.

### INTERPROFILE CONDITIONS

Because interprofile conditions relate choice sets for *different* preference profiles that might obtain, they occupy a very central position in *social* choice theory. A typical study of choice functions might concentrate on a function from $\mathfrak{X}$ into $\mathcal{P}(X)$. *Social* choice functions are essentially systems of choice functions, since $F : \mathfrak{X} \times \mathfrak{D} \to \mathcal{P}(X)$ can be viewed as a set of choice functions $F(\cdot, D)$, one for each $D$ in an index set $\mathfrak{D}$. The thing that distinguishes the study of social choice functions from other systems of choice functions that are defined on the same set $\mathfrak{X}$ is the nature of the index set $\mathfrak{D}$, and it is this nature that gives rise to the particular interprofile conditions that are used in the theory.

For interprofile conditions we do not make a distinction between active and passive conditions since all the interprofile conditions that we shall consider are essentially active. That is, the two or more $D$'s that appear in the statement of an interprofile condition will be related in a specific way.

Most of the common interprofile conditions use just two profiles at a time. This subclass includes the various monotonicity conditions, along with the following conditions of duality, neutrality, anonymity, and independence from infeasible alternatives:

if $Y \in \mathfrak{X}$ and if $D$ and its dual $D^*$ are in $\mathfrak{D}$ then $F(Y,D) \cap F(Y,D^*) \in \{\emptyset, Y\}$ ;

if $\sigma$ is a permutation on $X$, if $D$ and $D^\sigma$ (obtained from $D$, componentwise, by $\sigma$) are in $\mathfrak{D}$, and if $Y$ and $\sigma Y$ are in $\mathfrak{X}$, then $F(\sigma Y, D^\sigma) = \sigma F(Y,D)$ ; (14.1)

if $\sigma$ is a permutation on $\{1, \ldots, n\}$, if $D = (\succ_1, \ldots, \succ_n)$ and $D' = (\succ_{\sigma(1)}, \ldots, \succ_{\sigma(n)})$ are in $\mathfrak{D}$, and if $Y \in \mathfrak{X}$, then $F(Y,D') = F(Y,D)$ ; (14.2)

if $Y \in \mathfrak{X}$, if $D, D' \in \mathfrak{D}$, and if the restriction of $D$ on $Y$ equals the restriction of $D'$ on $Y$, then $F(Y,D') = F(Y,D)$. (14.3)

The final subclass, the multiprofile conditions, contains several conditions used in Part I, but explicit multiprofile conditions were not used in Part II. The three conditions from Part I that use more than two $D$'s in certain cases are noted at the bottom of Table 14.1. It is of some interest to recall that each of these three was used in connection with the Theorem of The Alternative, Theorem 3.2, in an analysis involving the existence of a solution for a set of linear inequalities. In the case of the special condition for representative systems (Definition 4.3), the Theorem of The Alternative was not applied directly to condition RS

Multiprofile conditions and the Theorem of The Alternative will be used again in Chapter 17.

## 14.3 SPECIAL ACTIVE INTRAPROFILE CONDITIONS

In the preceding section we noted that interprofile conditions serve to interrelate different choice functions $F(\cdot,D): \mathfrak{X} \to \mathcal{P}(X)$ for the various $D \in \mathfrak{D}$. These conditions have some interesting and powerful implications, provided that $\mathfrak{X}$ and $\mathfrak{D}$ are sufficiently rich. However, if fairly strong restrictions are placed on our basic sets, many of these implications cannot be derived due to a lack of structure.

A natural course to take in such restricted contexts is to modify the interprofile conditions such as neutrality and anonymity so that the modified versions will serve the intended purposes within the given structure. In other cases, such as when our primary interest is in a study of the binary relations $F_D$, it will suffice to introduce active intraprofile conditions that preserve much of the spirit of certain interprofile conditions.

To illustrate the latter course and to prepare for an analysis related to that in Chapters 9 through 11 that is given in the next section, we shall consider several specialized active intraprofile conditions.

FIVE ACTIVE INTRAPROFILE CONDITIONS

Of the five active intraprofile conditions that we shall present, three are based on previously introduced concepts. These are $x =_D y$ ($x \sim_i y$ for all $i$), $x >_D y$ ($x \succcurlyeq_i y$ for all $i$, $x >_i y$ for some $i$), and $xR_Dy$ ($x$ ties or beats $y$ by simple majority). One new relation is needed:

$$(x,y) \geq^D (z,w) \Leftrightarrow (\text{for each } i, \ z >_i w \Rightarrow x >_i y \ \& \ z \sim_i w \Rightarrow x \succcurlyeq_i y).$$

Thus, $(x,y) \geq^D (z,w)$ if every person who prefers $z$ to $w$ also prefers $x$ to $y$, and if every person who likes $z$ as much as $w$, also likes $x$ as much as $y$. From $\geq^D$ we define $=^D$ as follows:

$$(x,y) =^D (z,w) \Leftrightarrow (x,y) \geq^D (z,w) \quad \text{and} \quad (z,w) \geq^D (x,y).$$

The proof of the following is left to the reader.

LEMMA 14.1. $(x,y) =^D (z,w) \Leftrightarrow (\text{for each } i, \ x >_i y \Leftrightarrow z >_i w, \ \text{and } y >_i x \Leftrightarrow w >_i z)$.

We recall that $xF_Dy \Leftrightarrow x \neq y \ \& \ F(\{x,y\},D) = \{x\}$. The five conditions are summarized in the following list. Condition Ak holds if and only if the given statement holds for all $\{x,y\} \in \mathfrak{X}$ (or $\{x,y\},\{z,w\} \in \mathfrak{X}$) and all $D \in \mathfrak{D}$.

A1. $x =_D y \Rightarrow F(\{x,y\},D) = \{x,y\}$.
A2. $(x,y) =^D (z,w) \Rightarrow (xF_Dy \Leftrightarrow zF_Dw, \ \text{and } yF_Dx \Leftrightarrow wF_Dz)$.
A3. $(x,y) \geq^D (z,w) \ \text{and } zF_Dw \Rightarrow xF_Dy$.
A4. $x \geq_D y \Rightarrow not \ yF_Dx$.
A5. $xR_Dy \Rightarrow not \ yF_Dx$.

All of these hold if $F$ agrees with simple majority, and all but A5 agree with any fixed representative system. Collectively, they do not imply that $F$ agrees with simple majority. Each has a fairly straightforward interpretation that should be evident from its statement. The following lemma shows that they are not independent of one another.

LEMMA 14.2. A3 $\Rightarrow$ A2 $\Rightarrow$ A1. A5 $\Rightarrow$ A4 $\Rightarrow$ A1. A3 $\Rightarrow$ A4.

*Proof.* If $(x,y) =^D (z,w)$ then $(x,y) \geq^D (z,w)$ and $(z,w) \geq^D (x,y)$ by definition, and $(y,x) \geq^D (w,z)$ and $(w,z) \geq^D (y,x)$ by Lemma 14.1. It then follows that A3 $\Rightarrow$ A2. If $x =_D y$ then $(x,y) =^D (y,x)$, so that A2 and the asymmetry of $F_D$ imply A1. Since $x \geq_D y \Rightarrow xR_Dy$, A5 $\Rightarrow$ A4. Since $x =_D y \Rightarrow x \geq_D y \ \& \ y \geq_D x$, A4 $\Rightarrow$ A1. The proof that A3 $\Rightarrow$ A4 is left to the reader. ◆

We shall now observe that sufficiently rich structural conditions and several two-profile conditions imply the active intraprofile conditions A1–A5. The interprofile conditions that we shall use are independence (14.3), neutrality (14.1), monotonicity (Definition 13.1), and anonymity (14.2).

THEOREM 14.1. *Suppose that $\mathfrak{D}$ contains all n-tuples of strict partial orders on $X$ and that $F: \mathfrak{X} \times \mathfrak{D} \to \mathcal{P}(\mathfrak{X})$ is a social choice function. Then*

*$F$ is independent and neutral $\Rightarrow$ A1, A2;*
*$F$ is independent, neutral and monotonic $\Rightarrow$ A3, A4;*
*$F$ is independent, neutral, monotonic and anonymous $\Rightarrow$ A5.*

*Proof.* A1. Assume that $F$ is independent and neutral and that $x =_D y$ and $\{x,y\} \in \mathfrak{X}$. Contrary to A1 suppose that $xF_Dy$. Let $\sigma(x) = y$, $\sigma(y) = x$ and $\sigma(t) = t$ otherwise. Then, by neutrality, $yF_{D^\sigma}x$. But by independence (since $x =_D y$), $F(\{x,y\},D) = F(\{x,y\},D^v)$, a contradiction. Hence, not $xF_Dy$. Similarly, not $yF_Dx$. Therefore $F(\{x,y\},D) = \{x,y\}$.

A2. Assume that $F$ is independent and neutral and that $\{x,y\}$, $\{z,w\} \in \mathfrak{X}$ and $(x,y) =^D (z,w)$. Suppose first that $xF_Dy$. Then $x \neq y$, and by A1, $x >_i y$ or $y >_i x$ for some $i$. Therefore $z >_i w$ or $w >_i z$ for some $i$ so that $z \neq w$. Let $\sigma(x) = z$, $\sigma(z) = x$, $\sigma(y) = w$, $\sigma(w) = y$ and $\sigma(t) = t$ otherwise. Then $zF_{D^\sigma}w$ by neutrality. By independence, $zF_{D}w$ since the restriction of $D$ on $\{z,w\}$ equals the restriction of $D^\sigma$ on $\{z,w\}$ according to $\sigma$ and $(x,y) =^D (z,w)$. Hence $xF_Dy \Rightarrow zF_Dw$. The other implications in the conclusion of A2 are proved similarly.

A3. Assume that $F$ is independent, neutral, and monotonic and that $\{x,y\}$, $\{z,w\} \in \mathfrak{X}$, $(x,y) \geq^D (z,w)$ and $zF_Dw$. If $(x,y) -^D (z,w)$ then the conclusion $xF_Dy$ follows from A2. Henceforth assume not $(x,y) -^D (z,w)$, so that either $x \sim_i y$ and $w >_i z$ for some $i$ or $x >_i y$ and $w \geq_i z$ for some $i$. Let $D'$ be obtained from $D$ by moving $x$ "down" in each such order so that $(x,y) =^{D'} (z,w)$, and let $D''$ be obtained from $D$ by moving $y$ "up" in each such order so that $(x,y) -^{D''} (z,w)$. By independence, $zF_{D'}w$ and $zF_{D''}w$. Then, by A2, $xF_{D'}y$ and $xF_{D''}y$. In going back from $D'$ to $D$, $x$ is moved "up" in certain orders and therefore, by monotonicity, $x \in F(\{x,y\},D') \Rightarrow x \in F(\{x,y\},D)$. In going back from $D''$ to $D$, $y$ is moved "down" in certain orders and therefore, by the other part of monotonicity, $y \notin F(\{x,y\},D'') \Rightarrow y \notin F(\{x,y\},D)$. Therefore $xF_Dy$.

A4. This follows from the preceding proof since A3 $\Rightarrow$ A4.

A5. Assume that $F$ is independent, neutral, monotonic, and anonymous and that $\{x,y\} \in \mathfrak{X}$ and $xR_Dy$. If $xI_Dy$, let $D' = D$. If

$xP_Dy$, get $D'$ from $D$ by moving $x$ "down" in just enough orders with $x >_i y$ to give $x \sim_i' y$ and $xI_{D'}y$. Then, by independence, neutrality, anonymity, and Lemma 5.1 (iii), $x \in F(\{x,y\},D')$. Monotonicity then gives $x \in F(\{x,y\},D)$, so that not $yF_Dx$. ◆

## 14.4 RESTRICTIONS ON TRIPLES

In this section we observe that certain structural and active intraprofile conditions imply part or all of certain passive intraprofile conditions. The development is based on notions used in Chapters 9 through 11. A sample corollary of the main theorem to be proved is:

$$\left. \begin{array}{l} \text{if } \mathfrak{X} \text{ contains all two-element} \\ \text{subsets of } X, \text{ if } (X,D) \text{ is single} \\ \text{peaked for all } D \in \mathfrak{D} \end{array} \right] \quad \text{structural}$$

$$\left. \begin{array}{l} \text{and if } F: \mathfrak{X} \times \mathfrak{D} \to \mathcal{P}(X) \text{ is} \\ \text{a social choice function that} \\ \text{satisfies A3} \end{array} \right] \quad \begin{array}{l} \text{active} \\ \text{intraprofile} \end{array}$$

$$\left. \begin{array}{l} \text{then } F_D \text{ is transitive for every} \\ D \in \mathfrak{D}. \end{array} \right] \quad \begin{array}{l} \text{passive} \\ \text{intraprofile} \end{array}$$

To complete our preparations for Theorem 14.2, it is first necessary to recall the characterizations of the seven independent categories of section 10.2. These are summarized in Table 10.1 and in Table 11.1, but will be repeated here for our convenience.

A slight change will be made in the definitions of section 10.2. We shall say that $D$ on a triple $\{x,y,z\}$ is in category $K$ if and only if every $>$ in $D$ that is not empty on $\{x,y,z\}$ satisfies statement $K$ in the following list (or satisfies a similar statement obtained by a permutation on $\{x,y,z\}$ and/or by taking duals):

    I. $x \sim y$
    II. $(y > x \ \& \ y > z)$ or $(x > y \ \& \ z > y)$ or $(x \sim y \ \& \ y \sim z)$
    III. $(xy)z$ or $z(xy)$ or $(xz)y$ or $y(xz)$ or $(yz)x$ or $x(yz)$
    IV. $xyz$ or $zyx$ or $(xz)y$ or $y(xz)$
    V. $x \geqslant y \ \& \ z \geqslant y$
    VI. $x \geqslant y \ \& \ (x > y$ or $x > z$ or $z > y)$
    VII. $y > x$ or $y > z$.

Seven theorems, one for each category, are included in the following.

THEOREM 14.2. *Suppose that* $\mathfrak{X}$ *contains every two-element subset of* $X$, *that* $\mathfrak{D}$ *is a set of n-tuples of strict partial orders on* $X$, *that* $\{x,y,z\}$ *is a triple in* $X$ *and that* $F: \mathfrak{X} \times \mathfrak{D} \rightarrow \mathcal{P}(X)$ *is a social choice function. If, in addition,*

| $D$ on $\{x,y,z\}$ is in | and $F$ satisfies | then $F_D$ on $\{x,y,z\}$ is |
|---|---|---|
| *category* I | A1 | *a suborder* |
| *category* II | A2 | *transitive* |
| *category* III | A5 | *a suborder* |
| *category* IV | A5 | *a suborder* |
| *category* V | A4 | *a suborder* |
| *category* VI | A3 | *a suborder* |
| *category* VII | A3 | *transitive.* |

The corollary stated earlier in this section follows from Theorem 14.2 VII, since category VII covers the single-peaked as well as the single-troughed cases. The only other category that invariably gives a transitive $F_D$ when conditions on $F$ that do not go beyond A1 through A5 are used is category II. In the terms used by Sen and Pattanaik, these two categories comprise the triple condition of "value restriction."

No essential change occurs in the conclusions of Theorem 14.2 when all $>$ in every $D$ are assumed to be weak orders. In particular, Lemma 10.2 and Theorem 10.1 do not apply in the present context since the proof of Lemma 10.2 depends explicitly on the assumption that $F$ agrees with simple majority.

However, even without assuming weak orders, the special limited agreement category VI' of section 11.1, characterized by

VI'. $x \geqslant y$, and $x > y$ if $\sim$ on $\{x,y,z\}$ is not transitive,

gives rise to a transitive $F_D$ on $\{x,y,z\}$ provided that one more active intraprofile condition is used. This condition is strong binary unanimity, written here as

A6. $x >_D y \Rightarrow xF_Dy$,

whenever $\{x,y\} \in \mathfrak{X}$ and $D \in \mathfrak{D}$.

THEOREM 14.3. *Suppose that the initial hypotheses of Theorem* 14.2 *hold, that* $D$ *on* $\{x,y,z\}$ *is in category* VI' *and that* $F$ *satisfies* A3 *and* A6. *Then* $F_D$ *on* $\{x,y,z\}$ *is transitive.*

*Proofs:*
Let the initial hypotheses of Theorem 14.2 hold. We shall use the displayed characterization of each category in proving the assertion for that category. The stated conditions for $F$ are assumed to hold in each case.

I. A1 implies not $xF_Dy$ and not $yF_Dx$. Therefore neither

$$(xF_Dy \ \& \ yF_Dz \ \& \ zF_Dx) \qquad \text{nor} \qquad (xF_Dz \ \& \ zF_Dy \ \& \ yF_Dx), \quad (14.4)$$

and $F_D$ on $\{x,y,z\}$ is a suborder.

II. $(y,x) =^D (y,z)$ under the characterization of category II. Hence, by A2, $yF_Dx \Leftrightarrow yF_Dz$ and $xF_Dy \Leftrightarrow zF_Dy$. Hence $xF_Dy \ \& \ yF_Dz$ and $yF_Dx$ & $zF_Dy$ are impossible, and each of the other four hypotheses for transitivity clearly imply the transitivity conclusion.

III. The nonempty orders on $\{x,y,z\}$ allowed under category III are orders 7 through 12 on Table 10.1 (single indifference). We have $xP_Dy \Leftrightarrow n_9 + n_{12} > n_{10} + n_{11}$, $yP_Dz \Leftrightarrow n_7 + n_{10} > n_8 + n_9$, and $xP_Dz$ $\Leftrightarrow n_7 + n_{12} > n_8 + n_{11}$. Because of the symmetry of this category, it will suffice to suppose that $F_D$ is not a suborder with the first expression of (14.4) holding. Then, by A5, $xF_Dy \Rightarrow xP_Dy$ and $yF_Dz$ $\Rightarrow yP_Dz$, so that addition and cancellation give $n_7 + n_{12} > n_8 + n_{11}$, which implies $xP_Dz$. But, by A5, $xP_Dz \Rightarrow$ not $zF_Dx$, so that the first expression of (14.4) is contradicted.

IV. The nonempty orders allowed under the characterization of category IV are 1, 6, 9, and 10, or $xyz$, $zyx$, $(xz)y$, and $y(xz)$. Suppose first that the first expression of (14.4) holds. Then $xF_Dy \Rightarrow xP_Dy$ and $yF_Dz \Rightarrow yP_Dz$ under A5, so that, with $xP_Dy \Leftrightarrow n_1 + n_9 > n_6 + n_{10}$ and $yP_Dz \Leftrightarrow n_1 + n_{10} > n_6 + n_9$, addition and cancellation give $n_1 > n_6$, which implies $xP_Dz$ and hence not $zF_Dx$ by A5. Hence A5 implies that the first expression of (14.4) is false. By a similar proof, A5 implies that the second expression in (14.4) is false. Hence $F_D$ on $\{x,y,z\}$ is a suborder.

V. Given $x \geqslant y \ \& \ z \geqslant y$ for each order, A4 implies not $yF_Dx$ and not $yF_Dz$. Hence neither expression in (14.4) can hold.

VI. Given $x \geqslant y \ \& \ (x > y$ or $x > z$ or $z > y)$ for each nonempty order on $\{x,y,z\}$, A4 (implied by A3) implies not $yF_Dx$. Therefore, $F_D$ on $\{x,y,z\}$ is not a suborder only if $xF_Dy \ \& \ yF_Dz \ \& \ zF_Dx$. As is easily checked, the characterization used here implies that $(z,y) \geq^D (z,x)$ and $(x,z) \geq^D (y,z)$. Hence, by A3, $zF_Dx \Rightarrow zF_Dy$ and $yF_Dz \Rightarrow xF_Dz$. Therefore $xF_Dy \ \& \ yF_Dz \ \& \ zF_Dx$ is false.

VII. Given $y > x$ or $y > z$ for each nonempty order on $\{x,y,z\}$, it follows from A3 that

(1) $xF_Dy \Rightarrow xF_Dz$ and $yF_Dz$
(2) $zF_Dy \Rightarrow zF_Dx$ and $yF_Dx$
(3) $xF_Dz \Rightarrow yF_Dz$
(4) $zF_Dx \Rightarrow yF_Dx$.

For example, for $xF_Dz \Rightarrow yF_Dz$, the only admissible orders with $x > z$ are $(xy)z$, $xyz$ and some with $y > x$ and $y > z$, and $y > z$ for each of these; and the only nonempty admissible orders with $x \sim z$ are $z \sim y > x \sim z$ and $x \sim y > z \sim x$ and $y(xz)$, and $y \geqslant z$ for each of these. The six hypotheses for transitivity are

| | |
|---|---|
| $xF_Dy$ & $yF_Dz$: | then $xF_Dz$ by (1). |
| $xF_Dy$ & $zF_Dx$: | inconsistent by (1). |
| $yF_Dx$ & $xF_Dz$: | then $yF_Dz$ by (3). |
| $yF_Dx$ & $zF_Dy$: | then $zF_Dx$ by (2). |
| $yF_Dz$ & $zF_Dx$: | then $yF_Dx$ by (4). |
| $zF_Dy$ & $xF_Dz$: | inconsistent by (2). |

VI'. (Theorem 14.3: A3, A6.) Given $x \geqslant y$, and $x > y$ if $\sim$ is not transitive on $\{x,y,z\}$, we get $zF_Dx \Rightarrow zF_Dy$ and $yF_Dz \Rightarrow xF_Dz$ under A3, as in VI above. Together, A1 (implied by A3) and A6 imply not $yF_Dx$. These results cover all but the last of the preceding six hypotheses for transitivity: the first two carry through and the next three are inconsistent. Transitivity fails for the sixth case ($zF_Dy$ & $xF_Dz$) only if not $xF_Dy$. Since $x \geqslant y$ for all orders, we can get not $xF_Dy$ under A6 only if $x \sim y$ for all orders. But the only two nonempty orders under VI' that have $x \sim y$ are $z(xy)$ and $(xy)z$, and A3 on these implies that $zF_Dy \Rightarrow zF_Dx$, contradicting the hypotheses of the sixth case. ◆

# CHAPTER 15

# Choice Functions and Passive
# Intraprofile Conditions

A CHOICE FUNCTION is a function from a nonempty set $\mathfrak{X}$ of nonempty subsets of a set $X$ into the power set $\mathcal{P}(X)$ of $X$, whose image for each $Y \in \mathfrak{X}$ is a nonempty subset of $Y$. A *social* choice function can be viewed as a collection $\{F(\cdot, D) : D \in \mathfrak{D}\}$ of choice functions. Although a distinguishing feature of social choice theory is the interrelations among the $F(\cdot, D)$, a subsidiary part of the theory concerns the study of choice functions.

Most of the sizable literature on choice functions has been developed apart from social choice theory, and it is impossible at this time to say how much of the general theory of choice functions will find its way into social choice studies. It is clear, however, that certain aspects of choice functions are relevant in social choice theory. The purpose of this chapter is to review some of these aspects.

The study of a singular choice function is a natural setting in which to discuss certain intraprofile conditions. In particular, we shall examine critically several passive intraprofile conditions. In this connection it should be said that much of the material on choice functions that we shall consider was developed in other contexts, such as revealed preference theory in consumer economics, and that our criticisms of various conditions from the social-choice viewpoint should not be taken as criticisms of these conditions in other contexts.

## 15.1 ORDER CONDITIONS FOR CHOICE FUNCTIONS

DEFINITION 15.1. $f : \mathfrak{X} \to \mathcal{P}(X)$ *is a* choice function *if and only if* $\mathfrak{X}$ *is a nonempty set of nonempty subsets of* $X$, *and* $\emptyset \neq f(Y) \subseteq Y$ *for every* $Y \in \mathfrak{X}$.

We shall be concerned with two types of conditions for a choice function $f$: structural conditions on $\mathfrak{X}$, and conditions on $f$ (referred to as $f$-conditions) that take the structure of $\mathfrak{X}$ as given. A third type of condition, related to our existential class of section 14.1, is the existential $f$-condition, an example of which is: $f(Y) \in \mathfrak{X}$ for all $Y \in \mathfrak{X}$.

In mathematics, a common $f$-condition is: $f(Y)$ is a unit subset of $Y$ for every $Y \in \mathfrak{X}$. In social choice this relates to strong decisiveness. Mirksy and Perfect (1966) review some of the literature on choice functions of this type.

A familiar structural condition is: $\mathfrak{X}$ contains every two-element subset of $X$.

DEFINITION 15.2. *A choice function* $f:\mathfrak{X} \to \mathcal{P}(X)$ *is* binary *if and only if* $\mathfrak{X}$ *contains every two-element subset of* $X$.

In this section we shall focus on binary choice functions. This will enable us to make an immediate tie-in to intraprofile conditions that use the binary relation $F_D$, where $xF_Dy$ if and only if $x \neq y$ and $F(\{x,y\},D) = \{x\}$. Sections 15.2 and 15.3 consider more general structures.

PASSIVE INTRAPROFILE CONDITIONS AND $f$-CONDITIONS

Given a binary choice function $f:\mathfrak{X} \to \mathcal{P}(X)$, let $f'$ be the binary relation on $X$ defined by

$$xf'y \Leftrightarrow x \neq y \text{ and } f(\{x,y\}) = \{x\}.$$

Four obvious candidates for $f$-conditions coincide with the four order relations of section 7.2:

1. $f'$ is a suborder
2. $f'$ is a strict partial order
3. $f'$ is a weak order
4. $f'$ is a linear order.

If any one of these holds and if $Y \in \mathfrak{X}$ is finite, then $\{x:x \in Y \text{ and } yf'x \text{ for no } y \in Y\}$ is not empty. As in the case of the Condorcet conditions of Chapter 12, we can consider $f$-conditions like

5. If $Y \in \mathfrak{X}$ then $f(Y) \subseteq \{x:x \in Y \text{ and } yf'x \text{ for no } y \in Y\}$ whenever $\{x: \cdots\} \neq \emptyset$,

regardless of whether any of the preceding $f$-conditions are adopted.

Each $f$-condition has a corresponding passive intraprofile condition in the social-choice context. Conversely, every passive intraprofile condition has a corresponding $f$-condition. Thus there is a one-to-one correspondence between $f$-conditions and passive intraprofile conditions. Some of the $f$-conditions, such as 1 through 4 above, deal only with binary choices. Others, like 5, involve choices from larger sets.

The corresponding passive intraprofile condition for condition 1 is: $F_D$ is a suborder for each $D \in \mathfrak{D}$. For the passive condition

for all triples $\{x,y,z\} \subseteq X$ and $D \in \mathfrak{D}$, if $x \in F(\{x,y\},D)$ and $y \in F(\{y,z\},D)$ then $x \in F(\{x,z\},D)$,

which is the same thing as saying that $F_D$ is a weak order for every $D \in \mathfrak{D}$, the corresponding $f$-condition is condition 3 above.

The purpose of the rest of this section is to examine critically the binary $f$-conditions in the context of social choice theory. We shall deal mainly with the first of these ($f'$ is a suborder) since it is the most general of the order conditions that are sometimes suggested as reasonable conditions for a social choice function. Our criticisms, many of which have been anticipated in Part II, will involve active intraprofile conditions for $D \in \mathfrak{D}$. In most cases the $D$ that we shall use fall outside of the restricted categories used in section 14.4.

### CRITICISMS OF SOCIAL ORDER CONDITIONS

Our first criticism of condition 1 above, or of its categorical correspondent "$F_D$ is a suborder for every $D \in \mathfrak{D}$," involves example (7.13) where individual indifference is not transitive. The active intraprofile condition involved in this case is strong binary unanimity:

$$x >_D y \Rightarrow x F_D y.$$

This says that if $\{x,y\}$ is the feasible set and if nobody prefers $y$ to $x$ and at least one person prefers $x$ to $y$ then $x$ will be the social choice from $\{x,y\}$. As noted before, if $n \geq 3$ and $\#X \geq 3$ then there are $n$-tuples $D$ of strict partial orders on $X$ such that $F_D$ is not a suborder when $F$ satisfies strong binary unanimity.

So as not to further "bias" our case with the use of intransitive individual indifference, we shall assume henceforth in this section that every individual preference order on $X$ is a weak order. We maintain the assumption that every two-element subset of $X$ is in $\mathfrak{X}$.

Perhaps the oldest argument against a passive intraprofile condition such as "$F_D$ is a suborder (or weak order, etc.) for every $D \in \mathfrak{D}$" is the argument for simple majority. One version of this goes as follows. Suppose that there are situations in which you feel that the following apply:

  (i)  $X$ contains more than two alternatives,

  (ii)  there are at least three voters,

  (iii)  any $n$-tuple of weak orders on $X$ might obtain,

  (iv)  if in fact only two candidates turn out to be feasible, then the choice between these two should be determined by simple majority.

Then $F_D$ cannot be a suborder for some $D$ that qualifies under (iii). Put differently, if one feels that $F_D$ should always be a suborder, then one must categorically reject the unrestricted use of simple majority for binary decisions as in (iv) in *all* situations that satisfy (i), (ii), and (iii).

Instead of simple majority, our third argument uses the weaker condition that $x$ must be elected in a contest between $x$ and $y$ whenever $x$ receives a sufficiently large proportion (such as 99 percent) of all available votes. With $\alpha n$ the proportion that guarantees a winner in a two-alternative contest, we stop short of unanimity by requiring that $\alpha$ be less than unity.

LEMMA 15.1. *Let* $\frac{1}{2} \leq \alpha < 1$. *Suppose that, for all* $\{x,y\} \in \mathfrak{X}$, $F(\{x,y\},D) = \{x\}$ *whenever* $\#\{i:x >_i y\} > \alpha n$. *Then there is an* $X$, $n$ *and n-tuple D of linear orders on* $X$ *such that* $F_D$ *on* $X$ *is not a suborder.*

*Proof.* The proof is a simple extension of the cyclic case where $n = 3$, $\#X = 3$ and $D = (xyz,zxy,yzx)$. Let $n$ be the smallest integer that exceeds $1/(1 - \alpha)$, let $\#X = n$ with $X = \{x_1, \ldots ,x_n\}$, and take $D = (x_1x_2 \cdots x_n, x_2x_3 \cdots x_nx_1, x_3x_4 \cdots x_1x_2, \cdots , x_nx_1 \cdots x_{n-1})$. Then, according to the binary choice rule for $F$, since $n - 1 > \alpha n$, $x_1F_Dx_2F_Dx_3F_D \cdots F_Dx_nF_Dx_1$. ◆

A slight modification of this method of proof yields the following companion of the preceding lemma.

LEMMA 15.2. *Let* $\frac{1}{2} \leq \alpha < 1$. *Suppose that, for all* $\{x,y\} \in \mathfrak{X}$ *for which* $x \neq y$, $xF_Dy$ *whenever* $\#\{i:x >_i y\} = n$ (*i.e., binary unanimity*) *and that not* $yF_Dx$ *whenever* $\#\{i:x >_i y\} > \alpha n$. *Then there is an* $X$, $n$ *and n-tuple D of linear orders on* $X$ *such that* $F_D$ *on* $X$ *is not a weak order.*

*Proof.* The prototype example for this proof is (8.5), which will serve when $\frac{1}{2} \leq \alpha < \frac{2}{3}$. In general, let $n$ equal the smallest integer that exceeds $1/(1 - \alpha)$, let $\#X = n + 1$ with $X = \{x_0,x_1, \ldots ,x_n\}$ and take $D$ as follows:

1. $x_1x_2 \cdots x_nx_0$
2. $x_2x_3 \cdots x_nx_0x_1$
3. $x_3x_4 \cdots x_0x_1x_2$
   .
   .
   .
$n.$ $x_nx_0x_1 \cdots x_{n-2}x_{n-1}.$

By unanimity, $x_nF_Dx_0$. By the other rule for $F_D$ in the lemma, not $x_1F_Dx_0$, not $x_2F_Dx_1$, $\ldots$ , not $x_nF_Dx_{n-1}$. If $F_D$ were a weak order then the application of negative transitivity (section 7.1) to this string of negations would give not $x_nF_Dx_0$, contradicting $x_nF_Dx_0$. Hence $F_D$ is not a weak order. ◆

Another argument against $F_D$ being a weak order for all $D \in \mathfrak{D}$ that appeals to some people is provided by Arrow's impossibility theorem (1963). This says that if $F$ satisfies unanimity, independence from infeasible alternatives, a nondictatorship condition and several inoffensive structural conditions, then $F_D$ cannot be a weak order for every $D$. (Weak orders for individuals are used in the theorem.) Because Arrow's theorem has played such an important part in the recent history of social choice theory, it will be presented in the next chapter along with a number of related impossibility theorems.

## 15.2 Inclusion Conditions for Choice Sets

In this section we shall examine $f$-conditions that do not directly rely on a binary relation and which presuppose no specific structure for $\mathfrak{X}$. As we shall see, these conditions have a close relationship to the $f$-conditions discussed in the preceding section.

Our new conditions are all concerned with the relationship between $f(Y)$ and $Y \cap f(Z)$ when $Y \subseteq Z$ and $Y,Z \in \mathfrak{X}$. Their statements answer questions such as: Should an alternative $y$ that is in the choice set from $Z$ also be in the choice set from every subset of $Z$ that contains $y$? Put more crudely: Should a "best" alternative in $Z$ remain "best" if other alternatives are deleted from $Z$?

We shall consider three conditions. The first two are discussed at length by Arrow (1959). The second and third are mentioned in Sen and Pattanaik (1969). They apply to all $Y,Z \in \mathfrak{X}$.

B1. $Y \subseteq Z$ and $Y \cap f(Z) \neq \emptyset \Rightarrow f(Y) = Y \cap f(Z)$.
B2. $Y \subseteq Z \Rightarrow Y \cap f(Z) \subseteq f(Y)$.
B3. $Y \subseteq Z$ and $f(Y) \cap f(Z) \neq \emptyset \Rightarrow f(Y) \subseteq f(Z)$.

Let $Y$ be a subset of $Z$ with $Y,Z \in \mathfrak{X}$. Then B1 says that if some element in the choice set from $Z$ is in $Y$ also, then the choice set from $Y$ shall consist of all such elements. Condition B2 weakens this by only requiring that all alternatives in $Y \cap f(Z)$, if any, be in $f(Y)$. If $Y \cap f(Z) \neq \emptyset$, B2 permits $f(Y)$ to contain alternatives in $Y$ that are not "best" in $Z$. Condition B3 says that if some $Y$ choice is a $Z$ choice then every $Y$ choice shall be a $Z$ choice.

There are other ways to state these conditions. Two of these for B2 are

B2'. $Y \subseteq Z \Rightarrow Y - f(Y) \subseteq Z - f(Z)$.
B2''. $Y \subseteq Z \Rightarrow f(Z) \cap (Y - f(Y)) = \emptyset$.

The equivalence of these to B2 is left as an exercise. In the form of B2' or B2'', B2 asserts that any alternative in $Y$ that is not "best" in $Y$ shall not be "best" in the superset $Z$ of $Y$. An equivalent expression for B3 is

B3'. $Y \subseteq Z$ and $x,y \in f(Y) \Rightarrow [x \in f(Z) \Leftrightarrow y \in f(Z)]$, which says that if two elements are in the choice set from $Y$ then either both or neither shall be in the choice set from $Z$.

As indicated in the preceding section, each of B1, B2, and B3 has a corresponding passive intraprofile condition in social choice theory, obtained by replacing $f(W)$ by $F(W,D)$ throughout the given $f$-condition.

### THEOREMS

The following theorem shows how the three conditions relate to one another. It does not presuppose any specific structure for $\mathfrak{X}$. The proof is very easy and is left to the reader.

THEOREM 15.1. B1 $\Leftrightarrow$ B2 & B3.

The next theorem shows that B1 gives rise to conditions based on the binary relation $f'$ of the preceding section.

THEOREM 15.2. *Suppose that* $f: \mathfrak{X} \to \mathcal{P}(X)$ *is a binary choice function. Then* B1 *implies that*

$$f(Y) = \{x : x \in Y \text{ and } yf'x \text{ for no } y \in Y\} \text{ for all } Y \in \mathfrak{X}. \quad (15.1)$$

*If, in addition,* $\mathfrak{X}$ *contains every triple in* $X$*, then* $f'$ *on* $X$ *is a weak order if* B1 *holds. Finally, if* $f$ *is a binary choice function and if* (15.1) *holds and* $f'$ *is a weak order then* B1 *holds.*

It should be observed that (15.1) applies regardless of whether $Y$ is finite or infinite. For example, if $Y = \{x_1, x_2, \ldots\}$ is denumerable then B1 and binary $f$ forbid the following linear order on $Y$ when $Y \in \mathfrak{X} : x_j f' x_k$ whenever $j > k$. If the order held for $f'$ on $Y$ then $\{x : x \in Y \text{ and } yf'x \text{ for no } y \subset Y\}$ would be empty.

We shall prove the final assertion of Theorem 15.2 first, by proving the following lemma.

LEMMA 15.3. *Suppose that* $f: \mathfrak{X} \to \mathcal{P}(X)$ *is a choice function and that there is a weak order* $f^*$ *on* $X$ *such that*

$$f(Y) = \{x : x \in Y \text{ and } yf^*x \text{ for no } y \in Y\} \text{ for all } Y \in \mathfrak{X}. \quad (15.2)$$

*Then* B1 *holds.*

*Proof of the lemma.* Let $Y, Z \in \mathfrak{X}$ with $Y \subseteq Z$ and $Y \cap f(Z) \neq \emptyset$. If $t \in Y \cap f(Z)$ then not $zf^*t$ for all $z \in Z$ by (15.2), and therefore $zf^*t$ for no $z \in Y$. Hence $t \in f(Y)$ so that $Y \cap f(Z) \subseteq f(Y)$. Now take $t \in Y \cap f(Z)$ and suppose that $y \in f(Y)$. Then not $tf^*y$, so that not $zf^*y$ for all $z \in Z$ by negative transitivity. Hence $y \in f(Z)$ by (15.2), and therefore $f(Y) \subseteq Y \cap f(Z)$. ◆

*Proof of the theorem.* For the first part of Theorem 15.2 let B1 hold for binary $f$. To verify (15.1) take $Y \in \mathfrak{X}$. Suppose first that $yf'x$ with

$x,y \in Y$. Then $x \notin f(Y)$, for otherwise a contradiction of B1 ($x \in f(Y)$ and $x \notin f\{x,y\}$) is obtained. Therefore, with $f'(Y)$ defined by

$$f'(Y) = \{x : x \in Y \text{ and } yf'x \text{ for no } y \in Y\},$$

we have proved that $f(Y) \subseteq f'(Y)$. This requires $f'(Y) \neq \emptyset$ since $f(Y) \neq \emptyset$ by definition. Suppose next that $x \in f'(Y)$ but that $x \notin f(Y)$. Then, for any $y \neq x$ in $f(Y)$, $f(\{x,y\}) = \{y\}$ by B1 so that $yf'x$, which contradicts $x \in f'(Y)$. Therefore $f'(Y) \subseteq f(Y)$ and hence $f(Y) = f'(Y)$, which is (15.1).

For the second part of the theorem let $Z = \{x,y,z\}$ be an arbitrary triple in $X$ if $\#X \geq 3$ and suppose $xf'y$. To verify negative transitivity we need $xf'z$ or $zf'y$. Since $xf'y$, B1 $\Rightarrow y \notin f(Z)$. If $z \in f(Z)$ then $zf'y$ by B1. If $z \notin f(Z)$ then $f(Z) = \{x\}$, so that $xf'z$. ◆

Theorem 15.2 looks somewhat fragmented. The following obvious corollary puts the matter in a simpler form.

COROLLARY 15.1. *Suppose that* $f : \mathfrak{X} \to \mathcal{P}(X)$ *is a choice function and that* $Y \in \mathfrak{X}$ *whenever* $\#Y \in \{2,3\}$ *and* $Y \subseteq X$. *Then* B1 *holds if and only if* $f'$ *on* $X$ *is a weak order and* (15.1) *holds.*

For condition B2 we have the following companion of Theorem 15.2.

THEOREM 15.3. *If* $f : \mathfrak{X} \to \mathcal{P}(X)$ *is a binary choice function then* (15.1) *implies* B2, *and* B2 *implies that*

$$f(Y) \subseteq \{x : x \in Y \text{ and } yf'x \text{ for no } y \in Y\} \text{ for all } Y \in \mathfrak{X}. \quad (15.3)$$

*If* $\mathfrak{X}$ *contains every nonempty finite subset of* $X$, *if* $f : \mathfrak{X} \to \mathcal{P}(X)$ *is a choice function, and if* B2 *holds, then* $f'$ *on* $X$ *is a suborder.*

*Remark.* Unlike the final assertion of Theorem 15.2, if $f : \mathfrak{X} \to \mathcal{P}(X)$ is a choice function, if $\mathfrak{X}$ contains every nonempty finite subset of $X$, and if $f'$ on $X$ is a weak order and (15.3) holds, then it is not necessarily true that B2 holds. To prove this, suppose that $X = \{x,y,z,t\}$, $\mathfrak{X} = \mathcal{P}(X) - \{\emptyset\}$, and $f' = \emptyset$. Then $f(\{u,v\}) = \{u,v\}$ for every two-element subset of $X$. But for every larger subset, $f(Y)$ can be defined however we wish ($\emptyset \neq f(Y) \subseteq Y$) and (15.3) will not be violated. In particular, we can take $f(\{x,y,z\}) = \{x\}$ and $f(X) = \{y\}$, which violate B2.

*Proof of the theorem.* Let $f$ be a binary choice function. Suppose first that (15.1) holds and $Y,Z \in \mathfrak{X}$, $Y \subseteq Z$ and $x \in Y \cap f(Z)$. Then not $zf'x$ for every $z \in Z$ and hence $x \in f(Y)$ by (15.1). Thus B2 holds. Suppose next that B2 holds and that $x,y \in Y$, $Y \in \mathfrak{X}$ and $yf'x$. Then, by B2, $\{x,y\} \cap f(Y) \subseteq \{y\}$. Therefore $x \notin f(Y)$, and (15.3) holds.

Assume that $\mathfrak{X}$ contains every nonempty finite subset of $X$ and that

$f$ is a choice function which satisfies B2. Suppose that $x_1 f' x_2 f' \cdots f' x_m f' x_1$. If $x_j \in f(\{x_1, \ldots, x_m\})$ then $x_j \in f(\{x_{j-1}, x_j\})$ by B2, contradicting $x_{j-1} f' x_j$. Hence, with $x_0 = x_m$, $x_j \notin f(\{x_1, \ldots, x_m\})$ for $j = 1, \ldots, m$, which contradicts the definition of a choice function. Therefore $x_1 f' x_2 f' \cdots f' x_m f' x_1$ is false, and $f'$ is a suborder. ◆

DISCUSSION

When viewed in the perspective of social choice theory, B1 and B2 have a certain intuitive appeal and indeed seem reasonable for some profiles $D \in \mathfrak{D}$. However, since they imply conditions such as 1 and 3 in the preceding section, they are liable to the criticisms given there. That is, there are some $n$-tuples of individual preference orders under which B1 and B2 may seem rather unreasonable.

Although B3 supplements B2 to produce B1, by itself it does not imply the types of conclusions stated in Theorems 15.2 and 15.3. In fact, B3 is trivially satisfied if $f(Y)$ is always a unit subset of $X$ (in which case B2 is equivalent to B1). Hence any criticism of B3 must use an $f(Y)$ that is not a singleton.

One example with B3 takes $y \sim_i x >_i z \sim_i y$ for every $>_i$ in $D$. Given $\{x,y\}$ and $\{x,y,z\}$ in $\mathfrak{X}$, it may seem reasonable to have

$$F(\{x,y\},D) = \{x,y\} \qquad \text{and} \qquad F(\{x,y,z\},D) = \{x\},$$

which violate B3 since $\{x,y\}$ is not a subset of $\{x\}$.

An example with linear orders that may cause some skepticism about B3 is obtained with $X = \{x,y,a,b,c\}$, $n = 6$, and the following linear orders for $D$:

1. $x\ a\ y\ b\ c$
2. $x\ c\ y\ a\ b$
3. $x\ b\ y\ c\ a$
4. $y\ a\ b\ c\ x$
5. $y\ c\ a\ b\ x$
6. $y\ b\ c\ a\ x$.

If $X \in \mathfrak{X}$, a "popular" choice would be $F(X,D) = \{y\}$. However, if only $x$ and $y$ were feasible, then $F(\{x,y\},D) = \{x,y\}$ may seem most appropriate since three individuals prefer $x$ to $y$, and the other three prefer $y$ to $x$. This would violate B3.

15.3 STRUCTURES AND EXTENSIONS

In Corollary 15.1 we observed that B1 implies that $f'$ is a weak order that satisfies (15.1) provided that $\mathfrak{X}$ contains all two-element and three-element subsets of $X$. What can be said about these things when $\mathfrak{X}$ does not contain all such subsets?

Consider first the following definition of $f'$, which is consistent with our usage in the preceding section:

$$xf'y \Leftrightarrow x \neq y, \{x,y\} \in \mathfrak{X} \text{ and } f(\{x,y\}) = \{x\}.$$

If $\{x,y\} \notin \mathfrak{X}$ then not $xf'y$ and not $yf'x$, and clearly B1 need not imply that $f'$ is a weak order or that (15.1) holds. However, it may be possible to define another binary relation $f^*$ on $X$ that agrees with $f'$ in the sense that

$$\{x,y\} \in \mathfrak{X} \Rightarrow (xf'y \Leftrightarrow xf^*y), \tag{15.4}$$

and which is in fact a weak order on $X$. Moreover, (15.2) might be true for $f^*$, where (15.2) is

$$f(Y) = \{x : x \in Y \text{ and } yf^*x \text{ for no } y \in Y\} \text{ for all } Y \in \mathfrak{X}. \tag{15.2}$$

In this section we shall present two theorems that deal with the existence of such an $f^*$. The second, which was proved by Richter (1966) and independently by Hansson (1968), gives an $f$-condition that is necessary and sufficient for the existence of a weak order $f^*$ on $X$ that satisfies (15.2) regardless of the structure of $\mathfrak{X}$. Such an $f^*$ must of course agree with $f'$ as in (15.4) and is therefore an extension of $f'$.

The new $f$-condition used in the second theorem will be referred to as B4: Richter (1966) calls it the Congruence Axiom. Since B4 implies a weak order $f^*$ that satisfies (15.2), we know by Lemma 15.3 that B4 implies B1. Therefore B4 is a stronger condition than each of B1, B2 and B3. On the other hand, if $\mathfrak{X}$ contains every two-element and three-element subset of $X$, then, by Theorem 15.2, it follows that B1 implies B4 so that the two are equivalent under this structure for $\mathfrak{X}$.

Before discussing B4 further we shall present a theorem, due to Hansson (1968), that focuses on the weaker condition B1. In the context of B1, Hansson's theorem shows what is required of $f : \mathfrak{X} \to \mathcal{P}(X)$ to be able to define a weak order extension $f^*$ of $f'$ that satisfies (15.2).

### EXTENSIONS

Since the theorems of this section involve extensions of binary relations and choice functions, several preliminaries are in order. The following lemma concerns the extension of certain binary relations.

LEMMA 15.4. *If $>$ on $X$ is a strict partial order then there is a linear order $>'$ on $X$ such that $> \subseteq >'$. If $\geqslant$ on $X$ is reflexive and transitive (i.e. a "quasi-order" or "preorder") then there is a connected and transitive binary relation $\geqslant'$ on $X$ such that $\geqslant \subseteq \geqslant'$ and $(x \geqslant y \text{ \& not } y \geqslant x) \Rightarrow \text{not } y \geqslant' x$, for all $x,y \in X$.*

The first statement of the lemma is due to Szpilrajn (1930), as noted in section 7.2. A proof is given also in Fishburn (1970, Theorem 2.4). Recall from Chapter 7 that $\succ \,\subseteq\, \succ'$ means that $x \succ y \Rightarrow x \succ' y$, for all $x,y \in X$.

The second part of the lemma is a variation of Szpilrajn's theorem. An explicit proof is given by Hansson (1968, Lemma 3). Since we have been dealing mainly with asymmetric and therefore irreflexive orders, it will be instructive to see how the second part of the lemma follows from the first part.

Suppose then that $\succcurlyeq$ on $X$ is *reflexive* and transitive. Reversing the process of definition used earlier, define $\sim$ and $\succ$ from $\succcurlyeq$ thus:

$$x \sim y \;\Leftrightarrow\; x \succcurlyeq y \;\&\; y \succcurlyeq x$$
$$x \succ y \Leftrightarrow x \succcurlyeq y \;\&\; \text{not } y \succcurlyeq x.$$

As one can easily show, $\sim$ is transitive and is therefore an equivalence on $X$, and $(\succcurlyeq)(\succ) \subseteq \succ$ and $(\succ)(\succcurlyeq) \subseteq \succ$, so that $\succ$ is transitive and $[(x \sim y \;\&\; y \succ z)$ or $(x \succ y \;\&\; y \sim z)] \Rightarrow x \succ z$.

With $\succcurlyeq'$ as in the conclusion of the lemma, we claim that $x \sim y \Rightarrow x \sim' y$ and $x \succ y \Rightarrow x \succ' y$. If not $x \succcurlyeq y$ & not $y \succcurlyeq x$, which can occur if $\succcurlyeq$ is not connected, then the extension $\succcurlyeq'$ must have either $x \succcurlyeq' y$ or $y \succcurlyeq' x$.

With $\sim$ an equivalence on $X$, let $\hat{x}$, $\hat{y}$, . . . denote equivalence classes in $X/\sim$. Define $\succ_1$ on $X/\sim$ by

$$\hat{x} \succ_1 \hat{y} \Leftrightarrow x \succ y \text{ for some (and hence for all) } x \in \hat{x} \text{ and } y \in \hat{y}.$$

It follows from above that $\succ_1$ on $X/\sim$ is a strict partial order. Therefore, by Szpilrajn's theorem, there is a linear order $\succ_2$ on $X/\sim$ that includes $\succ_1$. Let $\succ'$ on $X$ be the weak order defined from $\succ_2$ by

$$x \succ' y \Leftrightarrow \hat{x} \succ_2 \hat{y} \qquad \text{when} \qquad x \in \hat{x} \qquad \text{and} \qquad y \in \hat{y},$$

so that, with $x \sim' y \Leftrightarrow \text{not } x \succ' y \;\&\; \text{not } y \succ' x$ as in the Chapter 7 presentation, $x \sim' y \Leftrightarrow x \sim y$ ($x$, $y$ in same class in $X/\sim$). Taking $\succcurlyeq' = \succ' \cup \sim'$, it follows that $\succcurlyeq'$ is transitive and connected and it is easily seen to satisfy the conclusions of the second part of Lemma 15.4.

In addition to Lemma 15.4 we shall use a definition that applies to extensions of choice functions.

DEFINITION 15.3. *Let* $f : \mathfrak{X} \to \mathcal{P}(X)$ *be a choice function. Then* $g : \mathfrak{X}' \to \mathcal{P}(X)$ *is an* extension *of* $f : \mathfrak{X} \to \mathcal{P}(X)$ *if and only if* $g : \mathfrak{X}' \to \mathcal{P}(X)$ *is a choice function, every element in* $\mathfrak{X}'$ *is a subset of* $X$, $\mathfrak{X} \subseteq \mathfrak{X}'$ *and* $g(Y) = f(Y)$ *for all* $Y \in \mathfrak{X}$.

**199**

HANSSON'S THEOREM

With this definition, we are now ready to state the first of the two theorems.

THEOREM 15.4. *Suppose that $f: \mathfrak{X} \to \mathcal{P}(X)$ is a choice function. Then the following three statements are equivalent:*

(a) *There is a weak order $f^*$ on $X$ that satisfies* (15.2);

(b) *There is an extension $g: \mathfrak{X}' \to \mathcal{P}(X)$ of $f: \mathfrak{X} \to \mathcal{P}(X)$ such that B1 holds for $g$ and $Y, Z \in \mathfrak{X}' \Rightarrow Y \cup Z \in \mathfrak{X}'$;*

(c) *There is an extension $h: \mathfrak{X}^0 \to \mathcal{P}(X)$ of $f: \mathfrak{X} \to \mathcal{P}(X)$ such that B1 holds for $h$ and $\mathfrak{X}^0$ contains every nonempty finite subset of $X$.*

*Proof.* (a) $\Rightarrow$ (b). Assume that (a) holds. Let $\mathfrak{X}'$ be the closure of $\mathfrak{X}$ under nonempty finite unions. If $Y = \cup_{j=1}^{m} Y_j$ with each $Y_j \in \mathfrak{X}$, let $y_j \in f(Y_j)$ for each $j$. Since $f^*$ is a weak order, it follows that, for some $k \in \{1, \ldots, m\}$, $y_j f^* y_k$ for no $y_j$. Since not $y f^* y_j$ for every $y \in Y$ by (15.2), it follows from negative transitivity that not $y f^* y_k$ for every $y \in Y$. Therefore $g$ on $\mathfrak{X}'$ defined by

$$g(Y) = \{x : x \in Y \text{ and } y f^* x \text{ for no } y \in Y\} \text{ for all } Y \in \mathfrak{X}'$$

is a well-defined choice function that is an extension of $f$. B1 for $g$ is assured by Lemma 15.3.

(b) $\Rightarrow$ (c). Assume that (b) holds with $g: \mathfrak{X}' \to \mathcal{P}(X)$ as specified therein. Define $R_1$ on $X$ by

$$x R_1 y \Leftrightarrow \text{there is a } Y \in \mathfrak{X}' \text{ such that } x \in g(Y) \text{ and } y \in Y. \quad (15.5)$$

To show that $R_1$ is transitive, assume that $x R_1 y$ and $y R_1 z$. Then, by (15.5), there are $Y, Z \in \mathfrak{X}'$ such that $x, y \in Y$, $y, z \in Z$, $x \in g(Y)$ and $y \in g(Z)$. By (b), $Y \cup Z \in \mathfrak{X}'$. Take $t \in g(Y \cup Z)$. If $t \in Y$ then $x \in g(Y \cup Z)$ by B1 for $g$, and hence $x R_1 z$ by (15.5). If $t \in Z$ then $Z \cap g(Y \cup Z) = g(Z)$ by B1, so that $y \in g(Y \cup Z)$. Then, by B1 again, $Y \cap g(Y \cup Z) = g(Y)$ so that $x \in g(Y \cup Z)$ and $x R_1 z$.

We show next that

$$g(Y) = \{x : x \in Y \text{ and } x R_1 y \text{ for all } y \in Y\} \text{ for all } Y \in \mathfrak{X}'. \quad (15.6)$$

By (15.5), $g(Y) \subseteq R_1(Y) = \{x : x \in Y \text{ and } x R_1 y \text{ for all } y \in Y\}$. Contrary to (15.6), suppose that $t \in R_1(Y)$ and $t \notin g(Y)$. Then, for every $y \neq t$ in $Y$, there is a $T(y) \in \mathfrak{X}'$ such that $t, y \in T(y)$ and $t \in g(T(y))$. In particular, this is true for $x \in g(Y)$. So with $x \in g(Y)$ consider $Y \cup T(x) \in \mathfrak{X}'$, and take $v \in g(Y \cup T(x))$. Suppose first that $v \in T(x)$. Then, by B1, $t \in g(Y \cup T(x))$ so that, again by B1, $Y \cap g(Y \cup T(x)) = g(Y)$ and hence $t \in g(Y)$, which contradicts

$t \notin g(Y)$. Suppose then that $v \in Y$. Then $Y \cap g(Y \cup T(x)) = g(Y)$ by B1 so that $x \in g(Y \cup T(x))$. Since $x \in T(x)$ it follows from B1 that $T(x) \cap g(Y \cup T(x)) = g(T(x))$ and hence that $t \in g(Y \cup T(x))$ and then that $t \in g(Y)$ which again contradicts $t \notin g(Y)$. Therefore $R_1(Y) \subseteq g(Y)$ and the proof of (15.6) is complete.

Next, define $R_2$ on $X$ by

$$xR_2y \Leftrightarrow xR_1y \text{ or } x = y.$$

Then (15.6) holds for $R_2$ in place of $R_1$, and $R_2$ is transitive and reflexive. It follows from the second part of Lemma 15.4 that there is a transitive and connected $R_3$ on $X$ such that $R_2 \subseteq R_3$ and $(xR_2y$ & not $yR_2x) \Rightarrow$ not $yR_3x$. Moreover,

$$g(Y) = \{x : x \in Y \text{ and } xR_3y \text{ for all } y \in Y\} \text{ for all } Y \in \mathfrak{X}',$$

since $xR_2y$ for all $y \in Y \Rightarrow xR_3y$ for all $y \in Y$, and since if $t \in Y - g(Y)$ then not $tR_2y$ for some $y \in g(Y)$, since $R_2$ is transitive, and hence $yR_2t$ & not $tR_2y$, so that not $tR_3y$.

Finally, let $\mathfrak{X}^0$ equal $\mathfrak{X}'$ plus all nonempty finite subsets of $X$ and define $h : \mathfrak{X}^0 \to \mathcal{P}(X)$ by

$$h(Y) = \{x : x \in Y \text{ and } xR_3y \text{ for all } y \in Y\} \text{ for all } Y \in \mathfrak{X}^0.$$

Then $h(Y) = g(Y)$ for all $Y \in \mathfrak{X}'$, and $h(Y) \neq \emptyset$ for each $Y \in \mathfrak{X}^0 - \mathfrak{X}'$ by finiteness. If we define the binary relation $h^*$ on $X$ by $yh^*x \Leftrightarrow$ not $xR_3y$, or not $yh^*x \Leftrightarrow xR_3y$, then $h^*$ is a weak order, $h(Y) = \{x : x \in Y$ and $yh^*x$ for no $y \in Y\}$, and hence B1 holds for $h$ by Lemma 15.3.

(c) $\Rightarrow$ (a). This is immediate from Corollary 15.1.◆

A NECESSARY AND SUFFICIENT CONDITION

During the course of the preceding (b) $\Rightarrow$ (c) proof we have identified the binary relation that forms the basis of Richter's Congruence Axiom. As in (15.5), we define $R_1$ on $X$ for an arbitrary choice function $f : \mathfrak{X} \to \mathcal{P}(X)$ by

$$xR_1y \Leftrightarrow \text{there is a } Y \in \mathfrak{X} \text{ such that } x \in f(Y) \text{ and } y \in Y. \quad (15.7)$$

In a sense this says that "$x$ is directly revealed to be as good as $y$" if and only if $xR_1y$.

Richter's axiom uses the transitive closure $R_1^t$ of $R_1$ in the following way. The condition applies to all $Y \in \mathfrak{X}$.

B4. $x \in f(Y)$, $y \in Y$ and $yR_1^t x \Rightarrow y \in f(Y)$.

The expression $yR_1^t x$ can be interpreted to mean that "$y$ is indirectly revealed to be as good as $x$." Thus B4 says that if $x,y \in Y$, if $x$ is in the choice set $f(Y)$ and if "$y$ is indirectly revealed to be as good as $x$," then $y$ is in the choice set also.

THEOREM 15.5. *Suppose that $f: \mathfrak{X} \to \mathcal{P}(X)$ is a choice function. Then there is a weak order $f^*$ on $X$ for which (15.2) holds if and only if B4 holds.*

*Proof.* Suppose first that (15.2) holds with $f^*$ a weak order. With $xR_0y \Leftrightarrow$ not $yf^*x$, this is equivalent to

$$f(Y) = \{x : x \in Y \text{ and } xR_0y \text{ for all } y \in Y\} \text{ for all } Y \in \mathfrak{X}, \quad (15.8)$$

with $R_0$ transitive and connected. For B4, suppose that $x \in f(Y)$, $y \in Y$ and $yR_1^t x$. Then $yR_1z_1R_1 \cdots R_1z_mR_1x$ so that, by (15.7) and (15.8), $yR_0z_1R_0 \cdots R_0z_mR_0x$ and hence $yR_0x$ by transitivity. Since $xR_0v$ for all $v \in Y$, $yR_0v$ for all $v \in Y$ by transitivity, and therefore $y \in f(Y)$ by (15.8). Thus B4 holds.

Suppose next that B4 holds. For convenience let $W = R_1^t$, so that B4 reads (for all $Y \in \mathfrak{X}$)

B4. $x \in f(Y)$, $y \in Y$ and $yWx \Rightarrow y \in f(Y)$,

and let $W(Y) = \{x : x \in Y \text{ and } xWy \text{ for all } y \in Y\}$. $W$ is transitive by definition. Since $f(Y) \neq \emptyset$, B4 implies $W(Y) \subseteq f(Y)$. Take $x \in f(Y)$. Then $xR_1y$ for all $y \in Y$ by (15.7) so that $xWy$ for all $y \in Y$, and hence $f(Y) \subseteq W(Y)$. Thus $f(Y) = W(Y)$.

Define $W_1$ by $xW_1y \Leftrightarrow xWy$ or $x = y$. $W_1$ is reflexive and transitive, and $f(Y) = W_1(Y)$. By the latter part of Lemma 15.4, let $R_0$ be a connected and transitive binary relation on $X$ such that $W_1 \subseteq R_0$ and $(xW_1y \text{ \& not } yW_1x) \Rightarrow$ not $yR_0x$. As in the (b) $\Rightarrow$ (c) proof of Theorem 15.4, it follows easily that (15.8) holds. ◆

OTHER CONTRIBUTIONS

Additional theorems along the lines presented here are discussed in the aforementioned papers of Arrow (1959) and Hansson (1968), and in Wilson (1970) and Richter (1971). The last two of these summarize many of the earlier developments in this area and present several new theorems.

# CHAPTER 16

# Arrow's Impossibility Theorem

THE CONDITIONS in a set of conditions for a social choice function are incompatible, inconsistent or "impossible" if there is no social choice function that can simultaneously satisfy all conditions in the set. A number of such sets have been identified in preceding chapters. In Chapter 6 we noted that duality and strong decisiveness are incompatible. In Part II, each of Lemmas 7.2, 7.3, 8.2, 13.1 and Theorems 12.1, 12.2, and 12.3 can be viewed as an impossibility theorem.

In this chapter we shall examine Arrow's famous impossibility theorem and a number of its close relatives. The original theorem by Arrow (1950) differs in several respects from the version developed by Arrow and by Blau (1957) that appears in Arrow (1963, Theorem 2, p. 97) and which is stated here as Theorem 16.1. This theorem uses the passive intraprofile condition that $F_D$ on $X$ is a weak order for all $D \in \mathfrak{D}$. If individual strict partial orders are allowed, then, as we have seen in sections 7.3 and 15.1, we would have little to say since strong binary unanimity is inconsistent with this passive condition. But Arrow's theorem restricts $\mathfrak{D}$ by requiring that all individual preference orders be weak orders, and under this restriction the matter becomes more complex and much more interesting.

In general, it is assumed throughout the chapter that all individual preference orders are weak orders. Arrow's theorem is proved in the next section. Section 16.2 presents a modification of Arrow's theorem that retains all of his structural conditions but weakens weak order for $F_D$ to transitivity for $F_D$ and strengthens his nondictatorship condition to a no-vetoer condition. Section 16.3 notes a version of the impossibility theorem that was developed by Hansson (1972) and which uses a nonconstancy condition plus a condition of nonsuppression. The theorems in the first three sections assume that $\#X \geq 3$ and that $\mathfrak{X}$ contains all two-element subsets of $X$.

The final section discusses an impossibility theorem from Hansson (1969) which requires almost no structure for $\mathfrak{X}$. This theorem effectively assumes for $\mathfrak{X}$-structure that $\mathfrak{X}$ includes at least one subset of $X$ with more than two elements, and it does not require $\mathfrak{X}$ to contain any two-element subset of $X$.

## 16.1 A BASIC IMPOSSIBILITY THEOREM

In this section we shall first state Arrow's impossibility theorem and then discuss the conditions used in the theorem in more detail. The section concludes with two proofs of the theorem.

Working within the context of individual weak orders, we shall say that a triple $\{x,y,z\} \subseteq X$ is *free* in $\mathcal{D}$ if and only if for every $n$-tuple of weak orders on $\{x,y,z\}$ there is a $D \in \mathcal{D}$ whose restriction on $\{x,y,z\}$ is the given $n$-tuple. Because one of the structural conditions in the theorem says that every two-element subset of $X$ is in $\mathcal{X}$, $F_D$ as in (7.9) is well defined. This fact is used in later conditions.

THEOREM 16.1 (Arrow's Theorem). *Suppose that* $F: \mathcal{X} \times \mathcal{D} \to \mathcal{P}(X)$ *is a social choice function such that*

C1. *$n$ is a positive integer,*
C2. *$\#X \geq 3$ and $\mathcal{X}$ contains every two-element subset of $X$,*
C3. *$\mathcal{D}$ is a set of $n$-tuples of weak orders on $X$ and every triple in $X$ is free in $\mathcal{D}$.*

*Then at least one of the following conditions must be false:*

C4. *$F_D$ on $X$ is a weak order for every $D \in \mathcal{D}$,*
C5. *If $x,y \in X$, $D \in \mathcal{D}$ and $x \gg_D y$ then $xF_Dy$,*
C6. *If $x,y \in X$, $x \neq y$, $D,D' \in \mathcal{D}$ and if $D$ on $\{x,y\}$ equals $D'$ on $\{x,y\}$ then $F_D$ on $\{x,y\}$ equals $F_{D'}$ on $\{x,y\}$,*
C7. *There is no $i \in \{1, \ldots, n\}$ such that $(x,y \in X, D \in \mathcal{D}, x >_i y) \Rightarrow xF_Dy$.*

The seven conditions used in the theorem have the following classification according to Table 14.1:

Structural: C1, C2, C3
Passive Intraprofile: C4
Active Intraprofile: C5
Interprofile: C6
Existential: C7

Hence every class or subclass in Table 14.1 with the exception of the multiprofile class is represented in the theorem.

One should have no difficulty interpreting the conditions. C4 was discussed at length in section 15.1, C5 is binary unanimity, C6 is the binary version of independence from infeasible alternatives, and C7 is a binary nondictatorship condition.

The only condition that might appear to be redundant is C1. However, recall that the general definition of social choice function in

Definition 14.1 says nothing about $\mathcal{D}$ other than it is a nonempty set. With minor changes in terminology in C3 and C7, one might wish to assume that the set of voters is nonempty, and use this instead of C1. However, as shown in Fishburn (1970c), the theorem will then be false, since an infinite set of voters is consistent with conditions C2 through C7. Thus the stipulation that the set of voters is finite is crucial to the theorem.

Perhaps the greatest benefit of Arrow's theorem is the subsequent discussion and research it has generated. One direction that this research has taken appears in Chapters 9 through 11 and in section 14.4, which can be viewed as attempts to tighten C3 to such an extent that the remaining conditions (or modifications thereof) are compatible.

Arrow's theorem has led also to deeper examinations of conditions like C4 through C7 under the supposition that C1–C3 are acceptable in some situations. Some writers, who feel that each of C4 through C7 is acceptable, conclude that Arrow's theorem shows that there does not exist any reasonable or "rational" social choice procedure for some situations involving more than two alternatives. Others conclude that one or more of C4 through C7 is untenable as a general desideratum of social choice.

Most of the latter discussion has involved the condition of a social ordering (C4) and the condition of independence from infeasible alternatives (C6). For example, the arguments of section 15.1 suggest that C4 may be untenable, and some people feel that this viewpoint is further supported by Arrow's theorem. Others take issue with the independence condition, feeling that it causes the suppression of information about preferences that should be taken into account in determining the social choice. Closely allied to this is a potential disagreement with C3, which permits only certain types of information about voters to enter into the social choice function. For further comments on this point the reader is referred to the discussion of Chapter 1 and the references cited there.

PROOF PRELIMINARIES

We shall now consider two proofs of Theorem 16.1 that go at the matter from different directions. The first proof, which is used by Arrow (1963), shows that C1 through C6 imply the contradictory of C7. That is, C1 through C6 imply that some individual is a dictator. The second proof begins by assuming that no individual is a dictator and shows that C2 through C7 imply the contradictory of C1.

Several special definitions are used in the proofs. If $I$ is a nonempty subset of voters then $I$ is *decisive for $x$ over $y$* if $xF_D y$ whenever $x >_i y$

for all $i \in I$ and $y >_i x$ for all $i \notin I$. This is similar to the definition of section 4.1. For the first proof we shall write

$x \, i \, y \Leftrightarrow (x \, F_D \, y$ whenever $x >_i y$ and $y >_j x$ for all $j \neq i)$,
$x \, \bar{\imath} \, y \Leftrightarrow (x \, F_D \, y$ whenever $x >_i y)$.

$x \, i \, y$ says that $\{i\}$ is decisive for $x$ over $y$; and if $x \, \bar{\imath} \, y$ for a fixed $i$ and all $x, y \in X$ for which $x \neq y$, then $i$ is a dictator. The second proof used the "dual" of $x \, i \, y$ and another relation as follows:

$x \, i^* \, y \Leftrightarrow (x F_D y$ whenever $y >_i x$ and $x >_j y$ for all $j \neq i)$,
$x \cdot \mathbf{m} \, y \Leftrightarrow (x F_D y$ whenever $D$ is such that $m$ voters have $y >_i x$ and all others have $x >_i y)$.

$x \, i^* \, y$ says that $\{1, \ldots, i-1, i+1, \ldots, n\}$ is decisive for $x$ over $y$. If any subset that contains all but one of the voters is decisive for any alternative over any other alternative, then $x \, \mathbf{1} \, y$ whenever $x, y \in X$ and $x \neq y$.

In both proofs $\mathbf{n}$ *designates the set of all voters.*

ARROW'S PROOF

Let C1 through C6 hold. We show first that $a \, i \, b$ for some $i$ and some $a, b \in X$ with $a \neq b$. Using C5, $\mathbf{n}$ is decisive for $x$ over $y$ whenever $x, y \in X$ and $x \neq y$. It follows from C1 and C6 that there are $a \neq b$ and $\emptyset \subset I \subseteq \mathbf{n}$ such that $I$ is decisive for $a$ over $b$ and there is no smaller subset of $\mathbf{n}$ that is decisive for one alternative over another. Fix $i \in I$, take $x \notin \{a, b\}$ by C2, and use C3 to obtain a $D$ for which

$$x >_i a >_i b, a >_j b >_j x \text{ for all } j \in I - \{i\}, b >_j x >_j a \text{ otherwise.}$$

By construction, $aF_D b$. If $\{i\} \subset I$ then not $aF_D x$, for otherwise $I - \{i\}$ would be decisive for $a$ over $x$, using C6; but then $xF_D b$ by C4 and hence $x \, i \, b$, contrary to $\{i\} \subset I$. Hence $I = \{i\}$.

Given $a \, i \, b$, we now show that $i$ is a dictator. First, take $x \notin \{a, b\}$ by C2 and use C3 to obtain $D$ with

$$x >_i a >_i b \quad \text{and} \quad x >_j a, b >_j a \quad \text{for all} \quad j \neq i.$$

Then $aF_D b$ by $a \, i \, b$, and $xF_D a$ by C2 and C5, so that $xF_D b$ by C2 and C4. Since C3 allows any relationship between $x$ and $b$ for $j \neq i$ it follows from C6 that $x \, \bar{\imath} \, b$. A similar argument with $a >_i b >_i x$ and $b >_j x, b >_j a$ gives $a \, \bar{\imath} \, x$. Note that $x \, \bar{\imath} \, b \Rightarrow x \, i \, b$ and $a \, \bar{\imath} \, x \Rightarrow a \, i \, x$.

Beginning with $x, b$ in place of $a, b$, the preceding argument gives $a \, \bar{\imath} \, b$ and $x \, \bar{\imath} \, a$. Beginning with $a, x$ in place of $a, b$, the argument gives

$y \bar{\imath} x$ for $y \notin \{a,x\}$, which includes $b \bar{\imath} x$. Finally, $b,x$ in place of $a,b$ yields $b \bar{\imath} a$. This accounts for all distinct pairs in $X$, and hence $i$ is a dictator, contradicting C7. ◆

AN ALTERNATIVE PROOF

Let C2 through C7 hold. Suppose $\mathbf{n} \neq \emptyset$ and take any $i \in \mathbf{n}$. C2, C3, and C7 imply that $a >_i b$ and not $aF_D b$ for some $D$ and some $a,b \in X$. Take $x \notin \{a,b\}$ by C2 and let $D'$ agree with $D$ on $\{a,b\}$ with

$$a >'_i x >'_i b \qquad \text{and} \qquad a >'_j x, \, b >'_j x \qquad \text{for all} \qquad j \neq i. \quad (16.1)$$

Then not $aF_{D'}b$ by C6, $aF_{D'}x$ by C5, and hence $bF_{D'}x$ by C4, and $b \, i^* \, x$ by C6. A similar proof gives $x \, i^* \, a$. With $y \notin \{x,b\}$ let $D^1$ agree with $D'$ on $\{x,b\}$ and have $x >^1_i y >^1_i b$ and $y >^1_j b >^1_j x$ for $j \neq i$. Since $bF_{D^1}x$, and $yF_{D^1}b$ by C5, $yF_{D^1}x$ by transitivity, and $y \, i^* \, x$ by C6. This includes $a \, i^* \, x$. By a similar proof, $x \, i^* \, b$. Finally, take $D^2$ with $a >^2_i b >^2_i x$ and $b >^2_j x >^2_j a$ for $j \neq i$. Then $xF_{D^2}a$ by $x \, i^* \, a$, $bF_{D^2}x$ by C5, and hence $bF_{D^2}a$ by C4, and $b \, i^* \, a$ by C6. A similar proof gives $a \, i^* \, b$.

Since $i \in \mathbf{n}$ was arbitrary, $x \, \mathbf{1} \, y$ whenever $x,y \in X$ and $x \neq y$.

Suppose $\mathbf{n} \neq \emptyset$. Then $\#\mathbf{n} > 1$ is required by C5 and C7. Suppose $\#\mathbf{n} > m \geq 1$, and that $x \, \mathbf{k} \, y$ for all $k \leq m$ and all $x,y \in X$ with $x \neq y$. With $i \in \mathbf{n}$, $i \notin I$ and $\#I = m$ take $D$ with

$$y >_i x >_i a, \, a >_j y >_j x \text{ for all } j \in I, \, x >_j a >_j y \text{ otherwise.} \quad (16.2)$$

Then $a \, \mathbf{1} \, y \Rightarrow aF_D y$ and $x \, \mathbf{m} \, a \Rightarrow xF_D a$, so that $xF_D y$ by C4. This contradicts C5 if $\#\mathbf{n} = m + 1$. Hence $\#\mathbf{n} > m + 1$. Moreover, since $i$, $x$, and $y$ are arbitrary, $x(\mathbf{m} + 1)y$ for $x \neq y$ in $X$. It follows either that $\mathbf{n} = \emptyset$ or that $\#\mathbf{n} > m$ for all positive integers $m$, thus contradicting C1. ◆

## 16.2 VETOERS AND OLIGARCHIES

During the years since Arrow's original theorem appeared, there have been many variations on his impossibility theorem theme. Some of the more important variants of his theorem appear as numbered theorems in this and later sections. A few others will be noted in the text.

One type of modification weakens condition C4, that $F_D$ be a weak order for each $D \in \mathfrak{D}$. The following theorem, mentioned by Murakami (1968) and Schick (1969), replaces C4 by a transitivity condition and strengthens the nondictatorship condition C7 to a no-vetoer condition.

THEOREM 16.2. *Suppose that* $F: \mathcal{X} \times \mathcal{D} \rightarrow \mathcal{P}(X)$ *is a social choice function for which* C1, C2, *and* C3 *hold. Then at least one of the following conditions must be false:*

C4'. $F_D$ *on* $X$ *is transitive for every* $D \in \mathcal{D}$,
C5. (*Binary unanimity*),
C6. (*Binary independence from infeasible alternatives*),
C7'. *For each* $i \in \{1, \ldots ,n\}$ *there are* $x,y \in X$ *and* $D \in \mathcal{D}$ *such that* $x >_i y$ *and* $yF_Dx$.

Condition C7' says that no individual has unlimited veto power: that is, there is no $i$ such that not $yF_Dx$ whenever $x >_i y$, for all $x,y \in X$ for which $x \neq y$. C7' is therefore referred to as a no-vetoer condition. It is stronger than the nondictatorship condition (C7' $\Rightarrow$ C7, but not conversely) since a dictator is a vetoer, but not conversely.

*Proof.* In the second proof of the preceding section, negative transitivity for $F_D$ was required only in the sentence after (16.1). All other uses of C4 involved only the transitivity of $F_D$. By using C7' instead of C7 we obtain $a >_i b$ and $bF_{D'}a$ for use with (16.1): this and $aF_{D'}x$ then give $bF_{D'}x$ by C4'. Since C4' serves elsewhere in the proof and since C7' $\Rightarrow$ C7, the proof of Theorem 16.2 is complete. ◆

SOME OTHER MODIFICATIONS

Each of Theorems 16.1 and 16.2 can be modified by weakening C3 by requiring only one triple in $X$ to be free in $\mathcal{D}$. This weakening then requires a strengthening in C7 [or C7'] to the effect that no individual is a dictator (or vetoer) with respect to the three alternatives in some free triple. The foregoing proofs for Theorems 16.1 and 16.2 apply directly to a free triple with this property.

Another modification changes C3 by assuming only the presence of linear individual preference orders, with free triples in this context. Since individual indifference is not actually used in the proofs, the theorems remain valid under this slight weakening of C3.

A more interesting possibility is to weaken C4 or C4' to "$F_D$ is a suborder for each $D \in \mathcal{D}$," but we know of no simple modification of Theorem 16.2 for this case that gives an impossibility theorem of quite the same caliber as the preceding theorems. This does not say that there are no impossibility theorems for the suborder case. Indeed, with sufficiently strong conditions (approaching those used for simple majority agreement) such a theorem is readily obtained.

A somewhat different modification of Arrow's theorem has been developed by Blau (1971). His basic idea is to replace the binary version of independence, C6, by a weaker independence condition that applies to $m$-element subsets of $X$ where $2 \leq m < \#X$. For example, ternary independence says that if $\{x,y,z\}$ is a triple in $X$ and if $D$ on $\{x,y,z\}$ equals $D'$ on $\{x,y,z\}$ then $F_D$ on $\{x,y,z\}$ equals $F_{D'}$ on $\{x,y,z\}$. Strengthening C3 to admit all $n$-tuples of weak orders in $\mathfrak{D}$, Blau shows that the preliminary conditions of Theorem 16.1 along with C4 and $m$-ary independence, for any fixed $m$ with $2 \leq m < \#X$, imply binary independence (C6). Additional remarks on types of independence are found in Hansson (1972).

OLIGARCHIES

In general, when one of the conditions in Theorem 16.1 [Theorem 16.2] is omitted, the remaining conditions are compatible and any $F$ that satisfies them must satisfy also the contradictory of the omitted condition. For example, if $F$ satisfies all of C1 through C7 except for C5, then there must be $x,y \in X$ and $D \in \mathfrak{D}$ such that $x \gg_D y$ and not $xF_Dy$. Or if $F$ satisfies C1, C2, C3, C5, C6, and C7', then $F_D$ is not transitive for some $D$.

As several authors have shown, sets of compatible conditions sometimes give rise to other properties for a social choice function that may seem unusual or surprising. A good example of this is provided by a theorem attributed to A. Gibbard by Sen (1970b). Given C1, C2, C3, C5, and C6, we have noted that C4 and C7 are incompatible and that C4' and C7' are incompatible. However, simple examples show that C4' (transitivity) and C7 (nondictatorship) are compatible. However, as Gibbard has shown, there must then be an oligarchy. This is a nonempty subset of voters which is decisive for $x$ over $y$ whenever $x \neq y$, with each voter in the subset having veto power.

DEFINITION 16.1. *In the context of a social choice function* $F:\mathfrak{X} \times \mathfrak{D} \to \mathcal{P}(X)$ *for which* $\mathfrak{X}$ *contains every two-element subset of* $X$ *and* $\mathbf{n} = \{1, \ldots, n\}$, $I$ *is an* oligarchy *if and only if* $\emptyset \subset I \subseteq \mathbf{n}$ *and, for all distinct* $x$ *and* $y$ *in* $X$ *and* $D \in \mathfrak{D}$,

(i) $x \succ_i y$ *for all* $i \in I \Rightarrow xF_Dy$,
(ii) $x \succ_i y$ *for any* $i \in I \Rightarrow$ *not* $yF_Dx$.

If $\mathbf{n}$ itself is an oligarchy then not $xF_Dy$ and not $yF_Dx$ whenever someone prefers $x$ to $y$ and somebody else prefers $y$ to $x$. If some pair in $X$ is free in $\mathfrak{D}$, then it is easily seen that there can be at most one oligarchy.

THEOREM 16.3. *Suppose that* $F:\mathfrak{X} \times \mathfrak{D} \to \mathcal{P}(X)$ *is a social choice function that satisfies* C1, C2, C3, C4', C5, C6, *and* C7. *Then* $\mathbf{n}$ *includes an oligarchy.*

**209**

*Proof.* Let the conditions of the theorem hold for $F$. Suppose that $K \subseteq \mathbf{n}$ is decisive for some $a$ over $b$. Then, by an argument like that following (16.1), it is easily seen that $K$ is decisive for $x$ over $y$, for all distinct $x$ and $y$ in $X$.

By Theorem 16.2, C7′ must be false. Therefore, there is at least one $i \in \mathbf{n}$ who is a vetoer: for all distinct $x$ and $y$ in $X$ and $D \in \mathfrak{D}$, $x >_i y \Rightarrow$ not $yF'_D x$. Let $I$ be the set of all such $i$. Then Definition 16.1 (ii) holds for $I$, with $\emptyset \subset I \subseteq \mathbf{n}$.

By C5, $\mathbf{n}$ is decisive for $x$ over $y$ whenever $x \neq y$. Let $K$ be a smallest subset of $\mathbf{n}$ that is decisive for some alternative over another. Clearly $I \subseteq K$. Contrary to $I = K$ suppose that $k \in K - I$. Since $k \notin I$, there are distinct $a$ and $b$ in $X$ and $D \in \mathfrak{D}$ such that $a >_k b$ and $bF_D a$. The proof following (16.1) (replace not $aF_{D'}b$ by $bF_{D'}a$ in the sentence after (16.1) and use C4′) shows that $x\, k^*\, y$ ($xF_D y$ whenever $y >_k x$ and $x >_j y$ for all $j \neq k$) for all distinct $x$ and $y$ in $X$. For definiteness let $K$ be decisive for $c$ over $d$, and use C2 and C3 to obtain a $D \in \mathfrak{D}$ that has

$$c >_k d >_k x,\ x >_i c >_i d \text{ for all } i \in K - \{k\},\ d >_i x >_i c$$

otherwise.

Then $cF_D d$ by decisiveness, and $xF_D c$ by $x\, k^*\, c$, so that $xF_D d$ by C4′. But then $K = \{k\}$ is decisive for $x$ over $d$, contrary to our smallest assumption for the formation of $K$. Therefore $K - I = \emptyset$ and $K = I$, which with the initial paragraph of this proof gives Definition 16.1 (i). Hence $I$ is an oligarchy. ◆

## 16.3 SUPPRESSED INDIVIDUALS

In concluding our discussion of impossibility theorems that use the structure of Arrow's theorem, we shall prove a theorem of Hansson (1972) that drops the unanimity condition and adds conditions of nonconstancy and nonsuppression.

Within the context of C1, C2, and C3 we shall say that $F$ is *strongly nonconstant* if, for each pair $x,y \in X$ with $x \neq y$, there are $D$ and $D'$ in $\mathfrak{D}$ (which can depend on $x$ and $y$) such that $F(\{x,y\},D) \neq F(\{x,y\},D')$. This condition is closely related to Arrow's condition of *citizens' sovereignty*, which says that for each ordered pair $(x,y) \in X \times X$ there is a $D \in \mathfrak{D}$ such that $F(\{x,y\},D) = \{x\}$. Citizens' sovereignty implies strong nonconstancy, but $F$ can be strongly nonconstant and not satisfy citizens' sovereignty. Hence strong nonconstancy is the weaker of the two conditions.

Strong nonconstancy and citizens' sovereignty are generally felt to be desirable properties for a social choice function. In contrast to these we note three undesirable properties that are suggested by Hansson's developments. We shall say that $F$ is

(1) *flat*
(2) *perverse*
(3) *suppressive*

if and only if, for all $x,y \in X$ with $x \neq y$ and for all $D \in \mathfrak{D}$,

(1) not $xF_Dy$ and not $yF_Dx$
(2) $x \gg_D y \Rightarrow yF_Dx$
(3) there is an $i$ such that $x >_i y \Rightarrow yF_Dx$.

A flat social choice function yields a tie between $x$ and $y$ regardless of the individuals' preferences between $x$ and $y$. Flatness is ruled out by strong nonconstancy and by citizens' sovereignty.

A perverse social choice function selects $y$ over $x$ when everyone prefers $x$ to $y$, in sharp contrast to unanimity. A suppressive social choice function selects $y$ over $x$ whenever a given (suppressed) individual prefers $x$ to $y$, regardless of the other individuals' preferences. In a manner of speaking, a suppressed individual is a dictator turned upside down.

A suppressive function is perverse, but a perverse function need not be suppressive. Hence the *desirable* condition of *non*suppression is weaker than the condition of *non*perversion.

THEOREM 16.4. *Suppose that* $F: \mathfrak{X} \times \mathfrak{D} \to \mathcal{P}(X)$ *is a social choice function for which* C1, C2, *and* C3 *hold. Then at least one of the following conditions must be false:*

C4. $F_D$ *is a weak order for every* $D \in \mathfrak{D}$,
C6. *(Binary independence from infeasible alternatives),*
C7. *(Nondictatorship),*
C8. $F$ *is strongly nonconstant,*
C9. $F$ *is not suppressive.*

This shows that if C1, C2, and C3 hold and if we insist on weak orders for the $F_D$ along with independence, then either there is a dictator, or a suppressed individual, or else strong nonconstancy (and hence citizens' sovereignty) is violated.

*Proof.* We assume that all conditions except C9 hold and show that there must be a suppressed individual. Define three binary relations $A$, $B$, $C$ on $X$ as follows:

$$x \, A \, y \Leftrightarrow (x \gg_D y \Rightarrow xF_Dy)$$
$$x \, B \, y \Leftrightarrow (x \gg_D y \Rightarrow \text{not } xF_Dy \text{ \& not } yF_Dx)$$
$$x \, C \, y \Leftrightarrow (x \gg_D y \Rightarrow yF_Dx).$$

**211**

If $x \neq y$ then, under C6, exactly one of $x \, A \, y$, $x \, B \, y$ and $x \, C \, y$ holds. Given $x \neq y$ we note that

$$x \, A \, y \Rightarrow z \, A \, w \qquad \text{for all} \qquad z,w \in X \qquad (16.3)$$
$$x \, C \, y \Rightarrow z \, C \, w \qquad \text{for all} \qquad z,w \in X. \qquad (16.4)$$

First, $x \, A \, y \Rightarrow x \, A \, z$ for every $z \in X$. This is trivial if $z \in \{x,y\}$. Otherwise, suppose $x \, A \, y$ and not $x \, A \, z$, and consider a generic profile $D \in \mathfrak{D}$ in which the preferences between $y$ and $z$ are arbitrary, and $x \gg_D y$ and $x \gg_D z$. Then $x \, A \, y \Rightarrow xF_D y$, and not $x \, A \, z \Leftrightarrow (x \, B \, z$ or $x \, C \, z) \Rightarrow$ not $xF_D z$, so that $zF_D y$ by C4 (negative transitivity). Since the preferences between $y$ and $z$ are arbitrary, this violates C8 in light of C6. Hence $x \, A \, y \Rightarrow x \, A \, z$. A similar proof shows that $x \, A \, y \Rightarrow z \, A \, y$ for every $z \in X$. Then (16.3) follows, and (16.4) is proved in a similar manner.

By Arrow's theorem, C5 must be false. In view of (16.3) this says that $x \neq y \Rightarrow$ not $x \, A \, y$, or $x \neq y \Rightarrow (x \, B \, y$ or $x \, C \, y)$. Suppose $x \, C \, y$ for no distinct $x$ and $y$. Then $x \, B \, y$ for all pairs. A generic profile $D$ where $x$ and $y$ are arbitrarily distributed and $x \gg_D z$ and $y \gg_D z$ then gives not $xF_D z$ & not $zF_D x$ & not $yF_D z$ & not $zF_D y$, so that not $xF_D y$ & not $yF_D x$ by C4, which in view of C6 implies that $F$ is flat, which violates C8. Hence $x \, C \, y$ for some distinct $x$ and $y$, and $x \, C \, y$ for all $x,y \in X$ by (16.4). Therefore $F$ is perverse. Thus, if $F'_D$ is defined as the dual of $F_D$ ($xF'_D y \Leftrightarrow yF_D x$), then C1, C2, C3, C4, C5, and C6 hold for the $F'_D$ and therefore, by Arrow's theorem, there is a dictator for this dual case. By the definitions, this "dual dictator" is a suppressed individual with respect to $F$. ◆

## 16.4 Minimal $\mathfrak{X}$ Structure: Another Hansson Theorem

The impossibility theorems of the preceding sections presume that $\mathfrak{X}$ contains every two-element subset of $X$. The first major deviation from this pattern was made by Hansson (1969) for an impossibility theorem that does not assume that any two-element subset of $X$ is in $\mathfrak{X}$, but requires only that $\mathfrak{X}$ contain some subset of $X$ that has more than two elements. This subset may be finite or infinite. To avoid unnecessary notation and with no real loss in generality, we shall suppose that $X$ itself is in $\mathfrak{X}$.

In his proof of the following theorem, Hansson shows that if $F$ satisfies the conditions of the theorem then it is possible to define another social choice function that satisfies the conditions of Arrow's theorem. Since the latter are inconsistent, Hansson's conditions must be inconsistent.

THEOREM 16.5. *Suppose that* $F: \mathfrak{X} \times \mathfrak{D} \to \mathcal{P}(X)$ *is a social choice function such that*

D1. *$n$ is a positive integer,*
D2. *$\#X \geq 3$ and $X \in \mathfrak{X}$,*
D3. *$\mathfrak{D}$ is the set of all n-tuples of weak orders on $X$.*

*Then at least one of the following conditions must be false:*

D4. *If $x,y \in X$, $D \in \mathfrak{D}$ and $x \gg_D y$ then $y \notin F(X,D)$,*
D5. *If $D,D' \in \mathfrak{D}$, $\emptyset \subset Y \subseteq X$ and if $D$ equals $D'$ on $Y$ then either $Y \cap F(X,D) = Y \cap F(X,D')$ or else one of these two intersections must be empty,*
D6. *There is no $i \in \{1, \ldots, n\}$ such that $(x,y \in X$, $D \in \mathfrak{D}$, $x \succ_i y) \Rightarrow y \notin F(X,D)$.*

Condition D1 is C1, and D2 and D3 relate to C2 and C3 in an obvious way. The last three conditions make demands only on $F(X,D)$: if $\mathfrak{X}$ contains proper subsets of $X$, the behavior of $F$ on such subsets is immaterial.

Condition D4 is a unanimity condition, comparable to C5, and D6 is a nondictatorship condition, comparable to C7. If $X$ is infinite then D4 must be violated, since along with D3 it implies a $D$ for which $F(X,D) = \emptyset$.

The remaining condition, D5, is an interprofile condition that has no immediately obvious counterpart in the preceding system. It says that if individual preferences on $Y$ are the same in $D$ and $D'$ and if some alternative in $Y$ is "best" in $X$ under $D$, and some alternative in $Y$ is "best" in $X$ under $D'$, then every "best" $Y$ alternative in $X$ under $D$ will be a "best" alternative in $X$ under $D'$, and every "best" $Y$ alternative in $X$ under $D'$ will be a "best" alternative in $X$ under $D$. If one of $Y \cap F(X,D)$ and $Y \cap F(X,D')$ is empty and the other is not, D5 is not violated. This might be the case with $X = \{x,y,z\}$, $Y = \{x,y\}$, $n = 3$ and $D,D'$ as follows:

| $D$ | $D'$ |
|---|---|
| 1. $x\ y\ z$ | 1. $z\ x\ y$ |
| 2. $x\ y\ z$ | 2. $z\ x\ y$ |
| 3. $z\ y\ x$ | 3. $y\ z\ x$ |

$F(X,D) = \{x\}$ and $F(X,D') = \{z\}$ seem reasonable, in which case $Y \cap F(X,D) = \{x\}$ and $Y \cap F(X,D') = \emptyset$.

Condition D5 suggests the flavor of both the condition of independence from infeasible alternatives and a passive intraprofile condition such as B1 in the preceding chapter. As in the case of some of the passive intraprofile conditions, there are arguments (one of which may be Theorem 16.5 itself) that might cause some reservations about the general desirability of D5. For example, suppose $y \in F(X,D)$ and $D'$ is obtained from $D$ by lowering $y$ as much as possible in each individual order where $x >_i y$, and by raising $x$ as much as possible in each order without changing the order between $x$ and $y$. Then in some cases it may seem reasonable to have $x \in F(X,D')$ and $y \notin F(X,D')$.

A specific example that is partially built on this theme takes $X = \{x,y,a,b,c\}$, $n = 5$ and $D,D'$ as follows:

| $D$ | $D'$ |
|---|---|
| 1. $x\ y\ a\ b\ c$ | $x\ a\ b\ c\ y$ |
| 2. $y\ a\ c\ b\ x$ | $y\ x\ a\ b\ c$ |
| 3. $c\ a\ b\ x\ y$ | $c\ x\ a\ b\ y$ |
| 4. $x\ y\ a\ b\ c$ | $x\ b\ c\ a\ y$ |
| 5. $y\ b\ a\ c\ x$ | $y\ x\ b\ a\ c$ |

It seems to us rather reasonable to have $y \in F(X,D)$ and $x \notin F(X,D)$, and to have $x \in F(X,D')$ and $y \notin F(X,D')$. Since $D = D'$ on $\{x,y\}$, these selections would violate D5.

*Proof of Theorem* 16.5. The theorem is true if it is true when $\mathfrak{X} = \{X\}$, so assume that $X$ is the only element in $\mathfrak{X}$. Contrary to the theorem, we suppose that $F: \{X\} \times \mathfrak{D} \to \mathcal{P}(X)$ is a social choice function which satisfies D1 through D6. Let $\mathfrak{X}' = \mathcal{P}(X) - \{\emptyset\}$. We shall construct a social choice function $G: \mathfrak{X}' \times \mathfrak{D} \to \mathcal{P}(X)$ that satisfies C1 through C7. But this is impossible by Theorem 16.1, and the desired contradiction is obtained.

Given $D \in \mathfrak{D}$ and $\emptyset \subset Y \subseteq X$, define $D^Y \in \mathfrak{D}$ so that $D^Y = D$ on $Y$ and, for all $y \in Y$ and $x \in X - Y$, $y >_i^Y x$ for every $i$. Define $G$ by

$$G(Y,D) = Y \cap F(X,D^Y) \text{ for all } (Y,D) \in \mathfrak{X}' \times \mathfrak{D}. \quad (16.5)$$

Since $F(X,D^Y) \neq \emptyset$ and since $x \in X - Y \Rightarrow x \notin F(X,D^Y)$ by D4, $G(Y,D) \neq \emptyset$ and $G$ is a social choice function. We show next that $G$ satisfies

B1. $Y \subseteq Z$ and $Y \cap G(Z,D) \neq \emptyset \Rightarrow G(Y,D) = Y \cap G(Z,D)$

for each $D \in \mathfrak{D}$. Under the hypotheses of B1 we have

$$\emptyset \neq Y \cap G(Z,D) = Y \cap Z \cap F(X,D^Z) = Y \cap F(X,D^Z)$$
$$= Y \cap F(X,D^Y) = G(Y,D),$$

where the penultimate equality follows from D5 since $G(Y,D) \neq \emptyset$ and $D^Y = D^Z$ on $Y$.

Hence, by Corollary 15.1, $G_D$ on $X$ is a weak order for each $D \in \mathfrak{D}$. This verifies C4 for $G$. C1, C2, and C3 obviously hold.

To verify C5, C6, and C7, let $Y = \{x,y\}$ with $x \neq y$.

C5. Suppose $x \gg_D y$. Then $y \notin F(X,D^Y)$ by D4 and hence $y \notin G(Y,D)$ by (16.5). Thus $xG_Dy$.

C6. Take $D = D'$ on $Y$. Then $D^Y = D = D' = D'^Y$ on $\{x,y\}$. Hence, using D5,

$$\emptyset \neq G(Y,D) = Y \cap F(X,D^Y) = Y \cap F(X,D'^Y) = G(Y,D') \neq \emptyset.$$

C7. For $i$, let $x,y$ be as guaranteed by D6 with $x \succ_i y$ and $y \in F(X,D)$. Using D5, $\emptyset \neq Y \cap F(X,D) = Y \cap F(X,D^Y) = G(Y,D) \neq \emptyset$ and therefore $y \in G(Y,D)$. ◆

A CONSTANT FUNCTION

Hansson (1969, 1969b) presents several other interesting theorems. One of these produces a flatness conclusion by modifying the unanimity condition D4 in the following way:

D4'. If $x,y \in X$, $D \in \mathfrak{D}$, $x \gg_D y$ and if $y \in F(X,D)$ then $x \in F(X,D)$.

THEOREM 16.6. *Suppose that* $F: \{X\} \times \mathfrak{D} \to \mathcal{P}(X)$ *is a social choice function that satisfies* D1, D2, D3, D4', D5, *and* D6. *Then* $F(X,D) = X$ *for every* $D \in \mathfrak{D}$.

Clearly, $F \equiv X$ satisfies the conditions. To show that this is the only $F$, we assume that the cited conditions hold along with $F(X,D) \neq X$ for some $D \in \mathfrak{D}$, and show that this implies D4, thus giving a contradiction by Theorem 16.5. D6 is not used in this proof. Hence (D1, D2, D3, D4', D5) $\Rightarrow$ D4 when $F(X,D) \neq X$ for some $D$.

*Proof.* Let $F: \{X\} \times \mathfrak{D} \to \mathcal{P}(X)$ be a social choice function that satisfies D1, D2, D3, D4', and D5. Suppose further that there are $a,b \subset X$ and $D \in \mathfrak{D}$ such that $a \in F(X,D)$ and $b \notin F(X,D)$. Let $E = D^{\{a,b\}}$, using the definition of $D^Y$ in the preceding proof. By D4', $F(X,E)$ contains $a$ or $b$. Hence, by D5, $a \in F(X,E)$ and $b \notin F(X,E)$. It follows from D4' that $F(X,E) = \{a\}$.

Take any $x \neq a$ and let $D' = E$ on $X - \{x\}$ with $x \succ_i' y$ for every $y \neq x$ and all $i$. By D4', $x \in F(X,D')$. Take $u \notin \{x,a\}$. $E = D'$ on $\{u,a\}$. If $u \in F(X,D')$ then, by D5, $\{u,a\} \cap F(X,D') = \{u,a\} \cap F(X,E)$ and hence $u \in F(X,E)$, contradicting $F(X,E) = \{a\}$.

This shows that, for any $x \in X$ there is a $D \in \mathfrak{D}$ such that $x \in F(X,D)$ and $X \neq F(X,D)$.

To establish D4 take $x \gg_D y$. By the preceding result let $E \in \mathfrak{D}$ be such that $x \in F(X,E)$ and $u \notin F(X,E)$ for some $u \in X$. Suppose first

**215**

that $u \neq y$. By the initial analysis in this proof, $F(X,E^{\{x,u\}}) = \{x\}$. Since $E^{\{x,u\}}$ equals $D$ on $\{x,y\}$, D5 requires $y \notin F(X,D)$. Suppose next that $y = u$ is the only element not in $F(X,E)$. Take $t \notin \{x,y\}$. Then $x,t \in F(X,E)$ and $y \notin F(X,E)$. Let $D' = E$ on $X - \{x\}$ with $x >_i' a$ for all $a \neq x$ and all $i$. Then $x \in F(X,D')$ by D4'. Since $D' = E$ on $\{y,t\}$, D5 requires $y \notin F(X,D')$, for otherwise $y$ would be in $F(X,E)$. Since $D = D'$ on $\{x,y\}$, D5 requires $y \notin F(X,D)$, for otherwise $y$ would be in $F(X,D')$. Hence, in any event, $y \notin F(X,D)$, and this establishes D4. ◆

# CHAPTER 17

# Summation Social Choice Functions

A SOCIAL CHOICE function is a summation social choice function if, for each $(Y,D) \in \mathfrak{X} \times \mathfrak{D}$, numerical values can be assigned to the alternatives for each individual so as to preserve the individual preference orders in $D$ and to make $F(Y,D)$ equal to the subset of alternatives in $Y$ that have the largest value sum over the individuals. A precise definition and a unanimity-like necessary and sufficient condition are presented in section 17.1.

Section 17.2 then discusses a hierarchy of summation social choice functions. One branch in this hierarchy considers individual functions that do not depend on the particular feasible set $Y$ under consideration. It follows from the preceding chapter that social choice functions of this sort violate either the condition of independence from infeasible alternatives or the nondictatorship condition. These functions are examined briefly in section 17.5.

The intervening sections concentrate on summation social choice functions that, generally speaking, depend on the feasible set under consideration. Section 17.3 considers the case where the individual function for voter $i$ depends on $Y$ and on $\succ_i$ but not on other voters' preference orders. The effects of anonymity and neutrality within the voter independence context are noted in section 17.4. The Borda function of section 13.2 is a special case of this type.

*Throughout the chapter it is assumed that $X$ is finite.* For generality otherwise, we shall work with individual strict partial orders and will not assume that independence from infeasible alternatives holds. The effects of independence and of more specialized individual assumptions, such as weak orders, are generally left to the reader as exercises.

## 17.1 SUMMATION SOCIAL CHOICE FUNCTIONS

Our general definition of summation social choice function will, for simplicity, presuppose that $X$ *is finite* and that $\mathfrak{D}$ *is a set of n-tuples of strict partial orders on $X$.*

DEFINITION 17.1. $F: \mathfrak{X} \times \mathfrak{D} \to \mathcal{P}(X)$ *is a* summation social choice function *if and only if it is a social choice function and, for each $i \in \{1, \ldots, n\}$, there is a real-valued function $u_i$ on $X \times \mathfrak{X} \times \mathfrak{D}$ such that,*

**217**

*for all $i \in \{1, \ldots, n\}$ and $x, y \in X$ and $(Y, D) \in \mathfrak{X} \times \mathfrak{D}$,*

$$x \succ_i y \Rightarrow u_i(x, Y, D) > u_i(y, Y, D) \qquad (17.1)$$
$$x \approx_i y \Rightarrow u_i(x, Y, D) = u_i(y, Y, D) \qquad (17.2)$$

*and*

$$F(Y, D) = \{x : x \in Y \text{ and } \Sigma_{i=1}^n u_i(x, Y, D) \geq \Sigma_{i=1}^n u_i(y, Y, D)$$
$$\text{for all } y \in Y\}. \quad (17.3)$$

We have already discussed a special summation social choice function in detail, namely the Borda function of section 13.2, which the reader may wish to review before he continues with the present chapter. As we shall note later, Black's function, of section 13.3, is also a summation social choice function.

A main purpose of this section is to give an active intraprofile condition that is related to conditions (12.3) and (12.4) and is necessary and sufficient for $F$ to be a summation social choice function. Before doing this we shall examine some of the aspects of Definition 17.1.

### NUMERICAL REPRESENTATIONS AND INDEPENDENCE

Perhaps the main feature of the definition is its generality. Since each $u_i$ is defined on the three-fold product $X \times \mathfrak{X} \times \mathfrak{D}$, it is easily seen that the definition does not presuppose or imply the condition of independence from infeasible alternatives. Moreover, it allows the $u_i$ values for a given $i$ to change when $Y$ is held fixed and individual $i$'s preferences remain fixed but changes occur in some other individual's preference order. This is because the third argument in $u_i$ is the entire preference profile $D$ and not just the $i$th order $\succ_i$ from $D$.

Given strict partial orders for individuals, (17.1) and (17.2) require that $u_i$ preserve $\succ_i$ and $\approx_i$ as indicated. Although we could require $x \approx_i y \Leftrightarrow u_i(x, Y, D) = u_i(y, Y, D)$, as used in Theorem 7.1(2), the discussion of section 13.2 indicates that the $\Leftarrow$ part of $\Leftrightarrow$ is somewhat "forced," and we shall not require it. Recall that under strict partial orders, each $\approx_i$ on $X$ is an equivalence and if $a$ and $b$ are distinct equivalence classes in $X/\approx_i$ then either (1) $x \succ_i y$ for all $x \in a$ and all $y \in b$, or (2) $y \succ_i x$ for all $x \in a$ and all $y \in b$, or (3) $x \sim_i y$ and not $x \approx_i y$ for all $x \in a$ and all $y \in b$. If $\succ_i$ is a weak order, then $\approx_i$ is identical to $\sim_i$ and (17.1) and (17.2) require $x \sim_i y$ when $u(x) = u(y)$.

Apart from the obvious summation form, we note for (17.3) that the $u_i(x, Y, D)$ values for $x \notin Y$ play no part in the specification of $F(Y, D)$. However, there is a way in which preferences for elements not in $Y$ can affect $F(Y, D)$ within the context of the general form. This arises when $\succ_i$ is a strict partial order that is not also a weak order, and it comes from the fact that the definition of $\approx_i$ for (17.2) depends on all of $X$ ($x \approx_i y \Leftrightarrow [x \sim_i z \Leftrightarrow y \sim_i z$ for all $z \in X]$) and not just on $Y$. For example, if $Y = \{\dot{x},y\}$ and $x \sim_i y$, then $x \approx_i y$ *within the context of* $Y$, but, if there is a $z \in X - Y$ such that $z \sim_i x$ and $z >_i y$, then $x \approx_i y$ is false.

This analysis shows that an equivalent definition of a summation social choice function is obtained by only defining $u_i$ for $(x,Y,D) \in X \times \mathfrak{X} \times \mathfrak{D}$ for which $x \in Y$, and by modifying (17.1) and (17.2) to apply only to all $x,y \in Y$. On the other hand, an alternative definition that defines $u_i$ in the restricted sense and modifies (17.1) as indicated but changes (17.2) by requiring that $u_i(x,Y,D) = u_i(y,Y,D)$ whenever $x,y \in Y$ and ($x \sim_i z \Leftrightarrow y \sim_i z$ for all $z \in Y$), is not equivalent to Definition 17.1. However, it is easily seen that this alternative definition becomes equivalent to the original if $F$ is assumed to satisfy the condition of independence from infeasible alternatives and if $\mathfrak{D}$ is sufficiently rich. Under these conditions, if $x \approx_i y$ within $Y$ but not within $X$, we could consider a $D' \in \mathfrak{D}$ that agrees with $D$ on $Y$ but has $w >'_i z$ for every $w \in Y$, $z \in X - Y$ and for all $i$. Then, although $x \approx_i y$ is false, we have $x \approx'_i y$ and, by independence, can let the $u_i$ values for the $(w,Y,D')$ with $w \in Y$ serve also as the $u_i$ values for the $(w,Y,D)$ with $w \in Y$.

THE CONDORCET CONDITIONS

A specific illustration of the generality of Definition 17.1 is obtained by noting that it is wholly compatible with the weak Condorcet condition of Definition 12.1. For suppose that $P(Y,D) = \{x\}$ so that $x$ has a strict simple majority over every other alternative in $Y$ when $D$ obtains. Then $u_i$, values can be assigned in the $(Y,D)$ context so as to satisfy (17.1) and (17.2) along with the following:

$1 > u_i(y,Y,D)$ for all $y$, all $i$
$0 = u_i(x,Y,D)$ for all $i$
$-n > u_i(y,Y,D)$ when $x >_i y$, for all $i$ and $y$.

Since $\Sigma_i u_i(x,Y,D) = 0$ and $\Sigma_i u_i(y,Y,D) < -n + (n-1) = -1$ for every $y \in Y - \{x\}$, (17.3) gives $F(Y,D) = \{x\}$.

This shows that Black's function of section 13.3, which is a Condorcet social choice function, is a summation social choice function. If $P(Y,D) \neq \emptyset$, define the $u_i$ as above; if $P(Y,D) = \emptyset$, define the $u_i$ by the Borda method ($u_i = r_i$), which is consistent with (17.1), (17.2), and (17.3).

Although the weak Condorcet condition is consistent with the notion of a summation social choice function, the strong Condorcet condition is not. One can verify this with the example that precedes Theorem 12.2.

**219**

The condition that we shall use for a summation social choice function is a generalization of a unanimity condition. Letting $\gtrsim_i = \succ_i \cup \approx_i$, so that

$$x \gtrsim_i y \Leftrightarrow x \succ_i y \qquad \text{or} \qquad x \approx_i y, \tag{17.4}$$

the unanimity condition is: for all $(Y,D) \in \mathfrak{X} \times \mathfrak{D}$ and all $x,y \in Y$,

(1) $y \approx_i x$ for all $i$, and $x \in F(Y,D) \Rightarrow y \in F(Y,D)$;
(2) $y \gtrsim_i x$ for all $i$ and $y \succ_i x$ for some $i \Rightarrow x \notin F(Y,D)$.

Part (2) is a form of strong unanimity [but it is *not* the same as $y \succ_D x \Rightarrow x \notin F(Y,D)$], and (1) is a form of unanimity agreement. It says that, as far as the $\succ_i$ on $X$ are concerned, if all individuals regard $x$ and $y$ as equally desirable then either both $x$ and $y$ will be in the choice set $F(Y,D)$ or else neither will be in the choice set.

This simple unanimity condition is obviously necessary for a summation social choice function. It is also sufficient for a given $(Y,D)$ provided that $F(Y,D)$ is a singleton. For suppose that $F(Y,D) = \{x\}$, and consider the equivalence classes in $X/\approx_i$ for each $i$. Set $u_i(x',Y,D) = 0$ for all alternatives in the equivalence class that contains $x$; take $u_i(y,Y,D) < 1$ for all $y$; and for all alternatives in each class that is different from the class that contains $x$ and does not have an alternative preferred to $x$, make $u_i$ less than $-n$. This can be done so as to satisfy (17.1) and (17.2) for the given $(Y,D)$. If the foregoing unanimity condition holds then, for every $y \neq x$ that is in $Y$ there will be some $i$ with $u_i(y,Y,D) < -n$ and hence $\Sigma_i u_i(x,Y,D) > \Sigma_i u_i(y,Y,D)$.

The generalization of the unanimity condition that we shall use is designed to handle the cases for which $F(Y,D)$ contains more than one alternative.

DEFINITION 17.2. *A social choice function $F : \mathfrak{X} \times \mathfrak{D} \to \mathcal{P}(X)$ satisfies the* summation condition *if and only if the following holds for every $(Y,D) \in \mathfrak{X} \times \mathfrak{D}$. If $K$ is a positive integer, if $x_1, \ldots, x_K, y_1, \ldots, y_K \in Y$ and if, for each $i$, $\sigma_i$ is a permutation on $\{1, \ldots, K\}$ for which $y_{\sigma_i(k)} \gtrsim_i x_k$ for $k = 1, \ldots, K$, then*

(1) $y_{\sigma_i(k)} \approx_i x_k$ *for all $i$ and $k$, and $x_k \in F(Y,D)$ for all $k \Rightarrow y_k \in F(Y,D)$ for all $k$;*
(2) $y_{\sigma_i(k)} \succ_i x_k$ *for some $i$ and $k \Rightarrow x_k \notin F(Y,D)$ for some $k$.*

When $K = 1$, we have $\sigma_i(1) = 1$ for all $i$ and this part of the condition reduces to the foregoing unanimity condition. When $K > 1$, alternatives in $x_1, \ldots, x_K$ or in $y_1, \ldots, y_K$ may be replicated, but we could require that $\{x_1, \ldots, x_K\} \cap \{y_1, \ldots, y_K\} = \emptyset$ without affecting the condition. For if the condition is violated, a violation can be obtained when $\{x_k\} \cap \{y_k\} = \emptyset$ by reducing the original violation to this form. For example, if $x_j = y_k$ then, with $\sigma_i^*$ the inverse of $\sigma_i$, $y_{\sigma_i(j)} \succsim_i x_j$ & $x_j \succsim_i x_{\sigma_i^*(k)} \Rightarrow y_{\sigma_i(j)} \succsim_i x_{\sigma_i^*(k)}$, with $\succ_i$ in the conclusion if $\succ_i$ in either hypothesis. The two original statements are then collapsed into one for each $i$, with a corresponding deletion of $x_j$ and $y_k$.

As noted earlier, the summation condition bears a resemblance to (12.3) and (12.4). It is an active intraprofile condition. Its necessity for a summation social choice function follows easily from the assumption that (17.1) through (17.3) hold. Then the hypotheses of (1) require $\Sigma_k \Sigma_i u_i(y_k, Y, D) = \Sigma_k \Sigma_i u_i(x_k, Y, D)$: if $x_k \in F(Y, D)$ for every $k$ then we cannot have $\Sigma_i u_i(y_k, Y, D) > \Sigma_i u_i(x_k, Y, D)$ for any $k$ and hence must have $\Sigma_i u_i(y_k, Y, D) = \Sigma_i u_i(x_k, Y, D)$ for every $k$. The hypotheses of (2) give $\Sigma_k \Sigma_i(y) > \Sigma_k \Sigma_i(x)$, which requires $\Sigma_i u_i(y_k, Y, D) > \Sigma_i u_i(x_k, Y, D)$ for some $k$, so that $x_k \notin F(Y, D)$ by (17.3).

It thus remains to prove sufficiency for the following theorem.

THEOREM 17.1. *Suppose that* $F: \mathfrak{X} \times \mathfrak{D} \to \mathcal{P}(X)$ *is a social choice function. Then it is a summation social choice function if and only if it satisfies the summation condition.*

*Proof.* Assume that the summation condition holds, and let $(Y, D)$ be a generic pair in $\mathfrak{X} \times \mathfrak{D}$. As noted earlier, we need only consider $u_i(x, Y, D)$ for $x \in Y$. Then (17.1) through (17.3) will hold for the given $(Y, D)$ if and only if there are numbers $u_i(x, Y, D)$ for $i \in \{1, \ldots, n\}$ and $x \in Y$ such that

$$\Sigma_i u_i(x, Y, D) > \Sigma_i u_i(y, Y, D) \quad \text{when} \quad x \in F(Y, D),\ y \in Y - F(Y, D),$$
$$\Sigma_i u_i(x, Y, D) = \Sigma_i u_i(y, Y, D) \quad \text{when} \quad x, y \in F(Y, D) \quad \text{and} \quad x \neq y,$$
$$u_i(x, Y, D) > u_i(y, Y, D) \quad \text{when} \quad x, y \in Y \quad \text{and} \quad x \succ_i y,$$
$$u_i(x, Y, D) = u_i(y, Y, D) \quad \text{when} \quad x, y \in Y,\ x \neq y \quad \text{and} \quad x \approx_i y.$$

With $\#Y = m$ and $n$ voters there are $mn$ values $u_i(x, Y, D)$ to consider for the given $(Y, D)$. Let $\rho \in Re^{mn}$ with each $\rho_j$ corresponding to one of the $u_i(x, Y, D)$. Transposing terms in the foregoing display after selecting one order ($xy$ or $yx$) for each pair of $x \neq y$ involved in an equality statement, the preceding system can be written as

$$\rho \cdot a^t > 0 \quad \text{for the } x \in F(Y, D),\ y \in Y - F(Y, D) \text{ cases,}$$
$$\rho \cdot a^t = 0 \quad \text{for the } x, y \in F(Y, D),\ x \neq y \text{ cases,}$$
$$\rho \cdot a^t > 0 \quad \text{for the } x \succ_i y \text{ statements,}$$
$$\rho \cdot a^t = 0 \quad \text{for the } x \approx_i y,\ x \neq y \text{ statements,}$$

where $t$ runs through the integers $t = 1, \ldots, T$. Each $a^t \in Re^{mn}$ is a vector of zeros, ones, and minus ones, with $1 \cdot a^t = 0$.

Suppose that there is no $\rho$ solution for this system. Then, by Theorem 3.3, there are integers $r_1, \ldots, r_T$ such that

$$\Sigma_{t=1}^{T} r_t a_j^t = 0 \qquad \text{for} \qquad j = 1, 2, \ldots, mn, \qquad (17.5)$$

with $r_t \geq 0$ when $a^t$ corresponds to a $> 0$ statement, and at least one of these $r_t > 0$. If $r_t < 0$ for an $a^t$ involved in an $= 0$ statement, inversion of the chosen order for the $x,y$ pair replaces $a^t$ with $-a^t$, and a corresponding replacement of $r_t$ by $-r_t$ leaves things as they were. So all $r_t$ may be taken as nonnegative integers. Using replicates of alternatives for the $r_t > 1$, it follows from (17.5) and the original $u_i$ statements that, for each $i$, there are two sequences

$$x_1, \ldots, x_a, y_1, \ldots, y_b, z_{i1}, \ldots, z_{ia_i}, w_{i1}, \ldots, w_{ib_i}$$
$$x_1', \ldots, x_a', y_1', \ldots, y_b', z_{i1}', \ldots, z_{ia_i}', w_{i1}', \ldots, w_{ib_i}'$$

such that the second is a rearrangement of the first with

$$\begin{aligned} x_\alpha \in F(Y,D), \; x_\alpha' \in Y - F(Y,D) \qquad & \alpha = 1, \ldots, a \\ y_\beta, y_\beta' \in F(Y,D) \text{ and } y_\beta \neq y_\beta' \qquad & \beta = 1, \ldots, b \\ z_{i\alpha} >_i z_{i\alpha}' \qquad & \alpha = 1, \ldots, a_i \\ w_{i\beta} \approx_i w_{i\beta}' \text{ and } w_{i\beta} \neq w_{i\beta}' \qquad & \beta = 1, \ldots, b_i. \end{aligned}$$

Since $r_t > 0$ for at least one of the $>0$ statements in the system, either $a > 0$ or $a_i > 0$ for some $i$.

We now reduce the sequences as follows without changing their characteristics. If $x_\alpha = y_\beta'$ then delete $x_\alpha$ and $y_\beta'$ and replace the $(x_\alpha, x_\alpha')$, $(y_\beta, y_\beta')$ pairs by the pair $(y_\beta, x_\alpha')$ which has $y_\beta \in F(Y,D)$ and $x_\alpha' \notin F(Y,D)$. A similar replacement is made if $x_\alpha' = y_\beta$, or if $y_\beta = y_\gamma'$. After all such reductions are made we obtain, after the appropriate changes in subscripting and reduction of $b$, $\{x_1, \ldots, x_a, y_1, \ldots, y_b\}$ $\cap \; \{x_1', \ldots, x_a', y_1', \ldots y_b'\} = \emptyset$. Since the value of $a$ is unchanged by this process, if $a > 0$ initially then this continues in effect.

These reductions on the first parts of the sequences hold uniformly for all $i$. Similar reductions, permitted by the transitivity of $\approx_i$ and by $(>_i)(\approx_i) \cup (\approx_i)(>_i) \subseteq >_i$, can be made in the $z_i$ and $w_i$ for each $i$, with $a_i > 0$ after the reduction if $a_i > 0$ before the reduction and with $\{z_{i\alpha}, w_{i\beta}\} \cap \{z_{i\alpha}', w_{i\beta}'\} = \emptyset$ after the reductions. Since the reductions delete identical elements in the two sequences, it follows that, for each $i$, we obtain two sequences of the form

$$x_1, \ldots, x_K, y_{i1}, \ldots, y_{iK}$$
$$y_1, \ldots, y_K, x_1, \ldots, x_K$$

where $y_{i1}, \ldots, y_{iK}$ is a rearrangement of $y_1, \ldots, y_K$, and where $K > 0$ with

$$x_k \in F(Y,D) \qquad k = 1, \ldots, K$$
$$y_{ik} \gtrsim_i x_k \qquad k = 1, \ldots, K \text{ and each } i,$$

with either $y_k \notin F(Y,D)$ for some $k$ (for $a > 0$ formerly) or else $y_{ik} >_i x_k$ for some $k$ and $i$ (for $a_i > 0$ formerly). If $y_{ik} >_i x_k$ for some $i$ and $k$ then part (2) of the summation condition is contradicted. And if $y_{ik} \approx_i x_k$ for all $i$ and $k$, we then require $y_k \notin F(Y,D)$ for some $k$ so that part (1) of the summation condition is contradicted.

Hence this use of the Theorem of The Alternative shows that the summation condition implies the existence of a $\rho$ solution for the system. Thus there are $u_i(x,Y,D)$ values that satisfy (17.1) through (17.3) for the given $(Y,D)$. Since this is true for every $(Y,D) \in \mathfrak{X} \times \mathfrak{D}$, the theorem is proved. ◆

## 17.2 CLASSES OF SUMMATION FUNCTIONS

Definition 17.1 accommodates a large variety of specialized types of social choice functions. In this section we shall comment briefly on several classes of summation social choice functions that will be examined in later sections.

A partial characterization of classes of summation social choice functions is given in Figure 17.1. The original $u_i$ form of Definition 17.1 is shown in the upper right. An arrow from one class to another means

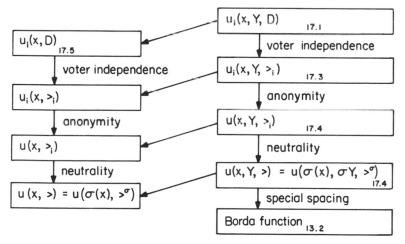

FIGURE 17.1. Some summation social choice functions

that the latter is a subclass of the former. The special classes in the right part of the figure retain dependence of $u_i$ on the feasible set $Y$ and are generally compatible with the condition of independence from infeasible alternatives. The classes on the left omit $Y$ as an argument of the function and are usually incompatible with the independence condition. We shall return to these momentarily.

### VOTER INDEPENDENCE AND OTHER SPECIALIZATIONS

In retaining the dependence of $u_i$ on $Y$, the first obvious specialization of the general summation form arises by requiring that $u_i(x, Y, D)$ $= u_i(x, Y, D')$ whenever $i$ has the same preference order on $X$ under both $D$ and $D'$, or whenever $>_i = >'_i$. This indicates that each $u_i$ depends only on the preferences of voter $i$ and not on the preferences of other voters, and it thus seems reasonable to refer to it as a form of "voter independence." When voter independence applies, each $u_i$ is defined on $X \times \mathfrak{X} \times \mathfrak{D}_i$, where $\mathfrak{D}_i$ is the set of strict partial orders for voter $i$ that obtain in one or more $D \in \mathfrak{D}$.

Black's function of section 13.3, which is a summation social choice function as noted in the preceding section, does not satisfy voter independence since the definition of $u_i$ depends on whether $P(Y, D) = \emptyset$, which clearly depends on the preference orders of other voters.

The voter independence case is considered in the next section. Section 17.4 then examines the effects of the conditions of anonymity and neutrality. When anonymity applies in the context of voter independence, all $u_i$ functions can be taken to be identical. Neutrality then allows the same set of values within individual orders obtained from one another by permutations on $X$.

Although the classes of functions in the next two sections are compatible with independence from infeasible alternatives, this condition will not be used. Except for a comment at the end of section 17.4, modifications under independence are left as exercises.

### DEPENDENCE ON INFEASIBLE ALTERNATIVES

Because the functions on the left of Figure 17.1 take no account of the specific set $Y$ of alternatives that are feasible in a particular realization of a situation, they might be said to be "dependent on infeasible alternatives." The most general subclass of such functions defines $u_i$ on $X \times \mathfrak{D}$ for each $i$. Defining $x f_D y \Leftrightarrow \Sigma_i u_i(x, D) > \Sigma_i u_i(y, D)$, $f_D$ on $X$ is a weak order for every $D \in \mathfrak{D}$, and

$$F(Y, D) = \{x : x \in Y \text{ and } y f_D x \text{ for no } y \in Y\} \text{ for all } (Y, D) \in \mathfrak{X} \times \mathfrak{D}$$

according to (17.3). It follows from Lemma 15.3 that condition B1 (or its social choice counterpart) holds for such functions. If $\mathfrak{X}$ contains every two-element subset of $X$ then $f_D \equiv F_D$ and we know from Arrow's theorem (see also Theorem 16.5) that, under appropriate structural conditions, there will either be a dictator or the independence condition will fail. Generally speaking, the failure of independence seems the lesser of "evils" in this case.

Additional conditions generate the further specializations of summation functions that are "dependent on infeasible alternatives" as shown on the left of Figure 17.1. We shall return to these in the final section of this chapter.

## 17.3 INDEPENDENCE AMONG VOTERS

To obtain a summation social choice function for which $u_i(x,Y,D) = u_i(x,Y,D')$ when $>_i = >'_i$, it should be clear that some interprofile condition is required. The special condition that we shall use for this case is a multiprofile condition according to Table 14.1. Since the summation form under consideration retains dependence on $Y$, we can state the condition for each $Y$ without taking account of other potential feasible sets.

For simplicity, the condition that follows is called the condition of voter independence. It is obviously a complicated version of the summation condition and thus asserts more than just a form of independence among voters.

DEFINITION 17.3. *A social choice function $F: \mathfrak{X} \times \mathfrak{D} \to \mathcal{P}(X)$ satisfies the* condition of voter independence *if and only if the following holds for every $Y \in \mathfrak{X}$. If $K$ is a positive integer, if $x_1, \ldots, x_K, y_1, \ldots, y_K \in Y$ and $D^1, \ldots, D^K \in \mathfrak{D}$ and if, for each $i$, $\sigma_i$ is a permutation on $\{1, \ldots, K\}$ for which $>_i^{\sigma_i(k)} = >_i^k$ and $y_{\sigma_i(k)} \gtrsim_i^k x_k$ for $k = 1, \ldots, K$, then*

(1) $y_{\sigma_i(k)} \approx_i^k x_k$ *for all $i$ and $k$, and $x_k \subset F(Y,D^k)$ for all $k \Rightarrow y_k \in F(Y,D^k)$ for all $k$;*

(2) $y_{\sigma_i(k)} >_i^k x_k$ *for some $i$ and $k \Rightarrow x_k \notin F(Y,D^k)$ for some $k$.*

To make sense of this we note first that the $K = 1$ case is the same as the $K = 1$ case of the summation condition, and that the summation condition results in general if we take $D^1 = D^2 = \cdots = D^K$. To illustrate the more general structure of the voter independence condition, take $Y = X = \{x,y,z\}$ and $K = n = 3$ with

$$
\begin{aligned}
(x_1,y_1) &= (x,y) & D^1 &= (zxy,yzx,yxz) \\
(x_2,y_2) &= (y,z) & D^2 &= (zxy,zyx,xyz) \\
(x_3,y_3) &= (z,x) & D^3 &= (xzy,yzx,xyz).
\end{aligned}
$$

For permutations on $\{1,2,3\}$ take $\sigma_1(1,2,3) = (2,1,3)$, $\sigma_2(1,2,3) = (3,2,1)$, and $\sigma_3(1,2,3) = (1,3,2)$. Consider voter 1 first. Since $>_1^2 = >_1^1$, $>_1^1 = >_1^2$ and $>_1^3 = >_1^3$, he satisfies $>_1^{\sigma_1(k)} = >_1^k$ for $k = 1$, 2, 3. In addition, since $y_2 = z >_1^1 x = x_1$, $y_1 = y \approx_1^2 y = x_2$ and $y_3 = x >_1^3 z = x_3$, we have $y_{\sigma_1(k)} \gtrsim_1^k x_k$ for $k = 1$, 2, 3, with $>_1^k$ at least once. Similar analyses with voters 2 and 3 show that they satisfy the hypotheses of the condition. It then follows from part (2) of the voter independence condition that either $x \notin F(X,D^1)$ or $y \notin F(X,D^2)$ or $z \notin F(X,D^3)$. In contrast to this, the summation condition allows $x \in F(X,D^1)$ and $y \in F(X,D^2)$ and $z \in F(X,D^3)$.

THEOREM 17.2. *Suppose that $F: \mathcal{X} \times \mathfrak{D} \to \mathcal{P}(X)$ is a social choice function, and let $\mathfrak{D}_i = \{>:> \text{ is the ith component of some } D \in \mathfrak{D}\}$, for $i = 1, \ldots, n$. Then the condition of voter independence holds if and only if, for each $i \in \{1, \ldots, n\}$, there is a real-valued function $u_i$ on $X \times \mathcal{X} \times \mathfrak{D}_i$ such that, for all $i \in \{1, \ldots, n\}$, $>_i \in \mathfrak{D}_i$, $x,y \in X$ and $(Y,D) \in \mathcal{X} \times \mathfrak{D}$,*

$$x >_i y \Rightarrow u_i(x,Y,>_i) > u_i(y,Y,>_i) \qquad (17.6)$$
$$x \approx_i y \Rightarrow u_i(x,Y,>_i) = u_i(y,Y,>_i) \qquad (17.7)$$

*and*

$$F(Y,D) = \{x : x \in Y \text{ and } \Sigma_{i=1}^n u_i(x,Y,>_i) \geq \Sigma_{i=1}^n u_i(y,Y,>_i)$$
$$\text{for all } y \in Y\}. \quad (17.8)$$

*Proof.* The necessity proof is left to the reader. To prove the sufficiency of the condition, we consider a generic $Y \in \mathcal{X}$ and assume that the voter independence condition holds. As in the proof of Theorem 17.1, we shall use the Theorem of The Alternative on a linear system. For the given $Y$ we take the following as an appropriate system, where (unlike the previous proof) $D$ varies over $\mathfrak{D}$:

| | | |
|---|---|---|
| $\Sigma_i u_i(x,Y,D) > \Sigma_i u_i(y,Y,D)$ | when | $x \in F(Y,D)$, $y \in Y - F(Y,D)$, |
| $\Sigma_i u_i(x,Y,D) = \Sigma_i u_i(y,Y,D)$ | when | $x,y \in F(Y,D)$ and $x \neq y$, |
| $u_i(x,Y,D) > u_i(y,Y,D)$ | when | $x,y \in Y$ and $x >_i y$, |
| $u_i(x,Y,D) = u_i(y,Y,D)$ | when | $x,y \in Y$, $x \neq y$ and $x \approx_i y$, |
| $u_i(x,Y,D) = u_i(x,Y,D')$ | when | $x \in Y$, $D \neq D'$ and $>_i = >_i'$. |

Apart from the changeability of $D$, the first four lines are the same as the former system. The last line asserts that each $u_i$ depends only on $(Y,>_i)$ and not on $(Y,D)$. This system is solvable if and only if (17.6) through (17.8) hold for the given $Y$.

Let $\#Y = m$ and let $\#\mathfrak{D} = p$. Since we are concerned about $u_i(x,Y,D)$ for all $x \in Y$, all $D \in \mathfrak{D}$ and all $i \in \{1, \ldots, n\}$, the appropriate $\rho$ vector is in $Re^{mnp}$, with a one-one correspondence between the components of $\rho$ and the $mnp$ $u_i(x,Y,D)$. The above system then converts into $\rho \cdot a^t > 0$ and $\rho \cdot a^t = 0$ statements, say for $t = 1, \ldots, T$. If there is no $\rho$ solution then, by Theorem 3.3, there are nonnegative (using inversion for equality statements if necessary) integers $r_1, \ldots, r_T$ with $r_t > 0$ for one of the $\rho \cdot a^t > 0$ statements such that

$$\Sigma_{t=1}^{T} r_t a_j^t = 0 \qquad \text{for} \qquad j = 1, 2, \ldots, mnp.$$

Similar to the analysis following (17.5), this implies that, for each $i$, there are sequences

$$(x_1,D^1), \ldots, (x_a,D^a), (z_{i1},D^{i1}), \ldots, (z_{ia_i},D^{ia_i}), (w_{i1},E^{i1}), \ldots,$$
$$(w_{ib_i},E^{ib_i})$$
$$(x_1',D^1), \ldots, (x_a',D^a), (z_{i1}',D^{i1}), \ldots, (z_{ia_i}',D^{ia_i}), (w_{i1},E^{i1*}), \ldots,$$
$$(w_{ib_i},E^{ib_i*})$$

such that the second is a rearrangement of the first with

$$\begin{aligned}
&x_\alpha \in F(Y,D^\alpha),\ x_\alpha' \in Y,\ x_\alpha' \neq x_\alpha &&\alpha = 1, \ldots, a\\
&z_{i\alpha} \gtrsim_i^{i\alpha} z_{i\alpha}',\ z_{i\alpha} \neq z_{i\alpha}' &&\alpha = 1, \ldots, a_i\\
&E_i^{i\alpha} = E^{i\alpha*},\ E^{i\alpha} \neq E^{i\alpha*} &&\alpha = 1, \ldots, b_i,
\end{aligned}$$

where $E_i$ is the $i$th component of $E$. Moreover, since $r_t > 0$ for one of the $> 0$ statements, either $x_\alpha' \notin F(Y,D)$ for some $\alpha$ or, for some $i$ and $\alpha$, $z_{i\alpha} >_i^{i\alpha} z_{i\alpha}'$. Without altering the permutation aspect or the other characteristics of the sequences, reductions can be made in the pairs of sequences so that $\{(x_\alpha,D^\alpha)\} \cap \{(x_\alpha',D^\alpha)\} = \emptyset$, $\{(z_{i\alpha},D^{i\alpha})\} \cap \{(z_{i\alpha}',D^{i\alpha})\} = \emptyset$ and $\{(w_{i\alpha},E^{i\alpha})\} \cap \{(w_{i\alpha},E^{i\alpha*})\} = \emptyset$. In addition, suppose that

$$(z_{i\alpha},D^{i\alpha}) = (w_{i\beta},E^{i\beta*}).$$

Then $w_{i\beta} \gtrsim_i^{i\alpha} z_{i\alpha}'$ with $>_i^{i\alpha}$ if $z_{i\alpha} >_i^{i\alpha} z_{i\alpha}'$, and $D^{i\alpha}$ and $E^{i\beta}$ have the same $i$th components, so that the pairs

$$\begin{aligned}
&(z_{i\alpha},D^{i\alpha}) &&(w_{i\beta},E^{i\beta})\\
&(z_{i\alpha}',D^{i\alpha}) &&(w_{i\beta},E^{i\beta*})
\end{aligned}$$

can be replaced by the single pair

$$\begin{aligned}
&(w_{i\beta},E^{i\beta})\\
&(z_{i\alpha}',D^{i\alpha}) &&w_{i\beta} >_i^{i\alpha} z_{i\alpha}',\ E_i^{i\beta} = >_i^{i\alpha}.
\end{aligned}$$

A similar reduction can be made if $(z_{i\alpha}',D^{i\alpha}) = (w_{i\beta},E^{i\beta})$. Since only identical pairs are deleted from the two sequences for individual $i$, these reductions imply that, for each $i$, there are sequences

$$\begin{aligned}
&(x_1,D^1), \ldots, (x_K,D^K), (y_{i1},D^{i1}), \ldots, (y_{iK},D^{iK})\\
&(y_1,D^1), \ldots, (y_K,D^K), (x_1,D^1), \ldots, (x_K,D^K)
\end{aligned}$$

227

where $(y_{i1}, D^{i1}), \ldots, (y_{iK}, D^{iK})$ is a rearrangement of $(y_1, D^1), \ldots,$ $(y_K, D^K)$, and where $K > 0$ with

$$x_k \in F(Y, D^k) \qquad k = 1, \ldots, K$$
$$y_{ik} \succsim_i^k x_k \qquad k = 1, \ldots, K \text{ and each } i$$
$$\succ_i^{ik} = \succ_i^k \qquad k = 1, \ldots, K \text{ and each } i,$$

with either $y_k \in F(Y, D^k)$ for some $k$ or else $y_{ik} \succ_i^k x_k$ for some $k$ and $i$. But this clearly contradicts the condition of voter independence. Hence, according to Theorem 3.3, there is in fact a $\rho$ solution for the system. ◆

## 17.4 ANONYMITY AND NEUTRALITY

We shall now examine the effects of anonymity (Definition 13.3) and neutrality (Definition 13.2) on the voter-independence representation (17.6) through (17.8) in Theorem 17.2. To do this in a reasonably efficient way we shall assume certain structure in addition to our continuing assumption that $X$ is finite. For anonymity it is assumed that $\mathfrak{D}$ is an $n$-fold product of a set of strict partial orders on $X$. The structure for neutrality is noted later. Theorems that are similar to those in this section but which use fewer structural assumptions are proved in Fishburn (1972).

### ANONYMITY

Let (17.6) through (17.8) hold and, for each strict partial order $\succ$ on $X$ define
$$u(x, Y, \succ) = \Sigma_{i=1}^n u_i(x, Y, \succ). \qquad (17.9)$$

It then follows that $x \succ_i y \Rightarrow u(x, Y, \succ_i) > u(y, Y, \succ_i)$, and that $x \approx_i y \Rightarrow u(x, Y, \succ_i) = u(y, Y, \succ_i)$.

For any $D^1 = (\succ_1, \ldots, \succ_n)$ let $D^2 = (\succ_2, \ldots, \succ_n, \succ_1)$, $D^3 = (\succ_3, \ldots, \succ_n, \succ_1, \succ_2), \ldots, D^n = (\succ_n, \succ_1, \ldots, \succ_{n-1})$. Suppose that $x \in F(Y, D^1)$. Then, by anonymity, $x \in F(Y, D^k)$ for $k = 2, \ldots, n$. Likewise, if $y \notin F(Y, D^1)$ then $y \notin F(Y, D^k)$ for $k = 2, \ldots, n$. It follows immediately from (17.8) and (17.9) that $x \in F(Y, D^1) \Leftrightarrow \Sigma_i u(x, Y, \succ_i) \geq \Sigma_i u(y, Y, \succ_i)$ for all $y \in Y$. This proves the following theorem.

THEOREM 17.3. *Suppose that* $F: \mathfrak{X} \times \mathfrak{D} \to \mathcal{P}(X)$ *is a social choice function that satisfies the conditions of voter independence and anonymity, and that* $D = S^n$ *where* $S$ *is a set of strict partial orders on* $X$. *Then* *there is a real-valued function u on $X \times \mathfrak{X} \times S$ such that, for all $i \in \{1, \ldots, n\}$, $>_i \in S$, $x,y \in X$ and $(Y,D) \in \mathfrak{X} \times \mathfrak{D}$,*

$$x >_i y \Rightarrow u(x, Y, >_i) > u(y, Y, >_i) \qquad (17.10)$$
$$x \approx_i y \Rightarrow u(x, Y, >_i) = u(y, Y, >_i) \qquad (17.11)$$

*and*

$$F(Y,D) = \{x : x \in Y \text{ and } \Sigma_{i=1}^n u(x, Y, >_i) \geq \Sigma_{i=1}^n u(y, Y, >_i)$$
$$\text{for all } y \in Y\}. \quad (17.12)$$

NEUTRALITY WITHOUT ANONYMITY

Departing slightly from the hierarchy on the right of Figure 17.1, we shall first consider neutrality without also assuming anonymity.

Structurally, we shall work with the set $\Lambda$ of all permutations $\sigma$ on $X$. Recall that $\sigma Y = \{\sigma(x) : x \in Y\}$ for any nonempty subset $Y \subseteq X$ and any $\sigma \in \Lambda$. It will be assumed that $Y \in \mathfrak{X} \Rightarrow \sigma Y \in \mathfrak{X}$ and that $D \in \mathfrak{D} \Rightarrow D^\sigma \in \mathfrak{D}$. With $D = (>_1, \ldots, >_n)$, $D^\sigma$ equals $(>_1^\sigma, \ldots, >_n^\sigma)$ where, for each $i$ and all $x,y \in X$, $x >_i y \Leftrightarrow \sigma(x) >_i^\sigma \sigma(y)$. In this setting neutrality says that, for all $(Y,D) \in \mathfrak{X} \times \mathfrak{D}$,

$$x \in F(Y,D) \Leftrightarrow \sigma(x) \in F(\sigma Y, D^\sigma). \qquad (17.13)$$

Since anonymity is not being assumed, we shall work separately with each $u_i$ in Theorem 17.2. To show the effect that neutrality will have on $u_i$ suppose for simplicity that $Y = X = \{x,y,z\}$. The 19 strict partial orders on $X$ are put into five groups as follows:

1. $xyz$, $xzy$, $yxz$, $yzx$, $zxy$, $zyx$   (linear)
2. $(xyz) = \emptyset$          (weak)
3. $(xy)z$, $(xz)y$, $(yz)x$   (weak)
4. $x(yz)$, $y(xz)$, $z(xy)$   (weak)
5. $x \sim y > z \sim x$, $x \sim z > y \sim x$, and the other four strict partial orders on $X$ that are not weak orders.

All orders in a given group can be obtained from one another by permutations $\sigma \in \Lambda$ that preserve order, and no order in one group can be obtained from an order in another group in this way. The effect of neutrality is to make the $u_i$ values for a given order in a group essentially the same as the $u_i$ values for any other order in its group, under the appropriate permutation. For example, if for $xyz$ in group 1, we have $u_i(x, X, xyz) = 3$, $u_i(y, X, xyz) = 1$, and $u_i(z, X, xyz) = 0$, then for the order $zxy$ in group 1 we will have $u_i(z, X, zxy) = 3$, $u_i(x, X, zxy) = 1$, and $u_i(y, X, zxy) = 0$. Or if

$$u_i(x, \ldots) = u_i(y, \ldots) = 5 \text{ and } u_i(z, \ldots) = 0$$

for the order $(xy)z$ in group 3, then the order $(xz)y$ in group 3 will have $u_i(x, \ldots) = u_i(z, \ldots) = 5$ and $u_i(y, \ldots) = 0$.

The same sort of thing applies when $Y \subset X$, except for the obvious fact that $Y$ itself gets transformed to $\sigma Y$ under $\sigma \in \Lambda$. In the general case, the effect of neutrality is to permit $u_i$ to be defined in the context of Theorem 17.2 so that

$$u_i(x, Y, >_i) = u_i(\sigma(x), \sigma Y, >_i^\sigma). \tag{17.14}$$

THEOREM 17.4. *Suppose that* $F: \mathfrak{X} \times \mathfrak{D} \to \mathcal{P}(X)$ *is a social choice function that satisfies the conditions of voter independence and neutrality, and that* $Y \in \mathfrak{X} \Rightarrow \sigma Y \in \mathfrak{X}$ *and* $D \in \mathfrak{D} \Rightarrow D^\sigma \in \mathfrak{D}$ *for all* $\sigma \in \Lambda$. *Then there are real-valued functions* $u_i$ *on* $X \times \mathfrak{X} \times \mathfrak{D}_i$ *that satisfy the representation of Theorem 17.2 and also satisfy (17.14) for all* $(x, Y, >_{i, \sigma}) \in X \times \mathfrak{X} \times \mathfrak{D}_i \times \Lambda$, *for each* $i$.

*Proof.* Let the $u_i$ satisfy (17.6) through (17.8) and define

$$v_i(x, Y, >_i) = \Sigma_{\sigma \in \Lambda} u_i(\sigma(x), \sigma Y, >_i^\sigma) \tag{17.15}$$

for all $(x, Y, >_i) \in X \times \mathfrak{X} \times \mathfrak{D}_i$. The structural assumptions assure that $(\sigma Y, >_i^\sigma) \in \mathfrak{X} \times \mathfrak{D}_i$ when $(Y, >_i) \in \mathfrak{X} \times \mathfrak{D}_i$. Since $(x, Y, >_i)$ is obtained from $(\sigma(x), \sigma Y, >_i^\sigma)$ by applying the inverse of $\sigma$ to the latter, it follows that (17.14) holds for $v_i$. Moreover, (17.6) and (17.7) hold for $v_i$ in view of the fact that $x >_i y \Leftrightarrow \sigma(x) >_i^\sigma \sigma(y)$.

It remains to verify (17.8) for the $v_i$, and this follows easily from (17.8) for the $u_i$, (17.13) and (17.15). ◆

ANONYMITY AND NEUTRALITY

Combining these two conditions, we obtain the following theorem. Its proof is obtained easily from Theorem 17.3 by defining $v(x, Y, >) = \Sigma_\Lambda u(\sigma(x), \sigma Y, >^\sigma)$, similar to (17.15).

THEOREM 17.5. *Suppose that* $F: \mathfrak{X} \times \mathfrak{D} \to \mathcal{P}(X)$ *is a social choice function that is anonymous, neutral and satisfies the condition of voter independence. Suppose further that* $Y \in \mathfrak{X} \Rightarrow \sigma Y \in \mathfrak{X}$ *and* $D \in \mathfrak{D} \Rightarrow D^\sigma \in \mathfrak{D}$ *for all* $\sigma \in \Lambda$, *and that* $\mathfrak{D} = S^n$ *where* $S$ *is a set of strict partial orders on* $X$. *Then there is a real-valued function* $u$ *on* $X \times \mathfrak{X} \times S$ *that satisfies the representation of Theorem 17.3 and also satisfies*

$$u(x, Y, >) = u(\sigma(x), \sigma Y, >^\sigma)$$

*for all* $(x, Y, >, \sigma) \in X \times \mathfrak{X} \times S \times \Lambda$.

When independence from infeasible alternatives also holds and the structure is sufficiently rich, the $u$ values for a given order on $Y$ can be taken to be the same as the $u$ values for any order on $Y'$ provided that

**230**

there is a one-one correspondence between $Y$ and $Y'$ that preserves order. For example, if $Y = \{x,y,z\}$ and $x >_i y >_i z$, and if $Y' = \{a,b,c\}$ and $a >_j b >_j c$, then $u$ for Theorem 17.5 can be made to satisfy $u(x,Y, >_i) = u(a,Y', >_j)$, $u(y,Y, >_i) = u(b,Y', >_j)$ and $u(z,Y, >_i) = u(c,Y', >_j)$. This may not be possible if independence from infeasible alternatives does not hold. For example, if there is no permutation $\sigma$ on $X$ such that $\sigma(x,y,z) = (a,b,c)$ and $>_i^\sigma = >_j$ on $X$, then we cannot reach the same conclusion with only the hypotheses of Theorem 17.5.

## 17.5 DEPENDENCE ON INFEASIBLE ALTERNATIVES

We now return briefly to the special summation functions on the left of Figure 17.1. Introductory remarks for these are given at the end of section 17.2.

The first case has the same representation as (17.1) through (17.3), except that $Y$ is deleted from the $u_i$ functions. This gives $u_i$ on $X \times \mathfrak{D}$ for each $i$ such that, for every $D$,

$$x >_i y \Rightarrow u_i(x,D) > u_i(y,D) \qquad \text{for all } i, x, y$$
$$x \approx_i y \Rightarrow u_i(x,D) = u_i(y,D) \qquad \text{for all } i, x, y$$
$$F(Y,D) - \{x : x \in Y \text{ and } \Sigma_i u_i(x,D) \geq \Sigma_i u_i(y,D)$$
$$\text{for every } y \in Y\} \qquad \text{for all } Y \in \mathfrak{X}.$$

The appropriate necessary and sufficient condition for this case considers each $D$ separately and lets $Y$ vary over $\mathfrak{X}$. It is, for each $D \in \mathfrak{D}$:

If $K$ is a positive integer, if $x_k, y_k \in Y_k \in \mathfrak{X}$ for $k = 1, \ldots, K$ and if, for each $i$, $\sigma_i$ is a permutation on $\{1, \ldots, K\}$ such that $y_{\sigma_i(k)} \gtrsim_i x_k$ for $k = 1, \ldots, K$, then

(1) $y_{\sigma_i(k)} \approx_i x_k$ for all $i$ and $k$, and $x_k \in F(Y^k, D)$ for all $k \Rightarrow y_k \in F(Y^k, D)$ for all $k$;

(2) $y_{\sigma_i(k)} >_i x_k$ for some $i$ and $k \Rightarrow x_k \notin F(Y^k, D)$ for some $k$.

This is easily seen to be necessary for the representation given above. The sufficiency proof is similar to the proof of Theorem 17.2 and is left to the reader.

If $\mathfrak{X}$ contains every binary subset of $X$, so that $F_D$ is well defined for each $D \in \mathfrak{D}$, then the conditions simplify slightly. For this special case we require $F_D$ to be a weak order for each $D$, with $F(Y,D) = \{x : x \in Y$ and $y F_D x$ for no $y \in Y\}$ for all $(Y,D) \in \mathfrak{X} \times \mathfrak{D}$, along with the following for each $D \in \mathfrak{D}$:

If $K$ is a positive integer, if $x_k, y_k \in X$ for $k = 1, \ldots, K$, and if, for each $i$, $\sigma_i$ is a permutation on $\{1, \ldots, K\}$ such that $y_{\sigma_i(k)} \gtrsim_i x_k$ for $k = 1, \ldots, K$, then

(1) $y_{\sigma_i(k)} \approx_i x_k$ for all $i$ and $k \Rightarrow$ either (not $x_k F_D y_k$ & not $y_k F_D x_k$) for all $k$, or $x_k F_D y_k$ for some $k$;

(2) $y_{\sigma_i(k)} >_i x_k$ for some $i$ and $k \Rightarrow y_k F_D x_k$ for some $k$.

### VOTER INDEPENDENCE

The next step indicated on Figure 17.1 is to remove the dependence of $u_i$ on other individuals' preference orders, so that $u_i(x,D)$ is replaced by $u_i(x, >_i)$. We shall consider only the simplest structural setting for this case, assuming that $\mathfrak{X} = \mathcal{P}(X) - \{\emptyset\}$ and that $\mathfrak{D}$ is the set of all $n$-tuples of strict partial orders on $X$.

As in the case just considered, $F_D$ is taken to be a weak order for each $D \in \mathfrak{D}$, with $F(Y,D) = \{x : x \in Y$ and $y F_D x$ for no $y \in Y\}$ for all $(Y,D) \in \mathfrak{X} \times \mathfrak{D}$. Two more conditions suffice for the $u_i(x, >_i)$ representation. They are the unanimity condition stated immediately after (17.4) and the following special voter independence condition:

If $K$ is a positive integer, if $x_1, \ldots, x_K, y_1, \ldots, y_K \in X$ and $D^1, \ldots, D^K \in \mathfrak{D}$ and if, for each $i$, $\sigma_i$ is a permutation on $\{1, \ldots, K\}$ for which

$$(y_{\sigma_i(k)}, >_i^{\sigma_i(k)}) = (x_k, >_i^k) \qquad k = 1, \ldots, K,$$

then $x_k F_{D^k} y_k$ for some $k \in \{1, \ldots, K\} \Leftrightarrow y_j F_{D^j} x_j$ for some $j \in \{1, \ldots, K\}$.

The main difference between this multiprofile condition and the voter independence condition of Definition 17.3 is that the new condition takes $y_{\sigma_i(k)} = x_k$, whereas the other has $y_{\sigma_i(k)} \gtrsim_i^k x_k$ (and $\approx_i^k$ uniformly, or $>_i^k$ for some $i$, $k$) in its hypotheses. Thus the new condition avoids the inclusion of a unanimity-type extension such as the summation condition. As we shall see momentarily, the simple unanimity condition after (17.4) is all that is needed in the present context.

The special voter independence condition also bears a strong resemblance to the condition of strong duality (Definition 5.2) used in Part I to obtain a weighted majority social choice function. Indeed, if $X = \{x,y\}$, then the conditions used here along with duality imply that $F$ is a weighted majority social choice function.

The proof that the $u_i(x, >_i)$ representation follows from the conditions given above proceeds as follows. Using Theorem 3.3 on the $F_D$ statements obtained from $F$, it follows from the special voter independence condition and from $F_D$ a weak order for each $D \in \mathfrak{D}$ that there are real-valued functions $w_i$ on $X \times \{> : >$ is a strict partial order on $X\}$ for $i = 1, \ldots, n$ such that, for all $x$ and $y$ in $X$ and all $D \in \mathfrak{D}$,

$$x F_D y \Leftrightarrow \Sigma_{i=1}^n w_i(x, >_i) > \Sigma_{i=1}^n w_i(y, >_i). \qquad (17.16)$$

The $w_i$ functions do not necessarily satisfy $x \succ_i y \Rightarrow w_i(x, \succ_i) > w_i(y, \succ_i)$ and $x \approx_i y \Rightarrow w_i(x, \succ_i) = w_i(y, \succ_i)$. To obtain this, we use the unanimity condition following (17.4). Fix $a \in X$ and define $\delta_i$ on $X$ for each $i$ by

$$\delta_i(x) = w_i(a, \emptyset) - w_i(x, \emptyset) \qquad \text{for all} \qquad x \in X.$$

When $D = (\emptyset, \ldots, \emptyset)$, the unanimity condition requires not $xF_Da$ and not $aF_Dx$, so that

$$\Sigma_{i=1}^n \delta_i(x) = \Sigma_i w_i(a, \emptyset) - \Sigma_i w_i(x, \emptyset) = 0 \qquad (17.17)$$

by (17.16). We then define $u_i$ for each $i$ by

$$u_i(x, \succ_i) = \delta_i(x) + w_i(x, \succ_i).$$

According to (17.16) and (17.17),

$$xF_Dy \Leftrightarrow \Sigma_{i=1}^n u_i(x, \succ_i) > \Sigma_{i=1}^n u_i(y, \succ_i). \qquad (17.18)$$

To verify

$$x \succ_i y \Rightarrow u_i(x, \succ_i) > u_i(y, \succ_i) \qquad (17.19)$$
$$x \approx_i y \Rightarrow u_i(x, \succ_i) = u_i(y, \succ_i) \qquad (17.20)$$

for $i = 1$ let $D = (\succ_1, \emptyset, \ldots, \emptyset)$. Suppose first that $x \approx_1 y$. Then, by (17.18) and unanimity,

$$u_1(x, \succ_1) + \Sigma_{i=2}^n u_i(x, \emptyset) = u_1(y, \succ_1) + \Sigma_{i=2}^n u_i(y, \emptyset).$$

But $u_i(x, \emptyset) = w_i(a, \emptyset) = u_i(y, \emptyset)$ for all $i > 1$, and therefore $u_1(x, \succ_1) = u_1(y, \succ_1)$. On the other hand, if $x \succ_1 y$, then we get $>$ in the foregoing display and hence $u_1(x, \succ_1) > u_1(y, \succ_1)$. Since a similar proof holds for each $i$, this establishes the representation of (17.18) through (17.20).

### ANONYMITY AND NEUTRALITY

Continuing in the context of (17.18) through (17.20) with finite $\mathfrak{X} = \mathcal{P}(X) - \{\emptyset\}$ and $\mathfrak{D}$ the set of all $n$-tuples of strict partial orders on $X$, suppose that $F$ is anonymous. Then, by a proof like that for Theorem 17.3, it follows that we can obtain $u_1 = u_2 = \cdots = u_n$, giving the representation

$$xF_Dy \Leftrightarrow \Sigma_{i=1}^n u(x, \succ_i) > \Sigma_{i=1}^n u(y, \succ_i)$$
$$x \succ_i y \Rightarrow u(x, \succ_i) > u(y, \succ_i)$$
$$x \approx_i y \Rightarrow u(x, \succ_i) = u(y, \succ_i),$$

along with $F(Y, D) = \{x : x \in Y \text{ and } \Sigma_i u(x, \succ_i) \geq \Sigma_i u(y, \succ_i)$ for all $y \in Y\}$ by previous assumption. If neutrality holds also then, by a proof similar to that for Theorem 17.4, $u$ can be made to satisfy $u(x, \succ) = u(\sigma(x), \succ^\sigma)$ for all $x$, $\succ$ and all permutations $\sigma$ on $X$.

# CHAPTER 18

## Lotteries on Social Alternatives

A LOTTERY on social alternatives can be thought of as a process that selects a social alternative "at random" according to specified probabilities for the alternatives. If a wife and husband want to watch different programs on the TV at 10 p.m. one evening and agree to settle the matter with the toss of a coin, then they are using a lottery.

In abstract form, a lottery can be viewed as a simple probability distribution on the basic alternatives. Section 18.1 shows that our previous definition of social choice function applies in a straightforward way to lotteries. For $F(Y,D)$, $Y$ is a set of probability distributions on basic alternatives, $D$ is an $n$-tuple of strict partial orders on probability distributions, and $F(Y,D)$ is a nonempty subset of $Y$.

The second section discusses axioms on individual preference that arise in the probabilistic context. These are then used in section 18.3, which examines the structure of the set of admissible (undominated) probability distributions for a given $(Y,D)$ when $Y$ is the set of distributions on a finite subset of basic alternatives.

The role of simple majority in the lottery context is briefly considered in the final section along with a few remarks on summation procedures.

### 18.1 LOTTERIES ON SOCIAL ALTERNATIVES

If a choice set in a specific situation contains several alternatives, then some form of tie-breaking procedure must be used to make a "final" selection. One such procedure that might be considered fair is to choose an alternative from the choice set by a chance process. For example, if $\{a,b,c\}$ is the choice set, then "$a$," "$b$," and "$c$" could be put into a hat, from which one of the three will be drawn at random. The alternative whose name is drawn will then be implemented.

This chance process introduces a "new" alternative into the choice process. This "new" alternative is not one of the basic alternatives; instead, it is a lottery on the basic alternatives. In the preceding example, it is a lottery $x$ in which each of $a$, $b$, and $c$ has equal probability, namely $\frac{1}{3}$, of being the "winning ticket." We can express this by the functional correspondence $x(a) = x(b) = x(c) = \frac{1}{3}$. In these terms, a basic alternative can also be thought of as a lottery; thus, alternative $b$ corresponds to the lottery $z$ that has $z(b) = 1$.

Since individuals have preferences between lotteries, it is clear that we can expand our basic feasible set, say $B$, to include lotteries such as $x$. We might ask, for example, what the choice set from $B \cup \{x\}$ would be if the procedure used to obtain the choice set $\{a,b,c\}$ from $B$ were applied to $B \cup \{x\}$. For the sake of illustration, suppose that $\{b,x\}$ is the choice set from $B \cup \{x\}$. If the random process were then applied to this new choice set (put "$b$" and "$x$" into a hat and draw one at random; if "$x$" is drawn, then lottery $x$ is activated), a second lottery, say $y$, results. Lottery $y$ is a compound lottery since one of its initial "prizes" is the lottery $x$. However, $y$ corresponds to a simple lottery with probabilities $y(a) = y(c) = (\frac{1}{2})(\frac{1}{3}) = \frac{1}{6}$ and $y(b) = \frac{1}{2} + (\frac{1}{2})(\frac{1}{3}) = \frac{2}{3}$, which are the total probabilities for $a$, $b$, and $c$ under lottery $y$.

ANOTHER EXAMPLE

Pursuing the spirit but not the particulars of this example, it might seem reasonable to admit all lotteries on feasible alternatives into the choice process from the beginning. Since each lottery and each basic alternative corresponds to a simple probability distribution on the set $B$ of basic feasible alternatives, this suggests that the choice set for $B$ be some nonempty subset of the set of simple probability distributions on $B$.

It is precisely this suggestion that we shall pursue in this chapter. Although a random tie-breaking procedure was used to introduce lotteries, it should be emphasized that other reasons may suggest the use of probability distributions.

To illustrate, suppose that a three-member committee is responsible for selecting a new man for a certain position in their company. Their search has turned up four satisfactory candidates, Messrs. $a$, $b$, $c$, and $d$. The feelings of the committee members are as follows:

1. Mr. $a$ is terrific; Mr. $d$ is all right and is slightly better than Messrs. $b$ and $c$, who are satisfactory.
2. Mr. $b$ is terrific; Mr. $d$ is all right and is slightly better than Messrs. $a$ and $c$, who are satisfactory.
3. Mr. $c$ is terrific; Mr. $d$ is all right and is slightly better than Messrs. $a$ and $b$, who are satisfactory.

Now each member swears by the weak Condorcet condition of section 12.1 for choice procedures that do not use lotteries. In such a procedure, $\{d\}$ is the choice set since $d$ has a strict simple majority over each of $a$, $b$, and $c$.

However, the committee knows that they might use a lottery to make the choice, and none of the members has a moral aversion to such a procedure. Indeed, with $x$ the even-chance lottery on $\{a,b,c\}$, so that $x(a) = x(b) = x(c) = \frac{1}{3}$ and $x(d) = 0$, it turns out that each member prefers $x$ to $d$. Hence $x$ is unanimously preferred to $d$, and the committee agrees to use $x$ to make the final selection.

This conclusion may seem strange, since any candidate that $x$ might "choose" would lose to $d$ on a simple-majority comparison. However, the inescapable fact is that each committee member would rather gamble with $x$ on the chance that his "terrific" candidate will win than accept the compromise candidate $d$.

DEFINITIONS AND NOTATION

Throughout this chapter, $A$ will denote the set of basic alternatives. A typical feasible subset of basic alternatives is $B \subseteq A$.

To keep matters fairly simple, we shall work only with *simple* probability distributions on $A$. For our purposes it will suffice to define such a distribution as a function $x: A \to Re$ such that

$$x(a) \geq 0 \quad \text{for all } a \in A$$
$$x(a) = 0 \quad \text{for all but a finite number of } a \in A$$
$$\dot{\Sigma}_A x(a) = 1.$$

We shall not make any notational distinction between a basic alternative and the distribution that assigns probability 1 to this alternative. Thus, $b$ may denote either a basic alternative or the simple probability distribution that assigns probability 1 to $b$.

We shall let $X$ be the set of all simple probability distributions on $A$. If $x,y \in X$ and $0 \leq \lambda \leq 1$ then $\lambda x + (1 - \lambda)y$ is the *function* from $A$ to $Re$ for which

$$(\lambda x + (1 - \lambda)y)(a) = \lambda x(a) + (1 - \lambda)y(a) \quad \text{for all} \quad a \in A.$$

Under the stated conditions $\lambda x + (1 - \lambda)y$, a convex linear combination of the functions $x$ and $y$, is a simple probability distribution on $A$ since $\Sigma_A[\lambda x(a) + (1 - \lambda)y(a)] = \lambda\Sigma_A x(a) + (1 - \lambda)\Sigma_A y(a) = \lambda + (1 - \lambda) = 1$. To illustrate such a combination let $\lambda = .4$ with

$$x(a) = .3, \, x(b) = .7, \, x(d) = 0 \quad \text{for all} \quad d \in A - \{a,b\}.$$
$$y(a) = .5, \, y(c) = .5, \, y(d) = 0 \quad \text{for all} \quad d \in A - \{a,c\}.$$

Then, with $z = \lambda x + (1 - \lambda)y = .4x + .6y$,

$$z(a) = .42, \, z(b) = .28, \, z(c) = .30.$$

More generally, if $x_1, \ldots, x_m \in X$ and if $\lambda_1, \ldots, \lambda_m$ are nonnegative numbers that sum to 1, then $\Sigma_{k=1}^m \lambda_k x_k$, a convex linear combination of $x_1$ through $x_m$, is the function from $A$ to $Re$ whose values are defined by

$$(\Sigma_{k=1}^m \lambda_k x_k)(a) = \Sigma_{k=1}^m \lambda_k x_k(a) \quad \text{for all} \quad a \in A.$$

Under the stated conditions, $\Sigma_{k=1}^{m}\lambda_k x_k \in X$, and therefore $X$ is closed under convex linear combinations.

When $B$ is the basic feasible set, the corresponding feasible set of probability distributions in $X$ is

$$Y = Y(B) = \{x : x \in X \text{ and } \Sigma_B x(a) = 1\}.$$

$Y(B)$ simply denotes the dependence of $Y$ on $B$. The set of all potentially feasible subsets of $X$ will, as before, be written as $\mathfrak{X}$. In the present context,

$$\mathfrak{X} = \{Y(B) : B \text{ is a potentially feasible basic subset of } A\}.$$

Also as before, $D$ is an $n$-tuple of strict partial orders on $X$, and $\mathfrak{D}$ is a nonempty set of such $n$-tuples. As in Definition 14.1, a social choice function is a function $F : \mathfrak{X} \times \mathfrak{D} \to \mathcal{P}(x)$ with $\emptyset \subset F(Y,D) \subseteq Y$ for all $(Y,D) \in \mathfrak{X} \times \mathfrak{D}$.

Independence from infeasible alternatives reads the same as before: $F(Y,D) = F(Y,D')$ when the restriction of $D$ on $Y$ equals the restriction of $D'$ on $Y$. Under independence, the distributions in $X - Y$ are ignored and $D$ can be viewed in abbreviated form as an $n$-tuple of strict partial orders on the distributions in $Y$.

## 18.2 AXIOMS FOR INDIVIDUALS

As usual, we define other binary relations on $X$ from a preference order $>$ on $X$ as follows:

$x \sim y \Leftrightarrow \text{not } x > y \ \& \ \text{not } y > x$
$x \geqslant y \Leftrightarrow x > y \text{ or } x \sim y$
$x \approx y \Leftrightarrow (x \sim z \Leftrightarrow y \sim z, \text{ for all } z \in X)$
$x \gtrsim y \Leftrightarrow x > y \text{ or } x \approx y.$

If independence is assumed, one may wish to replace $X$ in the definition of $\approx$ by $Y = Y(B)$ when $B$ is taken as the feasible set of basic alternatives.

### INTRANSITIVE INDIFFERENCE

We shall assume in general that each individual preference order $>$ on $X$ is a strict partial order. To show one way that the use of probabilities can lead to intransitive indifference ($\sim$), suppose that an individual is involved in a decision to allocate a certain amount of money to a specific activity. Four elements in $A$ are \$10,000, \$14,000, \$14,200, and \$20,000. Our individual's preference increases as the amount increases, so that \$14,200 > \$14,000 for example. Let $x$ be an even-chance lottery on {\$10,000, \$20,000}. Then it is quite possible that he will not have a definite preference between \$14,000 and $x$, or between $x$ and \$14,200, in which case $\sim$ is not transitive.

## SURE-THING AXIOMS

Suppose that $x > y$. Let $z \in X$ and $0 < \lambda < 1$, and consider the combinations $\lambda x + (1 - \lambda)z$ and $\lambda y + (1 - \lambda)z$. Although these are simple probability distributions, they can be viewed as two-stage lotteries in the following way. For $\lambda x + (1 - \lambda)z$, a random device selects $x$ with probability $\lambda$ and $z$ with probability $1 - \lambda$. If $x$ is selected in the first stage then a final winner in $A$ is determined according to the probabilities given by $x$; likewise for $z$. The overall probability for $a \in A$ under this two-stage procedure is precisely $\lambda x(a) + (1 - \lambda)z(a) = (\lambda x + (1 - \lambda)z)(a)$. The other combination, $\lambda y + (1 - \lambda)z$, can be viewed in a similar fashion. Since $x > y$, it seems reasonable in view of the two-stage interpretation that $\lambda x + (1 - \lambda)z > \lambda y + (1 - \lambda)z$. However, it might be argued that if $\lambda$ is sufficiently near to zero then the two combinations will be so overwhelmed by the dilution term $(1 - \lambda)z$ that the individual will be indifferent between them. This seems to me to be a valid psychological point. However, from a normative point of view, it might be argued that, even though the combinations may be almost indistinguishable, the individual will wish to take $\lambda x + (1 - \lambda)z > \lambda y + (1 - \lambda)z$ when he prefers $x$ to $y$.

Although one later result (Theorem 18.1) could be derived from an axiom that is not as strong as the sure-thing (or independence, monotonicity, etc.) axiom that requires $\lambda x + (1 - \lambda)z > \lambda y + (1 - \lambda)z$ when $\lambda \in (0,1)$ and $x > y$, we shall use it in the sequel. Likewise, we shall use the companion axiom based on the equivalence $\approx$: If $x \approx y$ and $0 < \lambda < 1$ then $\lambda x + (1 - \lambda)z \approx \lambda y + (1 - \lambda)z$. Since here we are diluting two distributions that are virtually identical in preference to begin with, the dilution would not seem to change this state of affairs.

The following definition sets forth the things that will generally be assumed about individual preference on $X$ as characterized in this chapter.

DEFINITION 18.1. *A preference order $>$ on $X$ satisfies the* weak individual axiom *if and only if, for all $x,y,z \in X$ and $\lambda \in (0,1)$,*

1. *$>$ on $X$ is a strict partial order,*
2. *$x > y \Rightarrow \lambda x + (1 - \lambda)z > \lambda y + (1 - \lambda)z$, and*
   *$x \approx y \Rightarrow \lambda x + (1 - \lambda)z \approx \lambda y + (1 - \lambda)z$.*

The following lemma shows how the two parts of part 2 of the definition combine with part 1 to extend themselves to similar finite combinations. The lemma will be used in the next section.

LEMMA 18.1. *Suppose that $>$ on $X$ satisfies the weak individual axiom, that $x_k$, $y_k \in X$ and $x_k \gtrsim y_k$ and $\lambda_k \geq 0$ for $k = 1, \ldots, m$, and that $\Sigma_{k=1}^{m} \lambda_k = 1$. Then*

(1) $x_k \approx y_k$ *for all* $k \Rightarrow \Sigma_{k=1}^{m} \lambda_k x_k \approx \Sigma_{k=1}^{m} \lambda_k y_k$;
(2) $x_k > y_k$ *for some* $k$ *for which* $\lambda_k > 0 \Rightarrow \Sigma_{k=1}^{m} \lambda_k x_k > \Sigma_{k=1}^{m} \lambda_k y_k$.

*Proof.* Suppose first that $x_k \approx y_k$ for all $k$. We proceed by induction on $m$. For $m = 2$, part 2 of the weak individual axiom gives $\lambda_1 x_1 + \lambda_2 x_2 \approx \lambda_1 y_1 + \lambda_2 x_2 \approx \lambda_1 y_1 + \lambda_2 y_2$. Since $\approx$ is transitive when $>$ is a strict partial order, $\lambda_1 x_1 + \lambda_2 x_2 \approx \lambda_1 y_1 + \lambda_2 y_2$. (If $\lambda_1 = 1$ or $\lambda_2 = 1$, the conclusion is immediate.) Now suppose that (1) is true for $m = 2$, $\ldots$, $K - 1$. For the case of $m = K$ take $0 < \lambda_K < 1$, by resubscripting if necessary. Then by the induction hypothesis,

$$(1 - \lambda_K)^{-1} \Sigma_{k=1}^{K-1} \lambda_k x_k \approx (1 - \lambda_K)^{-1} \Sigma_{k=1}^{K-1} \lambda_k y_k,$$

and by the result just proved for $m = 2$,

$$(1 - \lambda_K)[(1 - \lambda_K)^{-1} \Sigma_{k=1}^{K-1} \lambda_k x_k] + \lambda_K x_K$$
$$\approx (1 - \lambda_K)[(1 - \lambda_K)^{-1} \Sigma_{k=1}^{K-1} \lambda_k y_k] + \lambda_K y_K,$$

which is the same as $\Sigma_{k=1}^{K} \lambda_k x_k \approx \Sigma_{k=1}^{K} \lambda_k y_k$.

For (2) assume for definiteness that $x_m > y_m$ and $0 < \lambda_m < 1$. (If $\lambda_m = 1$, the conclusion is obvious.) Then, with $m = 2$, the weak individual axiom gives $\lambda_1 x_1 + \lambda_2 x_2 > \lambda_1 y_1 + \lambda_2 y_2$. Proceeding by induction as before, $\Sigma_{k=1}^{K} \lambda_k x_k > \Sigma_{k=1}^{K} \lambda_k y_k$ follows in the obvious manner when $m = K \geq 2$.◆

THE STRONG INDIVIDUAL AXIOM

Most studies based on a formulation that uses lotteries employ somewhat stronger assumptions for individual preference than those in Definition 18.1. A typical set of stronger axioms, which are essentially the ones proposed by von Neumann and Morgenstern (1947) in their study of game theory, is identified in the following definition.

DEFINITION 18.2. *A preference order $>$ on $X$ satisfies the strong individual axiom if and only if, for all $x$, $y$, $z \in X$ and $\lambda \in (0,1)$:*

1. $>$ *on $X$ is a weak order,*
2. $x > y \Rightarrow \lambda x + (1 - \lambda)z > \lambda y + (1 - \lambda)z$,
3. $x > y \,\&\, y > z \Rightarrow \alpha x + (1 - \alpha)z > y$ *and* $y > \beta x + (1 - \beta)z$ *for some $\alpha$, $\beta \in (0,1)$.*

Part 3 is a so-called Archimedean axiom and has the effect of preventing any basic alternative from being "infinitely desirable" or "infinitely undesirable." To note a contrived example where it might fail, suppose that an individual is convinced that a new penny is a "fair coin." The penny is to be flipped $N$ times. He is asked to consider a choice between

   (i) receive \$1 regardless of the outcome of the $N$ flips;
   (ii) be executed if every flip results in a head, and receive \$2 otherwise.

Presuming that \$2 > \$1 > execution, our individual would violate part 3 of the strong individual axiom if he chose (i) over (ii) regardless of the size of $N$.

Although the $\approx$ part of the weak individual axiom is not stated in the strong individual axiom, it can be shown to follow from the latter. This is proved by Jensen (1967), who gives a proof of Lemma 18.2 also. Similar proofs are contained in Chapter 8 of Fishburn (1970). The attractiveness of the strong individual axiom arises partly from the convenient numerical representation expressed in the following lemma.

LEMMA 18.2. *Suppose that $>$ on $X$ satisfies the strong individual axiom. Then there is a function $u: A \rightarrow Re$ such that, for all $x, y \in X$,*

$$x > y \Leftrightarrow \Sigma_A x(a) u(a) > \Sigma_A y(a) u(a). \qquad (18.1)$$

*Moreover, a function $v: A \rightarrow Re$ satisfies this in place of $u$ if and only if there are real numbers $r > 0$ and $s$ such that $v(a) = ru(a) + s$ for all $a \in A$.*

The function $u$ of (18.1) is a "utility function," and $\Sigma_A x(a) u(a)$ is the "expected utility" of the probability distribution $x$. In these terms, (18.1) says that one distribution is preferred to another if and only if the first has the larger expected utility. Clearly, $u$ reflects both the individual's preferences between basic alternatives and his attitudes about taking chances. It shows that, under the strong individual axiom, there is a way to assign numerical values to the basic alternatives so that preferences between distributions are preserved by linear combinations or expectations of the basic alternatives' utilities.

The final part of the lemma states that the utility function in (18.1) is unique up to origin and positive scale transformation. Thus, the origin of $u$ can be changed by adding a constant to all $u(a)$ values, and (18.1) will remain valid. The same thing is true if every $u(a)$ value is multiplied by the same positive constant. If $u$ satisfies (18.1), then any $v: A \rightarrow Re$ that does not satisfy $v(a) = ru(a) + s$ (for all $a$) for some constants $r > 0$ and $s$, cannot satisfy (18.1).

Because only a simple preference relation $>$ is used in the lemma, many authors have warned against interpreting $u$ in (18.1) as a relative measure of preference intensity or strength-of-preference over the basic alternatives in $A$. It obviously measures something (as described above), but it is by no means evident that it has any direct connection to what most people would intuitively think of as a relative measure of preference intensity.

A MODERATE INDIVIDUAL AXIOM

In addition to the strong and weak individual axioms, there are several intermediate forms. One of these, which will be used later, is identified in the following definition.

DEFINITION 18.3. *A preference order $>$ on $X$ satisfies the* moderate individual axiom *if and only if, for all $x,y,z \in X$ and $\lambda \in (0,1)$,*

1. *$>$ on $X$ is a strict partial order,*
2. *$x > y \Leftrightarrow \lambda x + (1 - \lambda)z > \lambda y + (1 - \lambda)z$, and*
   *$x \approx y \Leftrightarrow \lambda x + (1 - \lambda)z \approx \lambda y + (1 - \lambda)z$.*

This adds two antidilution statements to the weak individual axiom, namely $\lambda x + (1 - \lambda)z > \lambda y + (1 - \lambda)z \Rightarrow x > y$, and $\lambda x + (1 - \lambda)z \approx \lambda y + (1 - \lambda)z \Rightarrow x \approx y$. The first of these seems less liable to objection than its converse since it says that if one distribution is preferred to another and if both have a "common" part then the preference must be a result of their different parts. On the other hand, the second seems more vulnerable than its converse, since a small $\lambda$ might give $\lambda x + (1 - \lambda)z \approx \lambda y + (1 - \lambda)z$ because of dilution when $x \approx y$ is false. Lemma 18.2 shows that the moderate individual axiom is implied by the strong individual axiom.

The usefulness of our new axiom in comparison with the weak individual axiom lies in the following addition to the results of Lemma 18.1.

LEMMA 18.3. *Suppose that $>$ on $X$ satisfies the moderate individual axiom, and that $x,y \in X$ and $x \neq y$. Let $L = \{\lambda x + (1 - \lambda)y : \lambda \in Re\}$, and let $L' = L \cap X$. If $x > y$ then $x' > y'$ whenever $x',y' \in L'$ and the sense from $x'$ to $y'$ along $L'$ is the same as the sense from $x$ to $y$. If $x \approx y$ then $x' \approx y'$ for all $x',y' \in L'$.*

*Proof.* Given $x \neq y$, $L'$ is the "line segment" in $X$ that contains $x$ and $y$. (Recall that $x$ and $y$ are simple distributions, so that $L'$ involves only a finite number of basic alternatives.) Let $x^*$ and $y^*$ be the extreme points in $L'$ so that $L' = \{\lambda x^* + (1 - \lambda)y^* : 0 \leq \lambda \leq 1\}$, with $\alpha > \beta$ and $x = \alpha x^* + (1 - \alpha)y^*$, $y = \beta x^* + (1 - \beta)y^*$.

Suppose that $x > y$. With $\alpha > \beta$, $x > y$ is the same as

$$\beta x^* + (1 - \beta)\left[\frac{\alpha - \beta}{1 - \beta} x^* + \frac{1 - \alpha}{1 - \beta} y^*\right] > \beta x^* + (1 - \beta)y^*$$

so that $\lambda x^* + (1 - \lambda)y^* > y^*$ by the moderate individual axiom. Again by this axiom, $x^* > y^*$. Now suppose that

$x' = px^* + (1 - p)y^*$ and $y' = qx^* + (1 - q)y^*$ with $1 \geq p > q \geq 0$.

Then $px^* + (1 - p)y^* > y^*$ by the weak individual axiom, and if $q > 0$ then

$$(q/p)[px^* + (1 - p)y^*] + (1 - q/p)[px^* + (1 - p)y^*]$$
$$> (q/p)[px^* + (1 - p)y^*] + (1 - q/p)y^*,$$

or $px^* + (1 - p)y^* > qx^* + (1 - q)y^*$. If $q = 0$, this result has already been established.

The proof for $\approx$ is similar. ◆

The moderate individual axiom does not give rise to a unidimensional expected-utility result along the lines of Lemma 18.2 since it omits an essential Archimedian axiom. For further discussion on this point, the reader should consult Hausner (1954), Aumann (1962–1964), Kannai (1963), and Fishburn (1970, Chapter 9).

18.3  ADMISSIBLE DISTRIBUTIONS

We shall now use the individual axioms to investigate the important concept of admissible distributions. Throughout this section we shall work with a generic $(Y,D) \in \mathfrak{X} \times \mathfrak{D}$ where $Y$ is based on the subset $B$ of basic alternatives, so that $Y = Y(B)$. Moreover, the condition of independence from infeasible alternatives will be assumed to hold so that $D$ can be viewed as an $n$-tuple of strict partial orders on $Y$. The relation $\approx_i$ for each $i$ is defined with respect to $Y$ rather than $X$.

Employing a notion used widely in the preceding chapter, we define

$$x \cdot >_D y \Leftrightarrow x \succsim_i y \text{ for all } i \text{ and } x >_i y \text{ for some } i, \qquad (18.2)$$

with the understanding that $x,y \in Y$. $x$ is said to *dominate* $y$ precisely when $x \cdot >_D y$.

DEFINITION 18.4. *The distribution $y \in Y$ is* admissible *with respect to $(Y,D)$ if and only if $x \cdot >_D y$ for no $x \in Y$.*

This obviously relates to the version of unanimity which says that $x,y \in Y$ and $x \cdot >_D y \Rightarrow y \notin F(Y,D)$. For this condition to be consistent with the definition of $F$, it must be true that some $y \in Y$ is admissible. Since $Y$ is infinite if $\#B > 1$, strict partial orders do not guarantee an admissible $y$ even when $B$ is finite. However, if certain conditions are assumed for individuals, then some $y$ is admissible when $B$ is finite. In fact, some $b \in B$ is admissible in this case.

THEOREM 18.1. *Suppose that B is finite and that each individual order in D satisfies the weak individual axiom with respect to* $Y = Y(B)$. *Then there is a* $b \in B$ *such that b is admissible with respect to* $(Y,D)$.

The proof is based on two lemmas, the first of which is

LEMMA 18.4. *Suppose that* $x_k,y_k \in Y$ *and* $x_k \cdot >_D y_k$ *and* $\lambda_k \geq 0$ *for* $k = 1, \ldots, m$, *with* $\Sigma_{k=1}^m \lambda_k = 1$, *and that each* $>_i$ *satisfies the weak individual axiom. Then* $\Sigma_{k=1}^m \lambda_k x_k \cdot >_D \Sigma_{k=1}^m \lambda_k y_k$.

*Proof.* Since $x_k \cdot >_D y_k$ for all $k$, $x_k \gtrsim_i y_k$ for all $i$ and $k$ and therefore $\Sigma \lambda_k x_k \gtrsim_i \Sigma \lambda_k y_k$ for all $i$ by Lemma 18.1. For some $\lambda_k > 0$ there is an $i$ such that $x_k >_i y_k$. Hence $\Sigma \lambda_k x_k >_i \Sigma \lambda_k y_k$ for this $i$, by Lemma 18.1(2). Hence $\Sigma \lambda_k x_k \cdot >_D \Sigma \lambda_k y_k$ by (18.2).◆

The second lemma can be easily proved using Theorem 3.2 as modified in the sentence that precedes its statement. Another proof is given by Rosenblatt (1962, pp. 44–52). In the theory of Markov processes, this lemma guarantees the existence of a stationary distribution $p$ in the finite context.

LEMMA 18.5. *Suppose* $x_1, \ldots, x_m$ *are probability distributions on* $C = \{1, \ldots, m\}$. *Then there is a probability distribution p on C such that*

$$p(k) = \Sigma_{j=1}^m p(j)x_j(k) \qquad for \qquad k = 1, \ldots, m.$$

*Proof of Theorem* 18.1. Let the hypotheses of the theorem hold with $B = \{b_1, \ldots, b_m\}$. Contrary to the conclusion, suppose that every $b_j$ is dominated, with $x_j \in Y$ and $x_j \cdot >_D b_j$ for $j = 1, \ldots, m$. Let $p \in Y$ be as guaranteed by Lemma 18.5 so that

$$p(b_k) - \Sigma_{j=1}^m p(b_j)x_j(b_k) \qquad for \qquad k - 1, \ldots, m.$$

Then $p = \Sigma p(b_j)b_j = \Sigma p(b_j)x_j$, so that $p \cdot >_D p$ by Lemma 18.4. But this contradicts the irreflexivity of some $>_i$, and hence it must be true that some $b_j$ is admissible.◆

THE SPACE OF ADMISSIBLE DISTRIBUTIONS

Throughout this subsection, the hypotheses of Theorem 18.1 will be assumed to hold. Our main purpose will be to examine the structure of the admissible distributions in $Y$. Let

$$Y_0 = \{x:x \in Y \text{ and } x \text{ is not admissible w.r.t. } (Y,D)\}$$
$$Y_1 = \{x:x \in Y \text{ and } x \text{ is admissible w.r.t. } (Y,D)\}.$$

By definition, $Y_0 \cap Y_1 = \emptyset$ and $Y = Y_0 \cup Y_1$. Theorem 18.1 says that $Y_1 \neq \emptyset$, and in fact $b \in Y_1$ for some $b \in B$.

A convenient way of developing the structure of $Y_1$ is to look first at

$Y_0$, the space of inadmissible distributions. A set $Y'$ of distributions in $Y$ is convex if and only if $Y'$ is closed under convex linear combinations; that is, $x, y \in Y'$ and $0 \leq \lambda \leq 1 \Rightarrow \lambda x + (1 - \lambda)y \in Y'$.

LEMMA 18.6. (1) $Y_0$ *is convex.*

(2) $b \in Y_0$ *and* $x(b) > 0 \Rightarrow x \in Y_0$.

(3) $x \in Y_0$ *and* $0 < \lambda < 1 \Rightarrow \lambda x + (1 - \lambda)y \in Y_0$.

Part (2) says that if the basic alternative $b \in B$ is inadmissible, then every distribution in $Y$ with positive probability for $b$ is inadmissible. Thus, for the example of section 18.1 where Mr. $d$ had a strict simple majority over each of Messrs. $a$, $b$ and $c$, but was dominated by $x$ with $x(a) = x(b) = x(c) = \frac{1}{3}$, every distribution that gives Mr. $d$ any chance of winning is dominated by some other distribution. Looking at this result from the standpoint of $Y_1$, it says that if $x \in Y_1$ then $x(b) = 0$ for every inadmissible $b$. Part (3), which is stronger than part (2), says that, if $x$ is dominated and if $0 < \lambda < 1$, then $\lambda x + (1 - \lambda)y$ is dominated, regardless of whether $y$ is admissible.

*Proof of the lemma.* Part (1) is a corollary of part (3), and (2) follows from (3) by observing that if $0 < x(b) < 1$ then $x = x(b)b + [1 - x(b)]x'$, where $x'(b) = 0$ and $x'(a) = x(a)/[1 - x(b)]$ for all $a \neq b$ in $B$. For (3), suppose that $z \cdot >_D x$ and $0 < \lambda < 1$. Then, by the proof method for Lemma 18.4, $\lambda z + (1 - \lambda)y \cdot >_D \lambda x + (1 - \lambda)y$. ◆

Although $Y_0$ is convex, $Y_1$ need not be convex. We shall illustrate this and more with two simple examples that take $B = \{a,b,c\}$, $n = 2$ and for convenience we will assume that the strong individual axiom holds for each of the two orders on $Y = Y(B)$. In each case the following matrices give the individual utility functions on $B$ that satisfy (18.1) for $Y$. From the viewpoint of the nonprobabilistic approach of previous chapters, these two matrices would be equivalent. In the present con-

|   | $u_1$ | $u_2$ |
|---|-------|-------|
| $a$ | 3 | 0 |
| $b$ | 1 | 1 |
| $c$ | 0 | 3 |

I

|   | $u_1$ | $u_2$ |
|---|-------|-------|
| $a$ | 3 | 0 |
| $b$ | 2 | 2 |
| $c$ | 0 | 3 |

II

text, $b$ is dominated by $\frac{1}{2}a + \frac{1}{2}c$ in I, but $b$ is not dominated in II.

Situations I and II are shown geometrically on Figure 18.1, where $Y$ is the plane simplex in $Re^3$ shown at the top of the figure. The points in $Y_1$ in each case are enclosed by the dashed lines. For I, $Y_1 = Y(\{a,c\})$; for II, $Y_1 = Y(\{a,b\}) \cup Y(\{b,c\})$. In each case $Y_0$ is the convex set that is left when $Y_1$ is taken out of $Y$. Although $Y_1$ is convex in I, $Y_1$ is

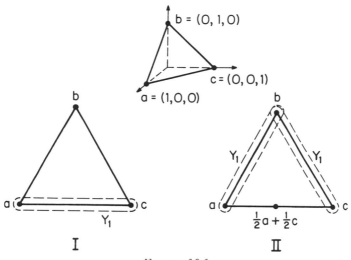

FIGURE 10.1

not convex in II. For example, $b \cdot >_D \frac{1}{2}a + \frac{1}{2}c$ in II since $u_i(b) > \frac{1}{2}u_i(a) + \frac{1}{2}u_i(c)$ for $i = 1, 2$, so that $\frac{1}{2}a + \frac{1}{2}c$ is not in $Y_1$ although $a$ and $c$ are.

Since $b$ is dominated in I, Lemma 18.6(2) says that $Y_1 \subseteq Y(\{a,c\})$ for this case. In view of the fact that $a >_1 c$ and $c >_2 a$ for I, $Y_1 = Y(\{a,c\})$.

Since $b \cdot >_D \frac{1}{2}a + \frac{1}{2}c$ in II, Lemma 18.6(3) shows that $Y_1 \subseteq Y(\{a,b\}) \cup Y(\{b,c\})$. That is, the points on any line through $\frac{1}{2}a + \frac{1}{2}c$ that are in $Y$ must be dominated, except perhaps for the extreme boundary points (where $\lambda = 0$ in the lemma). Lemma 18.6(3) implies also that if $\frac{1}{2}a + \frac{1}{2}b$ is admissible then every point on the line segment from $a$ to $b$, that is $Y(\{a,b\})$, is admissible. (This includes the end points $a$ and $b$. Why?) One can easily verify that $\frac{1}{2}a + \frac{1}{2}b$ is admissible in II. The same clearly holds for $\frac{1}{2}b + \frac{1}{2}c$ by symmetry.

This reasoning leads to a corollary of Lemma 18.6 that we include in a theorem. As before, with $C \subseteq B$,

$$Y(C) - \{x : x \in Y \text{ and } \Sigma_C x(b) - 1\}.$$

The *relative interior* (or interior) of $Y(C)$ is the set of all $x \in Y(C)$ for which $x(b)$ is positive for all $b \in C$: symbolically,

$$Y[C] = \{x : x \in Y(C) \text{ and } x(b) > 0 \text{ for all } b \in C\}.$$

The *relative boundary* (or boundary) of $Y(C)$ is $Y - Y[C]$. If $C$ is a unit subset of $B$, say $C = \{a\}$, then $Y(C) = Y[C] = \{a\}$ and the boundary of $\{a\}$ is empty.

**245**

THEOREM 18.2. *Suppose that the hypotheses of Theorem 18.1 hold. Then there is a nonempty subset $\mathcal{B}_1$ of nonempty subsets of B such that*

(1) $C, C' \in \mathcal{B}_1$ and $C \neq C' \Rightarrow$ not $C \subseteq C'$ & not $C' \subseteq C$,
(2) $Y_1 = \cup_{\mathcal{B}_1} Y(C)$.

*Moreover, if $Y_0 \neq \emptyset$ then there is a nonempty subset $\mathcal{B}_0$ of nonempty subsets of B such that*

(3) $C \in \mathcal{B}_0$ and $C \subseteq C' \subseteq B \Rightarrow C' \in \mathcal{B}_0$,
(4) $C_0 \in \mathcal{B}_0$ and $C_1 \in \mathcal{B}_1 \Rightarrow$ not $C_0 \subseteq C_1$,
(5) $Y_0 = \cup_{\mathcal{B}_0} Y[C]$, and $Y_0$ is convex.

This theorem includes all aspects of Theorem 18.1 and Lemma 18.6. For example, (1) and (2) require that $b \in Y_1$ for some $b \in B$. Because $Y(C) \subseteq Y(C')$ when $C \subseteq C'$, $\mathcal{B}_1$ contains only the maximal subsets of B whose $Y(C)$ are in $Y_1$. There is no similar expression for $\mathcal{B}_0$ since $Y[C] \cap Y[C'] = \emptyset$ if $C \neq C'$, even if $C \subset C'$. However, (4) states a noninclusion property between $\mathcal{B}_0$ and $\mathcal{B}_1$. It simply reflects the fact that $Y_0 \cap Y_1 = \emptyset$. Part (3) of the theorem follows easily from Lemma 18.6(3), for if $x$ is in the interior of $Y(C)$ and is inadmissible, and if $C \subset C'$ and $y$ is in the interior of $Y(C')$, then $\frac{1}{2}x + \frac{1}{2}y$ is inadmissible and in the interior of $Y(C')$. The line segments from $\frac{1}{2}x + \frac{1}{2}y$ to the boundary points of $Y(C')$ show by Lemma 18.6(3) that every point in $Y[C']$ is inadmissible.

A simple implication of Theorem 18.2(3,5) is that if $Y_0 \neq \emptyset$ then every point in the interior of $Y$ is in $Y_0$.

### THE MODERATE INDIVIDUAL AXIOM

One natural property of admissibility that has not yet been mentioned in our probabilistic setting is the dominance of each inadmissible distribution by an admissible distribution. We show first that this can be false under the weak individual axiom.

Let $B = \{a,b\}$ and let $x \in [0,1]$ be the distribution that has probability $x$ for $b$ and $1 - x$ for $a$. Taking $n = 1$, let $>$ satisfy $x > y > 1$ whenever $0 < x < y < 1$, and $0 \sim x$ for all $x \in (0,1]$. It is easily seen that the weak individual axiom holds. Since 0 is the only point that is not dominated, $Y_1 = \{a\}$. But $a \cdot >_D x$ for no $x \in (0,1]$, and therefore there is no point in $Y_1$ that dominates a point in $Y_0 = (0,1]$.

The moderate individual axiom of Definition 18.3 rectifies this anomaly.

THEOREM 18.3. *Suppose that B is finite and each individual order in D satisfies the moderate individual axiom. Then*

$$y \in Y_0 \Rightarrow x \cdot >_D y \text{ for some } x \in Y_1.$$

*Proof.* Let the hypotheses hold and, contrary to the conclusion, suppose that $y_1 \in Y_0$ and no admissible distribution dominates $y_1$. We shall obtain a contradiction to this by constructing a sequence $y_1$, $y_2$, $y_3$, . . . of points in $Y$ such that . . . $y_3 \cdot >_D y_2 \cdot >_D y_1$. The transitivity of $\cdot >_D$ gives $y_k \cdot >_D y_1$ for every $k > 1$, so that $y_k \in Y_0$ by our supposition. We let $C_k \subseteq B$ be such that $y_k \in Y[C_k]$. (See Theorem 18.2.)

Given $y_1$, determine $y_2$ as follows. If there is an $x \in Y[C_1]$ such that $x \cdot >_D y_1$, take $y_2$ as the point on the line $\{\lambda x + (1 - \lambda)y_1 : \lambda \in Re\}$ that is farthest from $y_1$ on the $x$ side of $y_1$ and is still in $Y$. It follows from Lemma 18.3 that $y_2 \cdot >_D y_1$ and, by construction with $y_2 \in Y[C_2]$, $C_2 \subset C_1$. [That is, $y_2$ is on the boundary of $Y(C_1)$ and hence will be in the interior of $Y(C_2)$ for some $C_2 \subset C_1$]. On the other hand, if $x \cdot >_D y_1$ for no $x \in Y[C_1]$, let $y_2$ be any point in $Y_0$ that dominates $y_1$. Since $Y_0$ is convex, $C_2$ will not be a subset of $C_1$ in this case.

Given $y_2$, precisely the same procedure is used to obtain $y_3 \cdot >_D y_2$. The construction proceeds in the same way for each $y_k$. Since $\cdot >_D$ is transitive, $y_k \cdot >_D y_j$ whenever $k > j$. Moreover, since $\cdot >_D$ is irreflexive, $y_k \neq y_j$ whenever $k \neq j$.

Suppose we are at $y_j$. Since $B$ is finite, and since $C_{k+1} \subset C_k$ if $x \cdot >_D y_k$ for some $x \in Y[C_k]$, after a finite number of steps we must reach a $k > j$ such that $x \cdot >_D y_k$ for no $x \in Y[C_k]$. And since $y_m \cdot >_D y_k$ for $m > k$ this means that $y_m \notin Y[C_k]$ *for all* $m > k$. It follows that there is an infinite sequence $k_1$, $k_2$, . . . with $k_1 < k_2 < . . .$ such that, for each $r \in \{1,2, . . .\}$, $y_m \notin Y[C_{k_r}]$ for all $m > k_r$. But this implies that no two $C_{k_r}$ are identical and hence that their number is infinite. We have thus reached the desired contradiction since $B$ has only a finite number of subsets. ◆

## A NONTHEOREM

As we have shown, $Y_1$ need not be convex. However, the first part of Theorem 18.2 states that $Y_1$ can be written as the union of several maximal convex sets, namely the $Y(C)$ for $C \in \mathcal{B}_1$. It might then be asked whether, under any of the individual axioms, each two subsets of $B$ that are in $\mathcal{B}_1$ contain a common basic alternative. For example, this would be true for case II of Figure 18.1 where $\mathcal{B}_1 = \{\{a,b\},\{b,c\}\}$, for the two subsets of $B$ in $\mathcal{B}_1$ both contain $b$.

Simple examples show that this can be false when only the weak individual axiom is used, provided that $\#B > 1$. Moreover, as we shall now show, it can be false even when the strong individual axiom is used, provided that $\#B > 3$.

Let $B = \{a,b,c,d\}$, $n = 2$, and suppose the following $u_i$ functions on $B$ satisfy (18.1). Then, as one can easily verify, each of $a$, $b$, $c$, and $d$

is in $Y_1$. Moreover, $c \cdot >_D \frac{1}{2}a + \frac{1}{2}b$, $d \cdot >_D \frac{1}{2}a + \frac{1}{2}c$ and $c \cdot >_D \frac{1}{4}b + \frac{3}{4}d$. By Theorem 18.2, this gives $Y_1 \subseteq Y(\{a,d\}) \cup Y(\{c,d\}) \cup$

|   | $u_1$ | $u_2$ |
|---|-------|-------|
| $a$ | 5 | 0 |
| $b$ | 0 | 5 |
| $c$ | 3 | 3 |
| $d$ | 4 | 2 |

$Y(\{b,c\})$. In fact, $Y_1$ can be shown to equal this union, so that $\mathcal{B}_1 = \{\{a,d\},\{c,d\},\{b,c\}\}$ with $\{a,d\} \cap \{b,c\} = \emptyset$.

This result is shown for the simplex $Y = Y(B)$ of Figure 18.2. Since

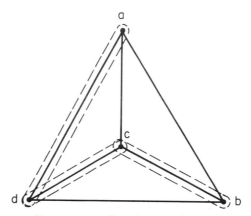

FIGURE 18.2. Regular tetrahedron

$Y$ is effectively 3-dimensional in this case, it can be viewed as a regular tetrahedron with $c$ lying above the plane that contains $a$, $b$ and $d$. (The tetrahedron represents part of the hyperplane $x(a) + x(b) + x(c) + x(d) = 1$ in 4-dimensional space.) As before, the points in $Y_1$, along three edges of the tetrahedron, are enclosed by dashed lines.

### SHOULD $F(Y,D)$ BE CONVEX?

Assume that the unanimity condition $x \cdot >_D y \Rightarrow y \notin F(Y,D)$ is imposed so that $F(Y,D) \subseteq Y_1$. Should $F(Y,D)$ be required to be convex also? If so, then $F(Y,D)$ must be a subset of one of the $Y(C)$ for $C \in \mathcal{B}_1$. This follows from Theorem 18.2 under the weak individual axiom.

Besides the purely esthetic attraction of a convex choice set, consideration of tie-breaking may support an argument in favor of convexity. Suppose for example that $x,y \in F(Y,D)$ and $x \neq y$. Then the distributions $x$ and $y$ both appear "fair" for "implementation," despite the obvious fact that some individuals may prefer $x$ to $y$ while others prefer $y$ to $x$. Hence $\lambda x + (1 - \lambda)y$ with $0 < \lambda < 1$ might also seem "fair," since when viewed as a two-stage lottery it results in either $x$ or $y$ at the first stage.

Of course, even when $F(Y,D)$ is convex, it does not fully resolve the issue if it contains more than one distribution. There is one qualification on this. If $x \sim_i y$ for every $i \in \{1, \ldots ,n\}$ and all $x,y \in F(Y,D)$, then it should make no difference to any individual which distribution in $F(Y,D)$ is actually used. In such a case it seems reasonable to say that $F(Y,D)$ fully resolves the issue at hand.

## 18.4   OTHER CONSIDERATIONS

Clearly, considerations besides admissibility will usually play a role when lotteries are allowed in a social choice procedure. For example, if a group has 100 individuals and if the situation of Figure 18.1 (II) has one individual with utility function $u_1$ and 99 with utility function $u_2$, then the social choice would probably not be the same as when 99 have $u_1$ and one has $u_2$, despite the fact that the admissible set in $Y$ is the same in both cases.

Corresponding to preceding investigations, several routes in the lotteries context might be pursued. These include an examination of conditions like those in Chapters 14 through 16, consideration of simple majority, and the determination of $F$ by summation as in the preceding chapter. In concluding our study, we shall comment on three things:

1. Conditions under which a basic alternative that has a strict simple majority over each other basic alternative is admissible;
2. The existence of a distribution $x \in Y$ that has a strict simple majority over every other distribution in $Y$;
3. Determination of $F(Y,D)$ by maximum utility sums.

The second of these has been studied by Zeckhauser (1969) and Shepsle (1970), and the third by Harsanyi (1955), Pattanaik (1968b), and Sen (1970c), among others. Two other papers of general interest which use expected utility in a social choice analysis are Coleman (1966) and Riker and Ordeshook (1968).

### BASIC MAJORITY ADMISSIBILITY

As in the preceding section, we shall work with a generic $(Y,D) \in \mathfrak{X} \times \mathfrak{D}$ with $Y = Y(B)$. The other conditions in the first paragraph of the preceding section are assumed here also.

As shown in section 18.1, a basic alternative (Mr. $d$) that has a strict simple majority over each other basic alternative may be inadmissible. A quick check will show that preferences on $a$, $b$, $c$, $d$ are not single-peaked in that example. When preferences on basic alternatives are single peaked, it will often be true that a "best" basic alternative by the weak Condorcet condition will be admissible. The combination of the weak Condorcet condition on $B$ and admissibility could reflect the following partial selection procedure. It is first determined whether one basic alternative has a strict simple majority over each other basic alternative. If there is a weak Condorcet "winner," say $b$, then $b$ will be implemented unless someone can propose a lottery that is "unanimously preferred" to $b$. In other words, each voter has veto power over any lottery that is put against $b$.

We shall consider two theorems that combine the weak Condorcet viewpoint on basic alternatives with admissibility. Both are based on single-peaked preferences on the basic alternatives in $B$. The notation of Chapter 9 will be used where appropriate.

THEOREM 18.4. *Suppose that each individual order in $D$ satisfies the weak individual axiom with respect to $Y = Y(B)$, that $(B,D)$ is single peaked under the linear order $<_0$ on $B$ and that for each $i$ there is an $a_i \in B$ such that $a_i >_i b$ for all $b \in B - \{a_i\}$. Then, if there is a basic alternative that has a strict simple majority over every other basic alternative, it is admissible.*

*Proof.* Let the hypotheses hold and assume that $bP_Da$ for all $a \in B - \{b\}$. Suppose first that $b = a_i$ for some $i$, so that $b >_i a$ for all $a \in B - \{b\}$. To show that $b$ is not dominated, let $x \in Y$ with $x \neq b$. If $x(b) = 0$ then, by Lemma 18.1, $\Sigma_{a \in B} x(a)b >_i \Sigma_{a \in B} x(a)a$, or $b >_i x$. If $0 < x(b) < 1$ then $x = x(b)b + [1 - x(b)]x'$ with $x'(b) = 0$. Hence $b >_i x'$ and therefore $b = [1 - x(b)]b + x(b)b >_i [1 - x(b)]x' + x(b)b = x$, or $b >_i x$. Hence $b >_i x$ for all $x \neq b$, so that $b$ cannot be dominated.

Suppose next that $b = a_i$ for no $i$. Let $a$ be the alternative in $\{a_1, \ldots, a_n\}$ that satisfies $[a <_0 b$ and $a <_0 a_i <_0 b$ for no $a_i]$, and let $c$ be the alternative in $\{a_1, \ldots, a_n\}$ that satisfies $[b <_0 c$ and $b <_0 a_i <_0 c$ for no $a_i]$. Since $bP_Da_i$ for all $i$, both $a$ and $c$ exist. Let $m = \#\{i : a_i <_0 b\}$ and $n - m = \#\{i : b <_0 a_i\}$. Then $bP_Da \Rightarrow m > n - m$, and $bP_Dc \Rightarrow n - m > m$, a contradiction. Hence the case supposed in this paragraph cannot arise. ◆

It should be noted that Theorem 18.4 says nothing about the size of $B$. In particular, it allows $B$ to be infinite, as does our next theorem. In this theorem the restriction on the nature of the peaks (unit subsets of $B$) is removed, but the individual assumptions are strengthened.

THEOREM 18.5. *Suppose that each individual order in $D$ is a weak order that satisfies the moderate individual axiom with respect to $Y =*

$Y(B)$, and that $(B,D)$ is single peaked under the linear order $<_0$ on $B$. Then, if there is a basic alternative that has a strict simple majority over every other basic alternative, it is admissible.

*Proof.* Let the hypotheses hold and assume $bP_Da$ for all $a \in B - \{b\}$. We shall let

$$I = \{i : b \succcurlyeq_i a \text{ for all } a \in B - \{b\}\}$$
$$B_i = \{a : a \sim_i b\} \text{ for each } i \in I.$$

Suppose first that $I = \emptyset$. Then either $b$ is at one end of $(B, <_0)$, in which case $a \succcurlyeq_i b$ for all $a$ and $i$, thus contradicting $bP_Da$, or else $a <_0 b <_0 c$ for some $a, c \in B$. In this case let $m$ individuals' "peaks" be $<_0 b$, and let $n - m$ have "peaks" on the other side of $b$. Then it is easily seen that there exist $a, c \in B$ such that $a <_0 b <_0 c$ with $a \succ_i b \succ_i c$ for $m$ individuals and $c \succ_i b \succ_i a$ for $n - m$. But this contradicts $bP_Da$ and $bP_Dc$. Therefore $I$ cannot be empty.

Given $I \neq \emptyset$ suppose that, contrary to the theorem, $x \cdot >_D b$ for some $x \in Y$. Since this requires $x \succcurlyeq_i b$ for each $i$, by the properties for the individual orders, it follows from these properties that $x(B_i) = 1$ for each $i \in I$. Therefore, with

$$C = \cap_I B_i, \qquad x(C) = 1 \text{ is required.} \tag{18.3}$$

Without loss in generality we can take $x(b) = 0$. Then suppose first that $C$ is on one side of $b$ under $<_0$, say $b <_0 c$ for all $c \in C$. To have $bP_Dc$ for each $c \in C$, there must be an $i$ whose "peak" is $\leq_0 b$. But then $b \succ_i c$ for all $c \in C$ and hence $b \succ_i x$ follows from (18.3), thus contradicting $x \cdot >_D b$. Suppose next that $a <_0 b <_0 c$ for some $a$, $c \in C$. Then there exist such $a$ and $c$ for which $a \sim_i b \sim_i c$ for all $i \in I$, and $a \succ_i b \succ_i c$ or $c \succ_i b \succ_i a$ for each $i \notin I$. But this contradicts $bP_Dc$ & $bP_Da$, and hence it must be false that $x \cdot >_D b$ for some $x$. ◆

SIMPLE MAJORITY BETWEEN LOTTERIES

In considering simple majorities between pairs of lotteries, or probability distributions on $B$, we shall note first that only a basic alternative can have a simple majority over every other lottery in $Y$.

THEOREM 18.6. *Suppose that each individual order in $D$ satisfies the weak individual axiom and that $x \in Y$ is such that $xP_Dy$ for every $y \in Y - \{x\}$. Then $x = b$ for some $b \in B$.*

*Proof.* Suppose that $xP_Dy$ for all $y \in Y - \{x\}$. Let $C = \{b : x(b) > 0\}$ so that $C$ is finite and $x \in Y[C]$. We shall prove that $C$ must be a unit subset of $B$.

**251**

To the contrary, suppose that $\#C > 1$. Because $x$ is in the interior of $Y(C)$, we can choose a $y \in Y[C]$ sufficiently close to but different than $x$ so that there are $t$ and $v$ in $Y[C]$ such that

$$x = \lambda t + (1 - \lambda)y$$
$$y = \lambda v + (1 - \lambda)x$$

with $\lambda \in (0,1)$ and small enough so that the results to be described will hold. In particular, $\lambda = .2$ will be a satisfactory value. This is shown on Figure 18.3, where $r_1 = \lambda t + (1 - \lambda)x$. An appropriate con-

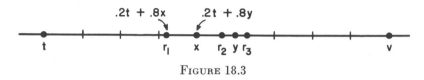

FIGURE 18.3

vex combination will give $\alpha r_1 + (1 - \alpha)v = x$, and for this $\alpha$ we take $r_2 = \alpha x + (1 - \alpha)v$. As shown on the figure, $r_2$ is between $x$ and $y$. Another combination will give $\beta x + (1 - \beta)v = r_2$, and for this we take $r_3 = \beta r_2 + (1 - \beta)v$, with $r_3$ to the right of $y$.

Now suppose that $x >_i y$. Then, by the weak individual axiom, $r_1 = \lambda t + (1 - \lambda)x >_i \lambda t + (1 - \lambda)y = x$, so that $r_1 >_i x$. Conversely, suppose that $r_1 >_i x$. Then with the combinations as described above, the weak individual axiom gives $x >_i r_2$, then $r_2 >_i r_3$, so that $x >_i r_3$ by transitivity. Since $y$ is a convex combination of $x$ and $r_3$, the weak individual axiom gives $x >_i y$. Hence $x >_i y \Leftrightarrow r_1 >_i x$. Reversing $>_i$ in each step here gives $y >_i x \Leftrightarrow x >_i r_1$. Therefore $xP_Dy \Leftrightarrow r_1P_Dx$. Hence, if $\#C > 1$, then $x$ cannot have a strict simple majority over every other distribution. ◆

In comparison with Theorems 18.4 and 18.5, it is easily seen that when $(B,D)$ is single peaked and $P(B,D) = \{b\}$, so that $b$ has a strict simple majority over every other basic alternative, there may be a distribution in $Y$ that has a strict simple majority over $b$. For example, if $B = \{a,b,c\}$, $n = 3$ and $u_i$ for (18.1) are as follows, then $(B,D)$ satisfies the conditions of Theorem 18.4, and $\{b\} = P(B,D)$ with $b$ admis-

|   | $u_1$ | $u_2$ | $u_3$ |
|---|---|---|---|
| $a$ | 3 | 0 | 0 |
| $b$ | 1 | 1 | 1 |
| $c$ | 0 | 3 | 0 |

sible. However, $\frac{1}{2}a + \frac{1}{2}c$ is preferred to $b$ by individuals 1 and 2, so that $\frac{1}{2}a + \frac{1}{2}c \, P_D \, b$. Zeckhauser (1969) and Shepsle (1970) investigate the three-alternative situation under the strong individual axiom in some detail, and the reader is referred to their papers for further information.

To simplify our discussion of summation in the lottery context, we shall assume that $B$ is finite and that the strong individual axiom holds for each order in $D$. Given $u_i$ for $i$ that satisfies (18.1) on $Y = Y(B)$, normalized so that max $\{u_i(b) : b \in B\} = 1$ and min $\{u_i(b) : b \in B\} = 0$ whenever $u_i$ is not constant on $B$, let

$$E_i x = \Sigma_B x(b) u_i(b)$$

for all $x \in Y$ and $i \in \{1, \ldots, n\}$. A typical procedure for determining $F(Y,D)$ by summation in this setting is to specify a positive number $\rho_i$ for each $i$ and take

$$F(Y,D) = \{x : x \in Y \text{ and } \Sigma_i \rho_i E_i x \geq \Sigma_i \rho_i E_i y \text{ for all } y \in Y\}. \quad (18.4)$$

As you can easily verify, $b \in F(Y,D)$ for some $b \in B$.

If one accepts such a procedure in principle, the question remains as to how the $\rho_i$ are to be specified. Various suggestions have been made on this point (see, for example, the papers cited early in this section), but there does not appear to be widespread agreement on any of these. We shall not go into them here.

There are other summation procedures besides those specified by (18.4) that qualify in the present context as summation social choice functions. For example, given $(Y,D)$ as supposed above, let $v_i : Y \to Re$ agree monotonically with $E_i$. $Y \to Re$, so that $v_i(x) > v_i(y)$ if and only if $E_i x > E_i y$. Then $v_i(x) > v_i(y) \Leftrightarrow x >_i y$ for all $x,y \in Y$ and all $i$. If it is true that

$$\{x : x \in Y \text{ and } \Sigma_i v_i(x) \geq \Sigma_i v_i(y) \text{ for all } y \in Y\} \quad (18.5)$$

is not empty, then $F(Y,D)$ could be taken to equal this subset of $Y$.

Simple examples that involve discontinuities show that (18.5) can be empty. Other examples show that when (18.5) is not empty, it need not contain any $b \in B$. For instance, let $B = \{a,b\}$ with $x \subset [0,1]$ representing the distribution that assigns probabilities $x$ to $a$ and $1 - x$ to $b$. Suppose that $n = 2$ with $a >_1 b$ and $b >_2 a$. Two $v_i$ functions that preserve the $>_i$ orders on $[0,1]$ are

$$v_1(x) = \sqrt{x}$$
$$v_2(x) = \sqrt{1 - x}.$$

The sum of these two functions is maximized by $x = \frac{1}{2}$, so that (18.5) contains only the even-chance distribution on $\{a,b\}$.

Alt, F., Über die Messbarkeit des Nutzens. *Zeitschrift für Nationalöko-nomie* 7 (1936) 161–169.

Armstrong, W. E., The determinateness of the utility function. *Economic J.* 49 (1939) 453–467.

Armstrong, W. E., Uncertainty and the utility function. *Economic J.* 58 (1948) 1–10.

Armstrong, W. E., Utility and the theory of welfare. *Oxford Economic Papers* N.S. 3 (1951) 259–271.

Arrow, K. J., A difficulty in the concept of social welfare. *J. Political Economy* 58 (1950) 328–346. Reprinted in Arrow and Scitovsky (1969) 147–168.

Arrow, K. J., Rational choice functions and orderings. *Economica* 26 (1959) 121–127.

Arrow, K. J., *Social choice and individual values*, second edition. New York: Wiley. 1963.

Arrow, K. J., and T. Scitovsky, *Readings in welfare economics*. Homewood, Illinois: Irwin. 1969.

Aumann, R. J., Utility theory without the completeness axiom. *Econometrica* 30 (1962) 445–462. A correction: *Econometrica* 32 (1964) 210–212.

Aumann, R. J., Subjective programming. In M. W. Shelly and G. L. Bryan (Eds.), *Human judgments and optimality*. New York: Wiley. 1964. 217–242.

Banzhaf, J. F. III, Weighted voting doesn't work: a mathematical analysis. *Rutgers Law Review* 19 (1965) 317–343.

Black, D., On the rationale of group decision-making. *J. Political Economy* 56 (1948) 23–34. Reprinted in Arrow and Scitovsky (1969) 133–146.

Black, D., *The theory of committees and elections.* Cambridge, England: Cambridge University Press. 1958.

Blau, J. H., The existence of social welfare functions. *Econometrica* 25 (1957) 302–313.

Blau, J. H., Arrow's theorem with weak independence. *Economica* 38 (1971) 413–420.

Borda, Jean-Charles de, Mémoire sur les élections au scrutin. *Histoire de l'Académie Royale des Sciences*. 1781.

Buchanan, J. M., and G. Tullock, *The calculus of consent*. Ann Arbor, Michigan: University of Michigan Press. 1962.

REFERENCES

Campbell, C. D., and G. Tullock, A measure of the importance of cyclical majorities. *Economic J.* **75** (1965) 853–857.

Churchman, C. W., On the intercomparison of utilities. In S. R. Krupp (Ed.), *The structure of economic science: essays on methodology.* Englewood Cliffs, New Jersey: Prentice-Hall. 1966. 243–256.

Coleman, J. S., The possibility of a social welfare function. *American Economic Review* **56** (1966) 1105–1122.

Condorcet, Marquis de, *Essai sur l'application de l'analyse à la probabilité des décisions rendues à la pluralité des voix.* Paris. 1785.

Copeland, A. H., A "reasonable" social welfare function. Mimeographed. *University of Michigan Seminar on Applications of Mathematics to the Social Sciences.* 1951.

Dahl, R. A., *A preface to democratic theory.* Chicago, Illinois: University of Chicago Press. 1956.

de Grazia, A., Mathematical derivation of an election system. *Isis* **44** (1953) 42–51.

DeMeyer, F., and C. R. Plott, The probability of a cyclical majority. *Econometrica* **38** (1970) 345–354.

Farquharson, R., *Theory of voting.* New Haven, Connecticut: Yale University Press. 1969.

Fishburn, P. C., *Utility theory for decision making.* New York: Wiley. 1970.

Fishburn, P. C., Conditions for simple majority decision functions with intransitive individual indifference. *J. Economic Theory* **2** (1970) 354–367. b.

Fishburn, P. C., Arrow's impossibility theorem: concise proof and infinite voters. *J. Economic Theory* **2** (1970) 103–106. c.

Fishburn, P. C., Intransitive indifference in preference theory: a survey. *Operations Research* **18** (1970) 207–228. d.

Fishburn, P. C., Utility theory with inexact preferences and degrees of preference. *Synthese* **21** (1970) 204–221. e.

Fishburn, P. C., Summation social choice functions. Unpublished manuscript, 1972. Forthcoming in *Econometrica.*

Frisch, R., Sur un problème d'économie pure. *Norsk Mathematisk Forenings Skrifter,* Serie 1, **16** (1926) 1–40.

Galton, F., One vote, one value. *Nature* **75** (1907) 414.

Garman, M., and M. Kamien, The paradox of voting: probability calculations. *Behavioral Science* **13** (1968) 306–316.

Goldman, A. J., Resolution and separation theorems for polyhedral convex sets. In H. W. Kuhn and A. W. Tucker (Eds.), *Linear inequalities and related systems.* Princeton, New Jersey: Princeton University Press. 1956. 41–51.

Goodman, L. A., On methods of amalgamation. In R. M. Thrall,

C. H. Coombs, and R. L. Davis (Eds.), *Decision processes*. New York: Wiley, 1954. 39–48.

Hansson, B., Choice structures and preference relations. *Synthese* **18** (1968) 443–458.

Hansson, B., Voting and group decision functions. *Synthese* **20** (1969) 526–537.

Hansson, B., Group preferences. *Econometrica* **37** (1969) 50–54. b.

Hansson, B., The independence condition in the theory of social choice. Working paper no. 2, The Mattias Fremling Society, Department of Philosophy, Lund, 1972.

Harary, F., Norman, R. Z., and D. Cartwright, *Structural models: an introduction to the theory of directed graphs*. New York: Wiley. 1965.

Harsanyi, J. C., Cardinal welfare, individualistic ethics, and interpersonal comparisons of utility. *J. Political Economy* **63** (1955) 309–321.

Harsanyi, J. C., A general theory of rational behavior in game situations. *Econometrica* **34** (1966) 613–634.

Hausner, M., Multidimensional utilities. In R. M. Thrall, C. H. Coombs, and R. L. Davis (Eds.), *Decision processes*. New York: Wiley. 1954. 167–180.

Inada, K.-I., The simple majority decision rule. *Econometrica* **37** (1969) 490 506.

Inada, K.-I., Majority rule and rationality. *J. Economic Theory* **2** (1970) 27–40.

Jensen, N. E., An introduction to Bernoullian utility theory. I. Utility functions. *Swedish J. Economics* **69** (1967) 163–183.

Kannai, Y., Existence of a utility in infinite dimensional partially ordered spaces. *Israel J. Mathematics* **1** (1963) 229–234.

Kendall, W., and G. W. Carey, The "intensity" problem and democratic theory. *American Political Science Review* **62** (1968) 5–24.

Lange, O., The determinateness of the utility function. *Review of Economic Studies* **1** (1934) 218–225; **2** (1934) 75–77.

Luce, R. D., Semiorders and a theory of utility discrimination. *Econometrica* **24** (1956) 178–191.

Luce, R. D., and H. Raiffa, *Games and decisions*. New York: Wiley. 1957.

May, K. O., A set of independent necessary and sufficient conditions for simple majority decision. *Econometrica* **20** (1952) 680–684.

May, R. M., Some mathematical remarks on the paradox of voting. *Behavioral Science* **16** (1971) 143–151.

McGarvey, D. C., A theorem on the construction of voting paradoxes. *Econometrica* **21** (1953) 608–610.

Mirski, L., and H. Perfect, Systems of representatives. *J. Mathematical Analysis and Applications* **15** (1966) 520–568.

REFERENCES

Murakami, Y., Some logical properties of Arrowian social welfare function. *J. Economic Behavior* **1** (1961) 77–84.

Murakami, Y., Formal structure of majority decision. *Econometrica* **34** (1966) 709–718.

Murakami, Y., *Logic and social choice*. London: Routledge and Kegan Paul. New York: Dover. 1968.

Niemi, R., and H. Weisberg, A mathematical solution for the probability of the paradox of voting. *Behavioral Science* **13** (1968) 317–323.

Pareto, V., *Manuel d'economie politique*, second edition. Paris: Marcel Giard. 1927.

Pattanaik, P. K., A note on democratic decision and the existence of choice sets. *Review of Economic Studies* **35** (1968) 1–9.

Pattanaik, P. K., Risk, impersonality, and the social welfare function. *J. Political Economy* **76** (1968) 1152–1169. b.

Pattanaik, P. K., On social choice with quasitransitive individual preferences. *J. Economic Theory* **2** (1970) 267–275.

Richter, M. K., Revealed preference theory. *Econometrica* **34** (1966) 635–645.

Richter, M. K., Rational choice. In J. S. Chipman, L. Hurwicz, M. K. Richter, and H. F. Sonnenschein (Eds.), *Preferences, utility, and demand*. New York: Harcourt Brace Jovanovich. 1971. 29–58.

Riker, W. H., and P. C. Ordeshook. A theory of the calculus of voting. *American Political Science Review* **62** (1968) 25–42.

Roberts, F. S., On nontransitive indifference. *J. Mathematical Psychology* **7** (1970) 243–258.

Rosenblatt, M., *Random processes*. New York: Oxford University Press. 1962.

Rothenberg, J., *The measurement of social welfare*. Englewood Cliffs, New Jersey: Prentice-Hall. 1961.

Schick, F., Arrow's proof and the logic of preference. *Philosophy of Science* **36** (1969) 127–144.

Sen, A. K., *Collective choice and social welfare*. San Francisco: Holden-Day. 1970.

Sen, A. K., The impossibility of a Paretian liberal. *J. Political Economy* **78** (1970) 152–157. b.

Sen, A. K., Interpersonal aggregation and partial comparability. *Econometrica* **38** (1970) 393–409. c.

Sen, A. K., and P. K. Pattanaik, Necessary and sufficient conditions for rational choice under majority decision. *J. Economic Theory* **1** (1969) 178–202.

Shepsle, K. A., A note on Zeckhauser's "Majority rule with lotteries on alternatives": the case of the paradox of voting. *Quarterly J. Economics* **84** (1970) 705–709.

Stearns, R., The voting problem. *Amer. Math. Monthly* **66** (1959) 761–763.

Suppes, P., and M. Winet, An axiomatization of utility based on the notion of utility differences. *Management Science* **1** (1955) 259–270.

Szpilrajn, E., Sur l'extension de l'ordre partiel. *Fundamenta Mathematicae* **16** (1930) 386–389.

von Neumann, J., and O. Morgenstern, *Theory of games and economic behavior*, second edition. Princeton, New Jersey: Princeton University Press. 1947.

Weldon, J. C., A note on measures of utility. *Canadian J. Economics and Political Science* **16** (1950) 227–233.

Wilson, R. B., An axiomatic model of logrolling. *American Economic Review* **59** (1969) 331–341.

Wilson, R. B., The finer structure of revealed preference. *J. Economic Theory* **2** (1970) 348–353.

Zeckhauser, R., Majority rule with lotteries on alternatives. *Quarterly J. Economics* **83** (1969) 696–703.